THE HUMAN FIGURE
A PHOTOGRAPHIC REFERENCE FOR ARTISTS

THE HUMAN FIGURE
A PHOTOGRAPHIC REFERENCE FOR ARTISTS

E. A. RUBY

A VNR Book
JOHN WILEY & SONS, INC.

New York   Chichester   Weinheim   Brisbane   Singapore   Toronto

Photographs by Sean Kerman

This text is printed on acid-free paper. ∞

Library of Congress Catalog Card Number 74-5948
ISBN 0-471-28949-3

98 99 25 24 23 22 21

Note: The even-numbered pages in this book are printed
in several orientations to the odd-numbered pages
due to the spiral binding of the original edition. Students
may wish to detach the pages, punch holes in the top
margins, and insert rings to duplicate the original version.

Contents

Author

Erik Ruby was born into a creative family. He entered the Paier School of Art in Hamden, Connecticut, where he studied in advertising together with other related subjects such as fine arts and illustration. He now works as both an illustrator and designer and his work has been used by many large corporations and has appeared in national magazines. The idea for *The Human Figure* came to him when he searched for a good book on drawing anatomy and found that traditional sources were mostly text and therefore useless, since one cannot draw from words.

He believes his book is the most complete on the subject and that it will be very useful for artists since it shows—in photographs—the figure in its natural state.

Drawing by the author.

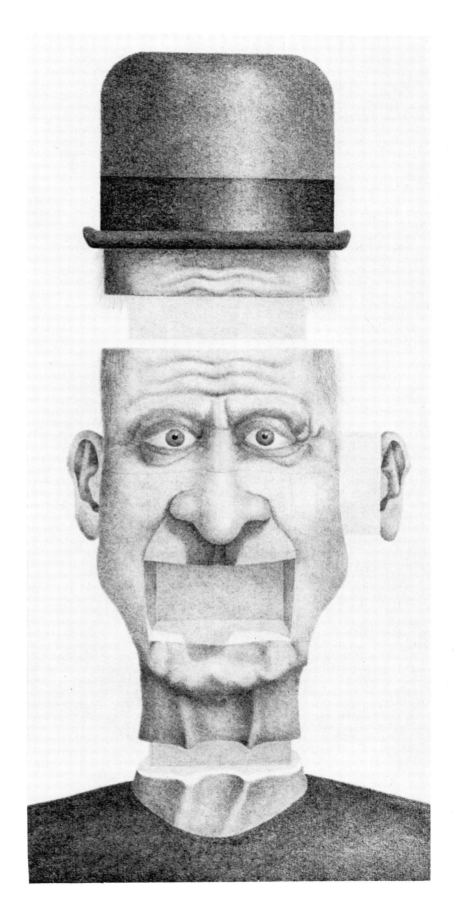

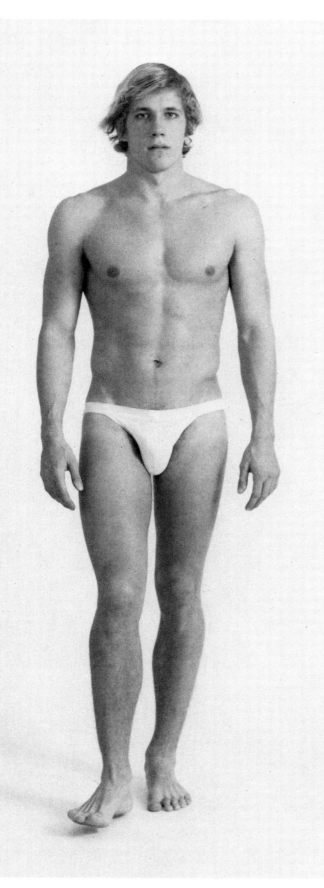 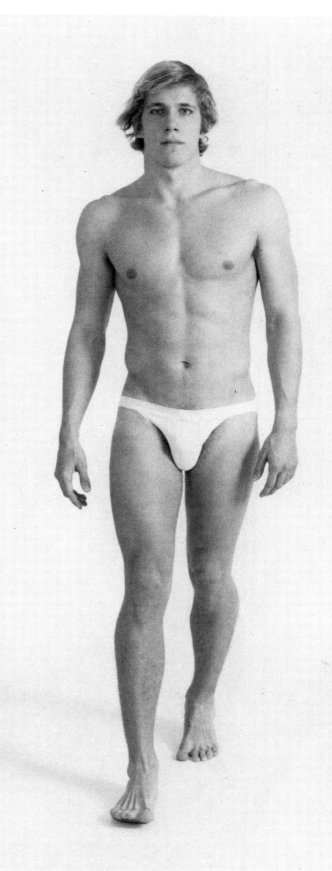

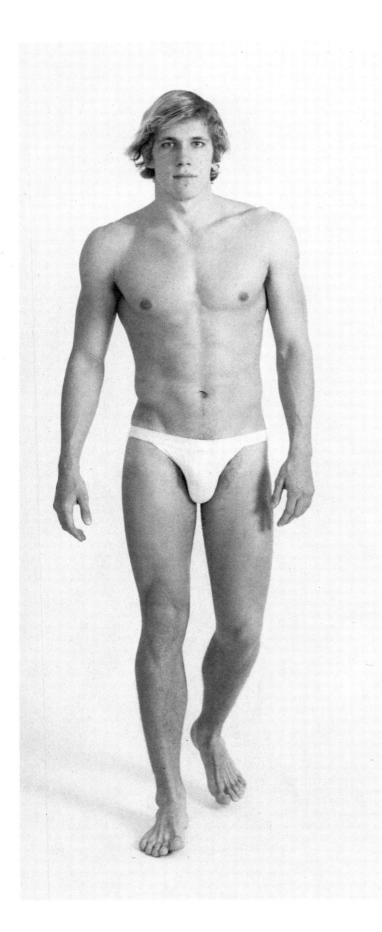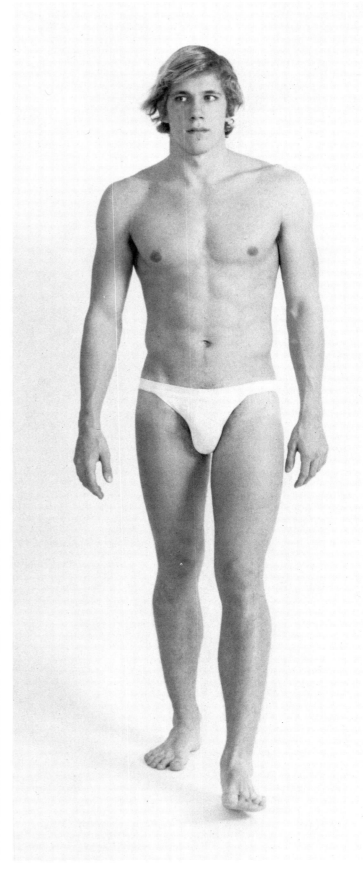

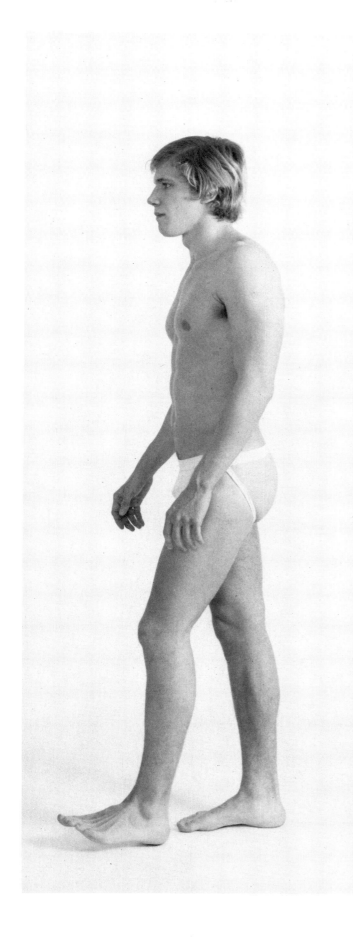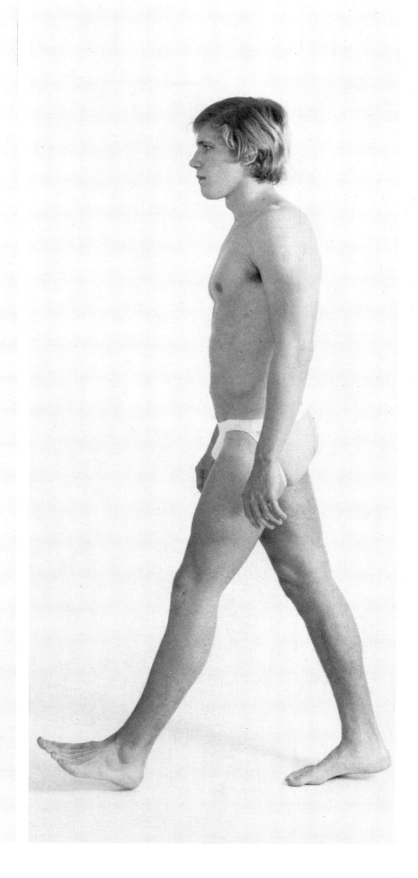

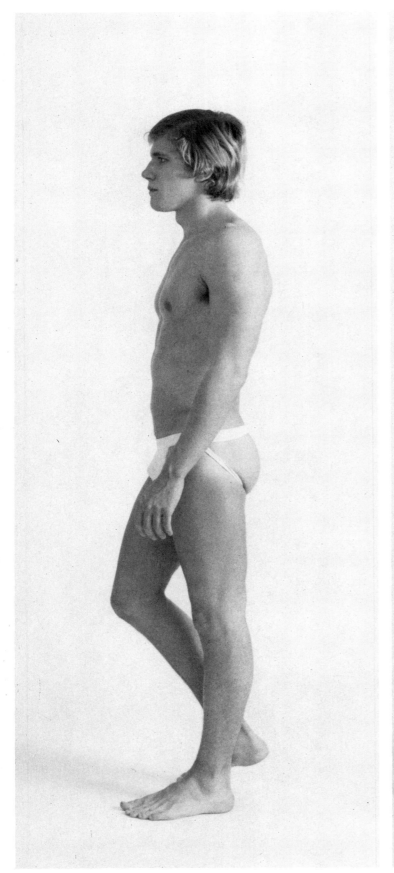 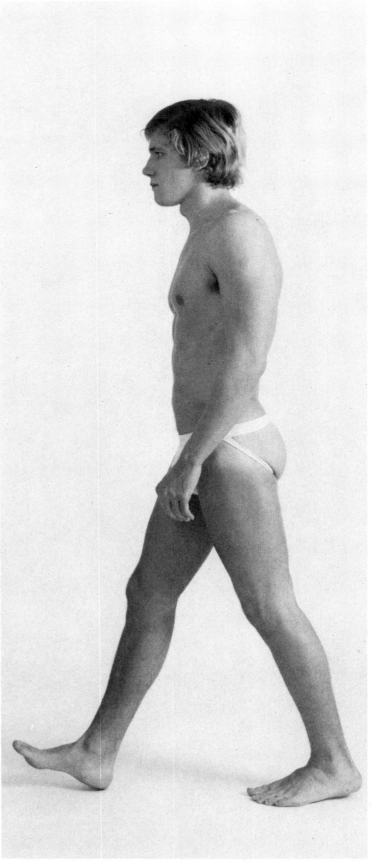

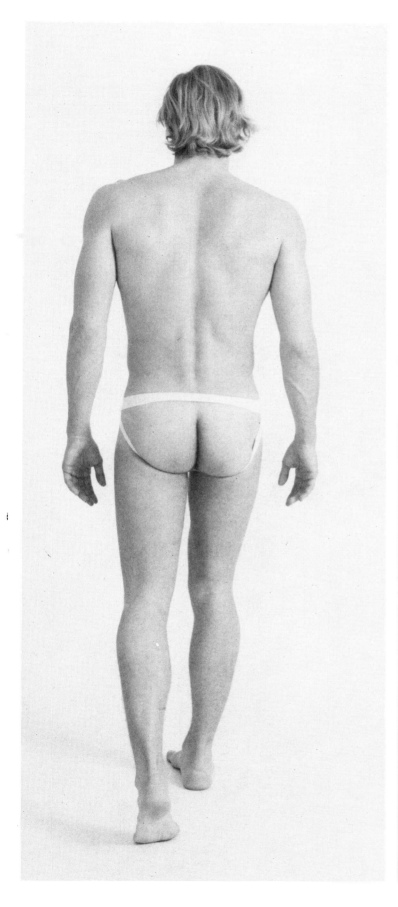
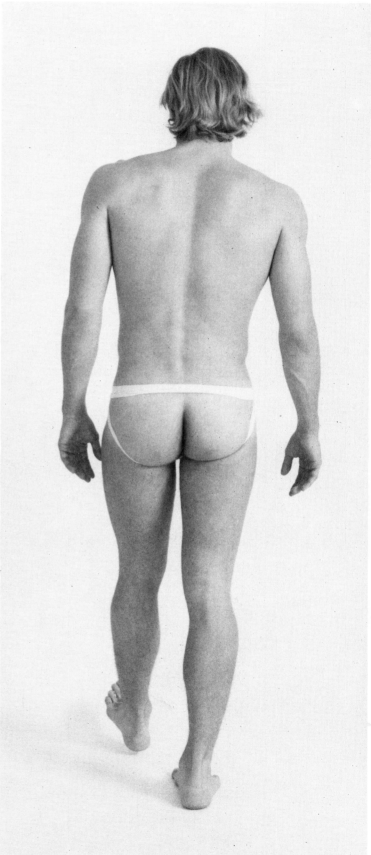

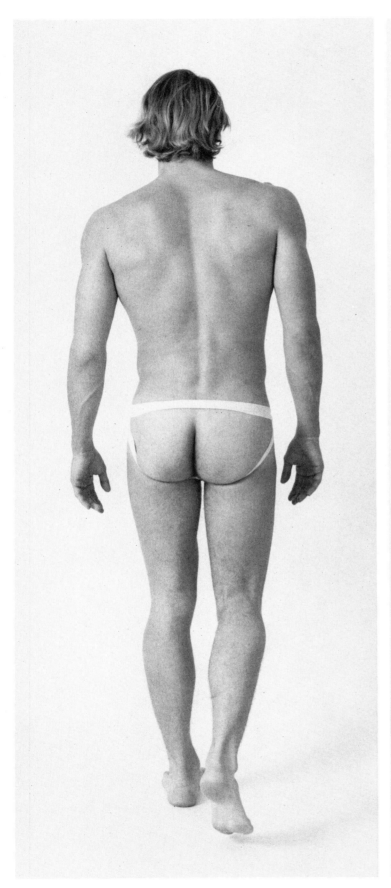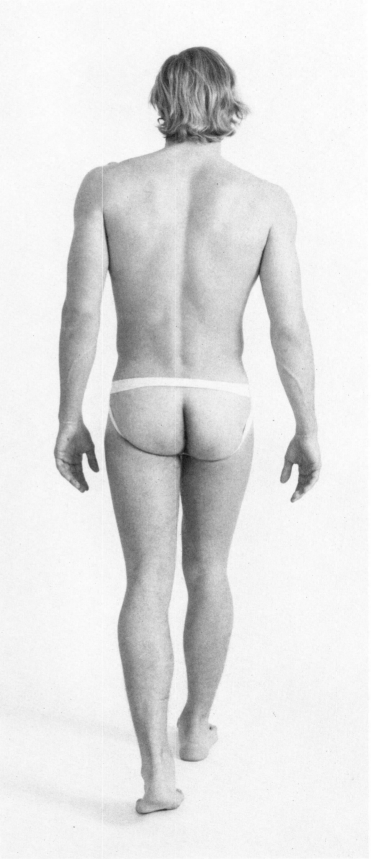

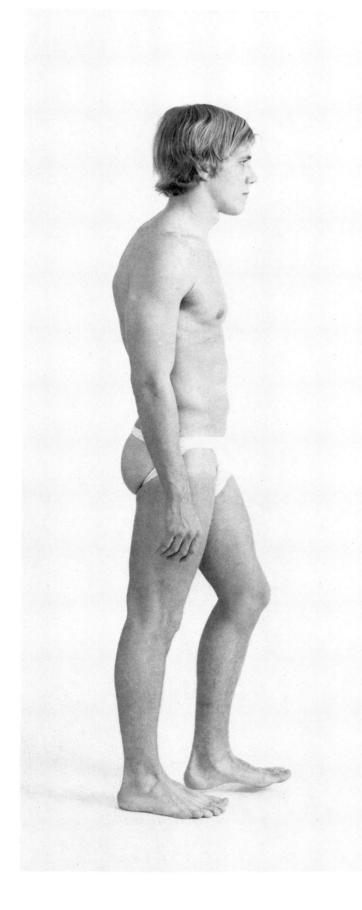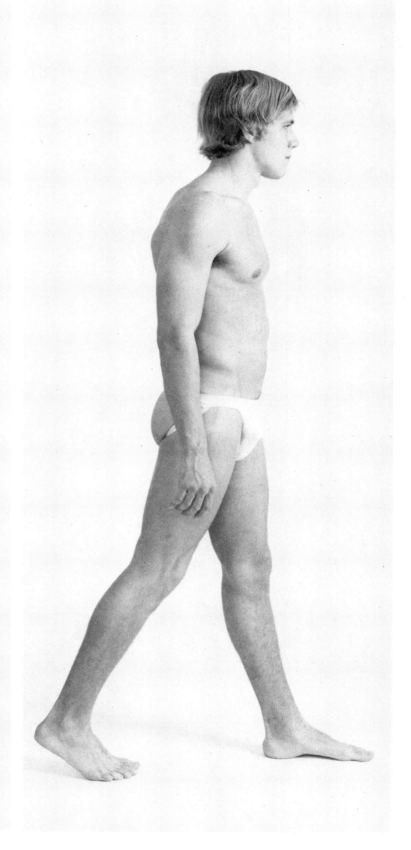

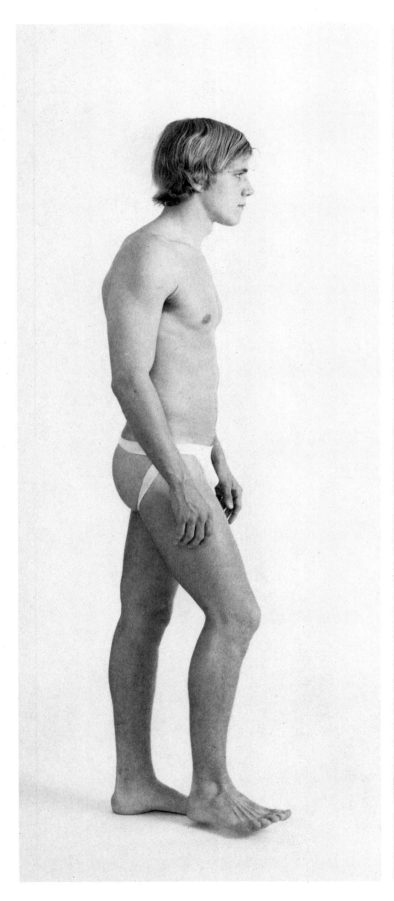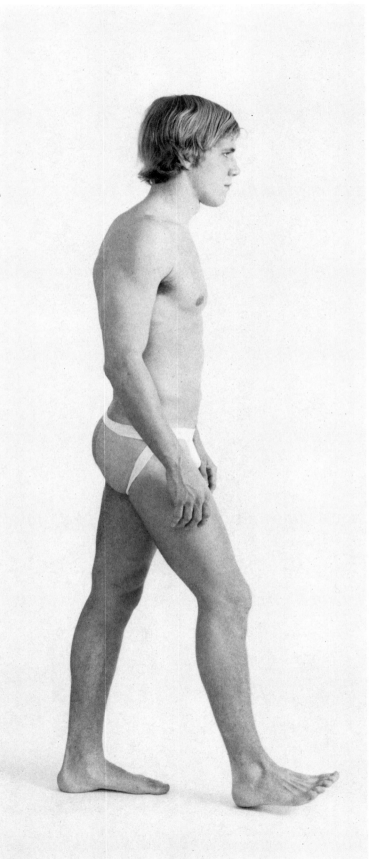

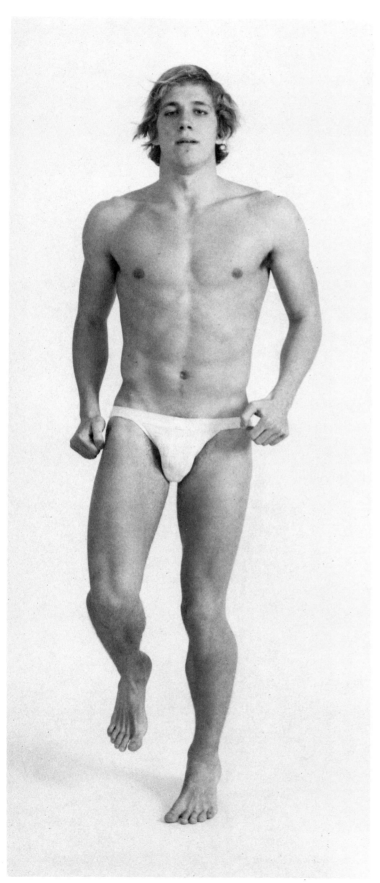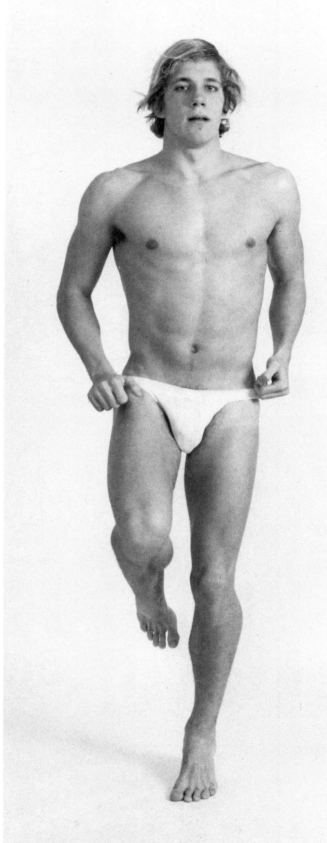

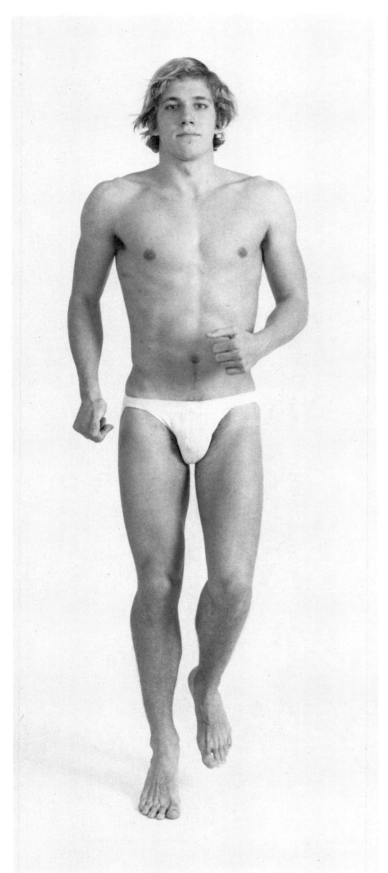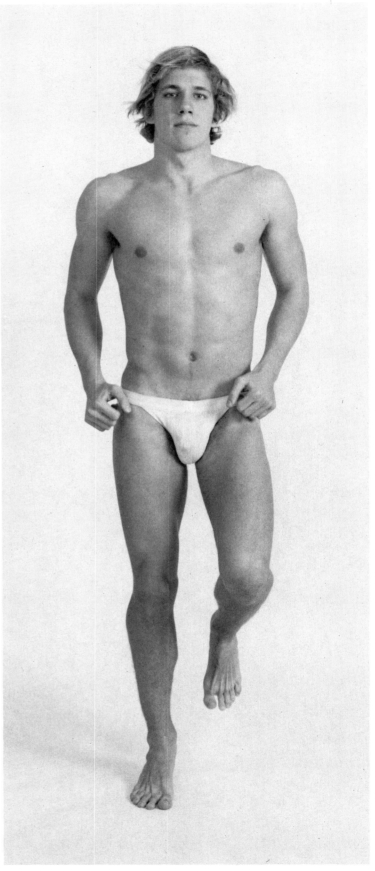

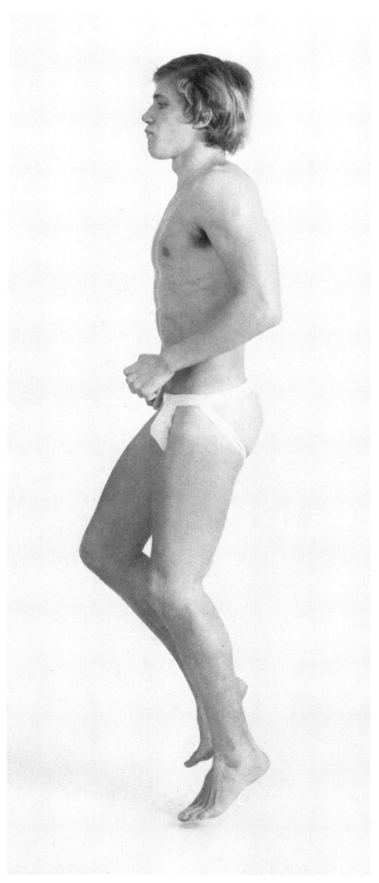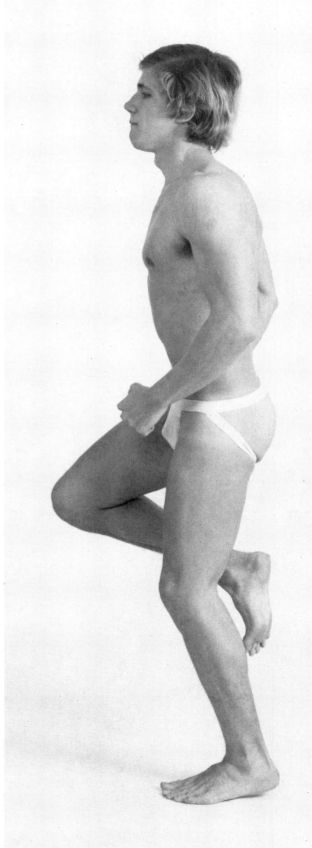

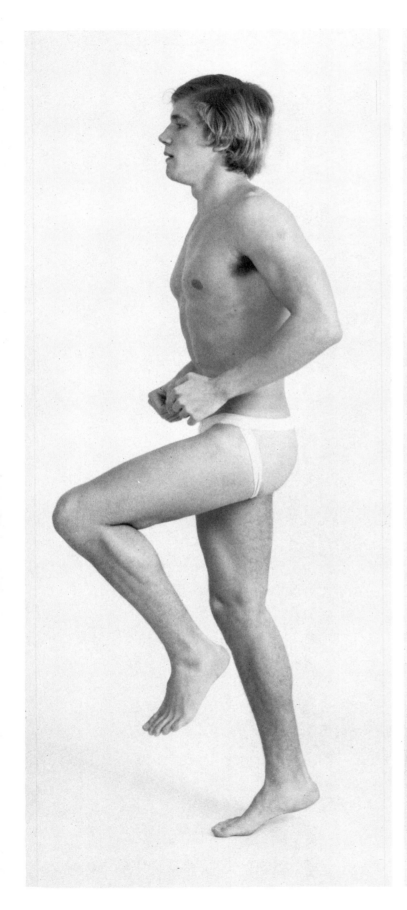
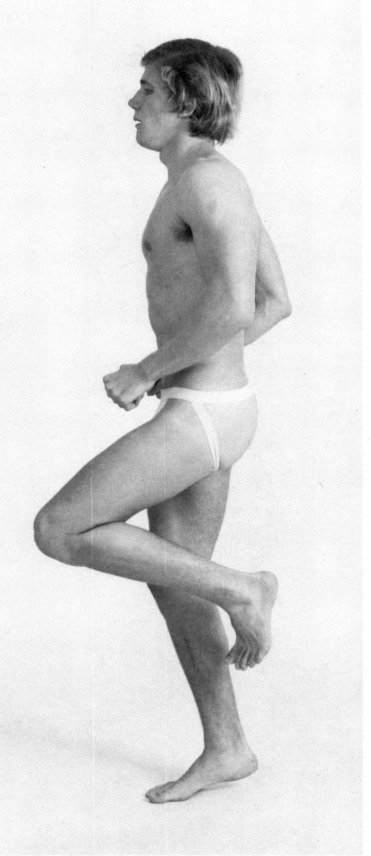

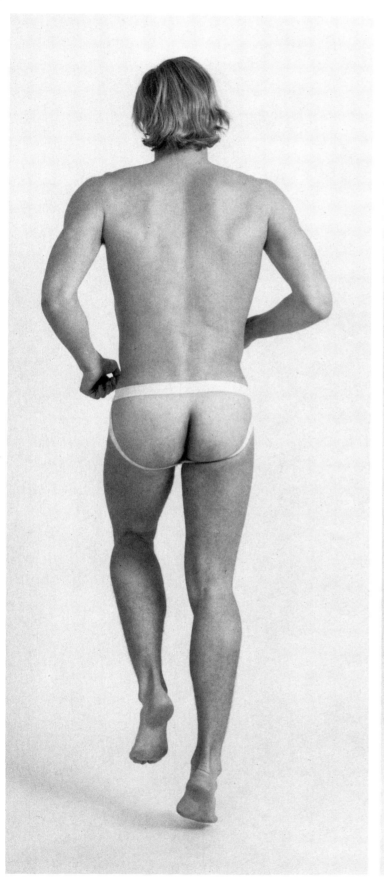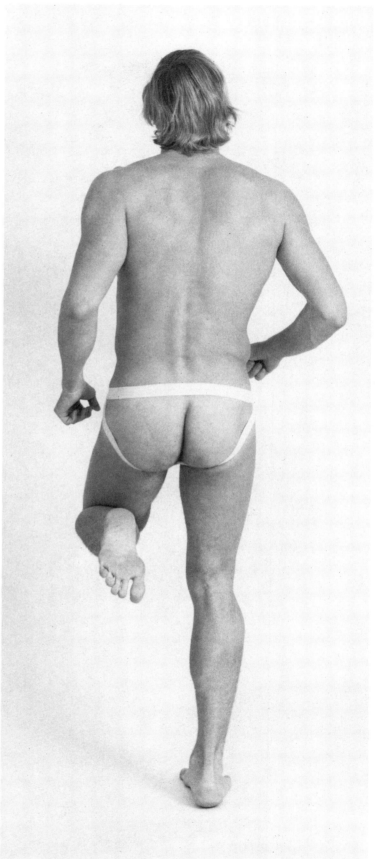

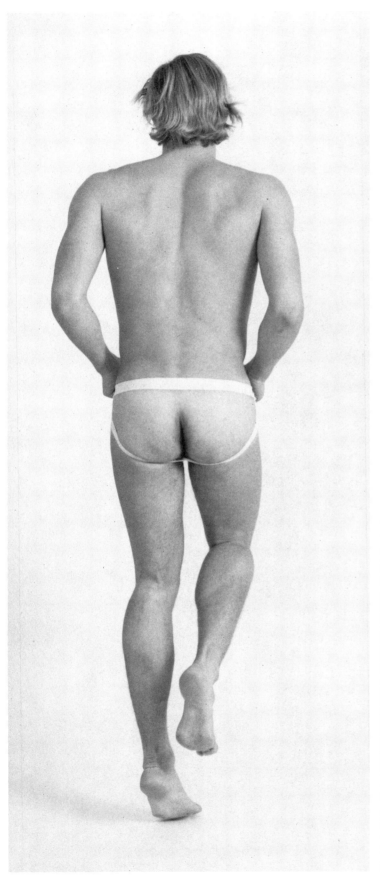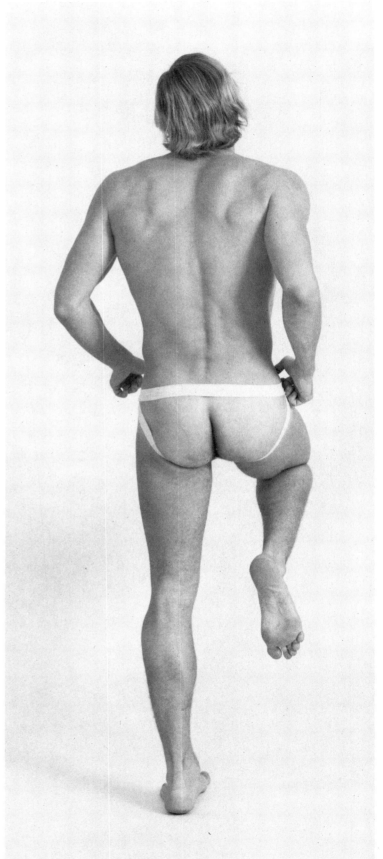

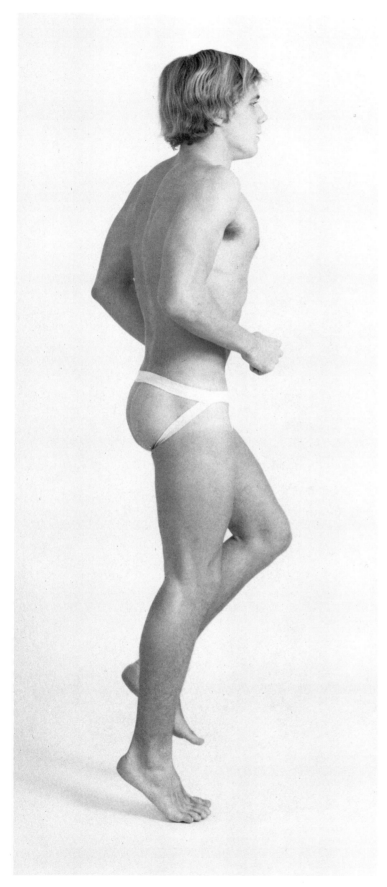
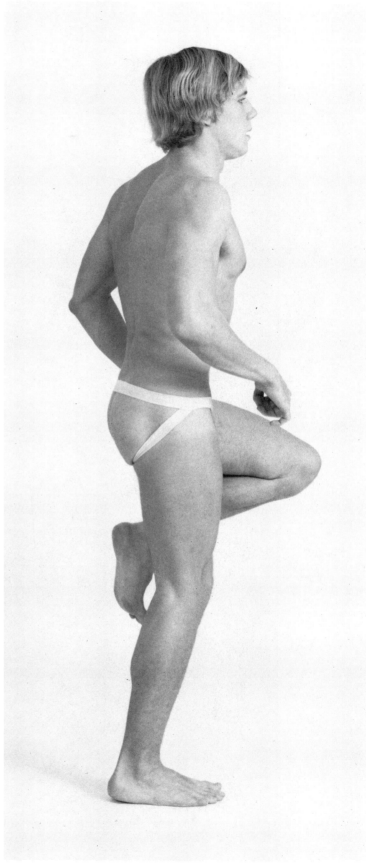

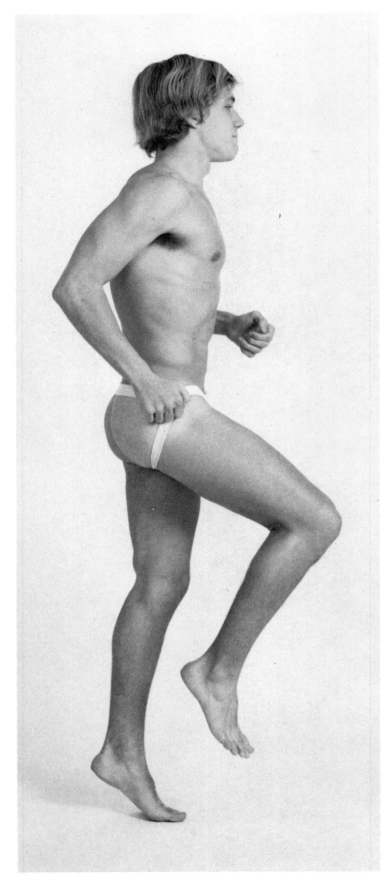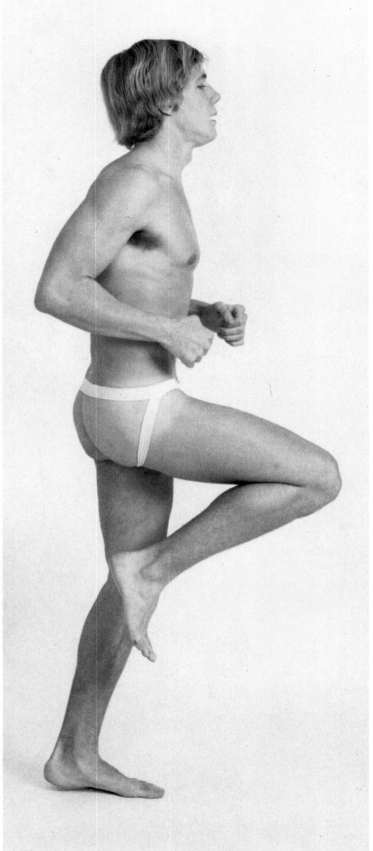

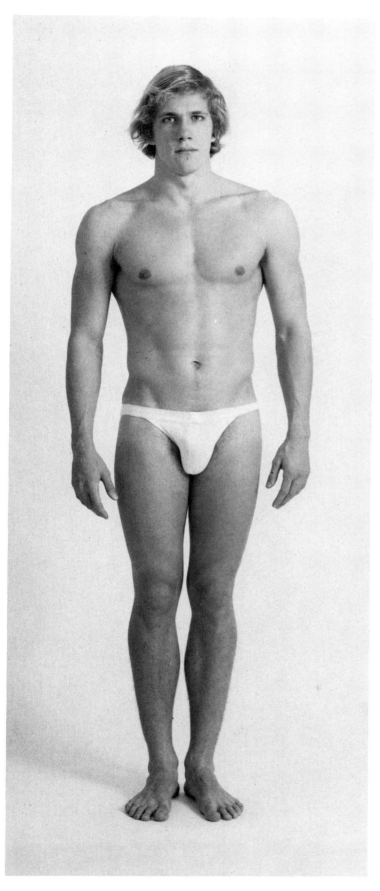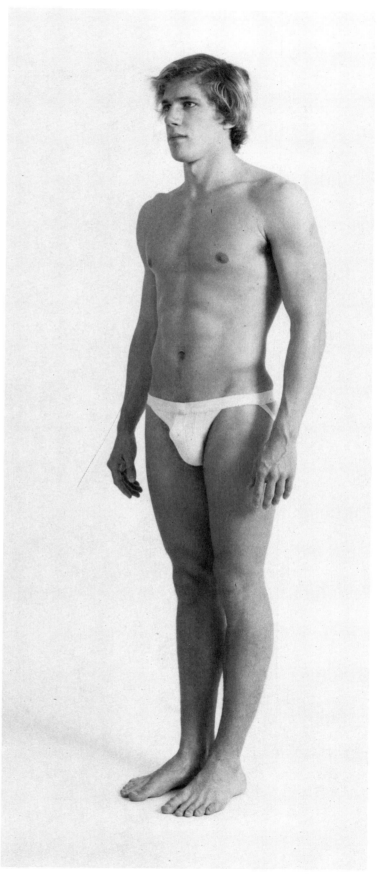

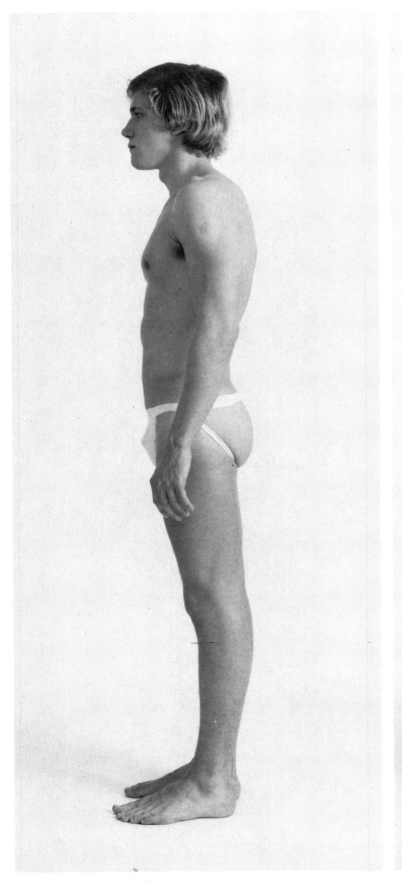
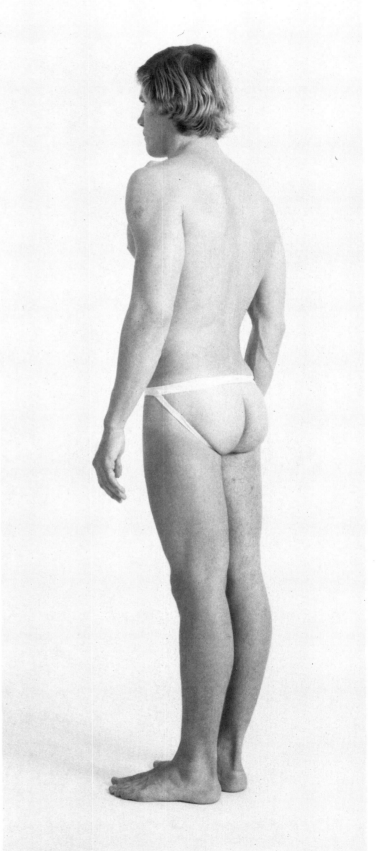

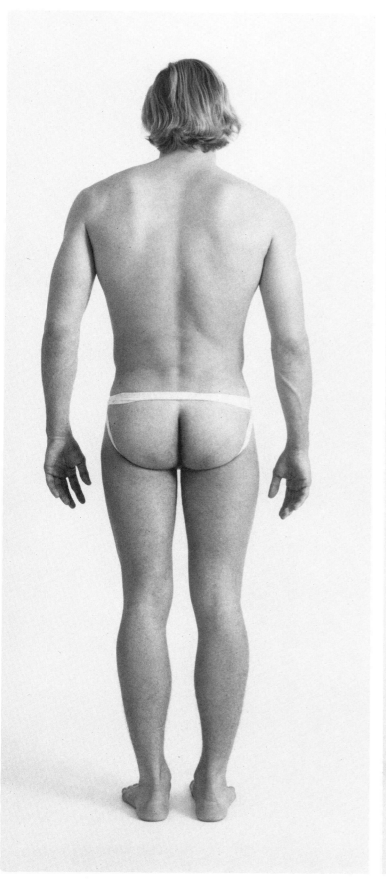
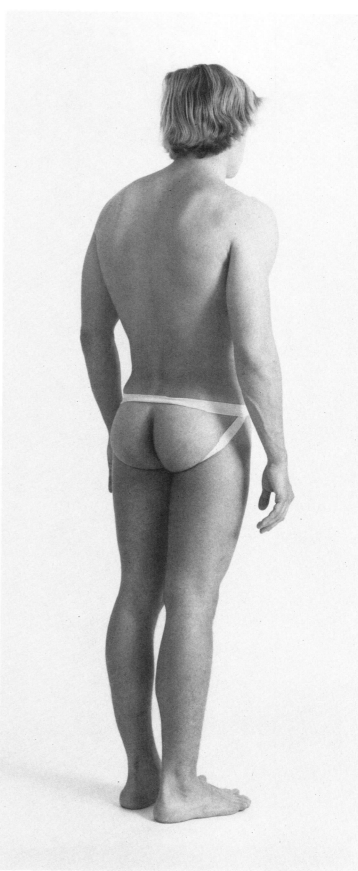

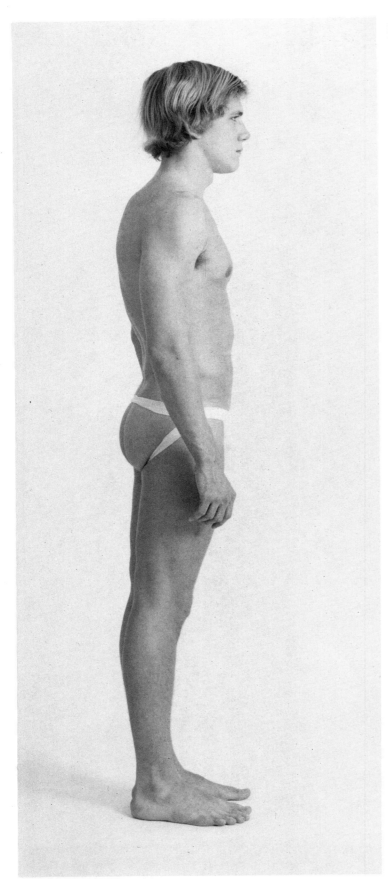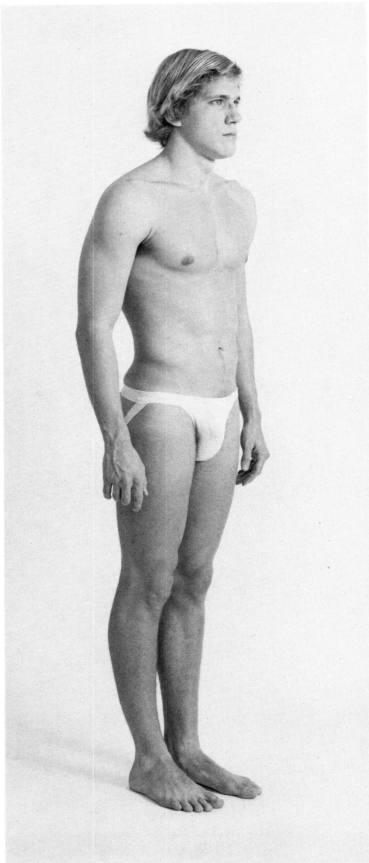

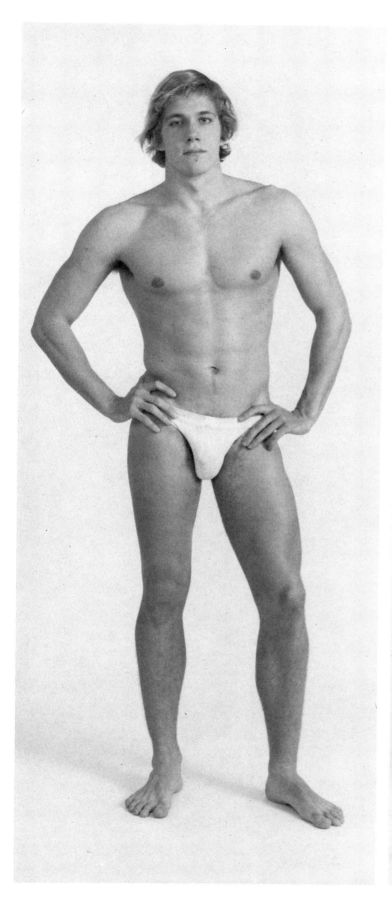
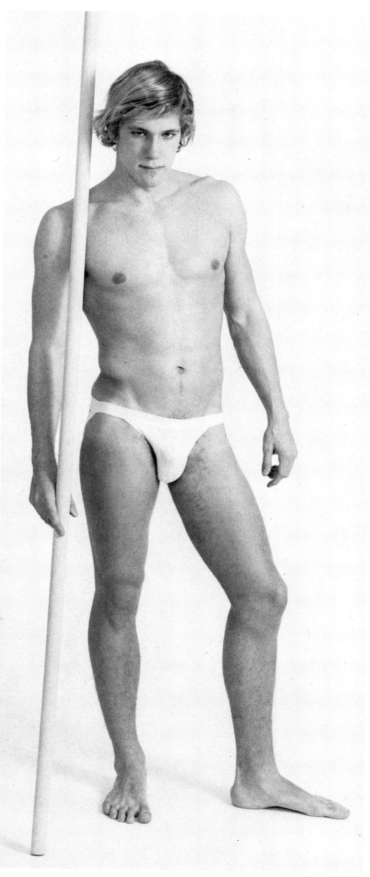

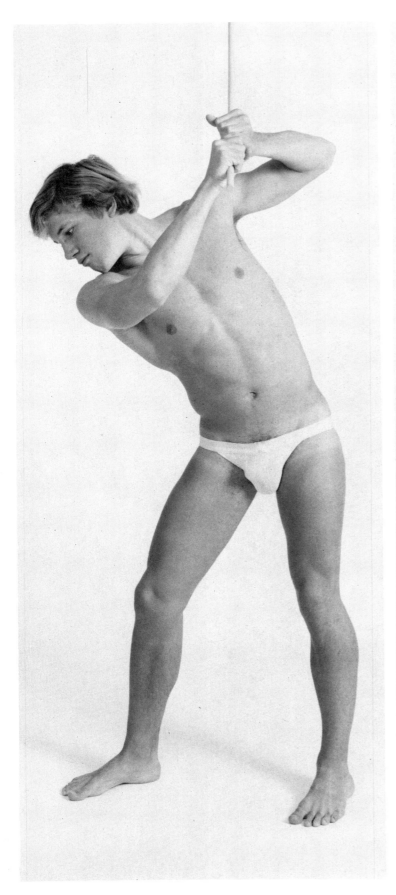
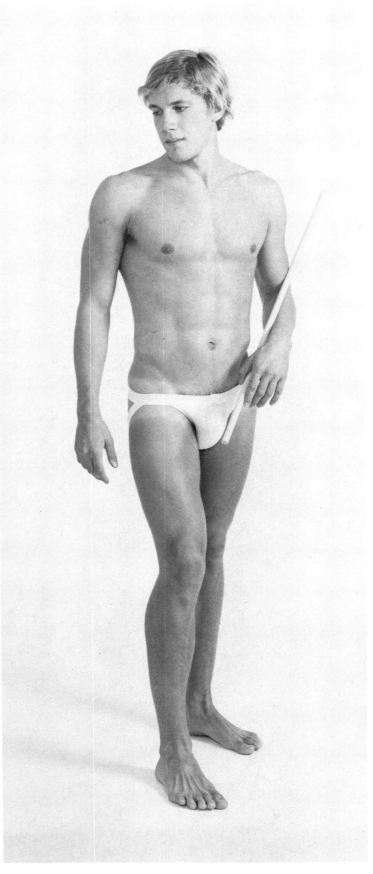

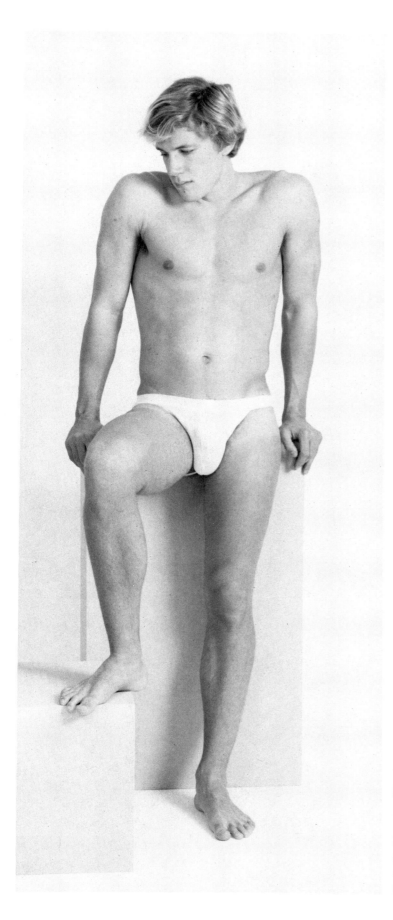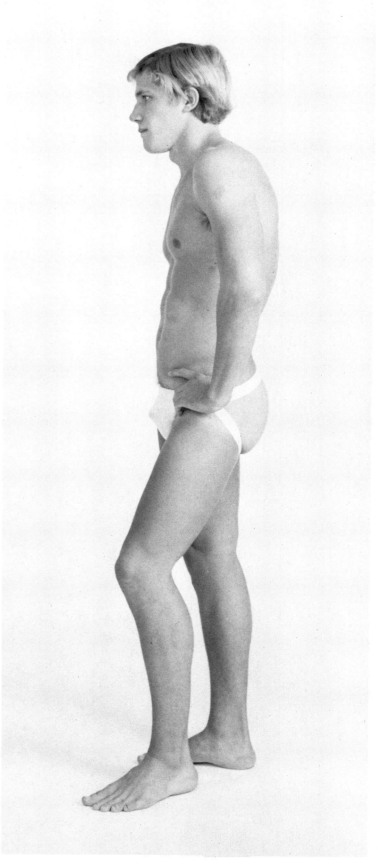

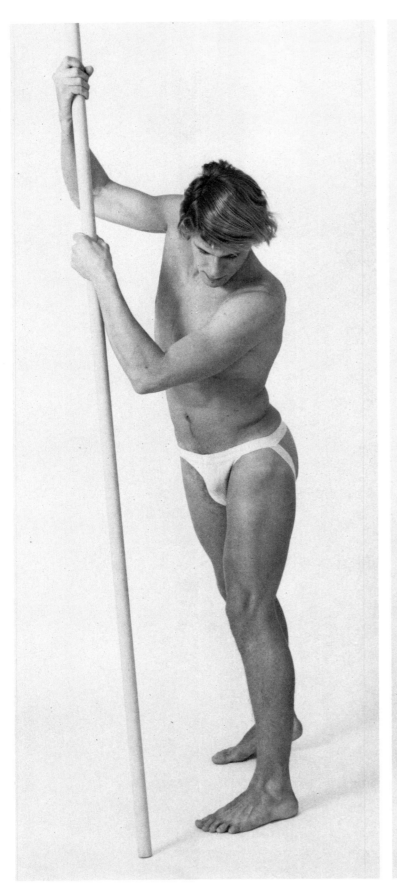
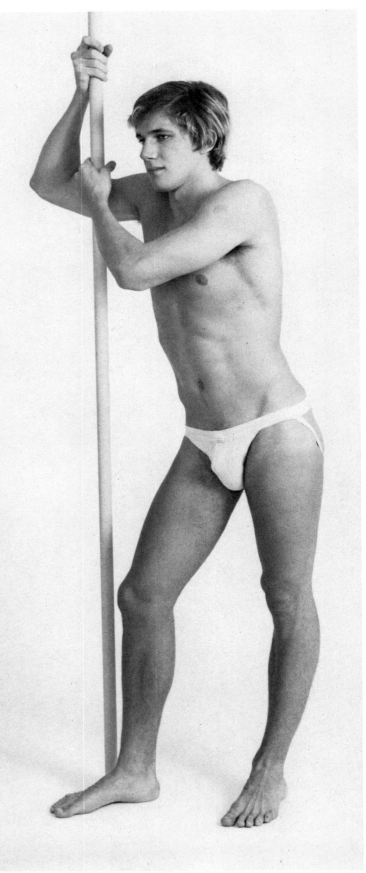

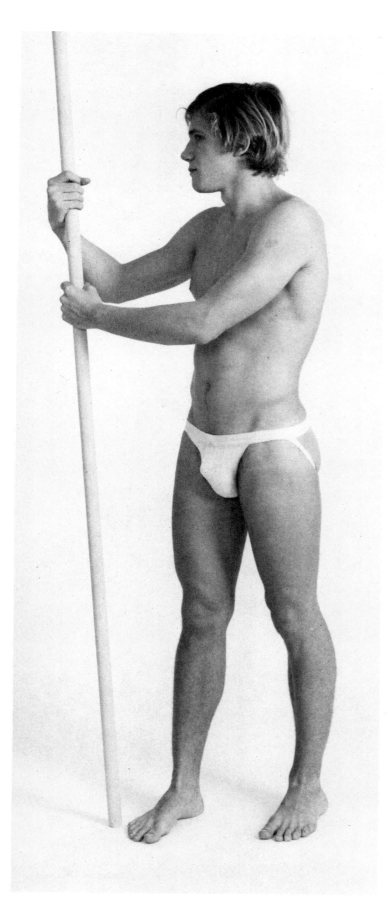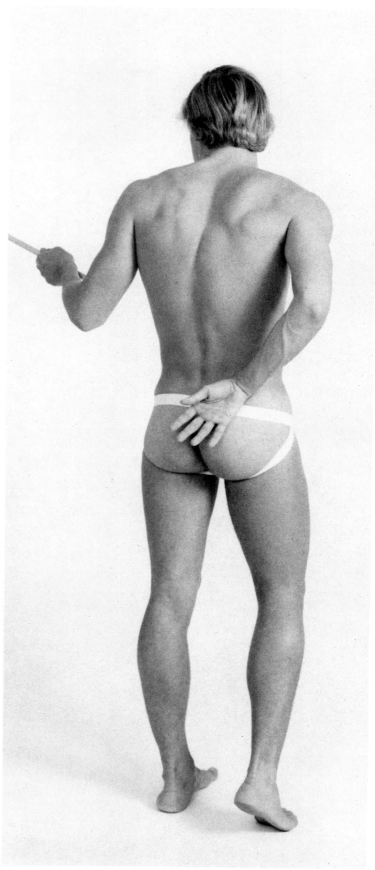

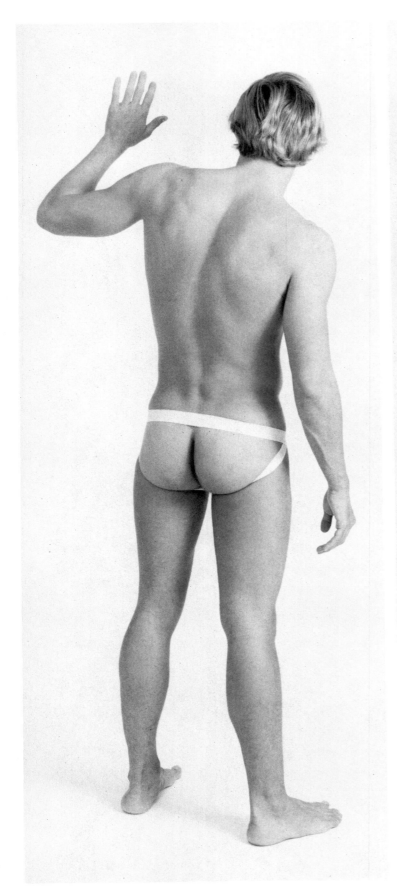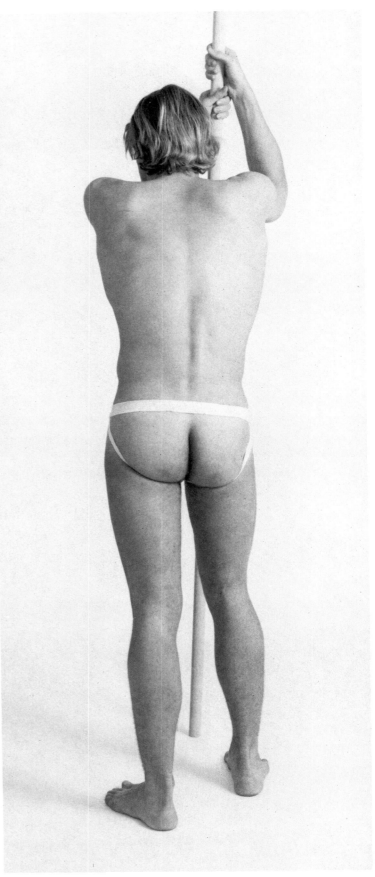

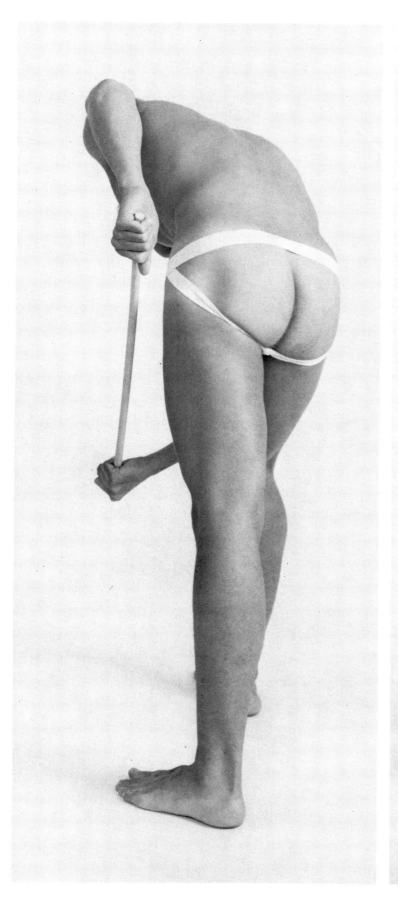
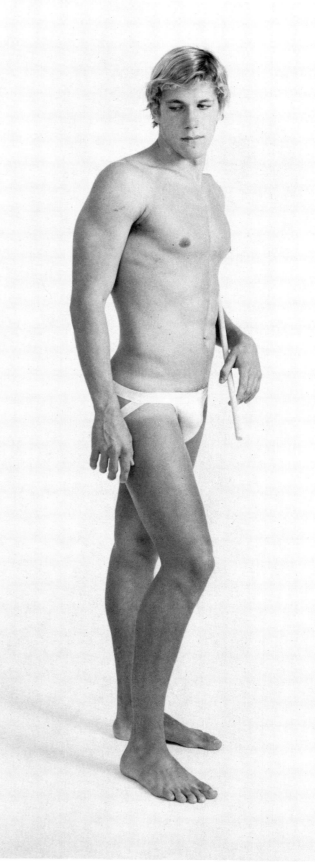

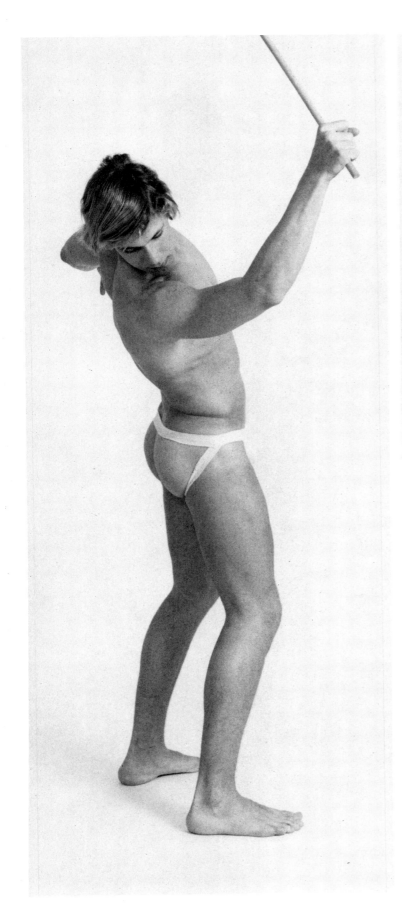
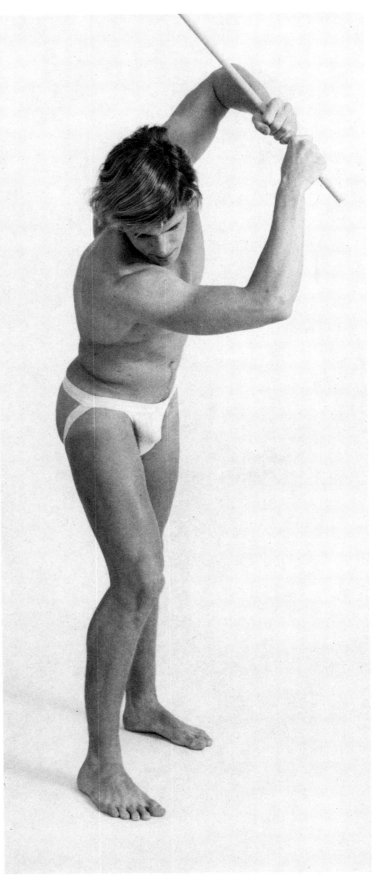

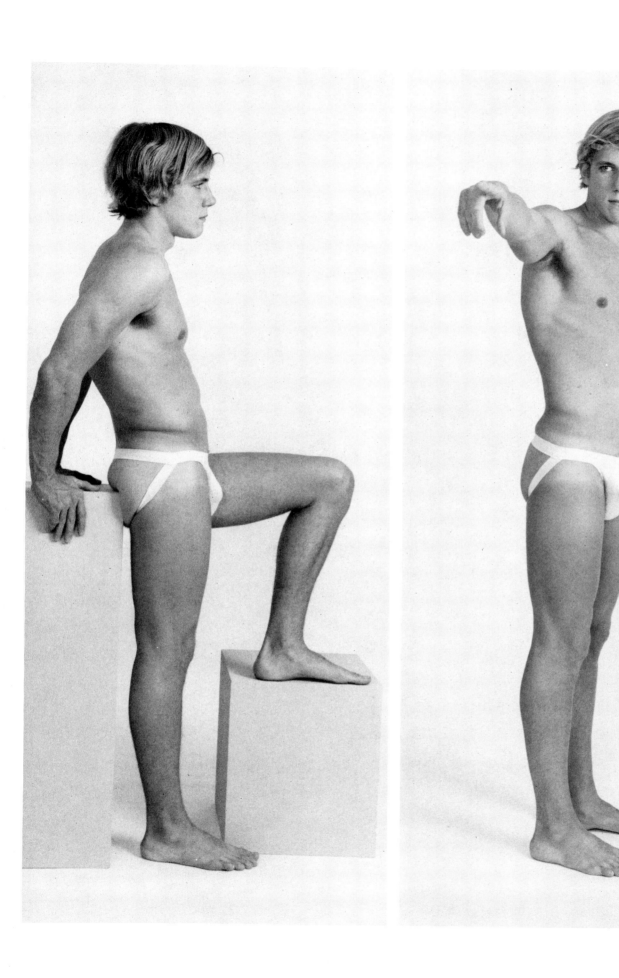

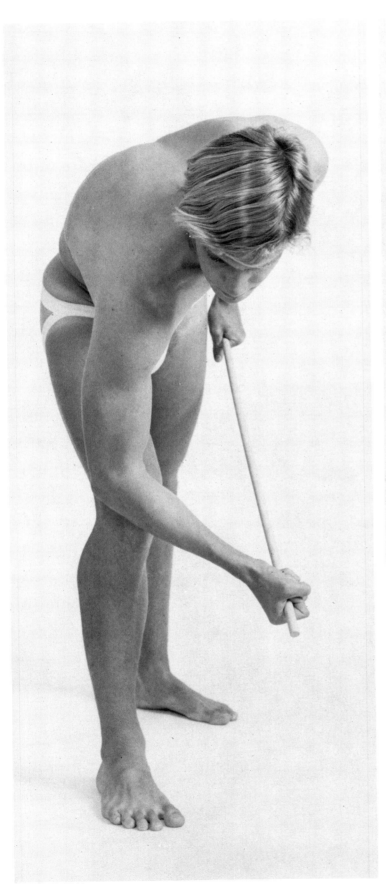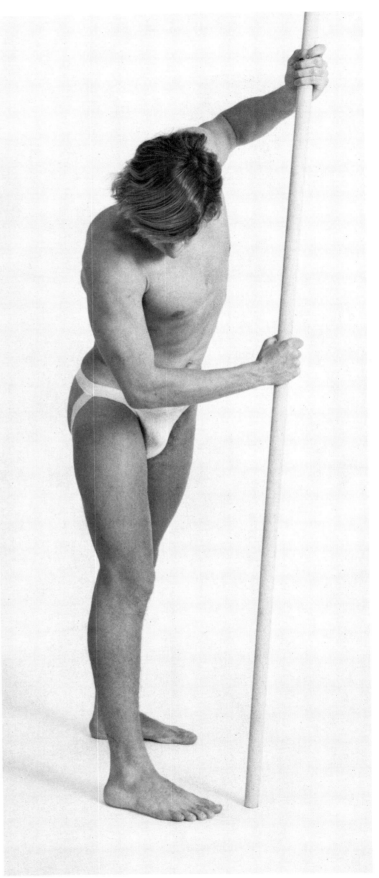

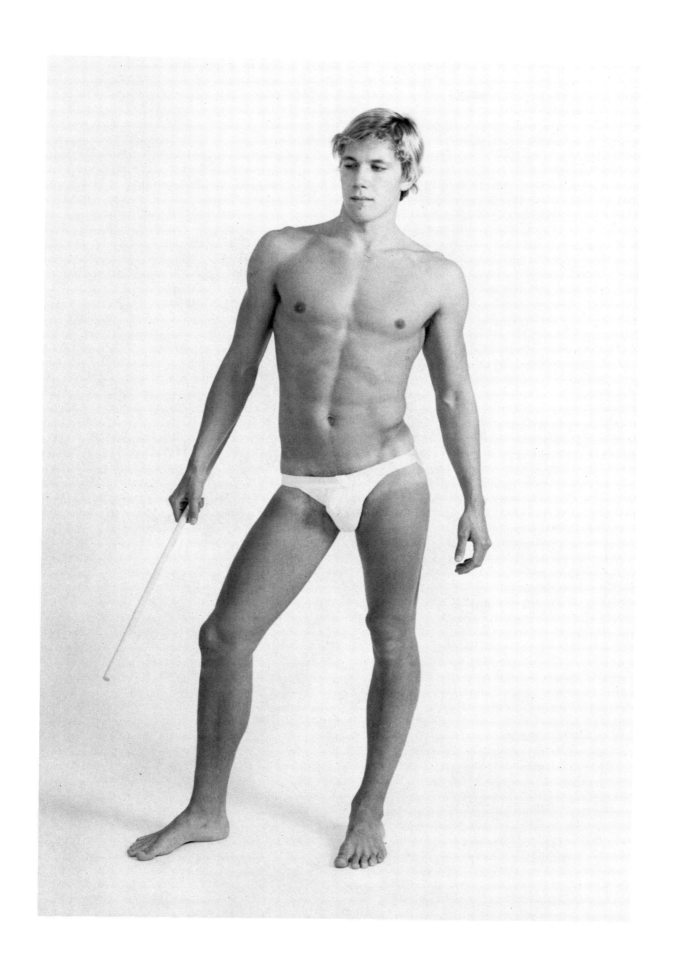

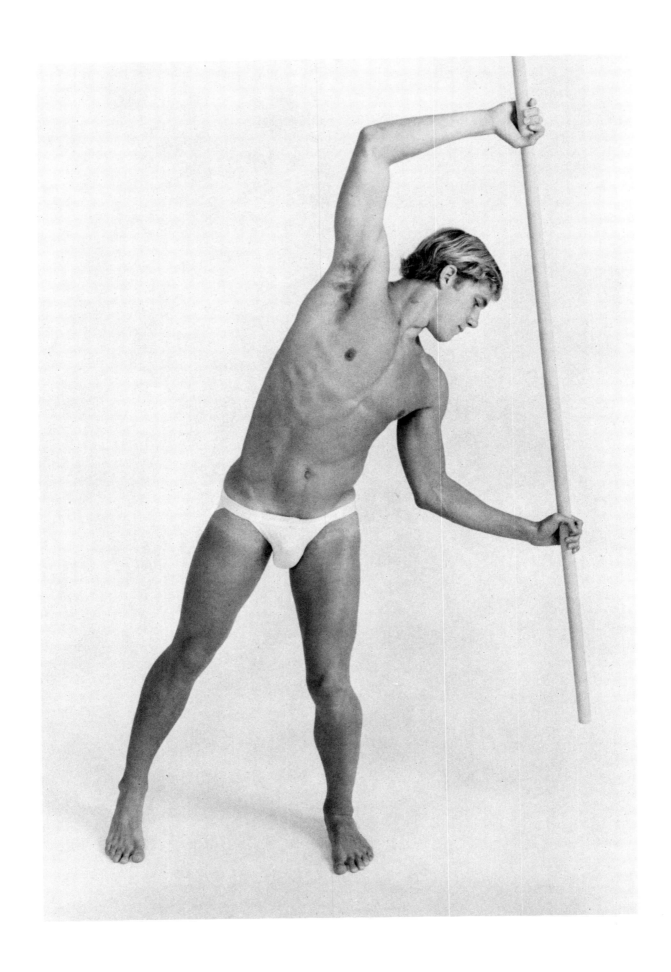

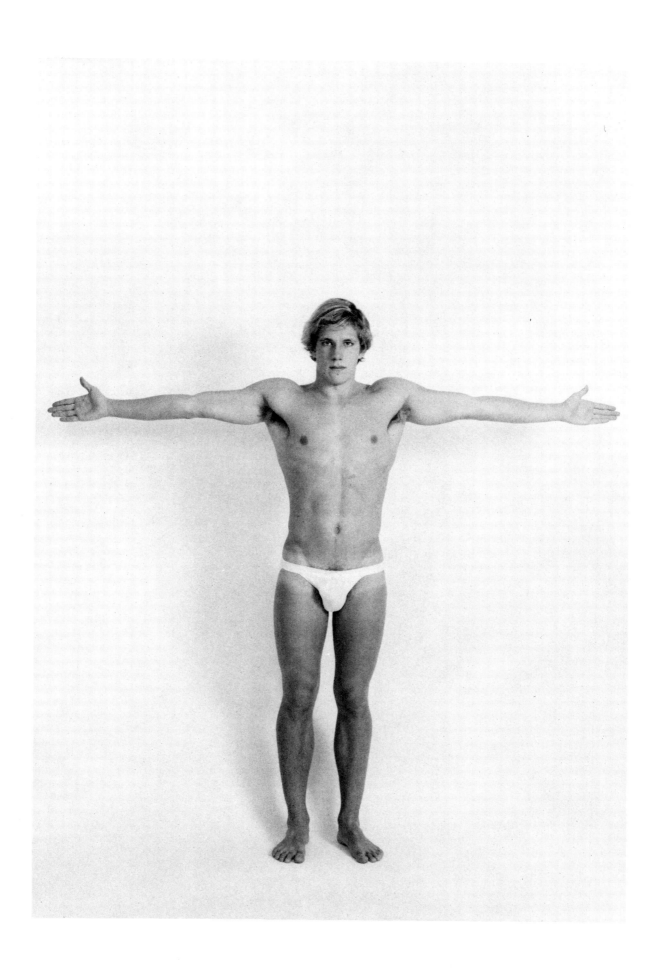

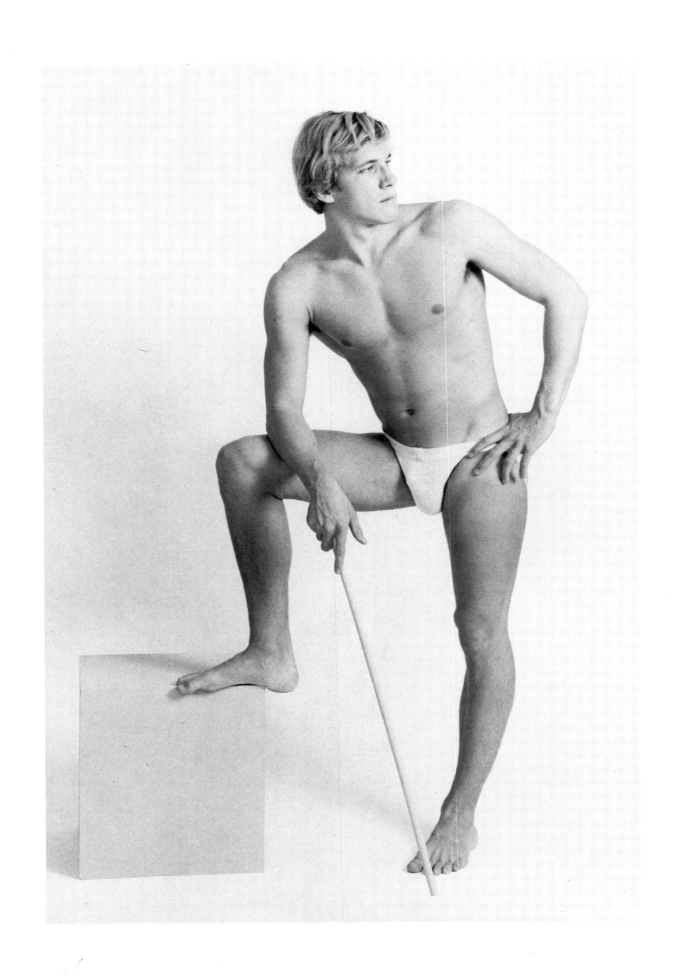

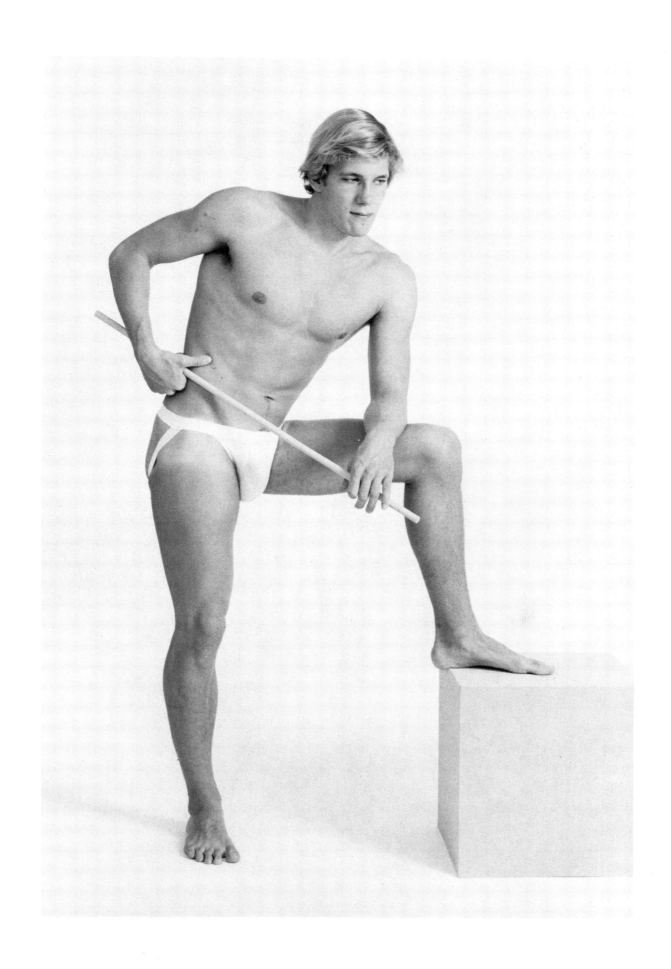

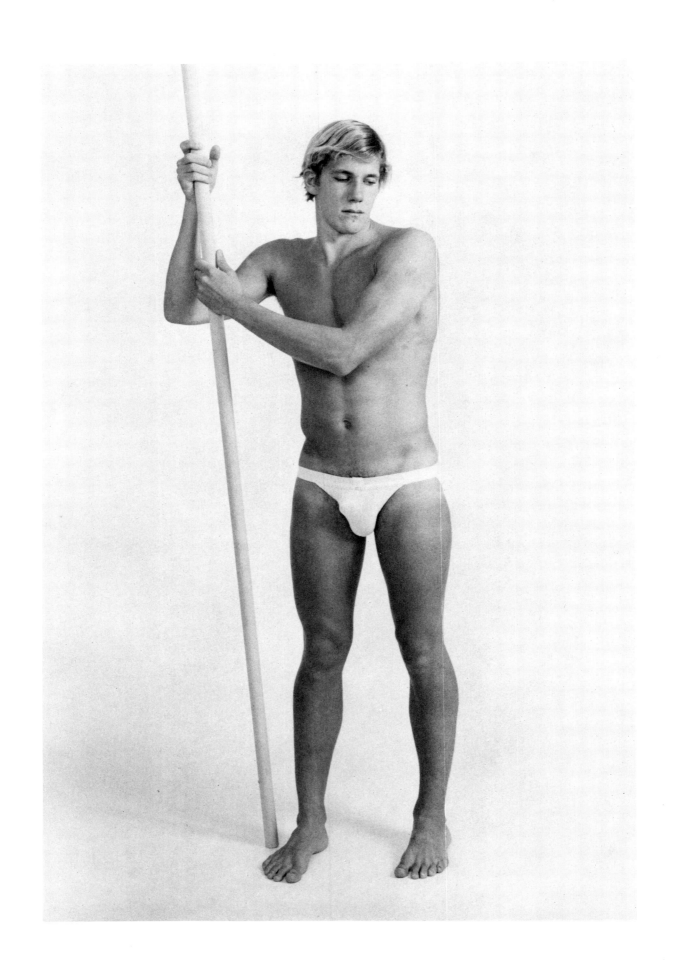

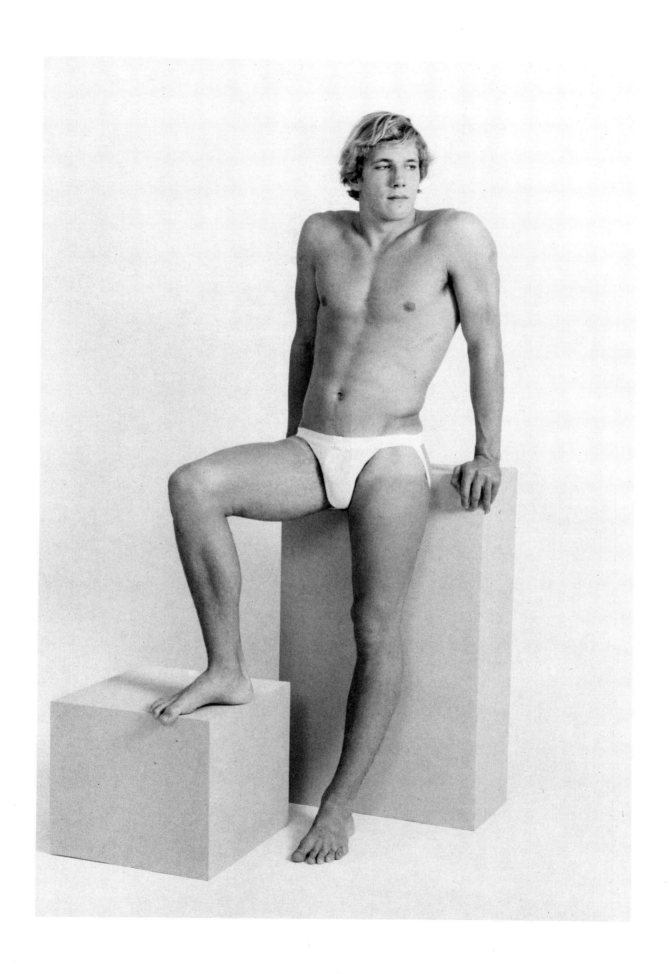

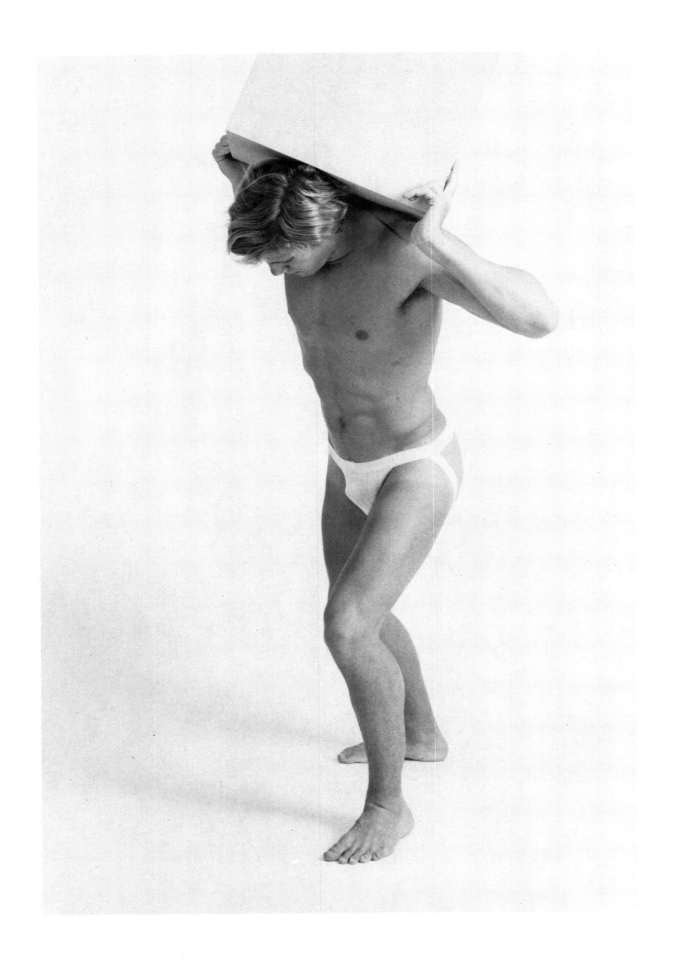

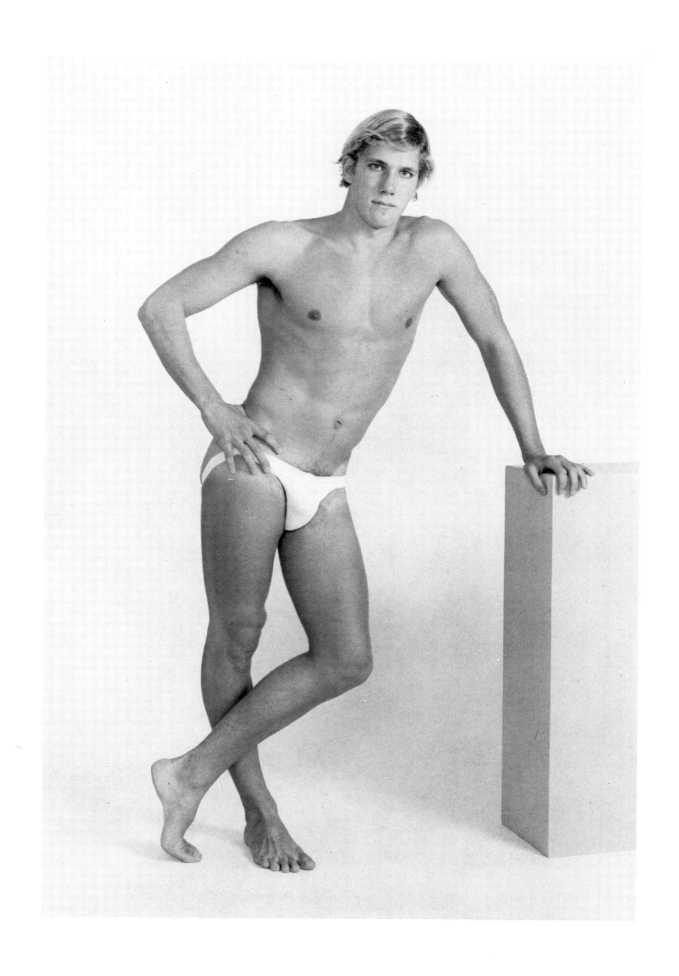

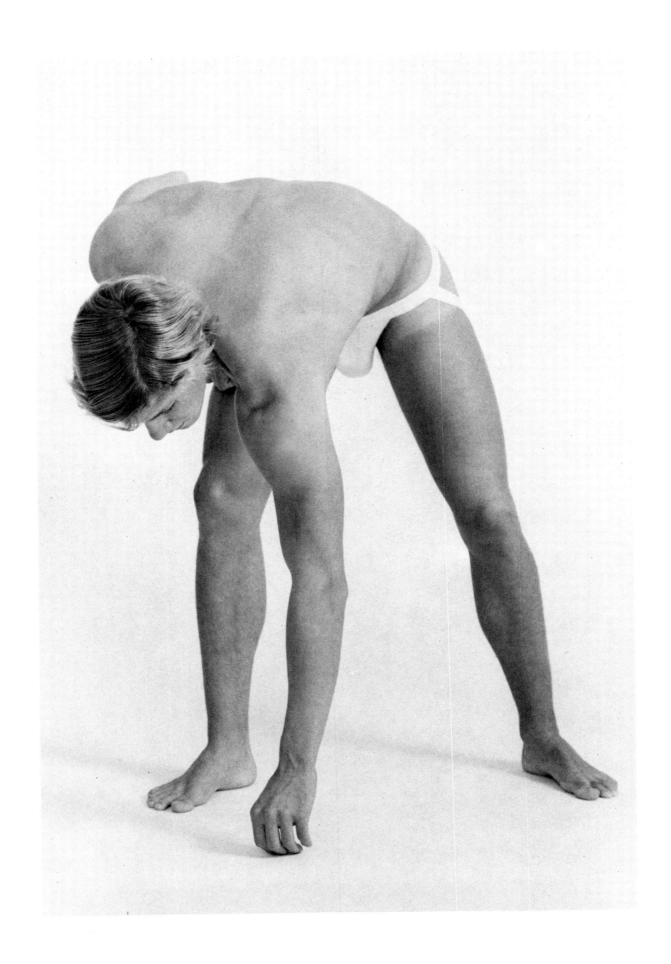

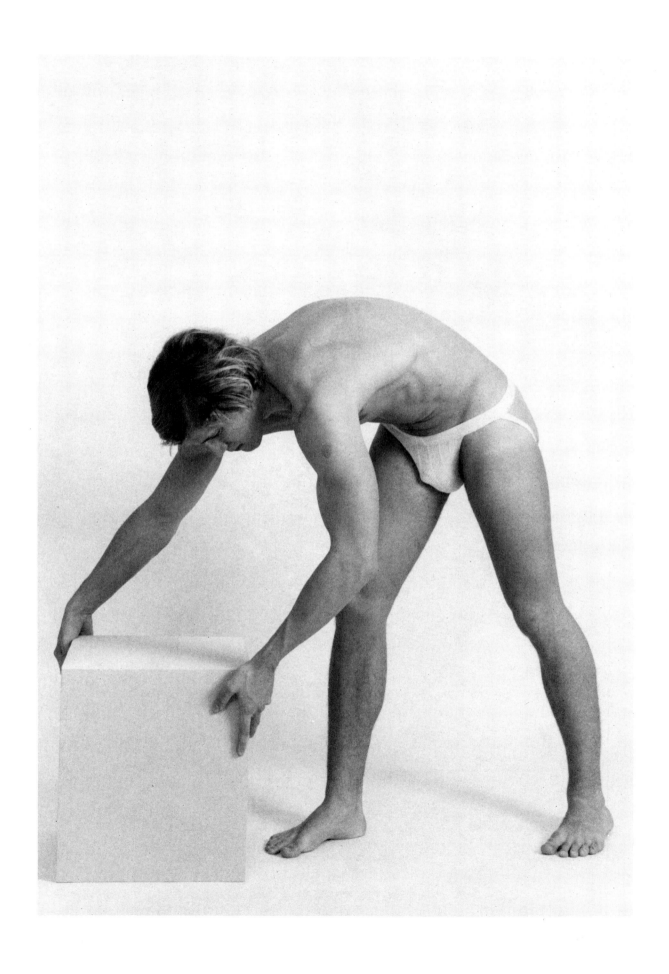

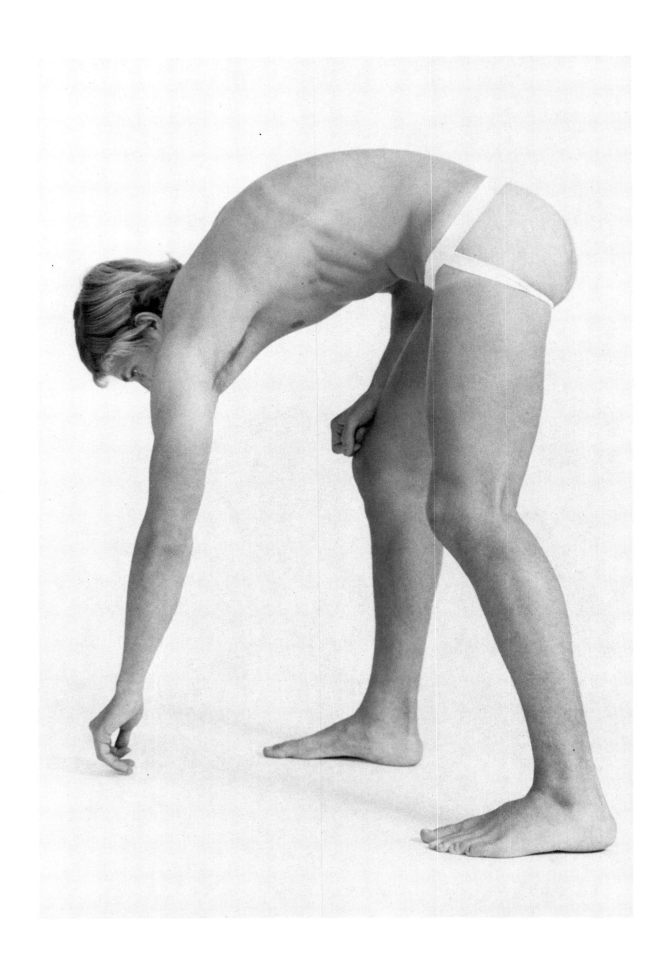

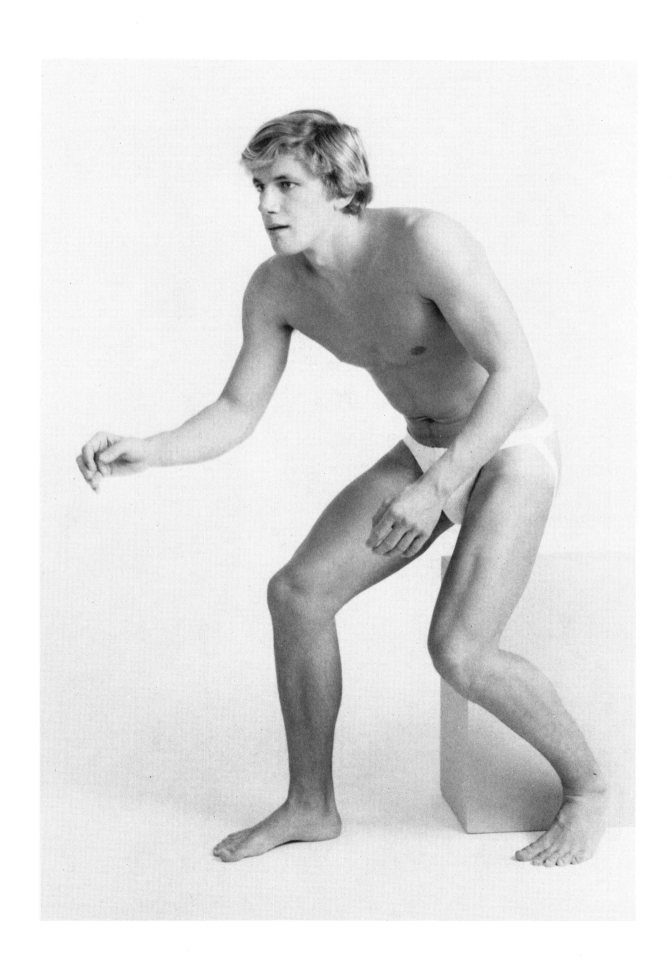

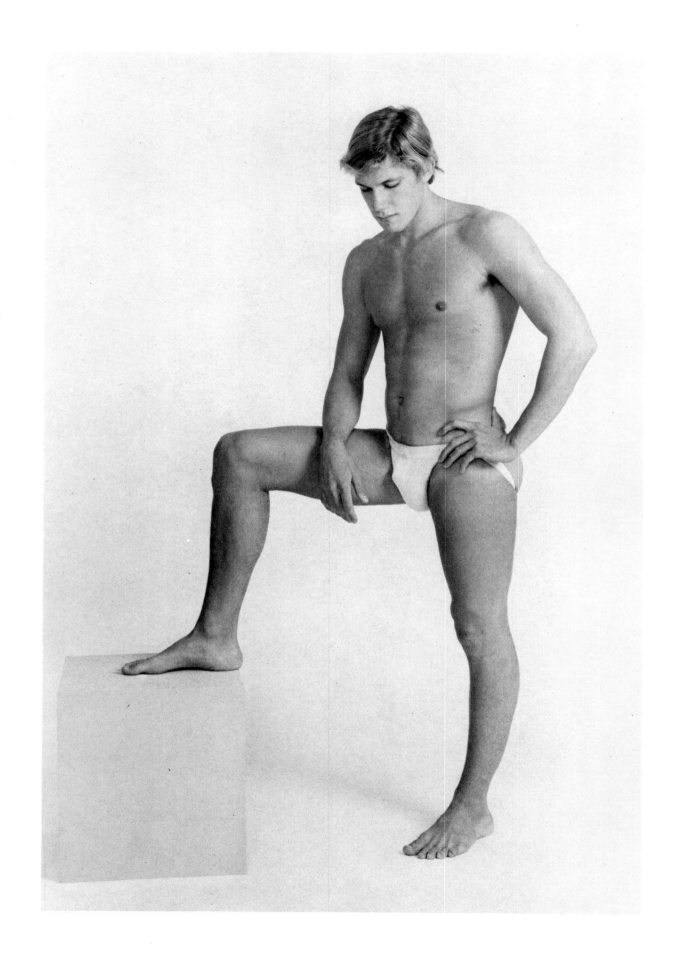

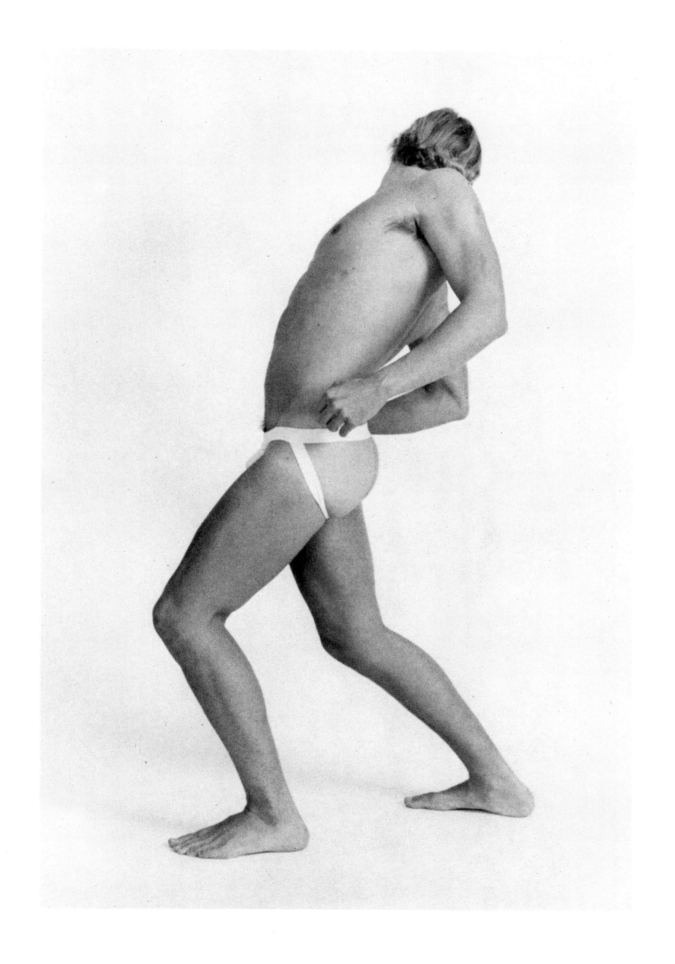

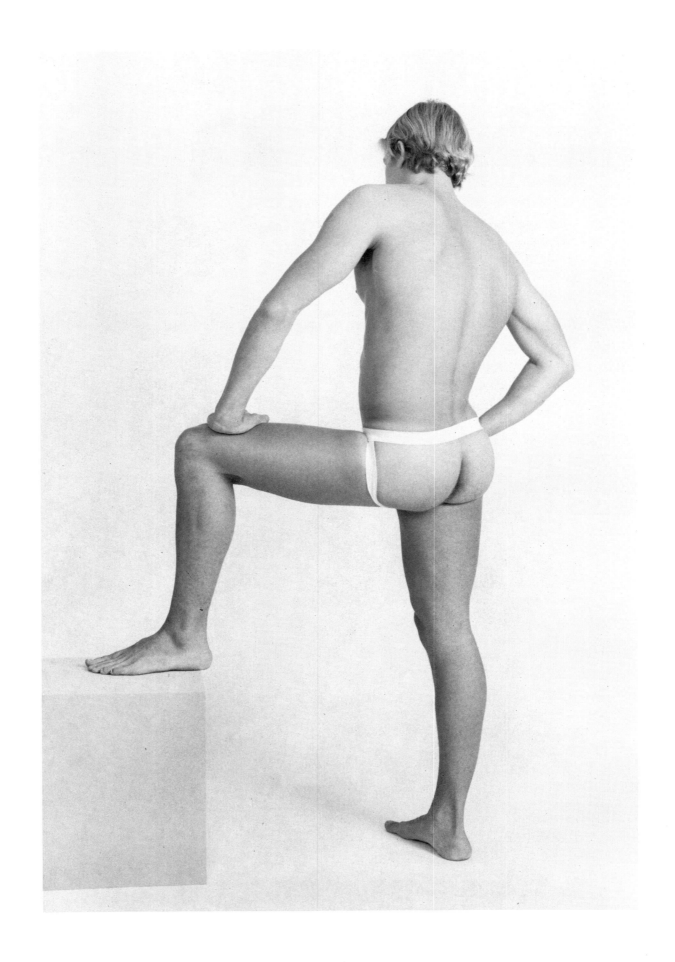

46

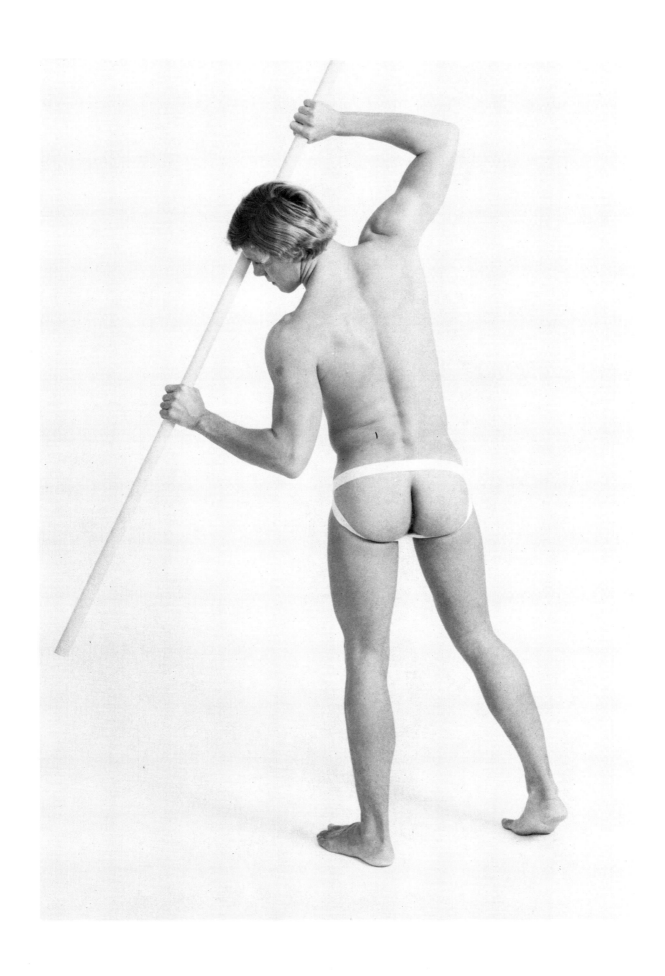

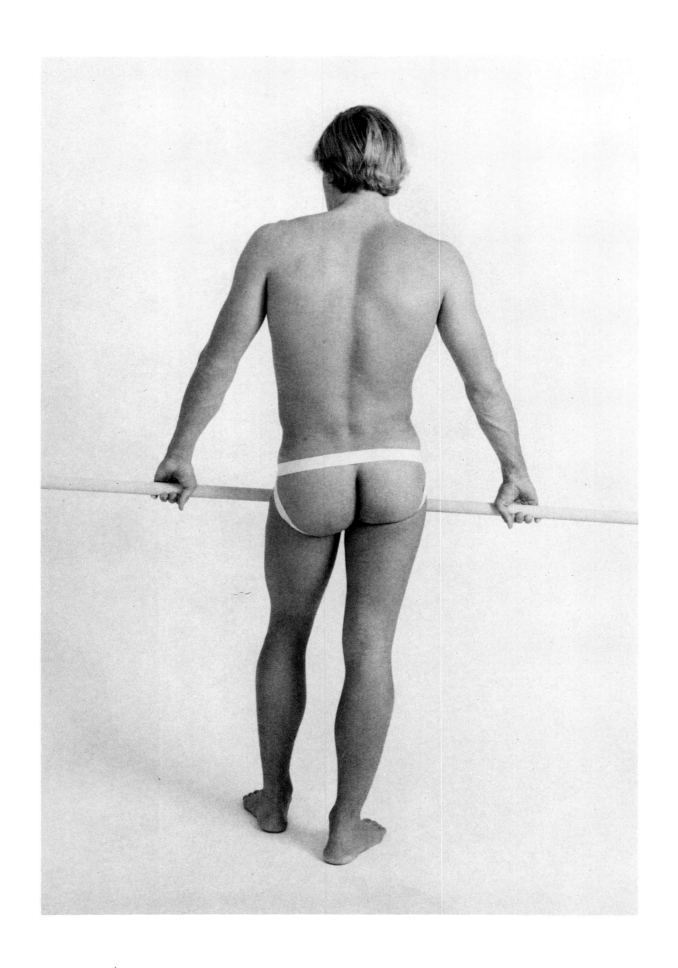

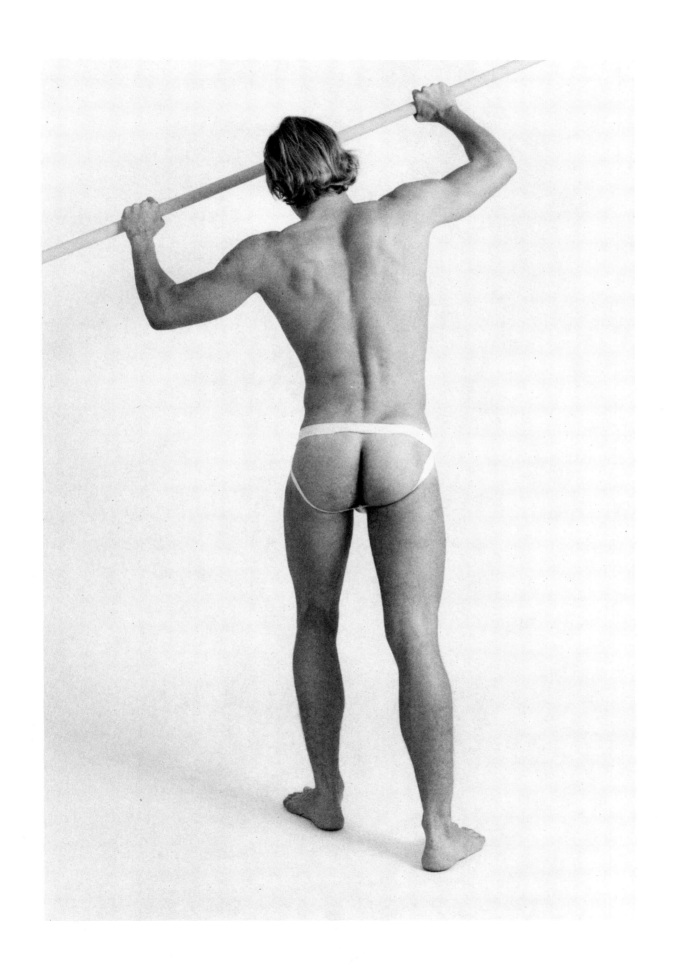

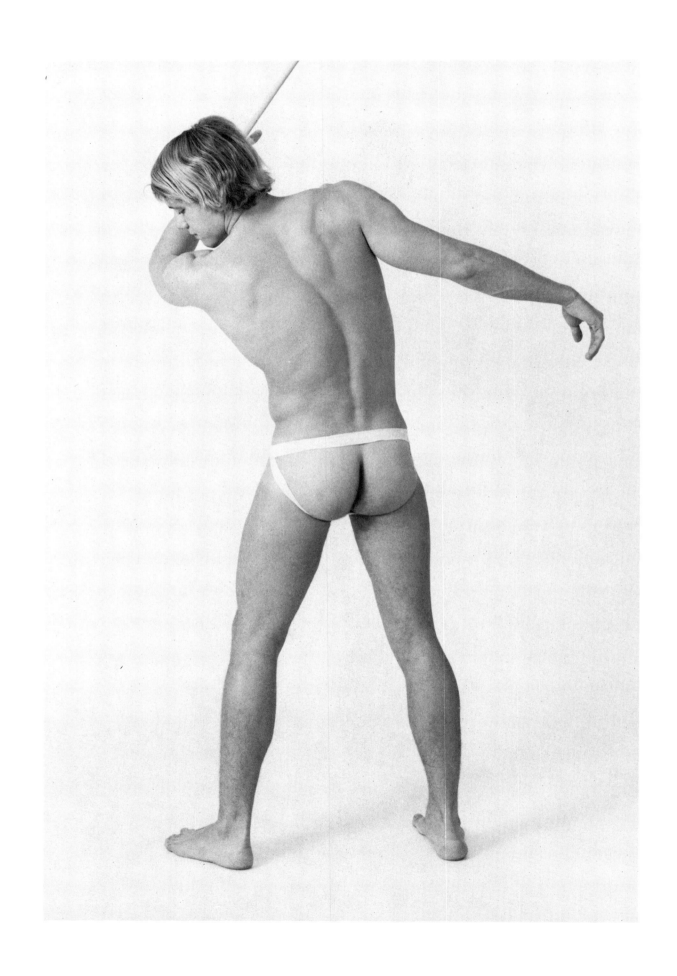

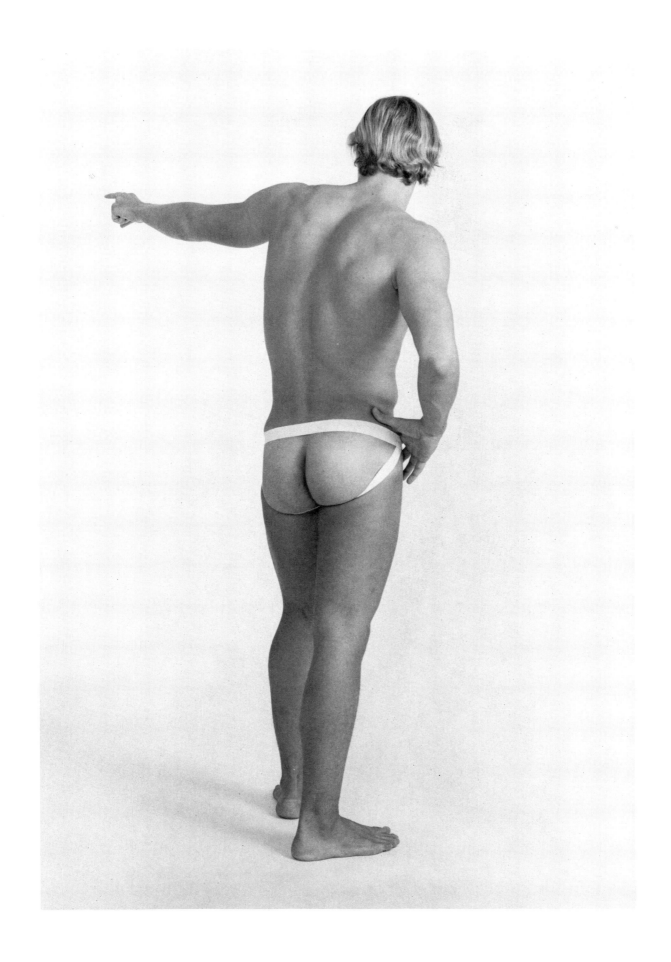

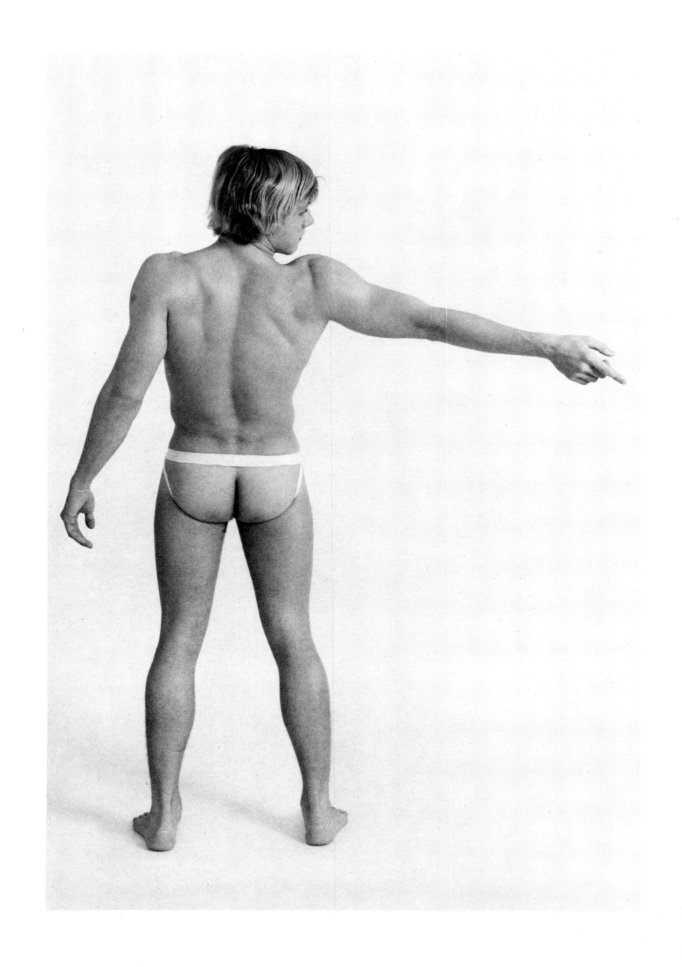

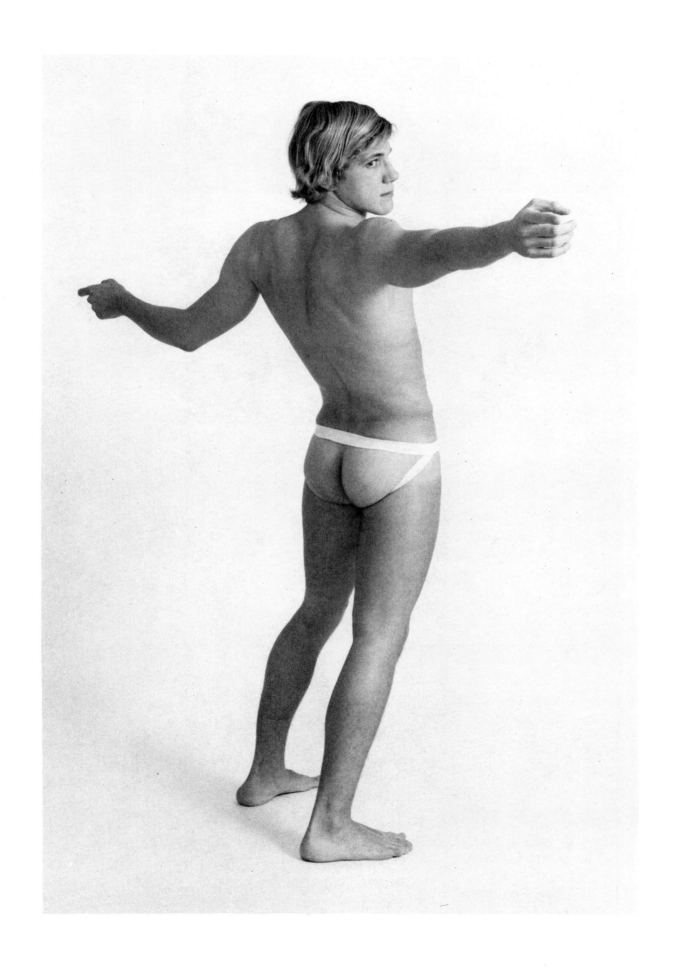

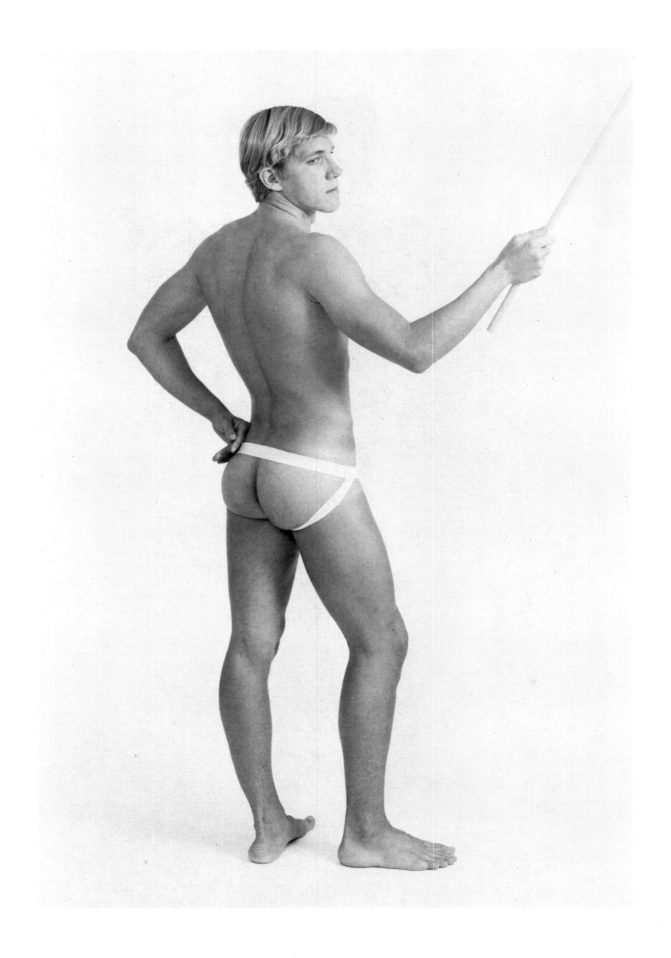

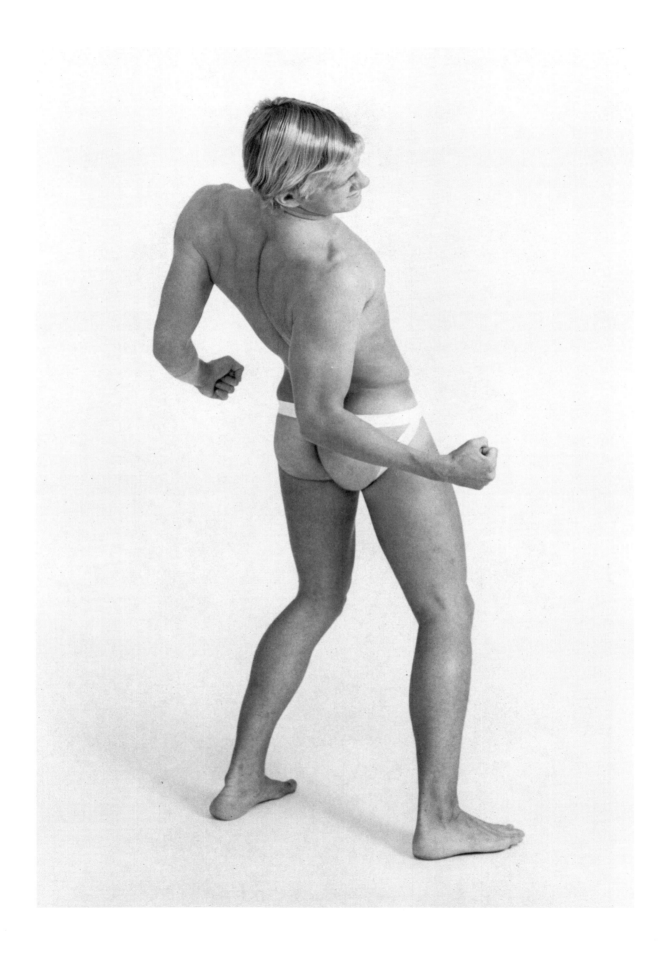

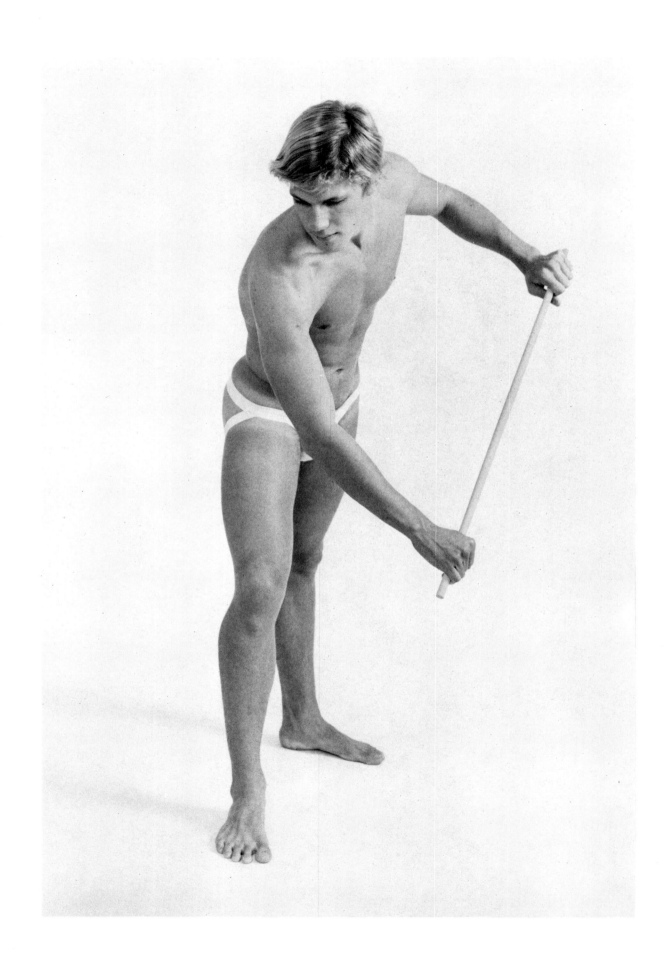

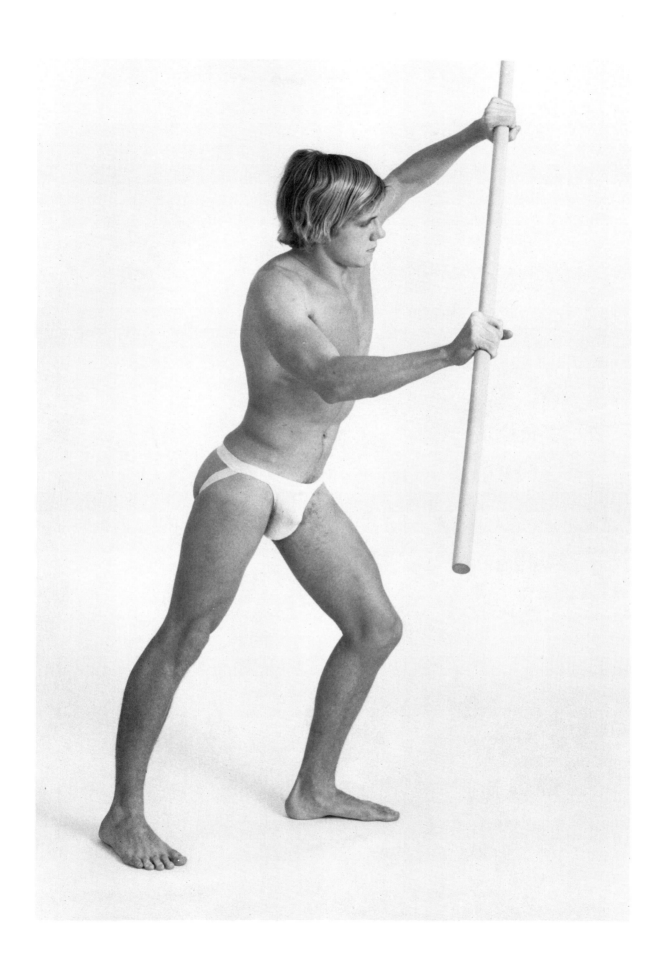

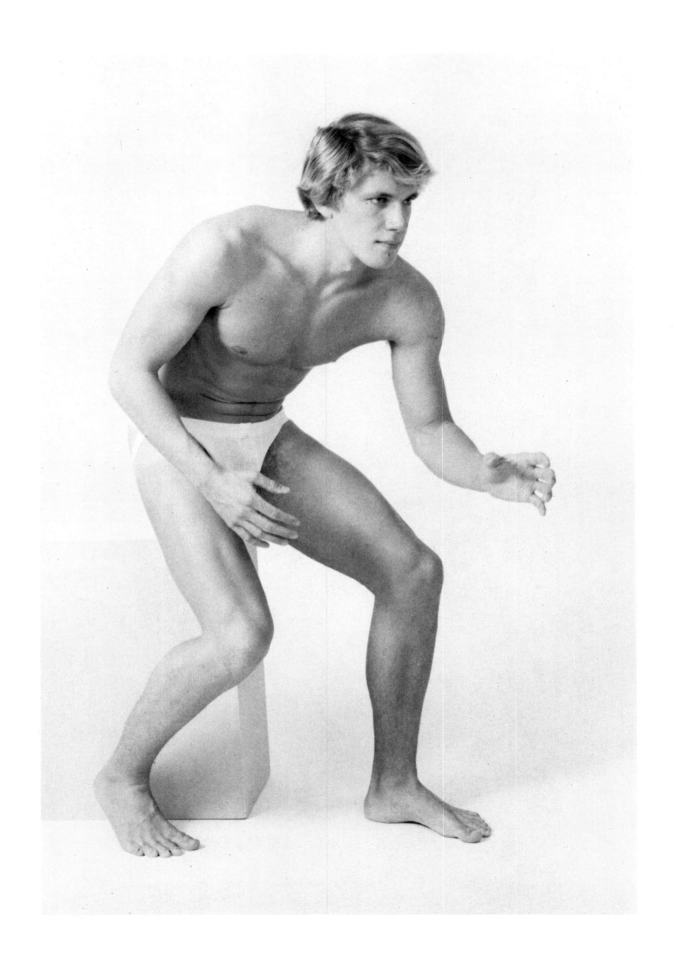

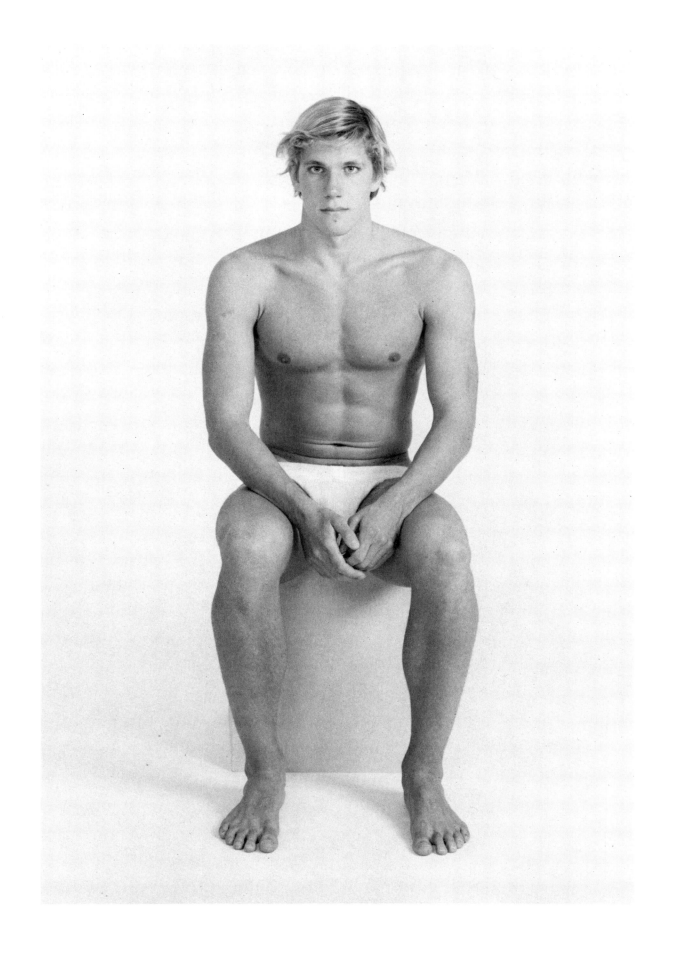

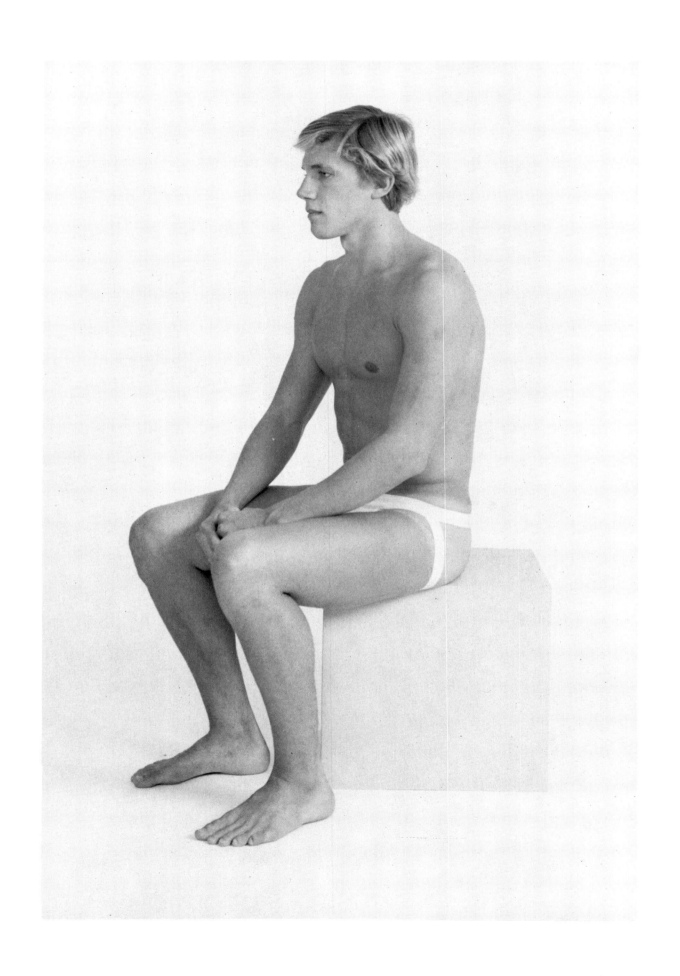

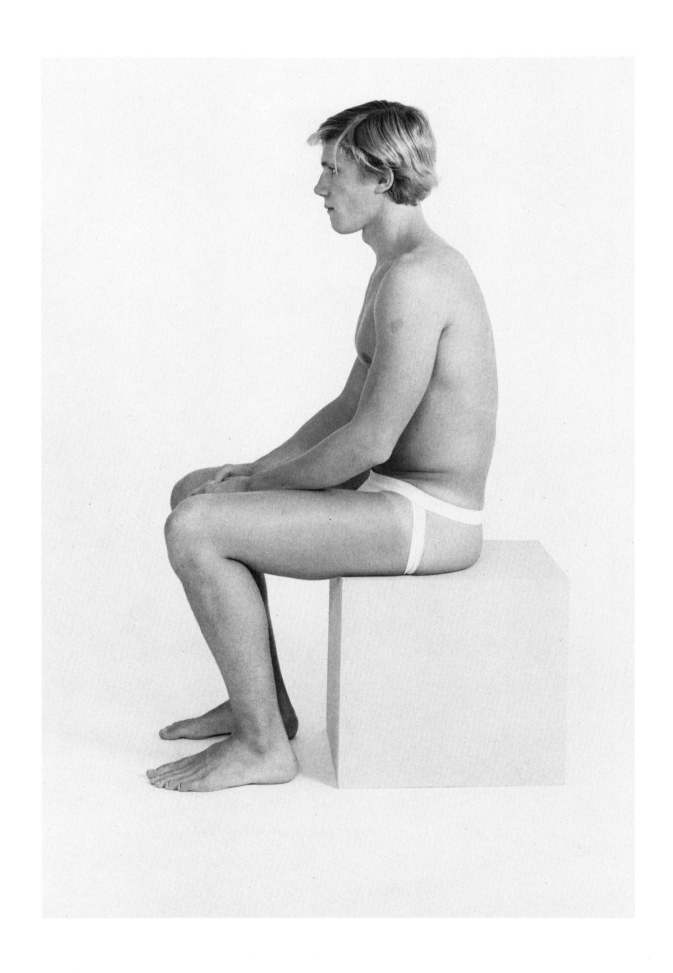

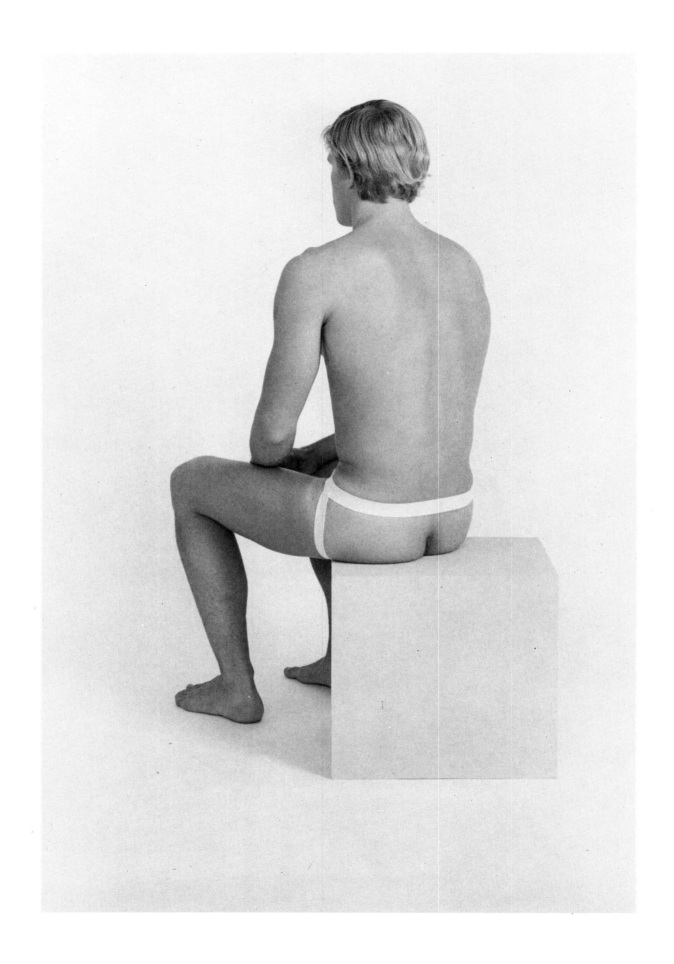

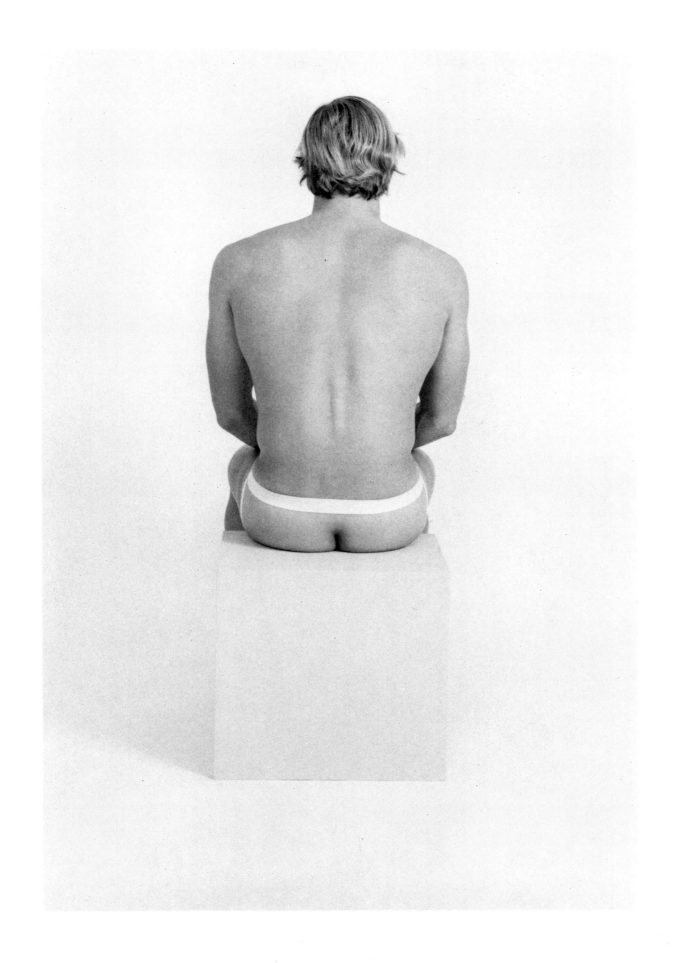

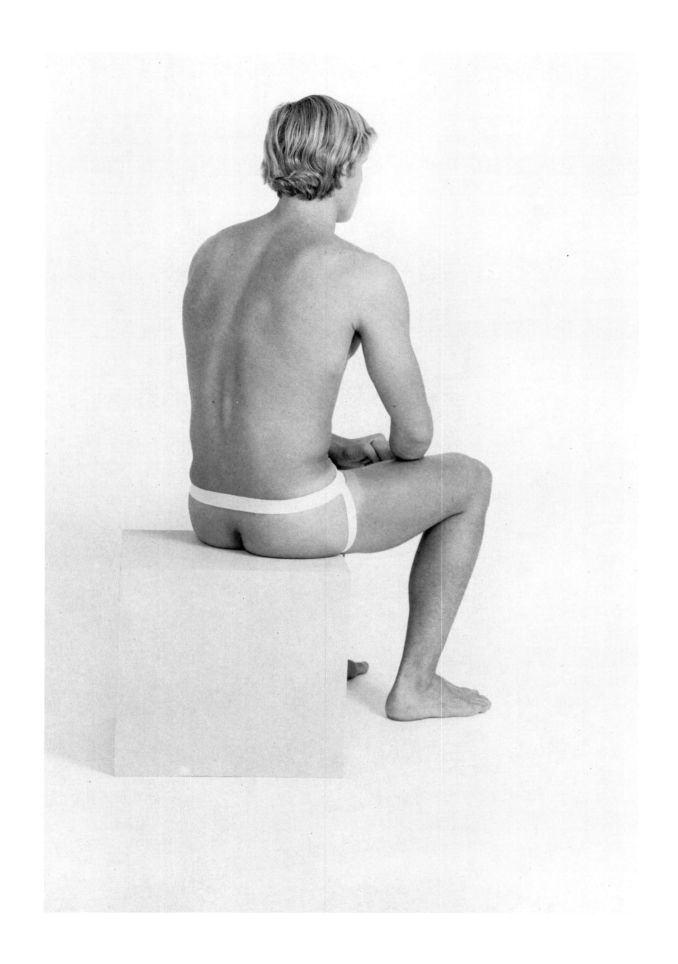

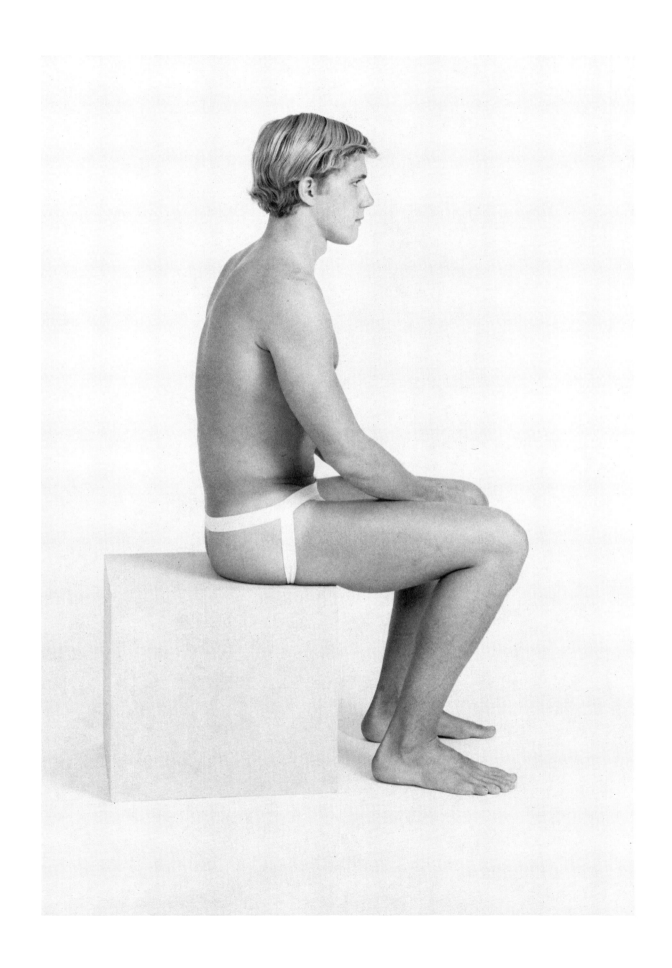

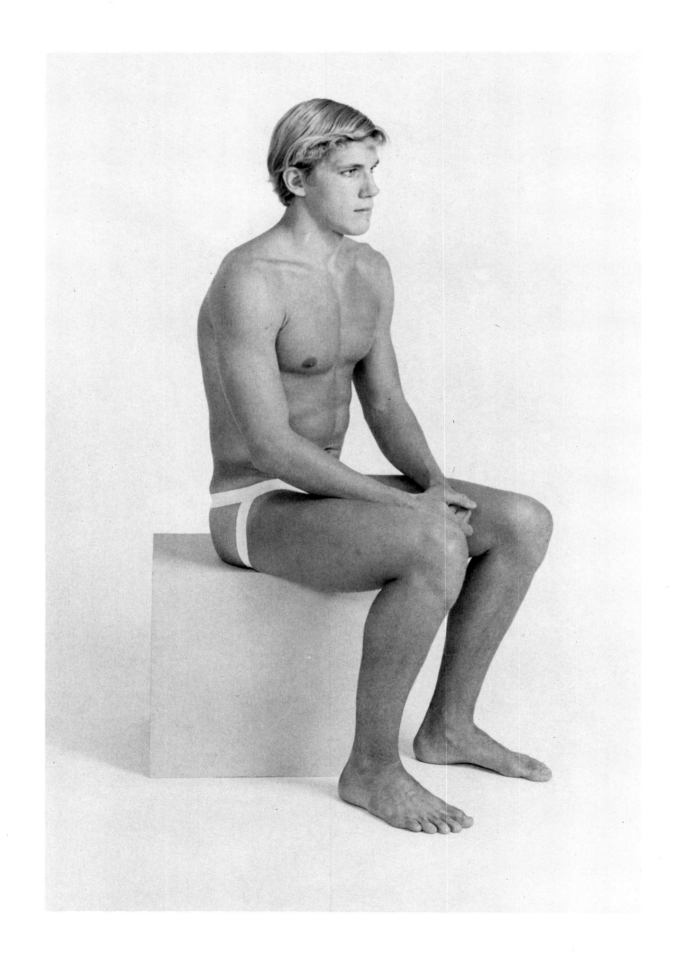

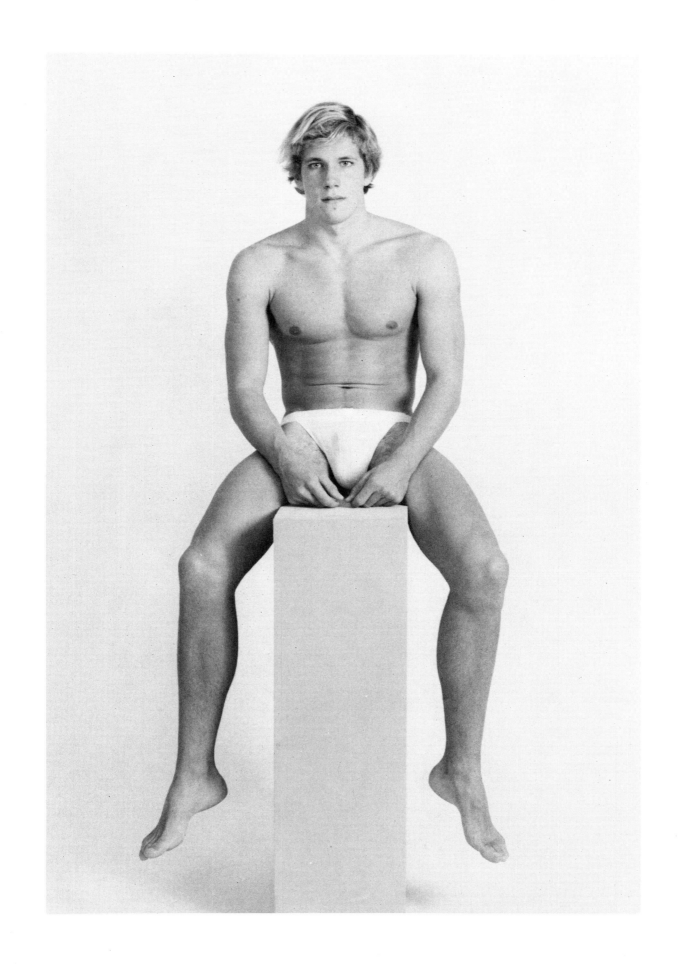

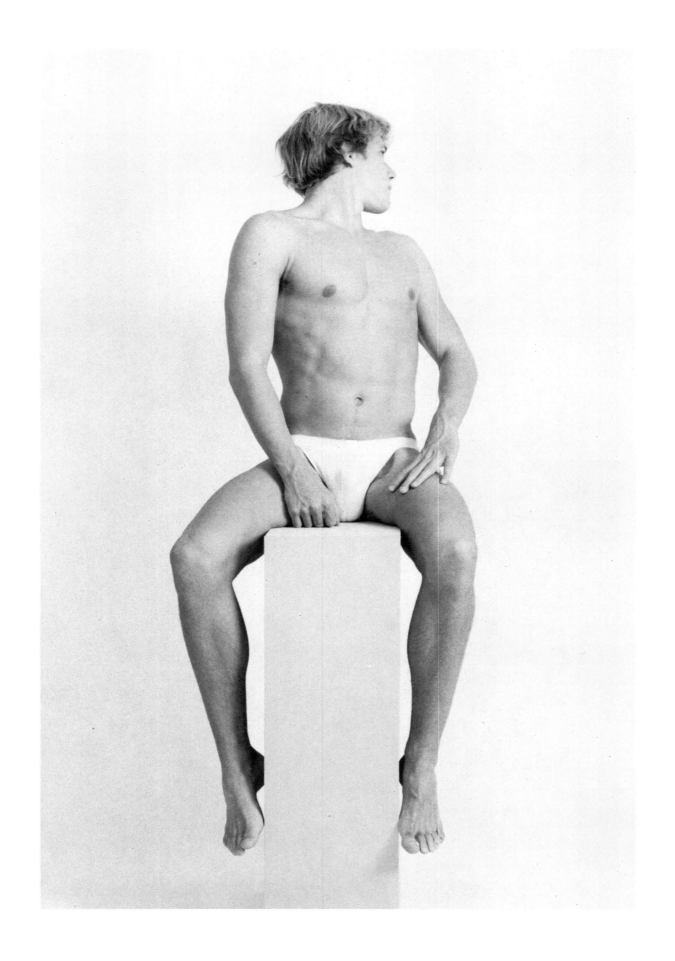

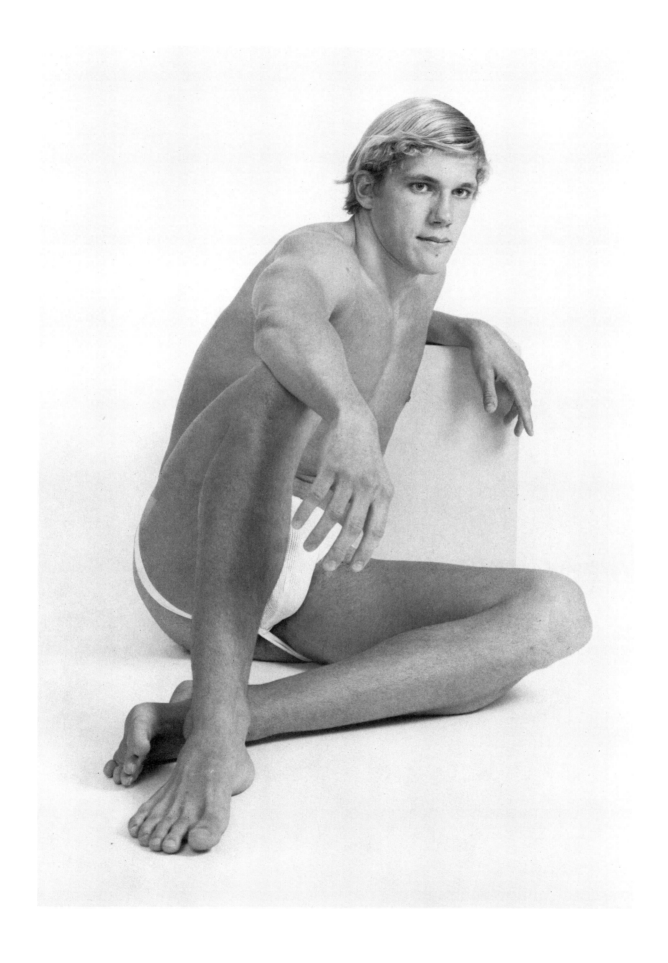

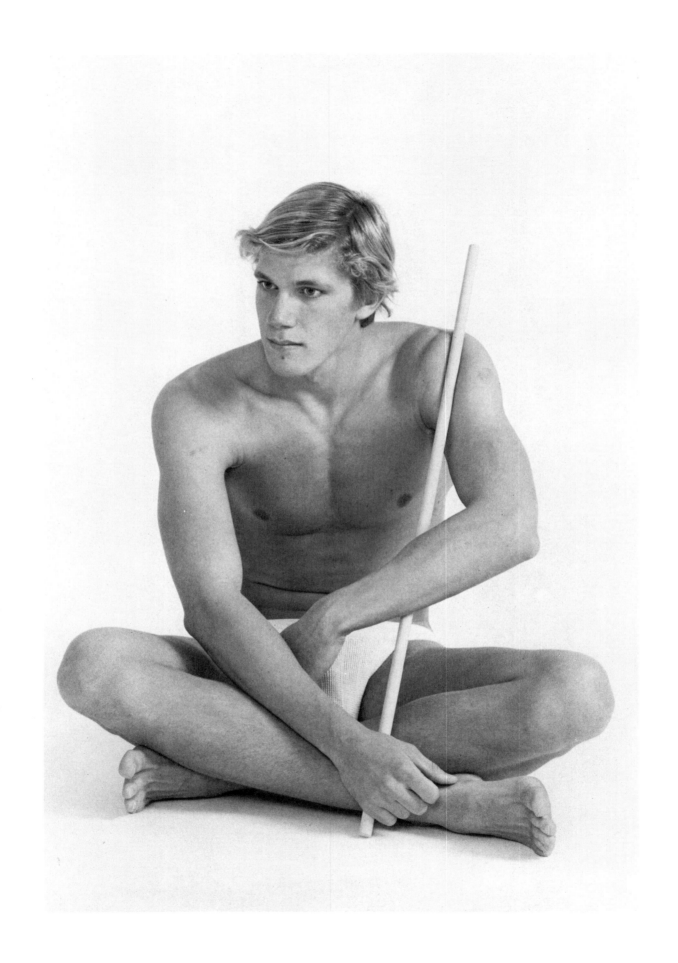

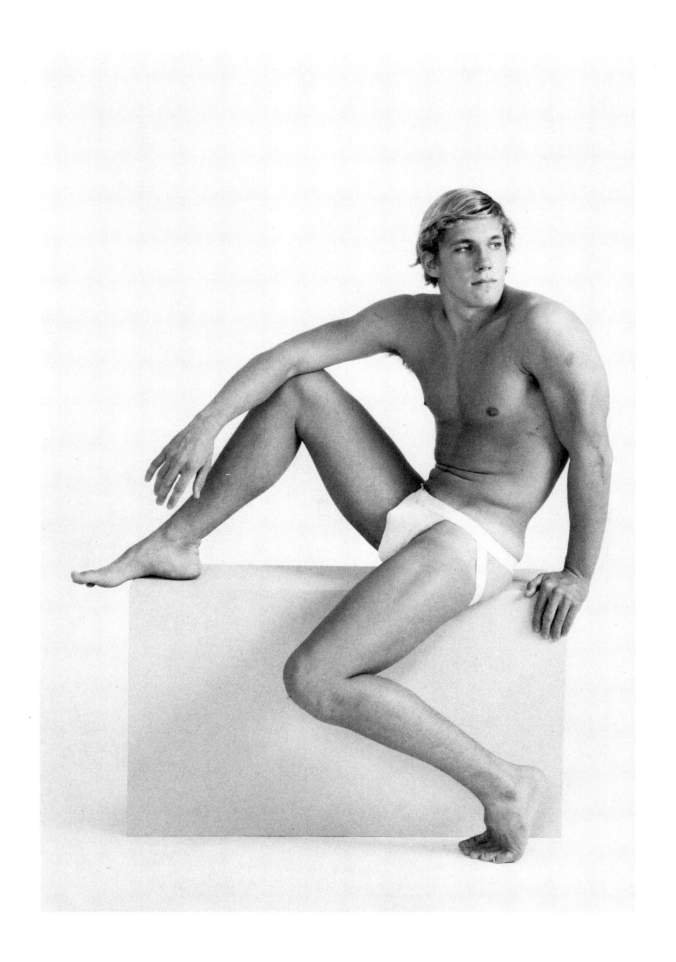

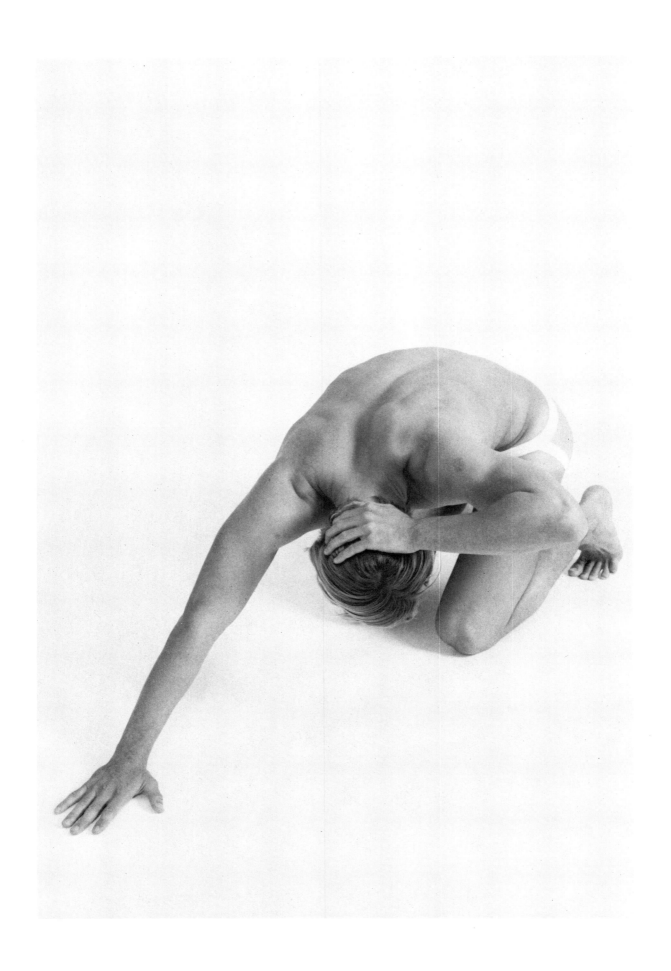

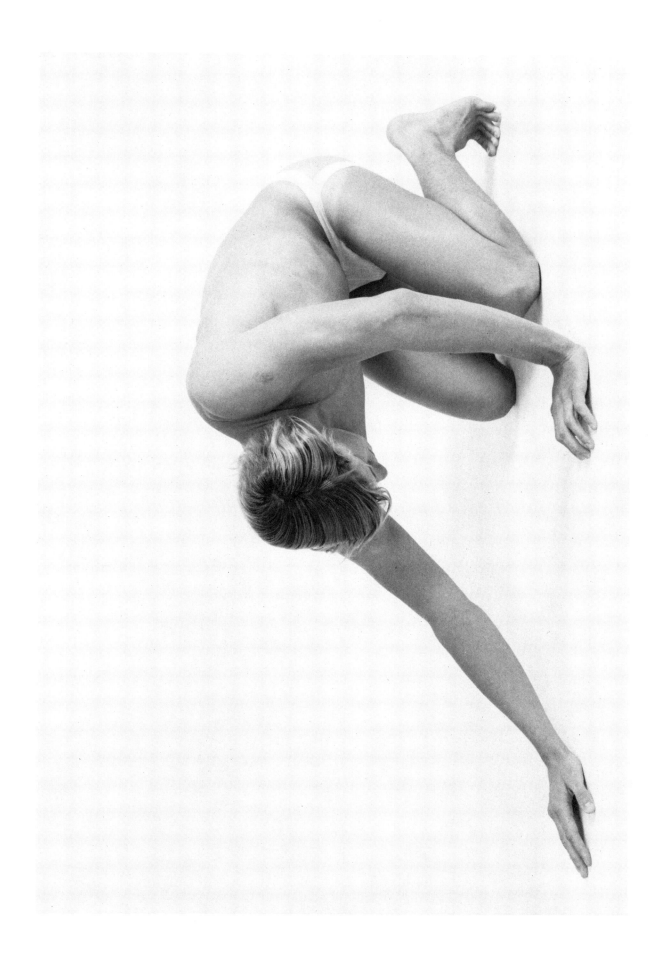

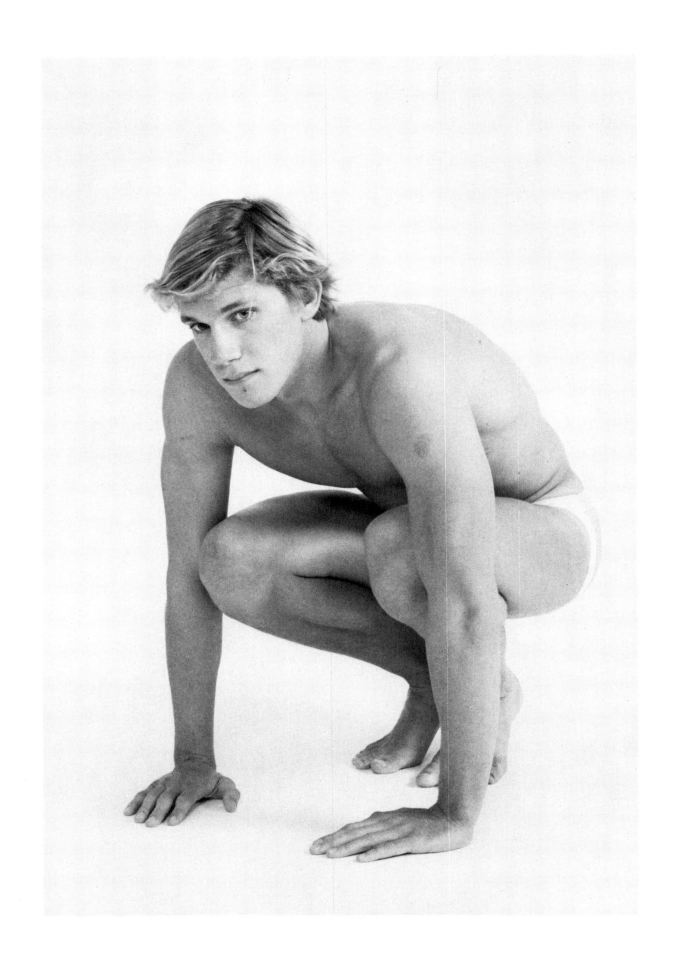

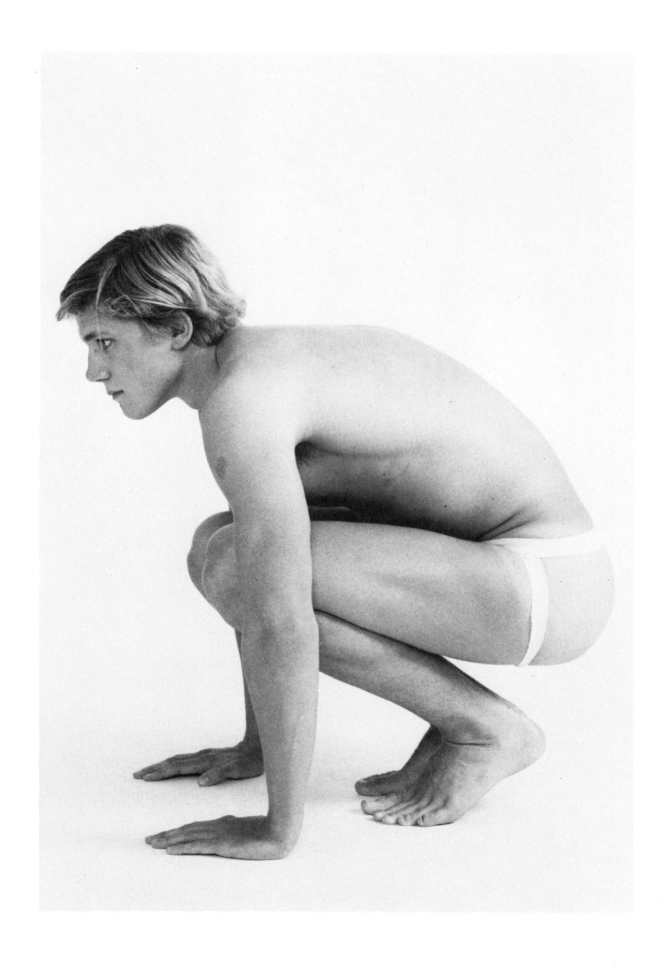

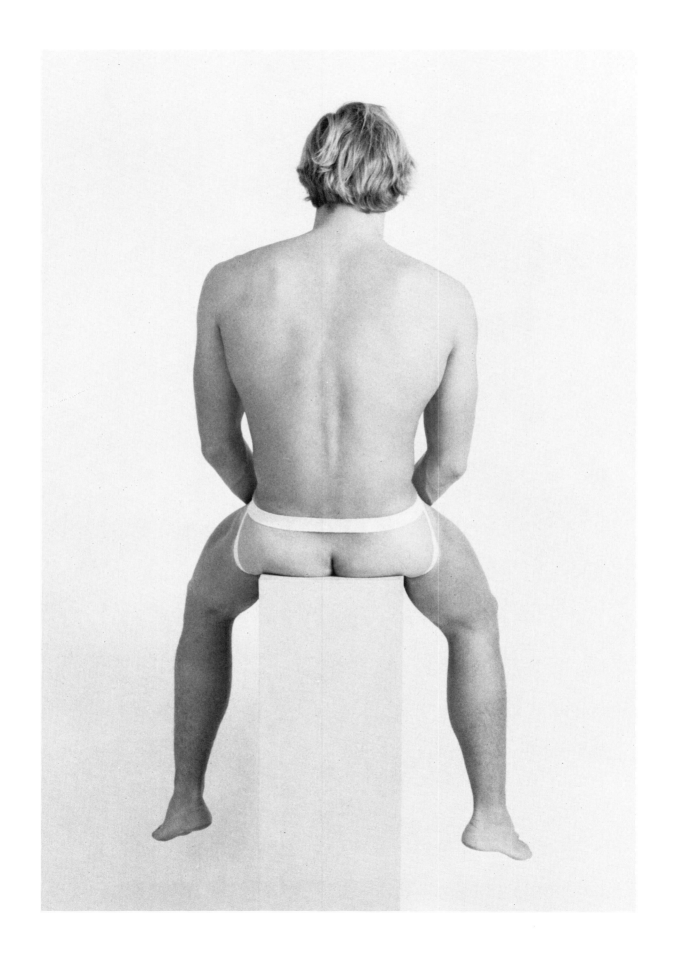

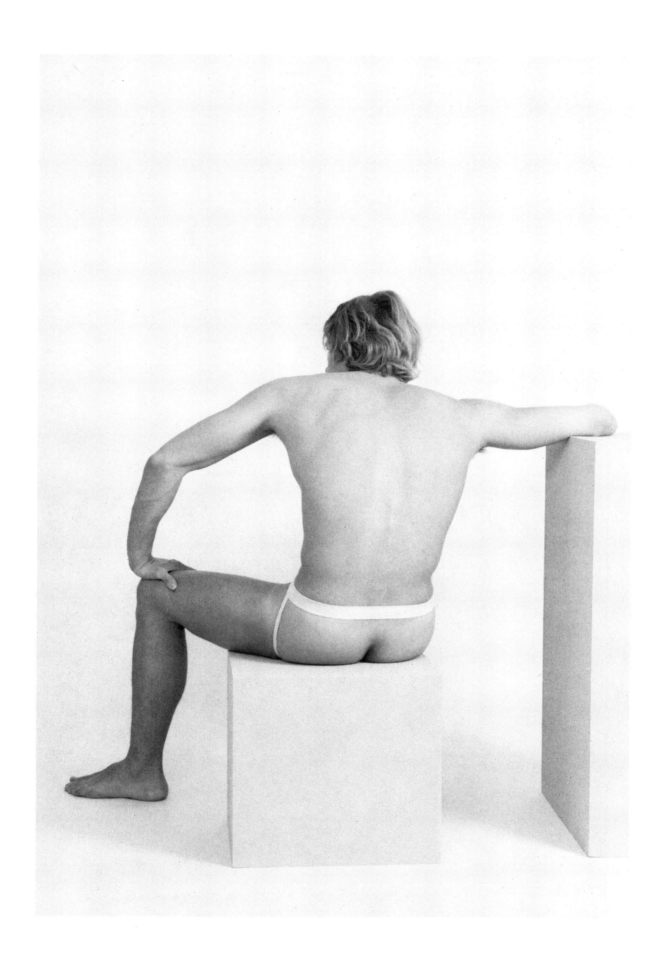

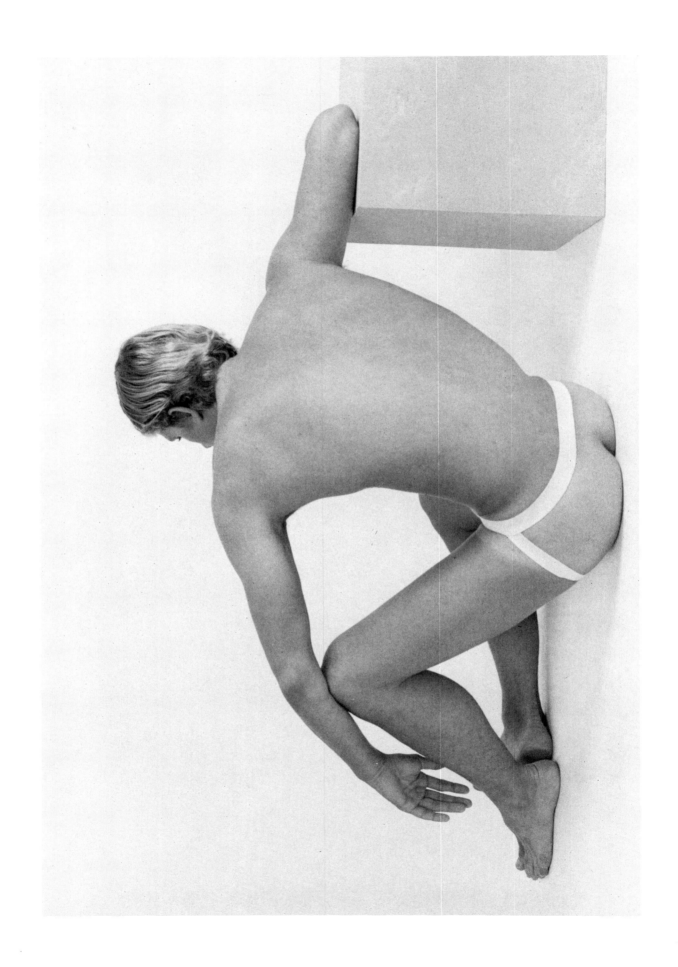

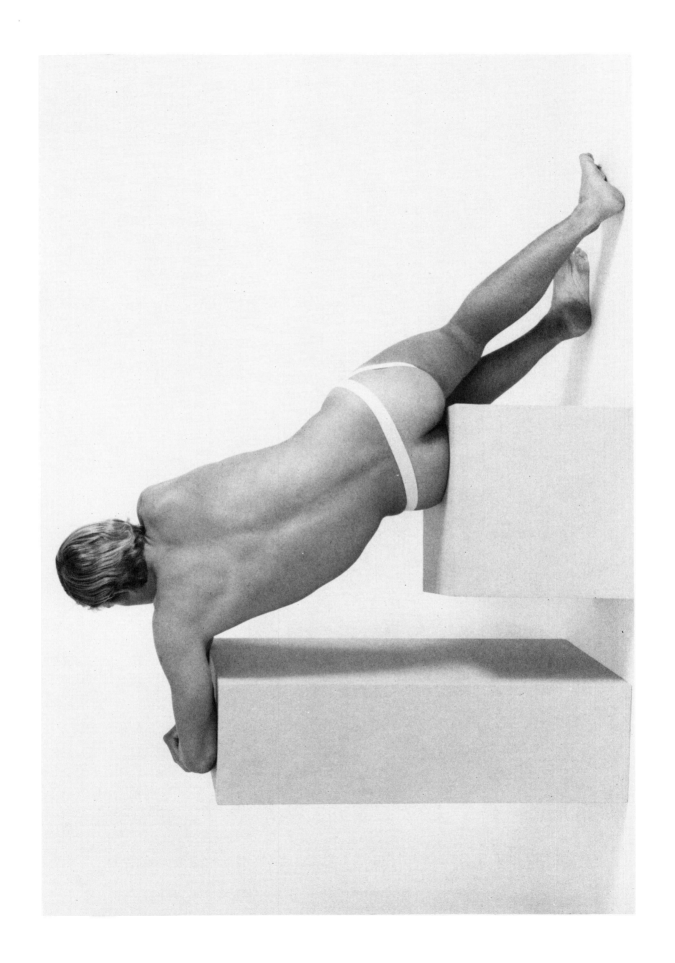

79

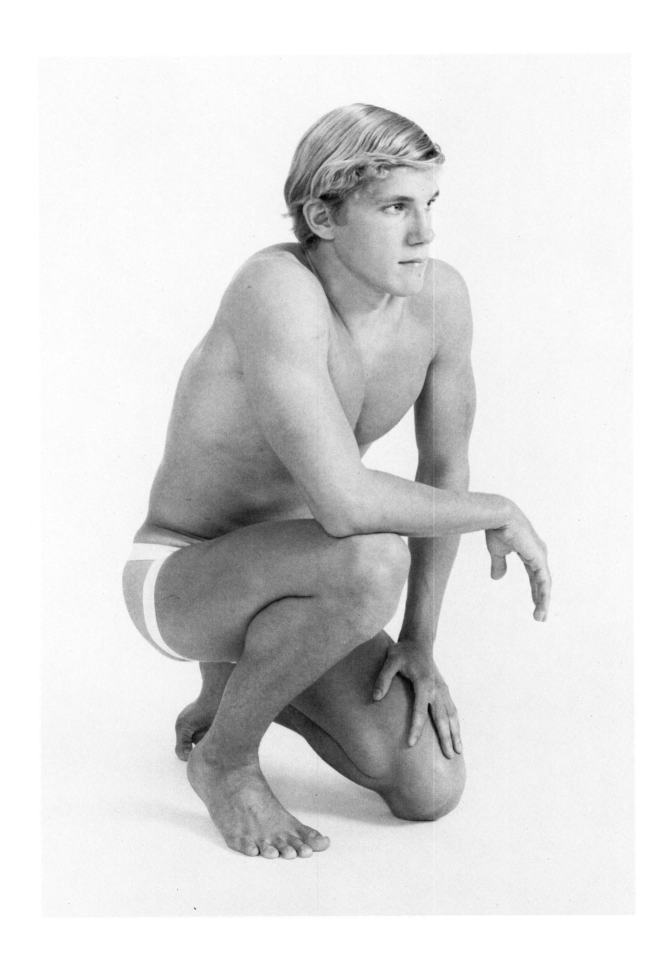

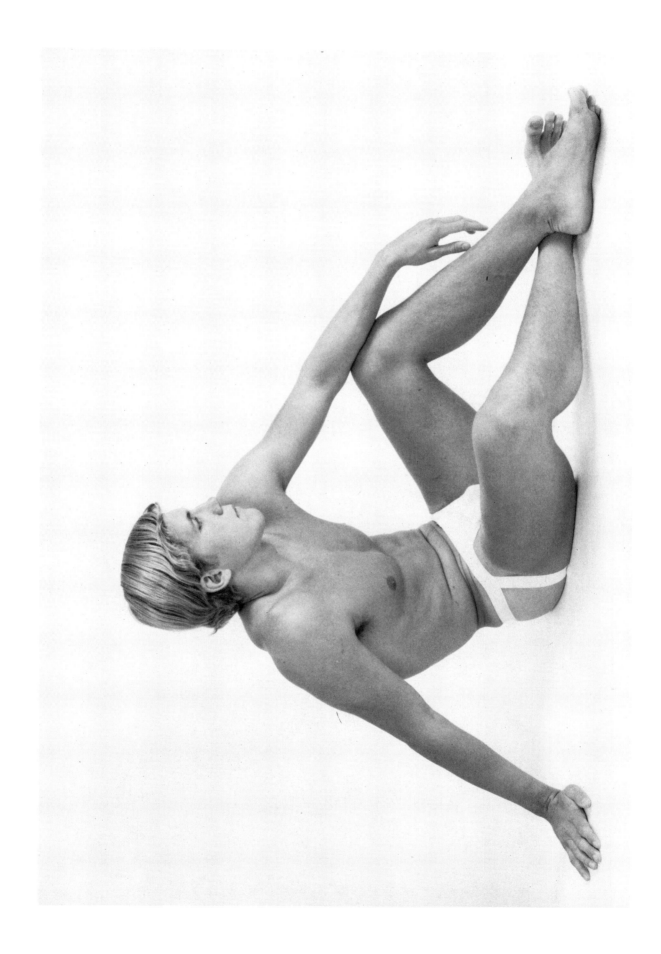

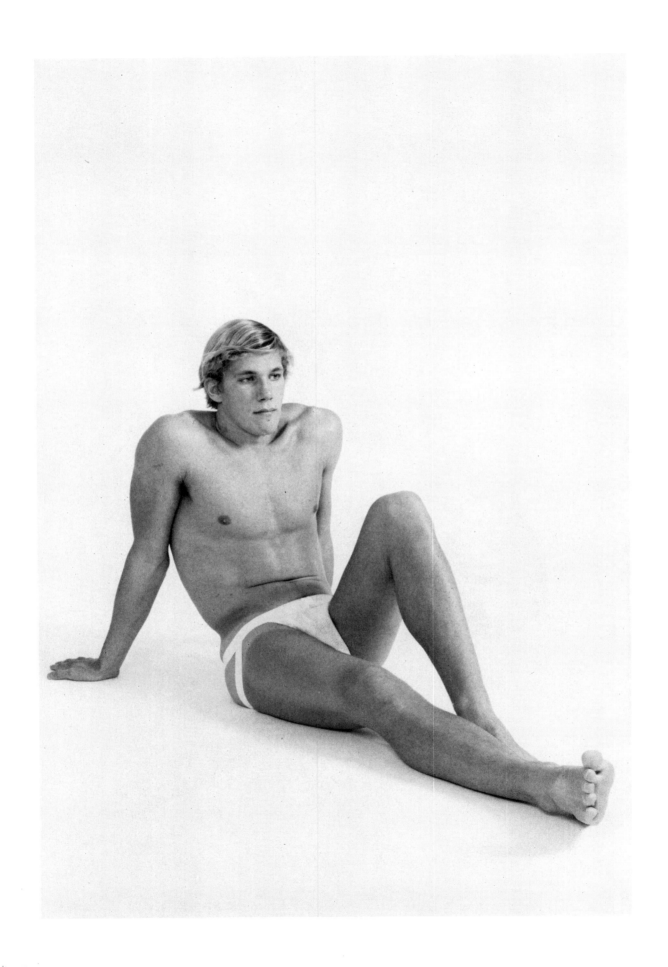

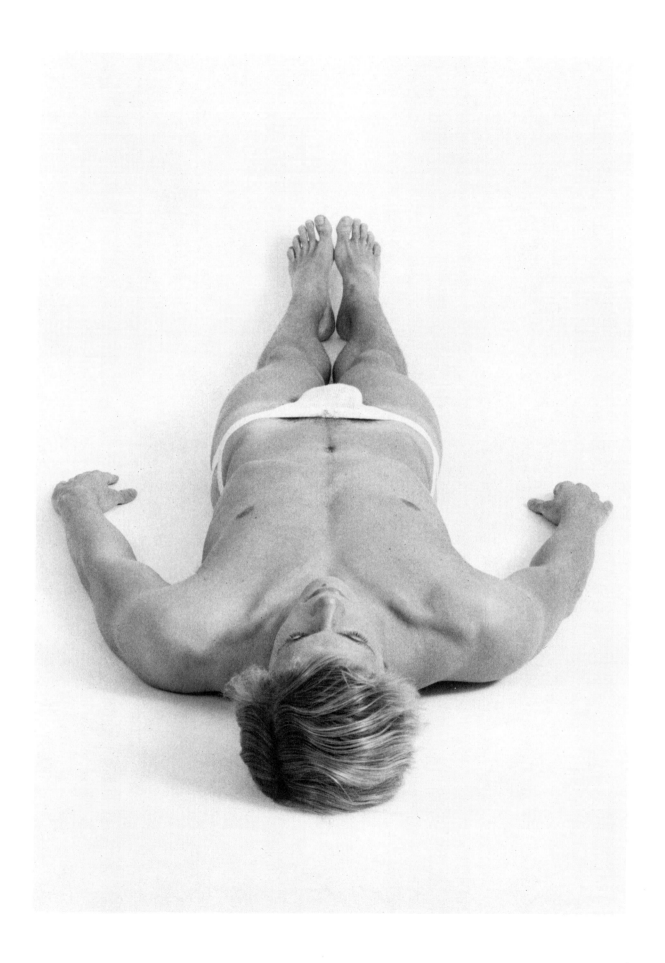

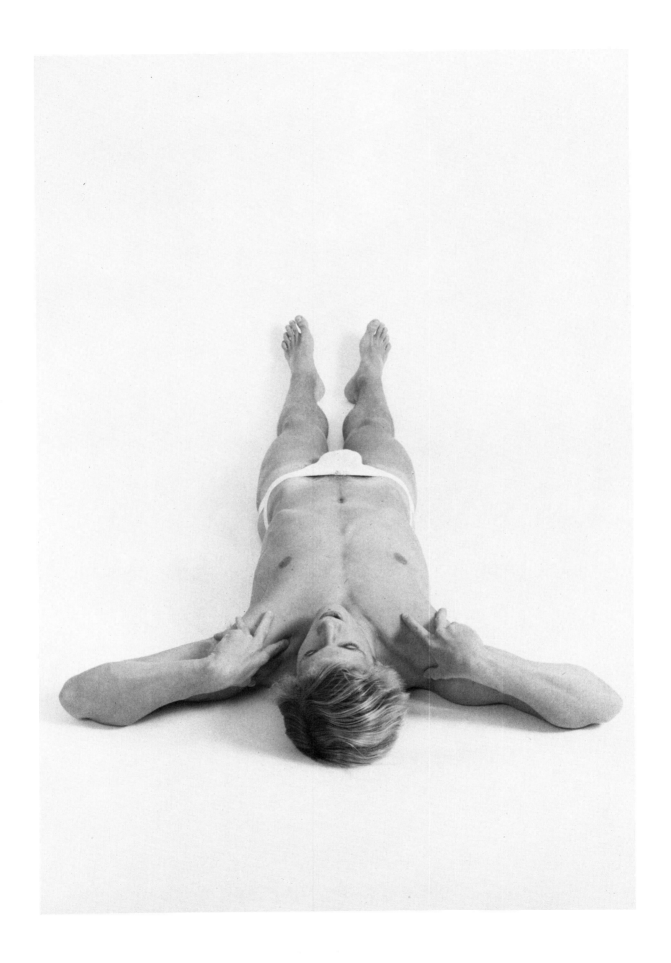

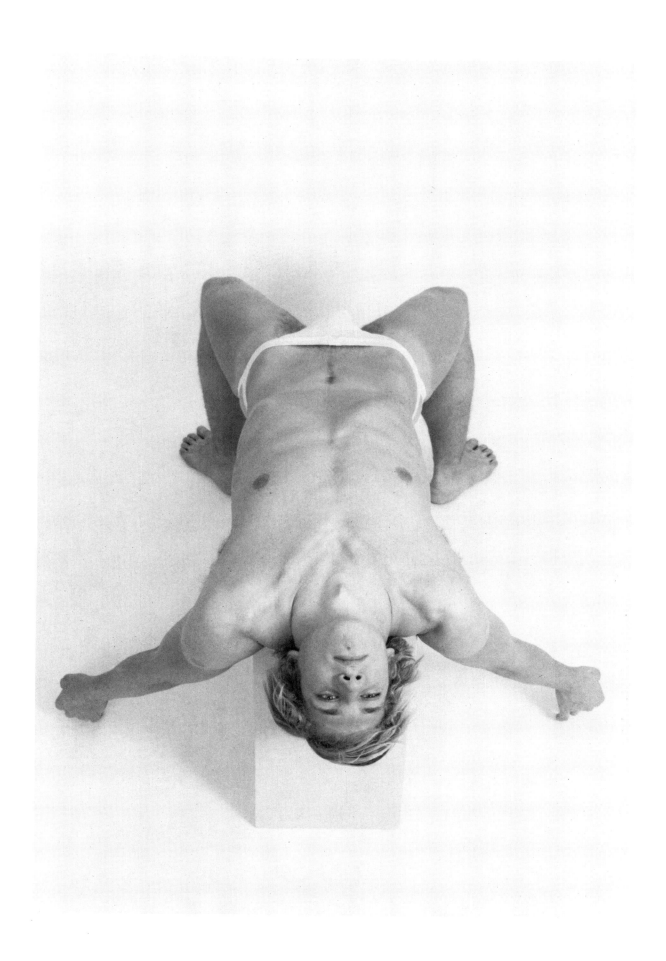

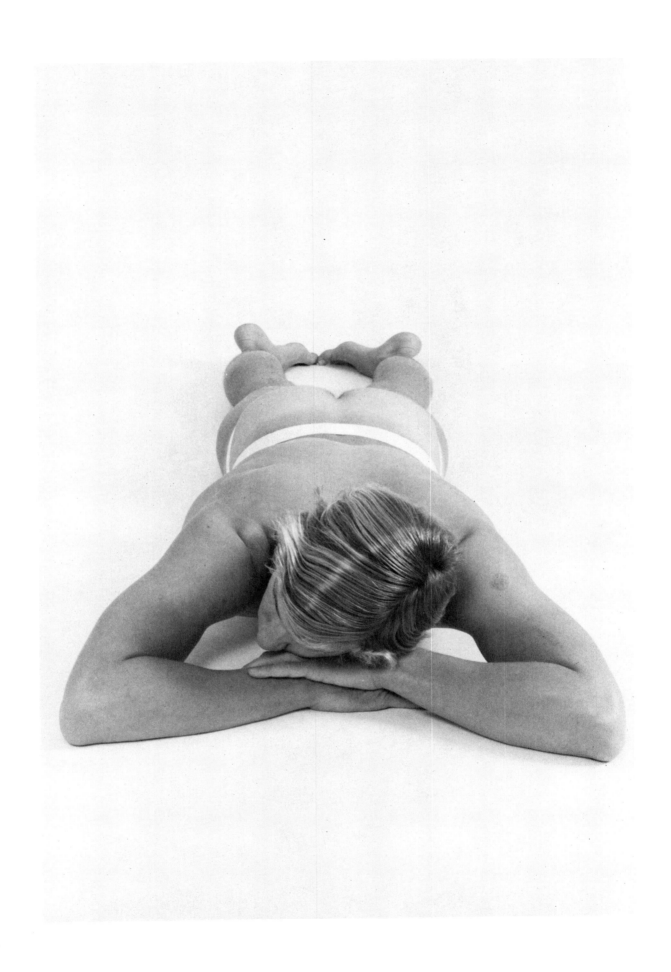

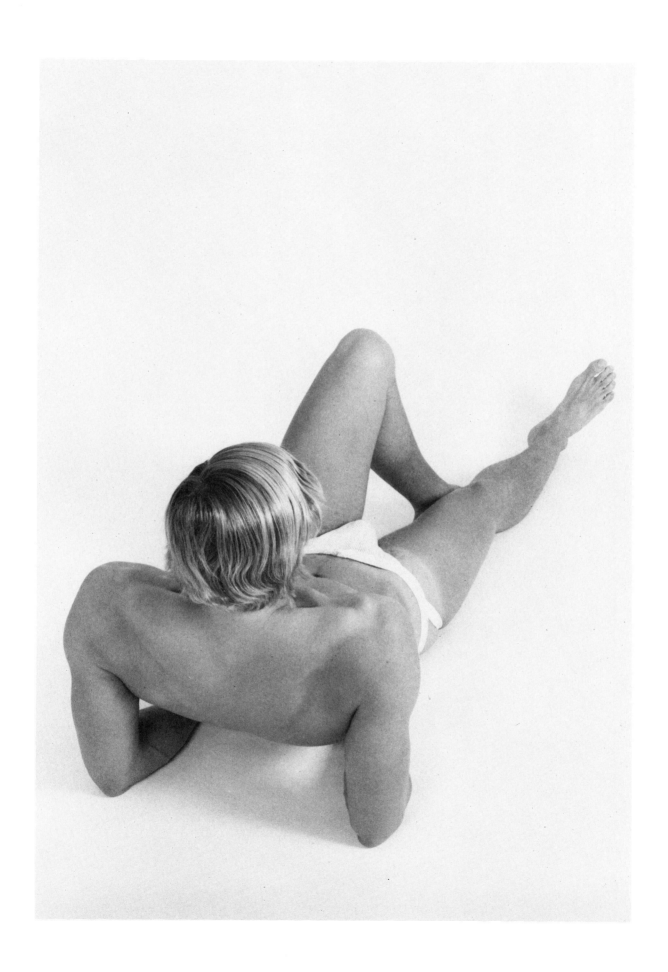

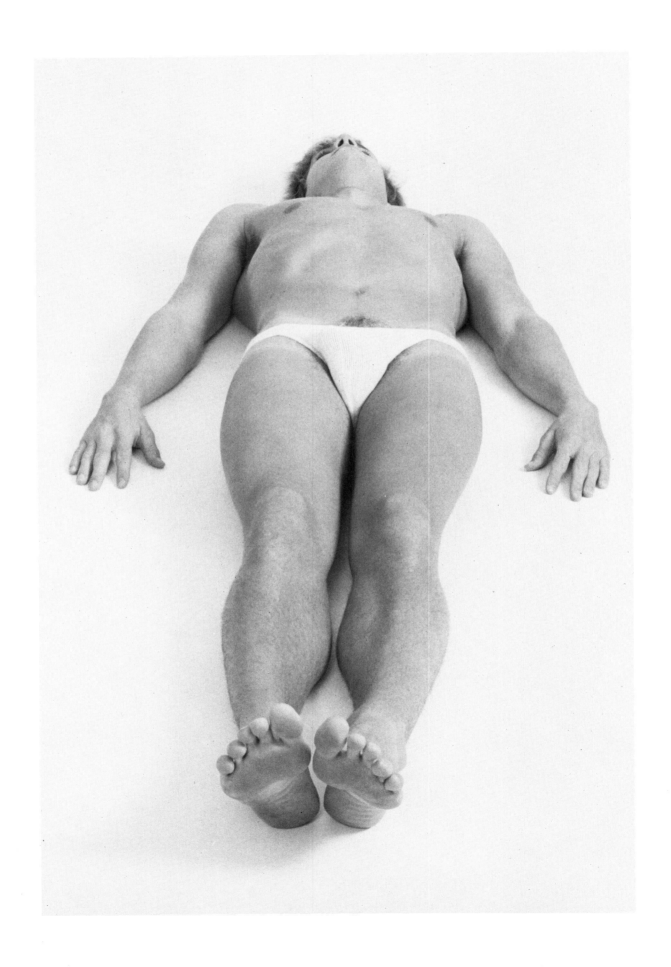

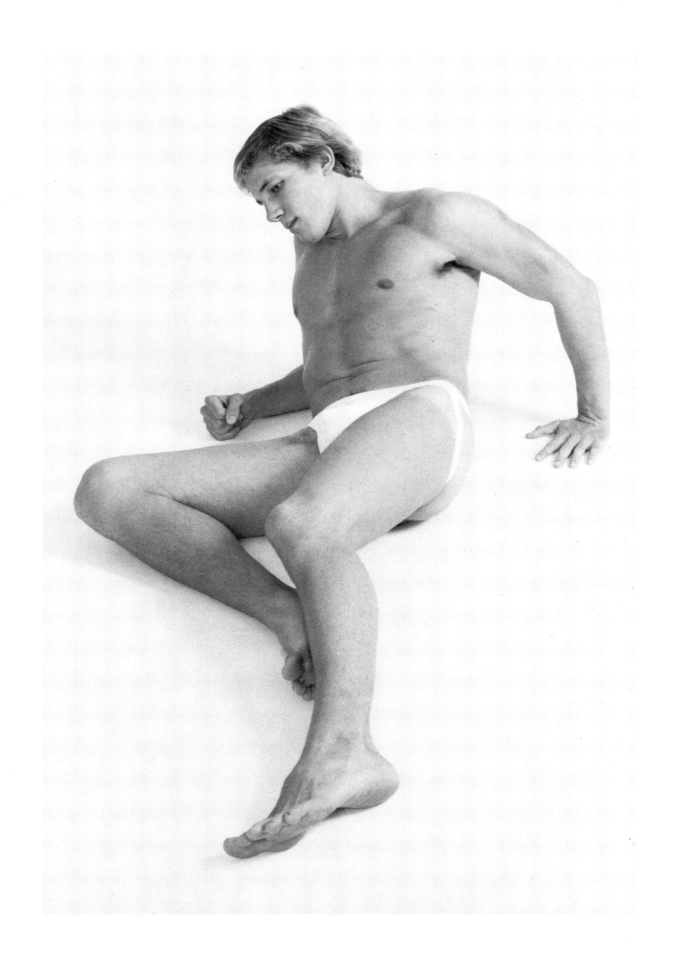

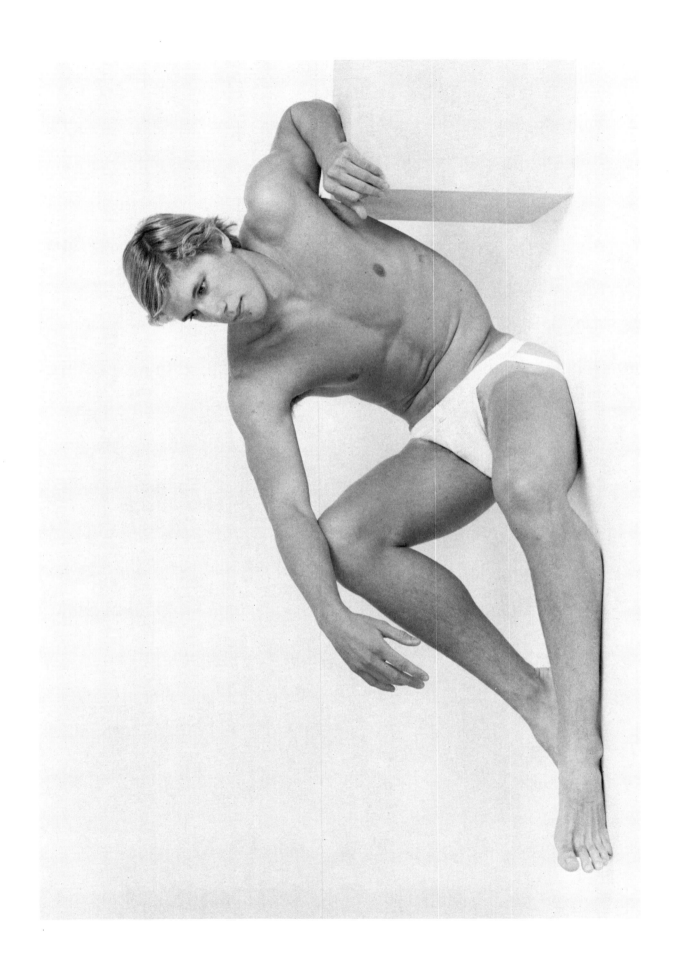

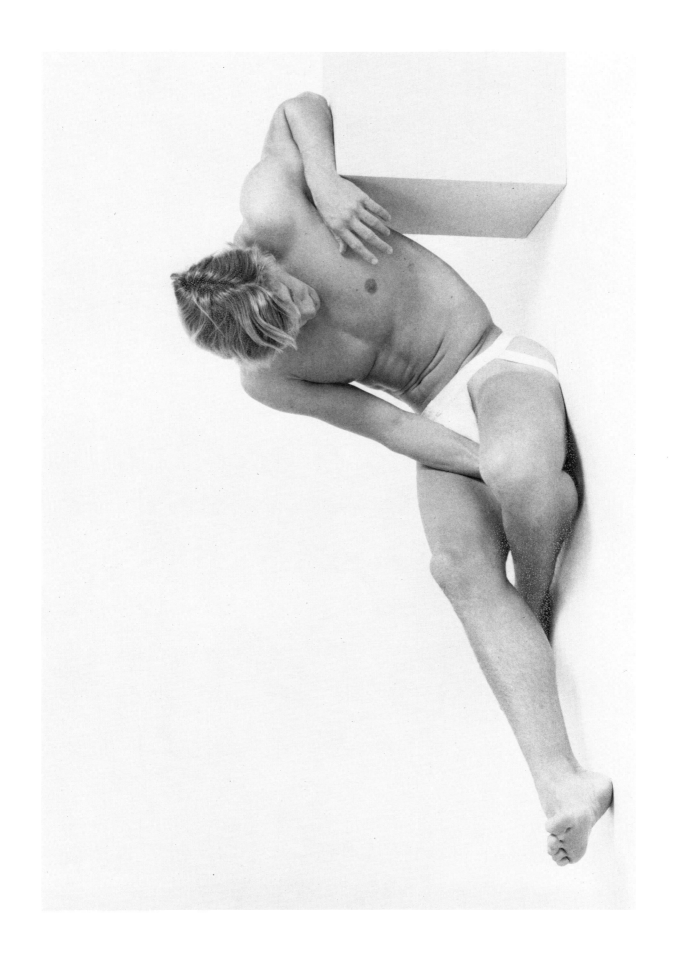

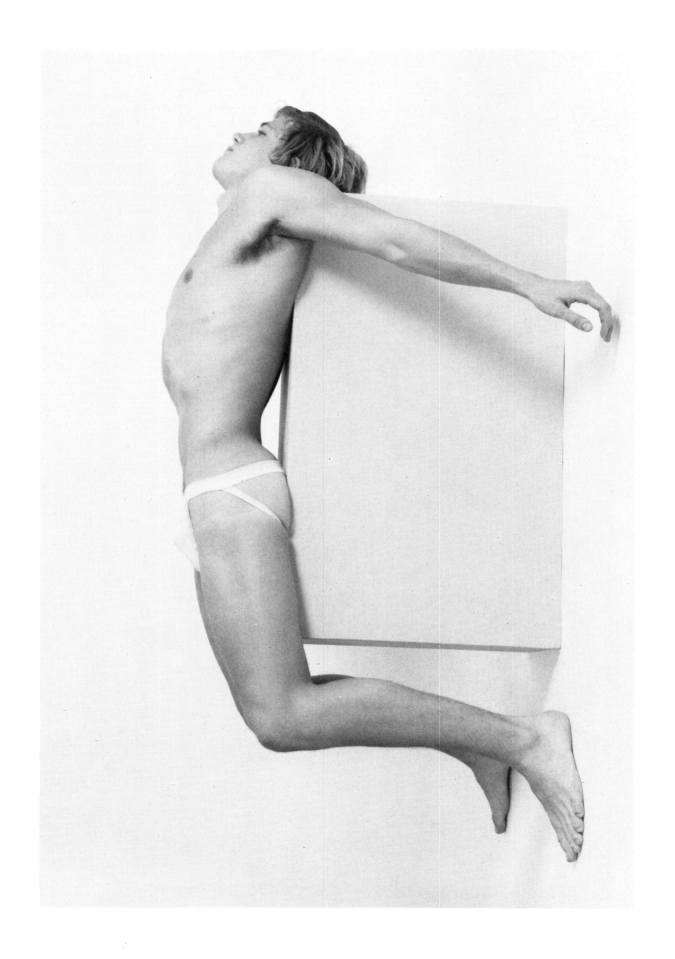

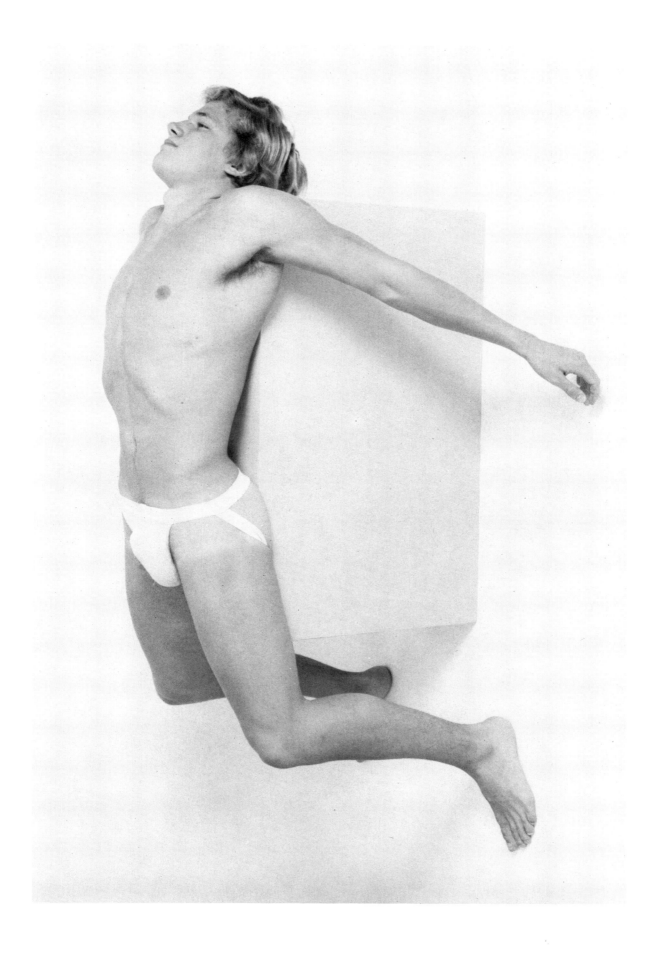

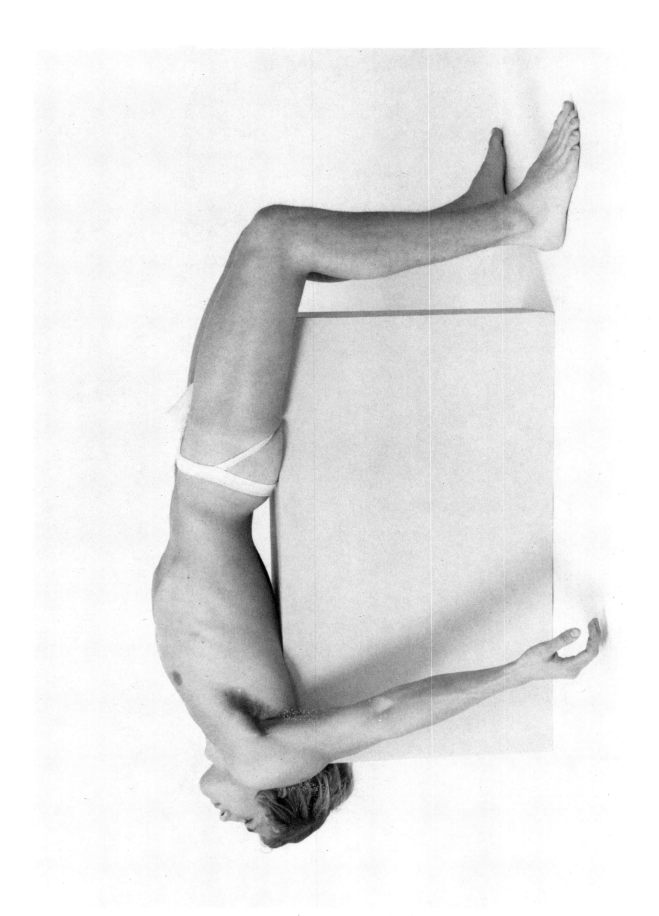

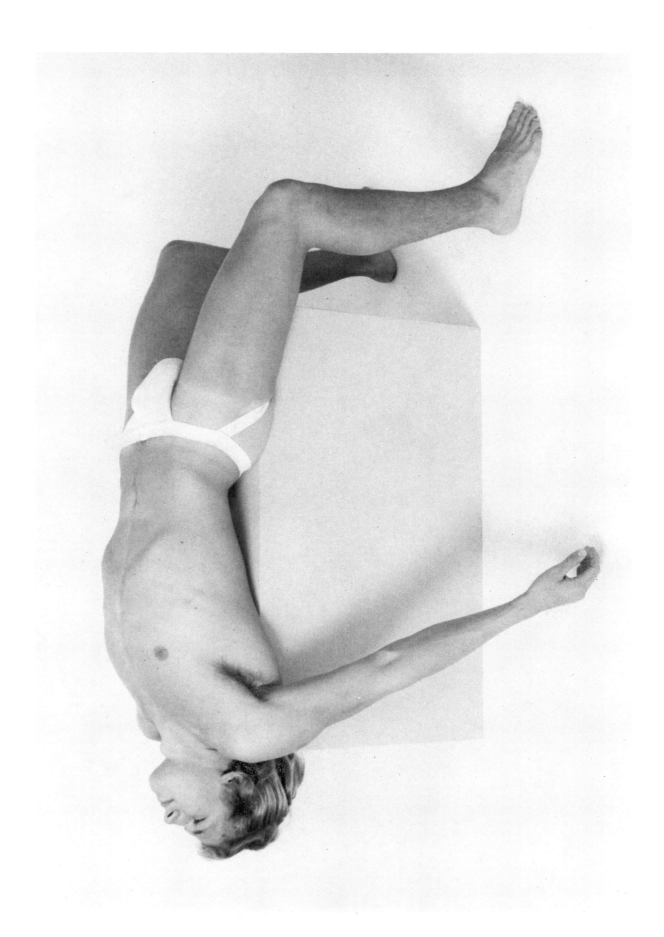

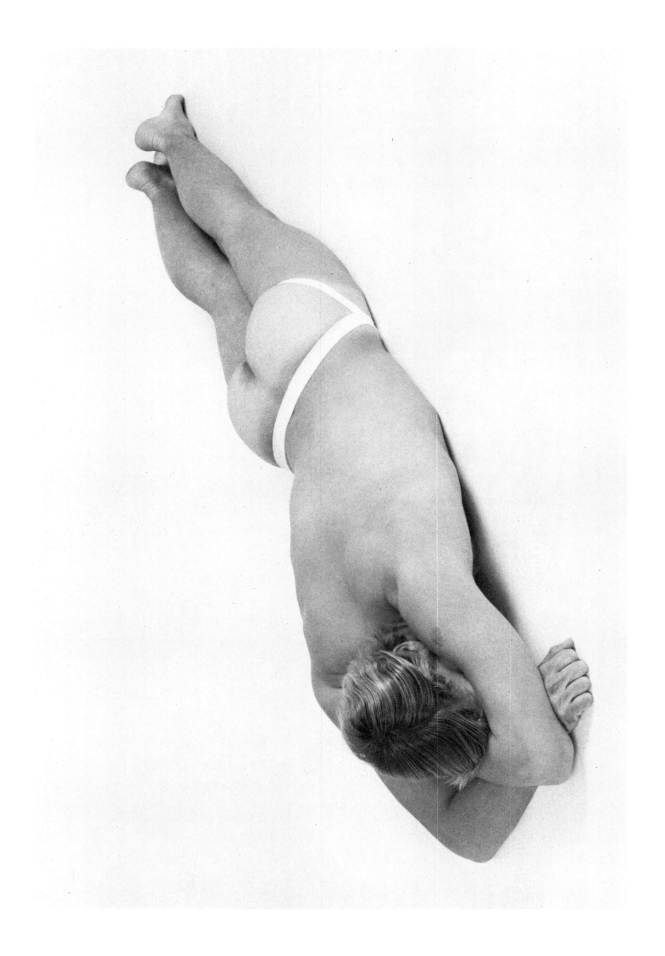

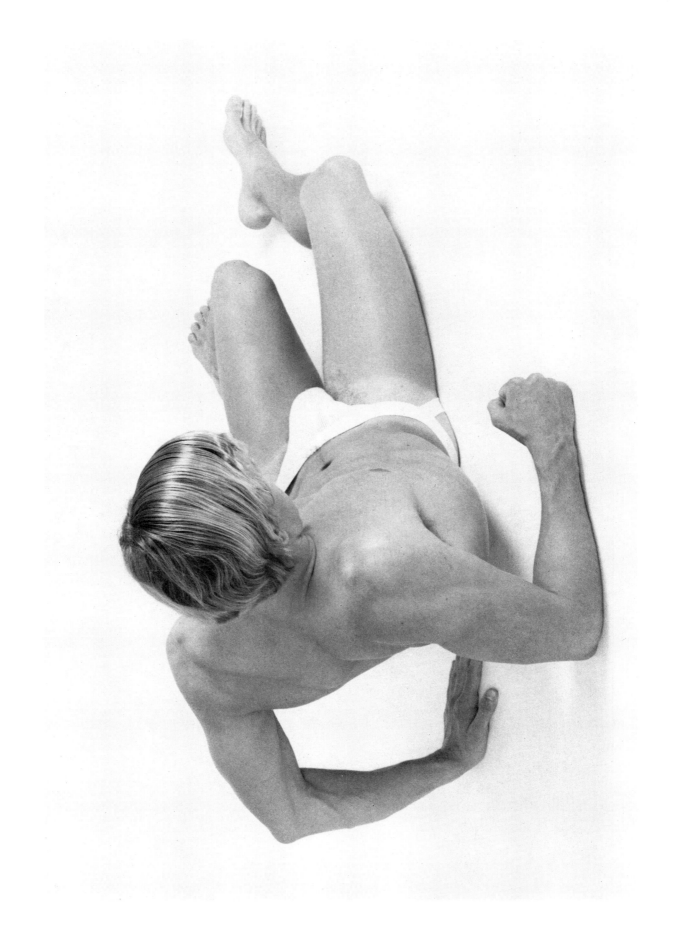

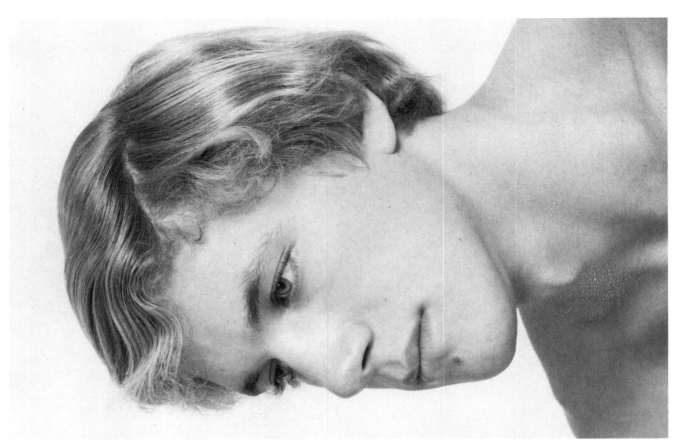

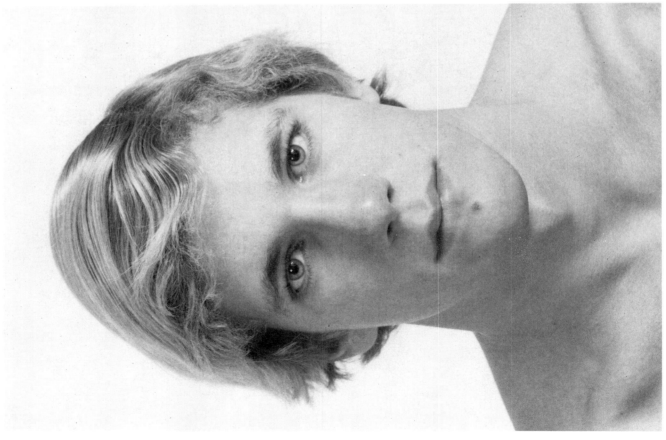

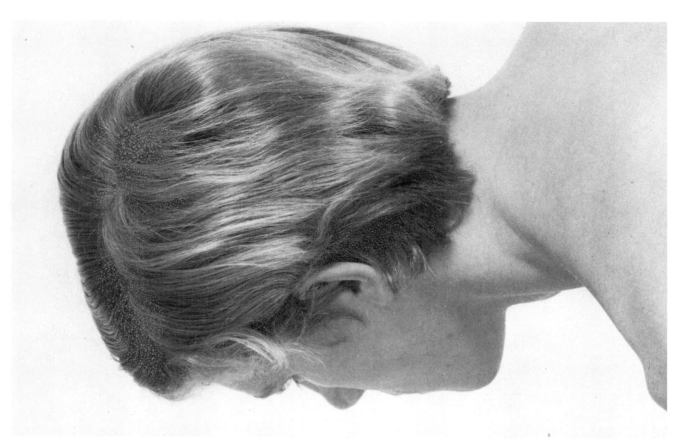

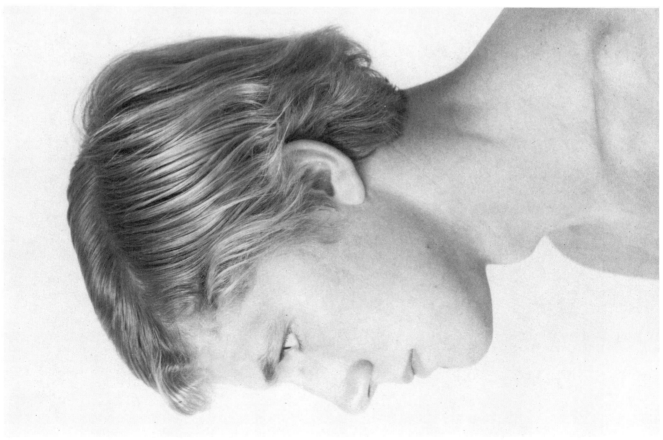

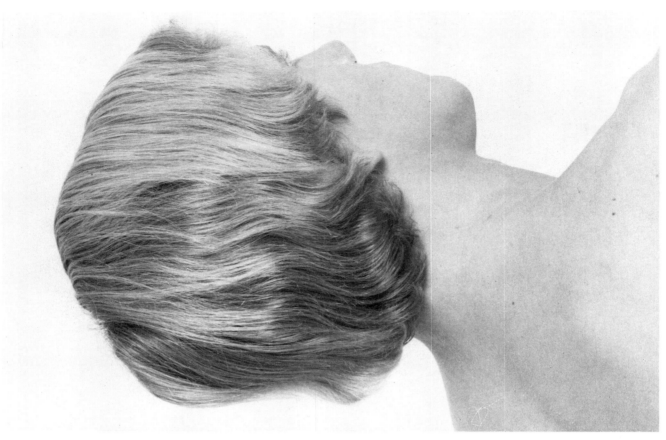

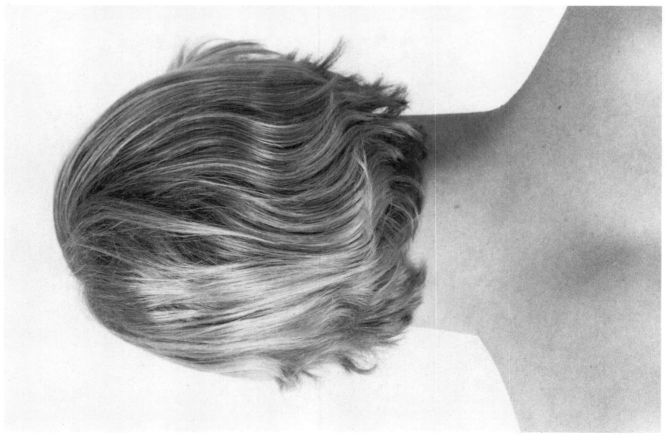

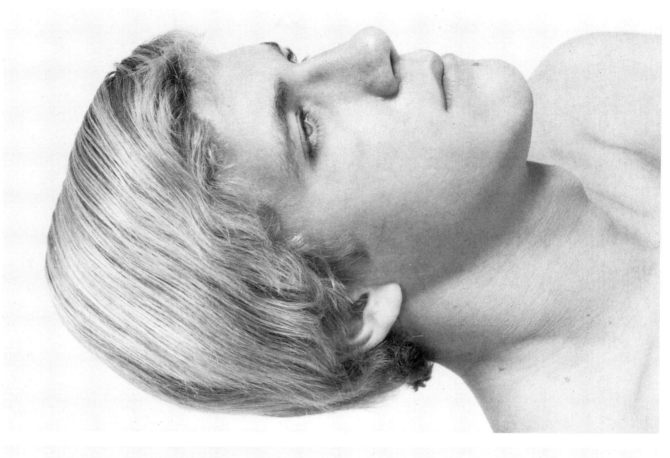

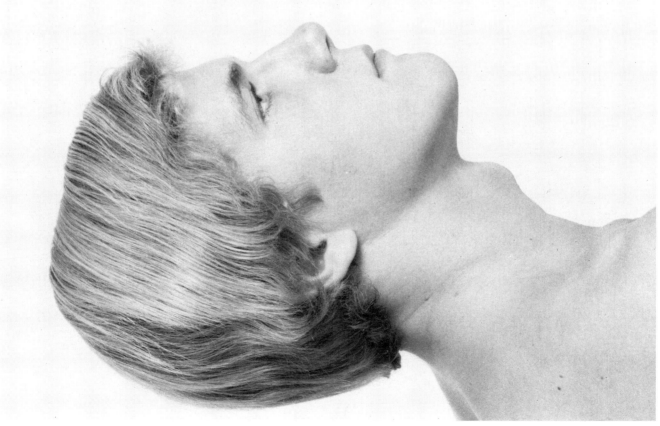

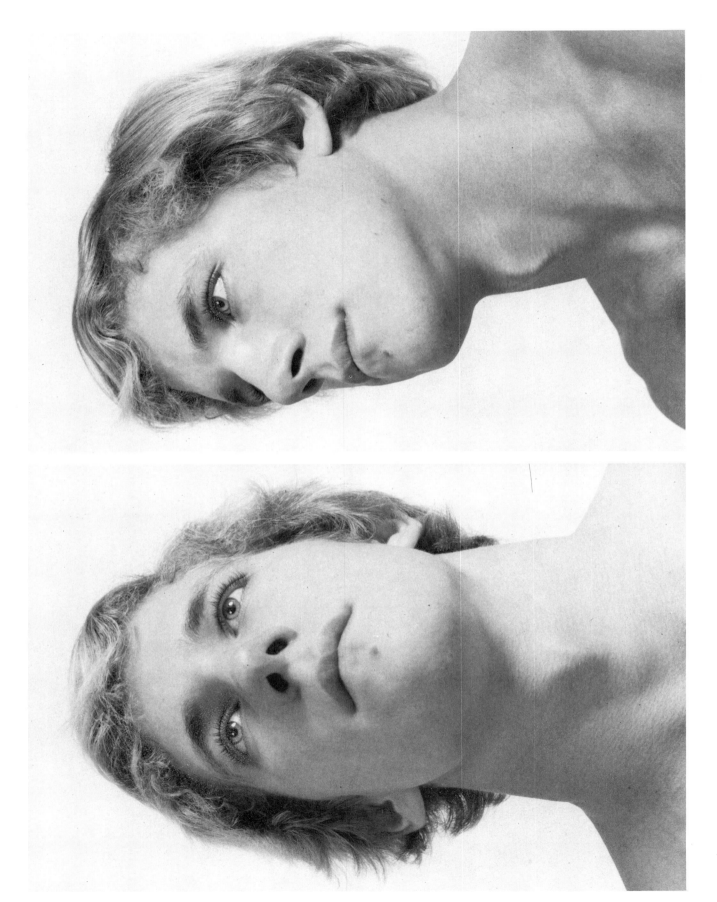

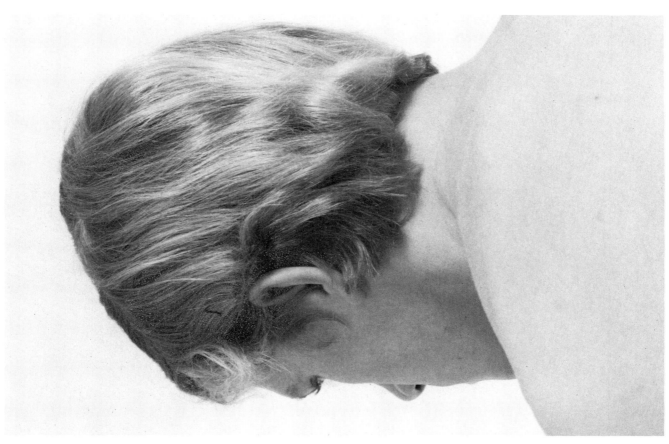

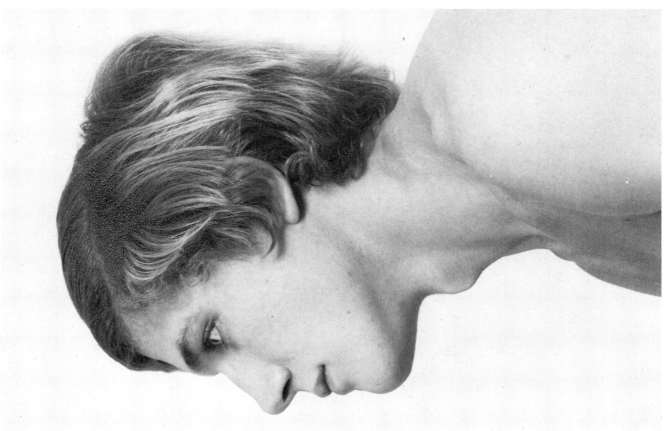

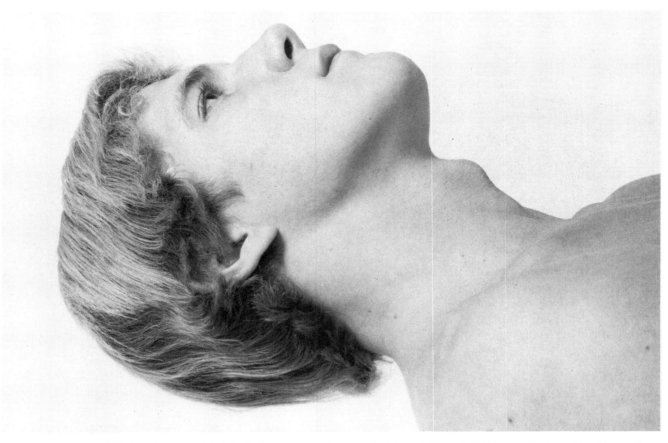

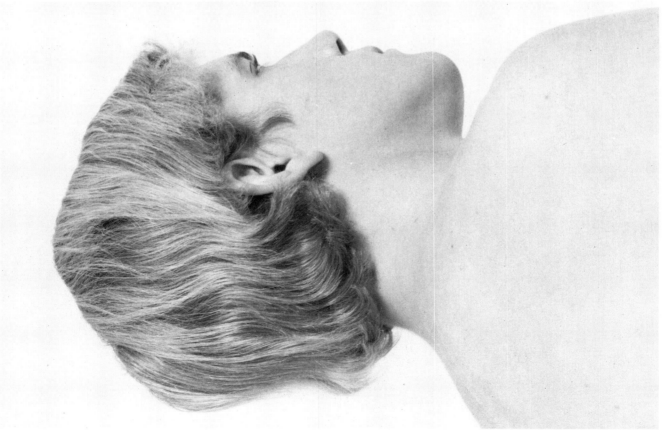

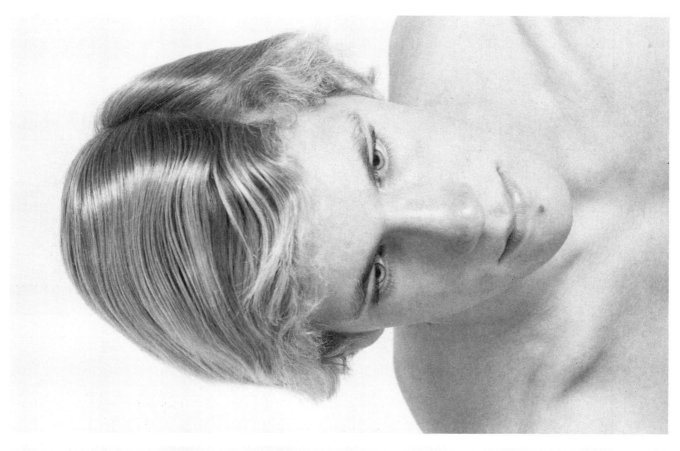

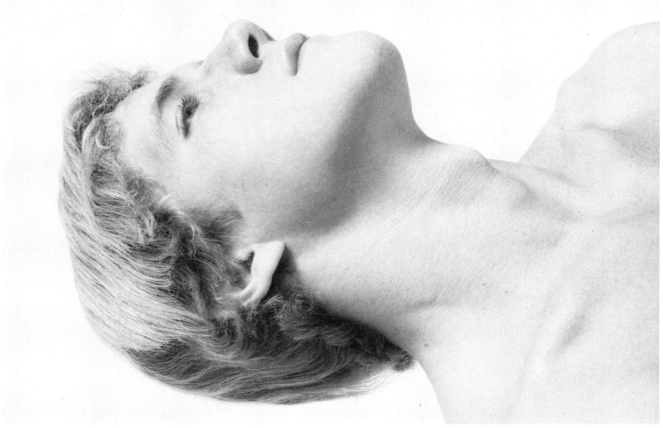

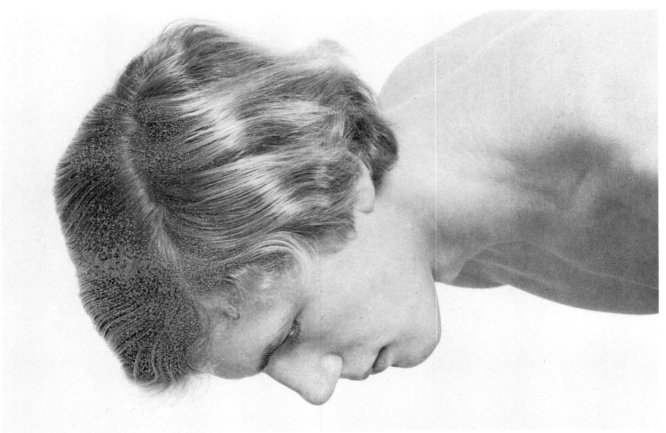

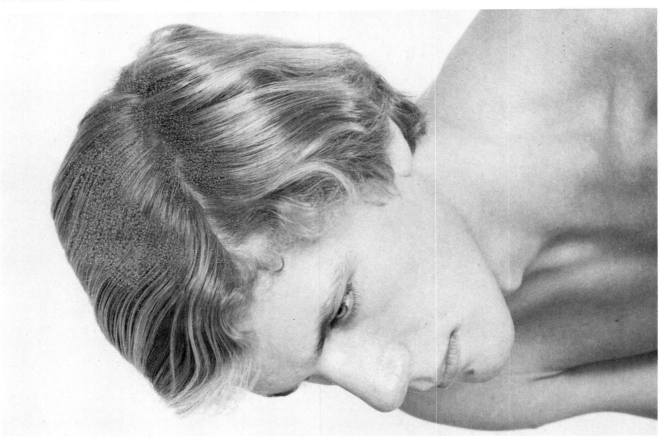

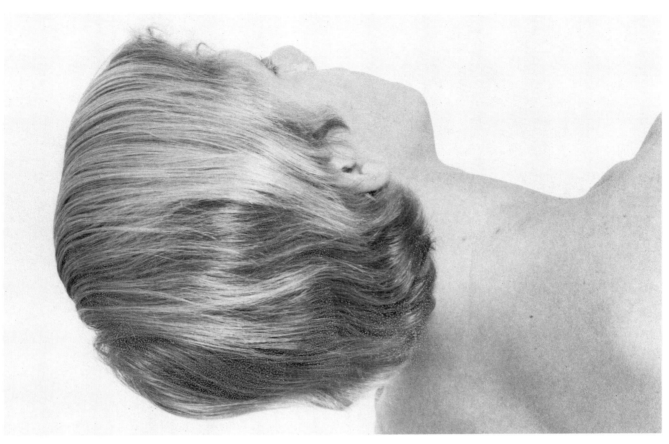

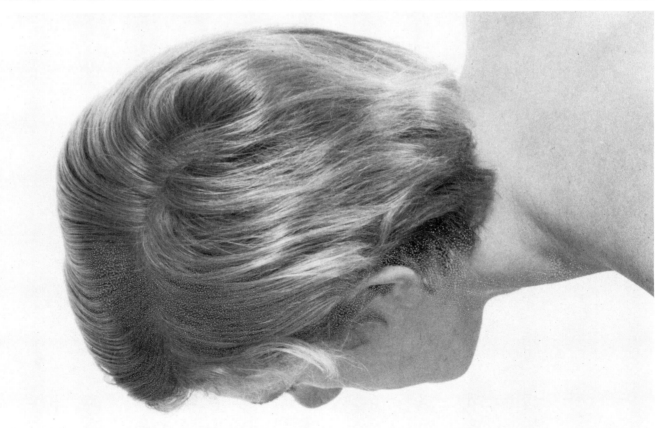

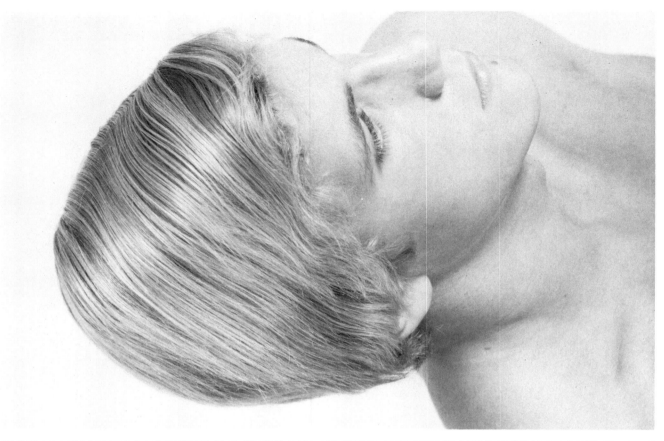

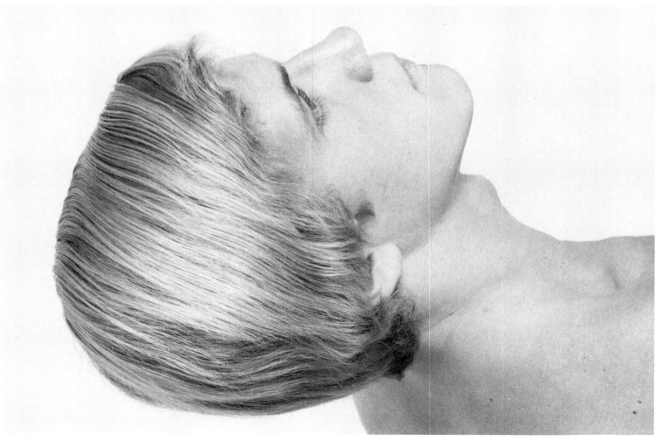

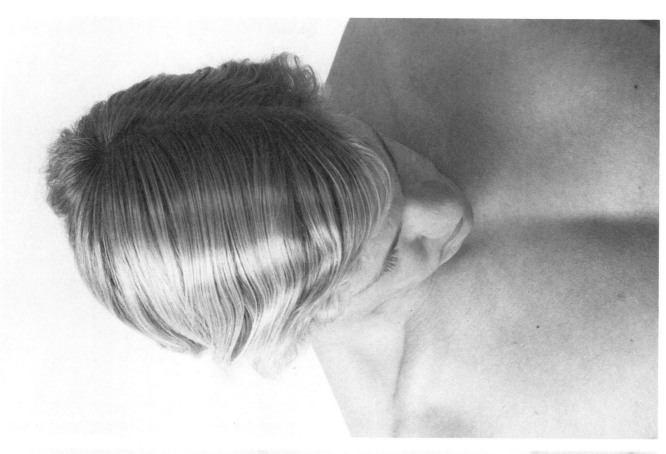

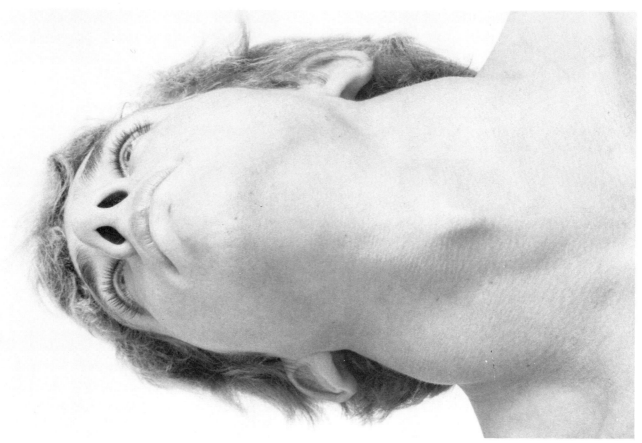

109

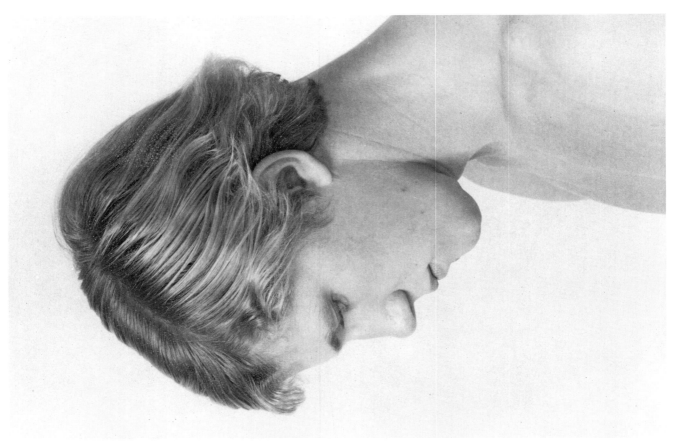

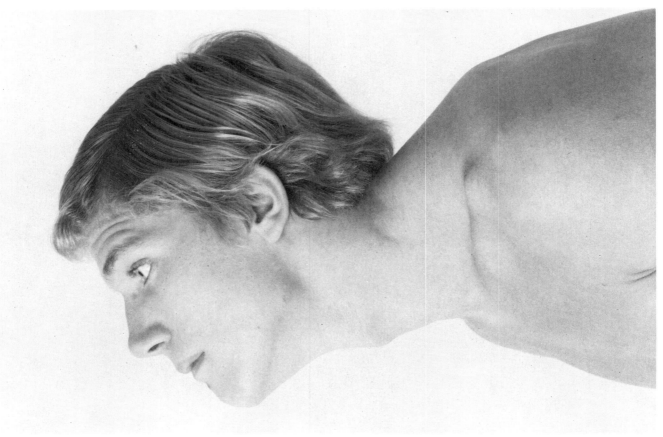

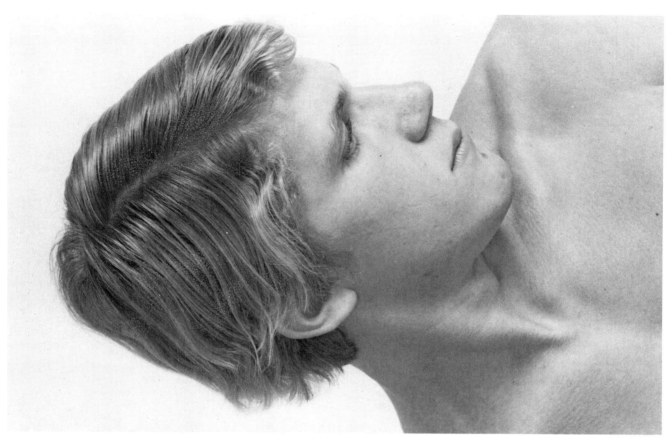

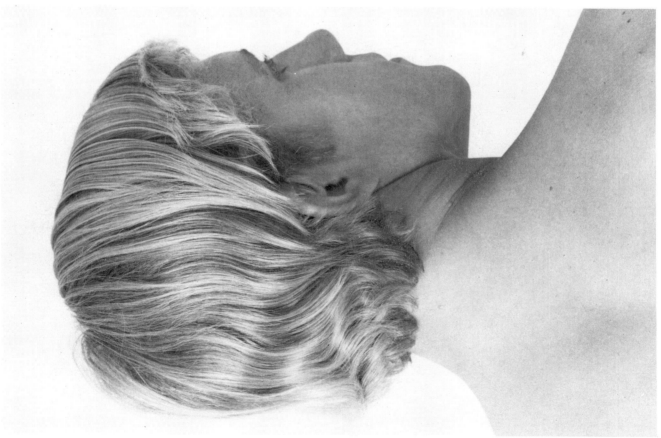

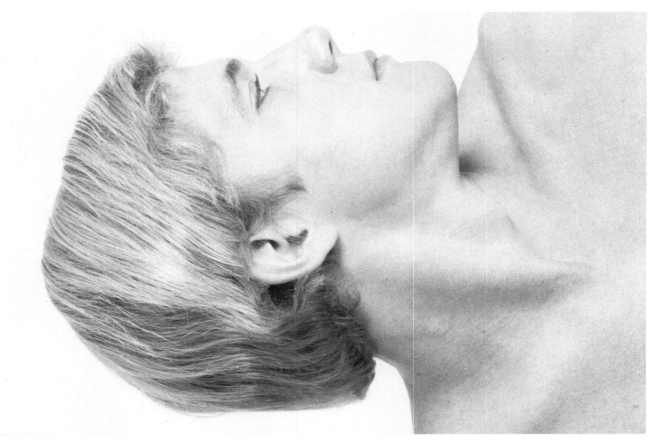

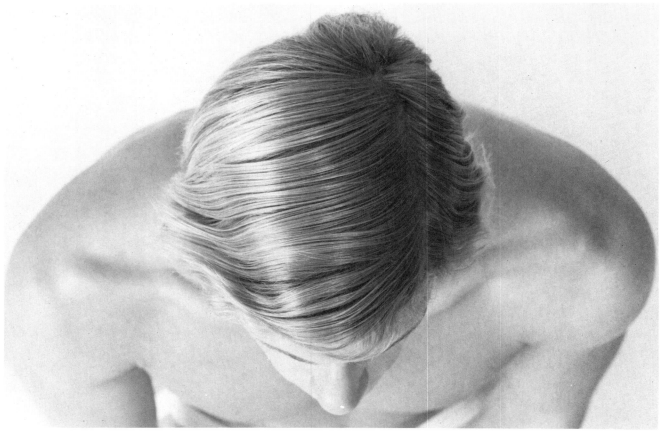

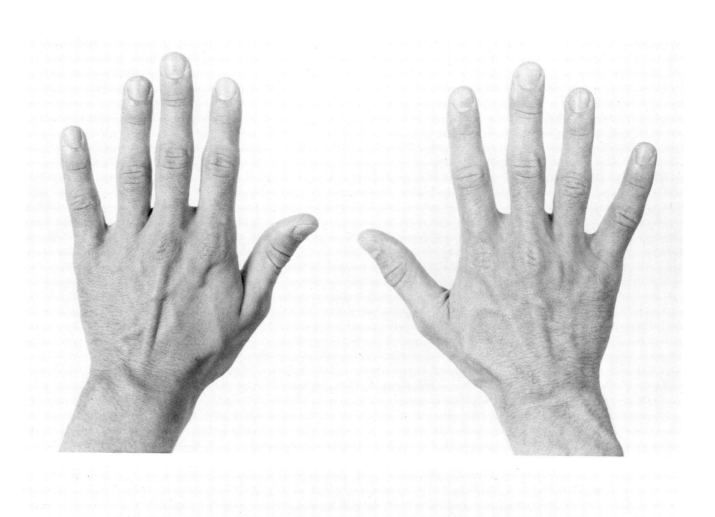
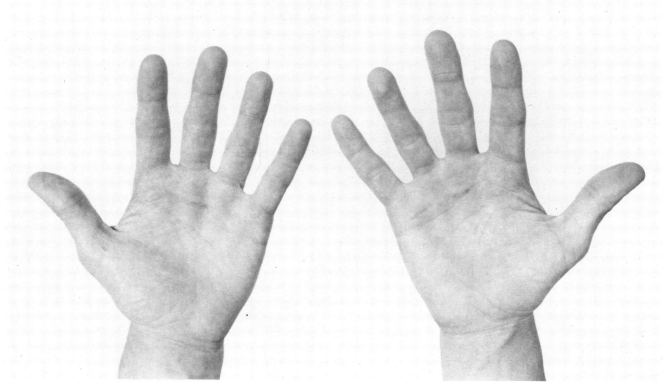

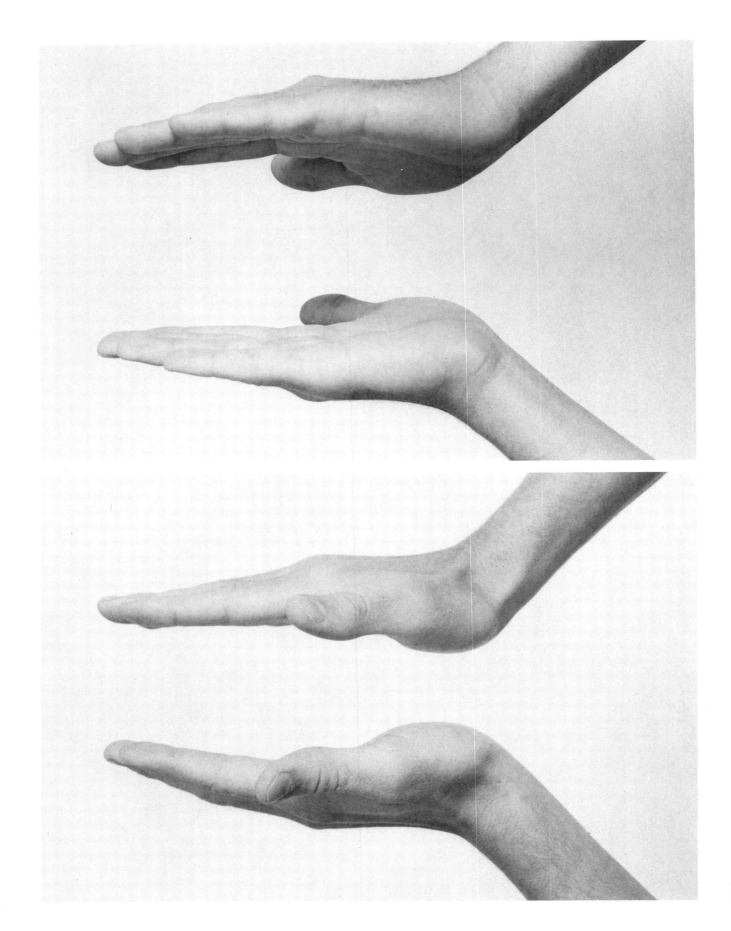

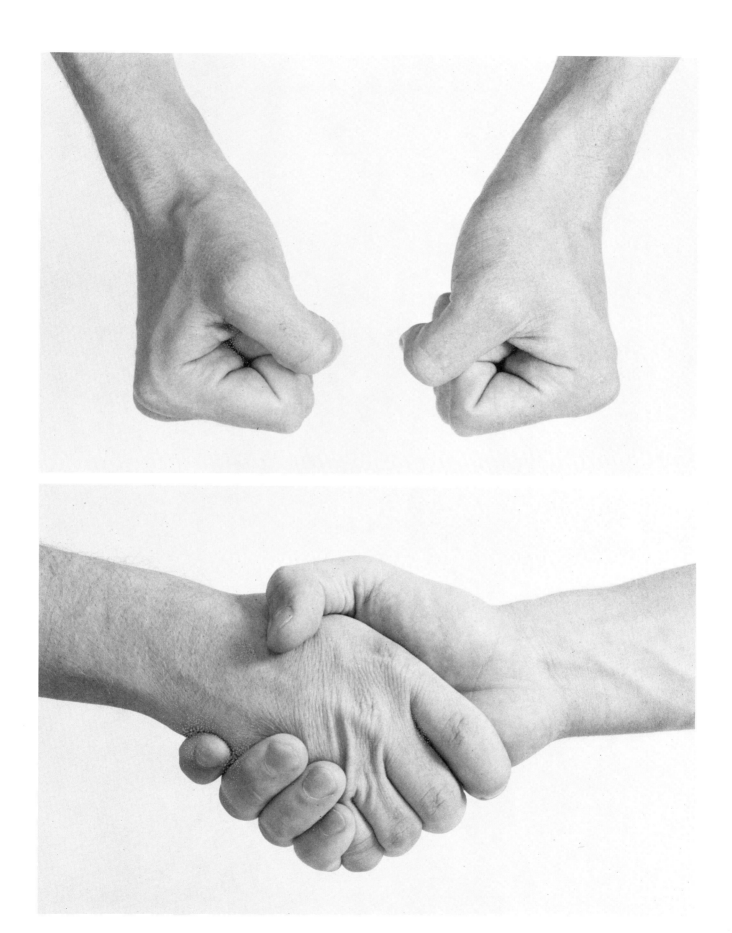

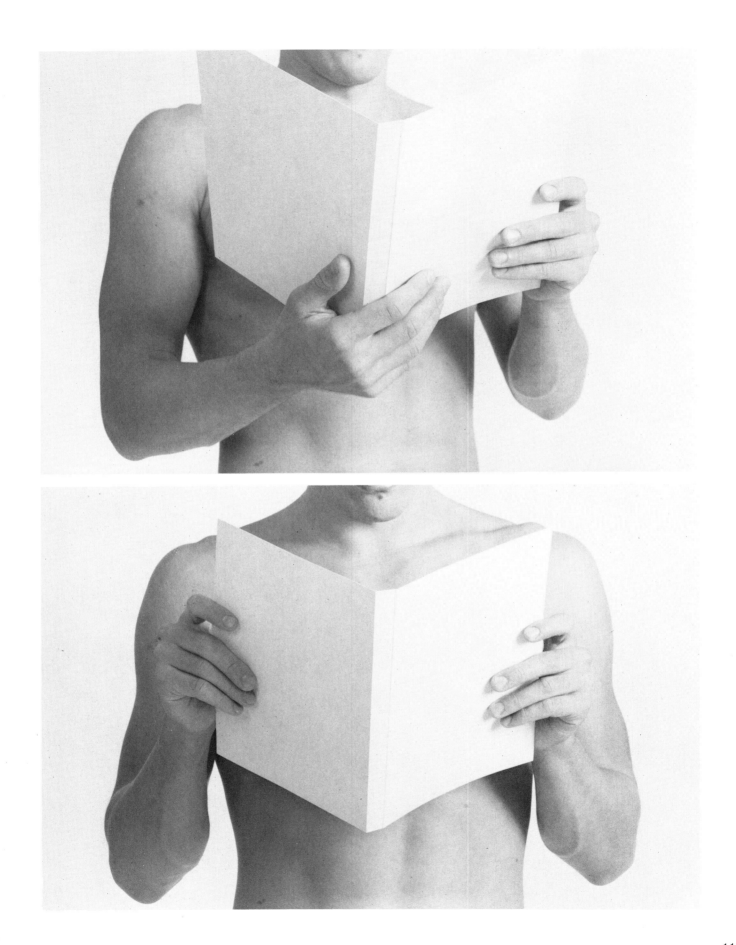

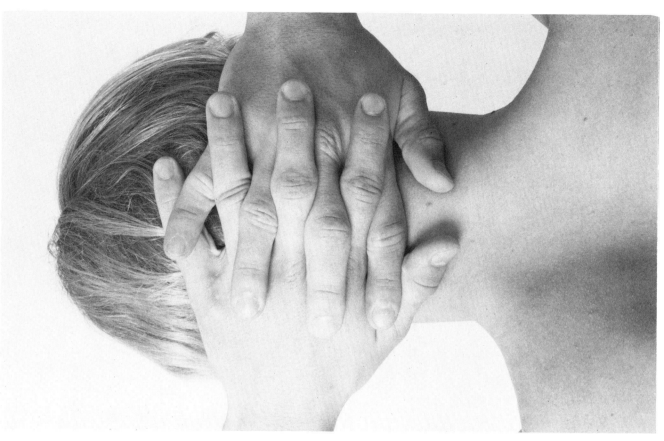

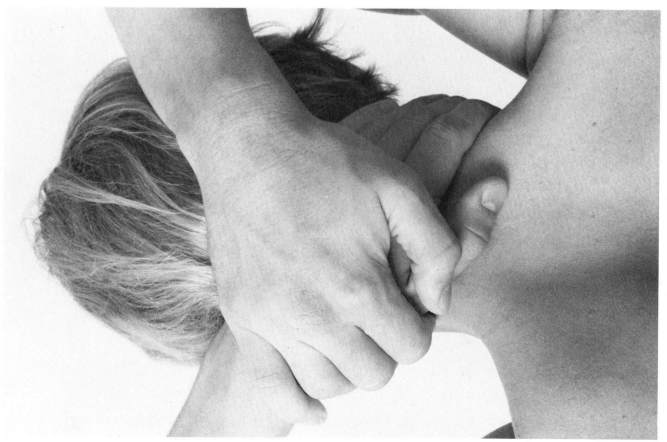

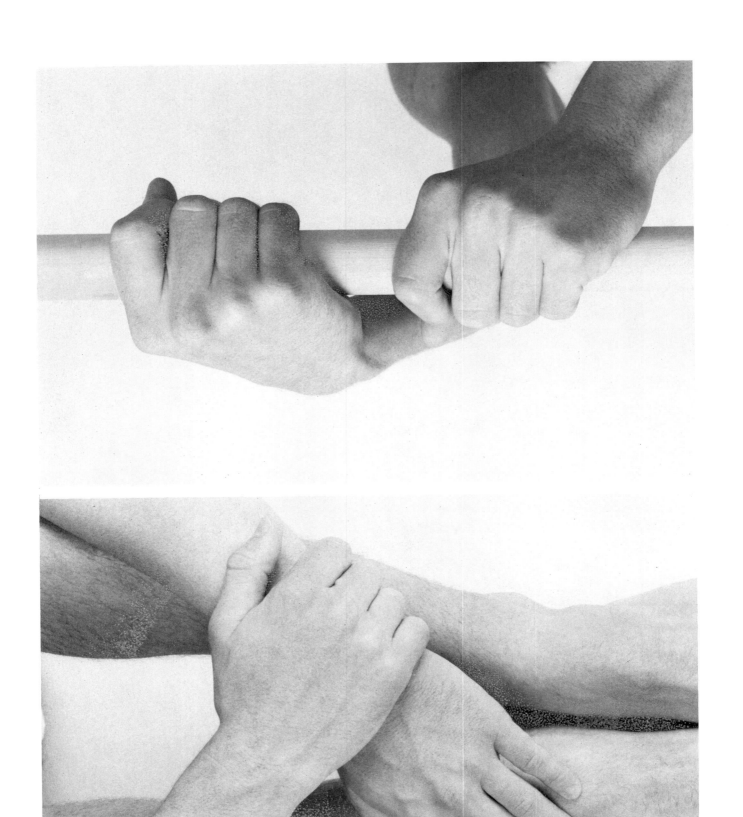

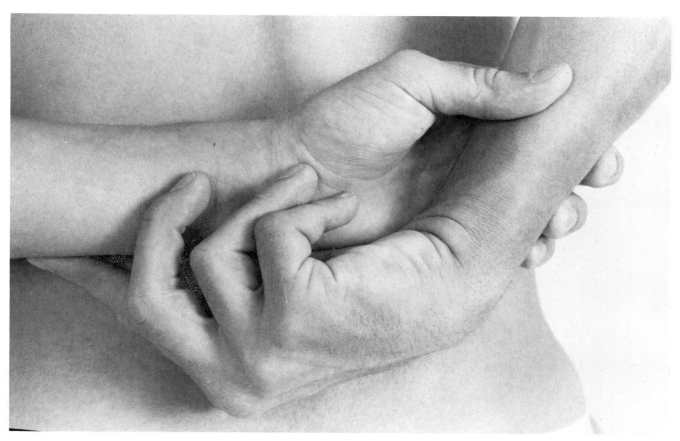

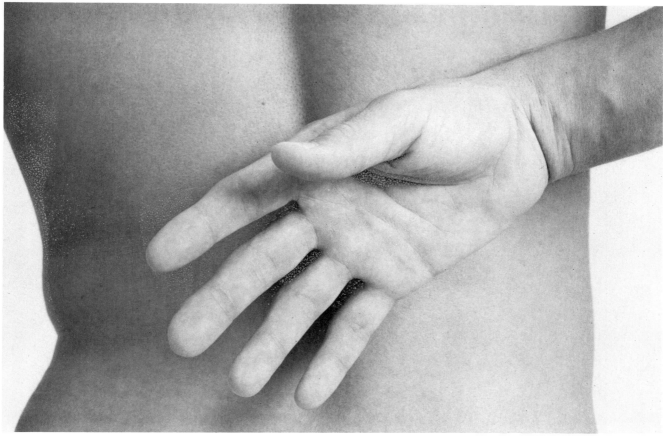

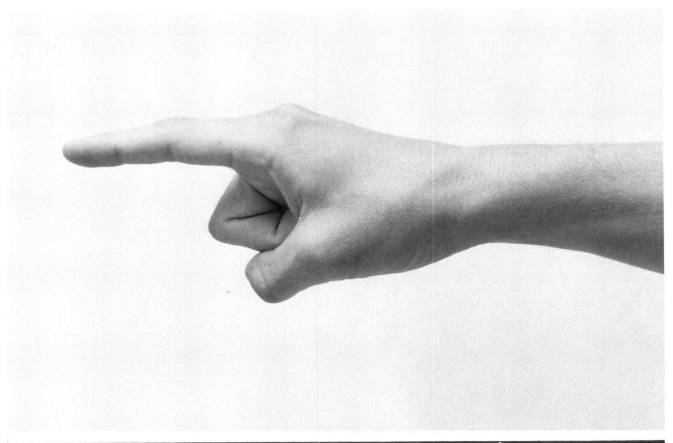

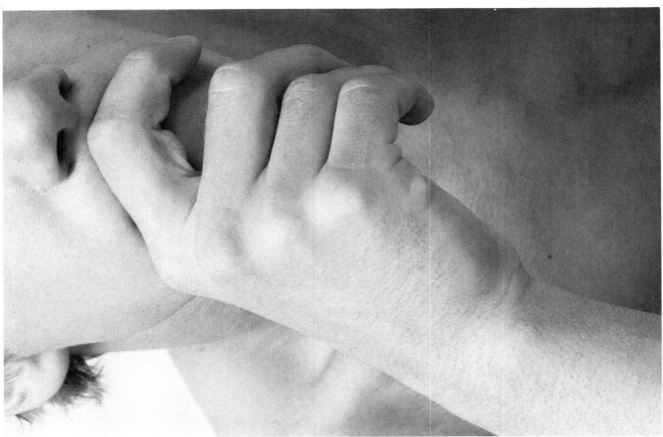

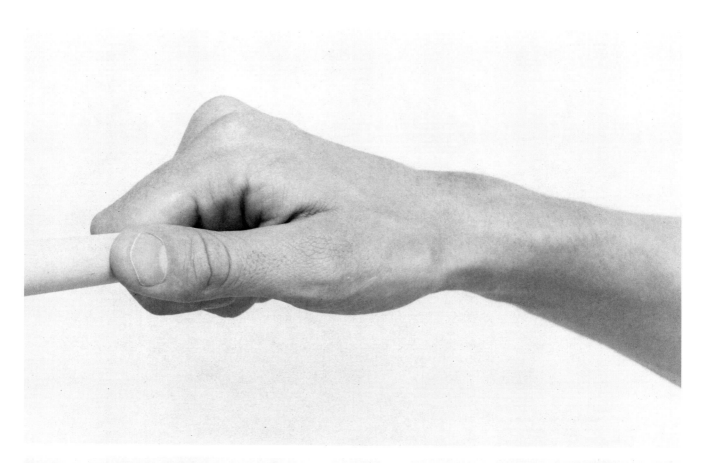

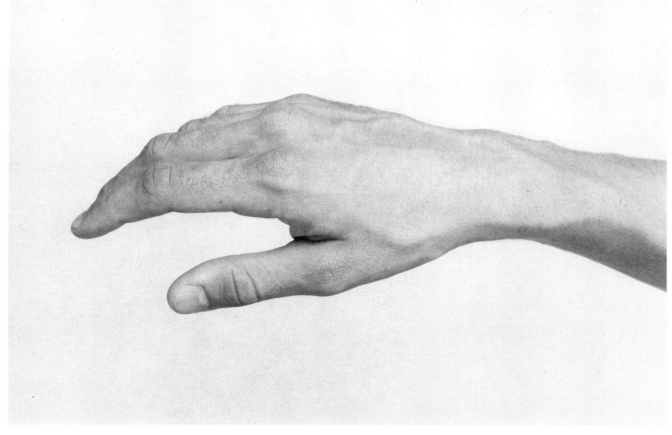

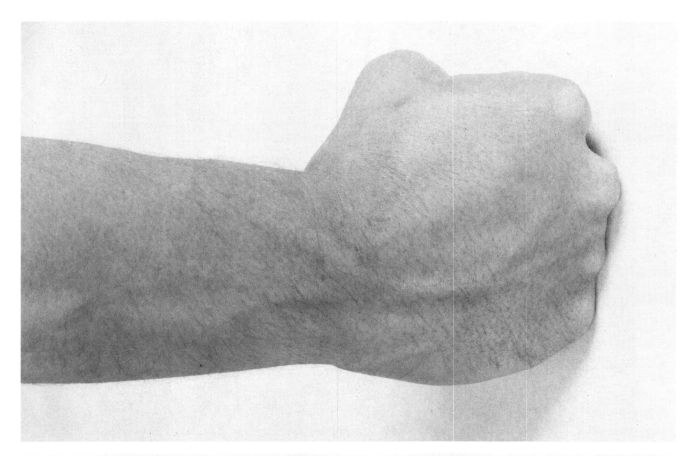

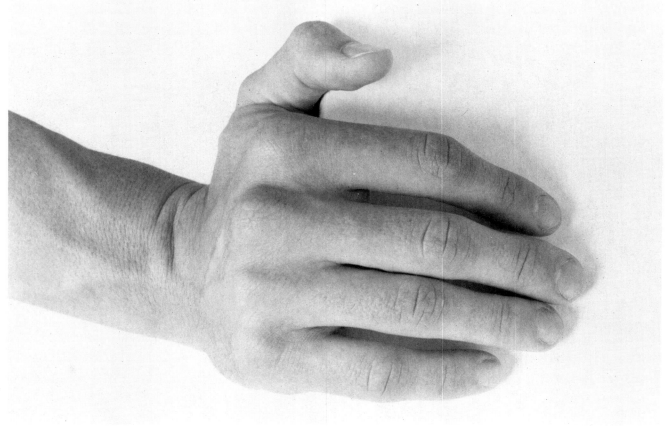

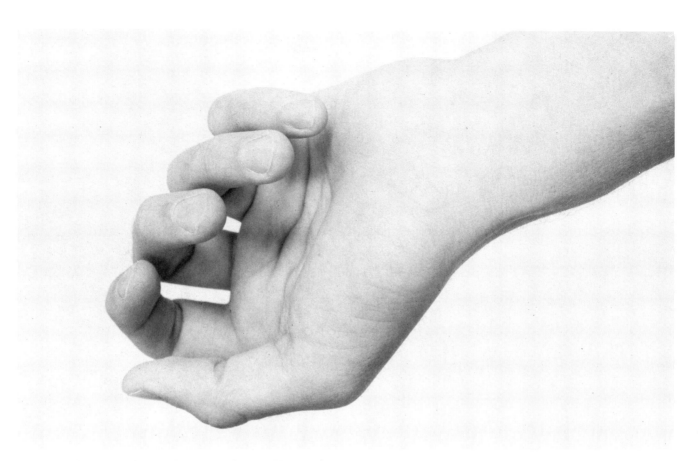

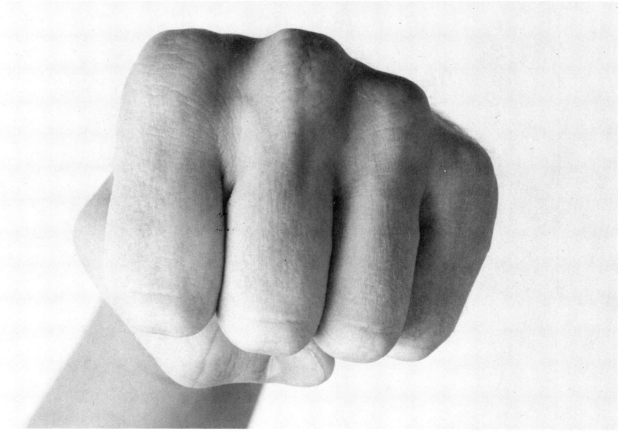

123

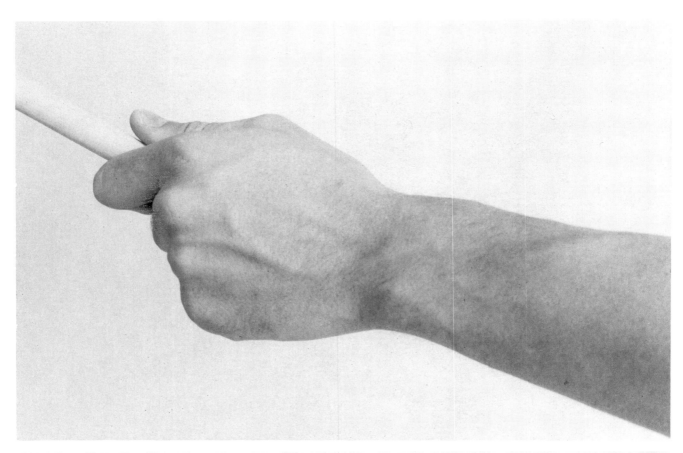

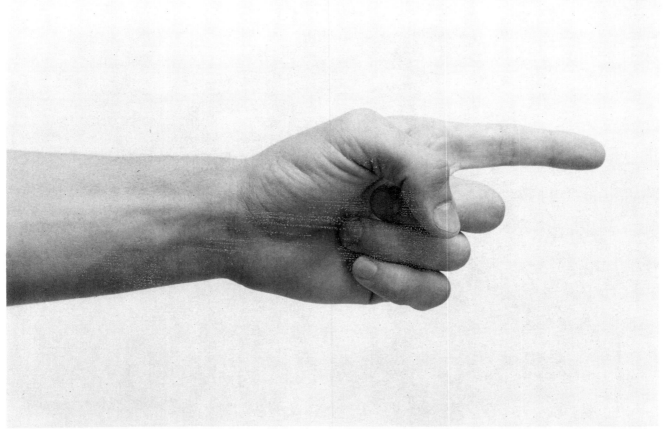

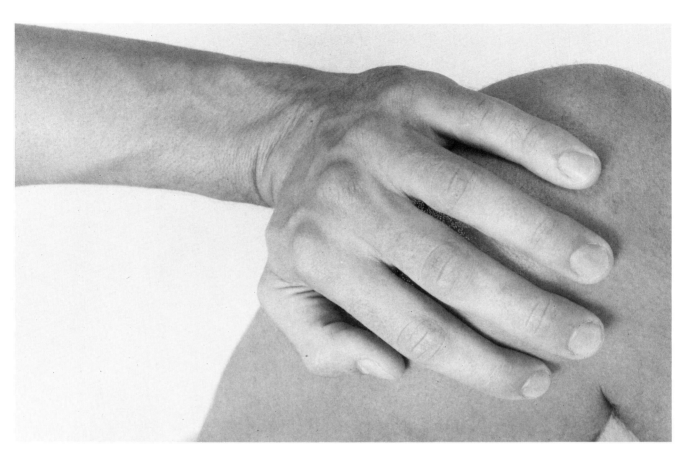

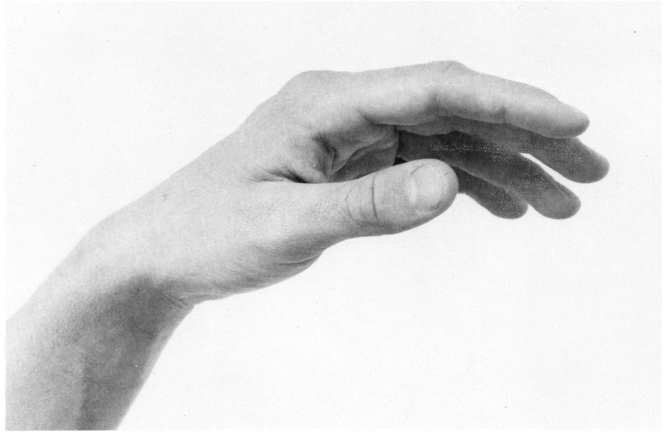

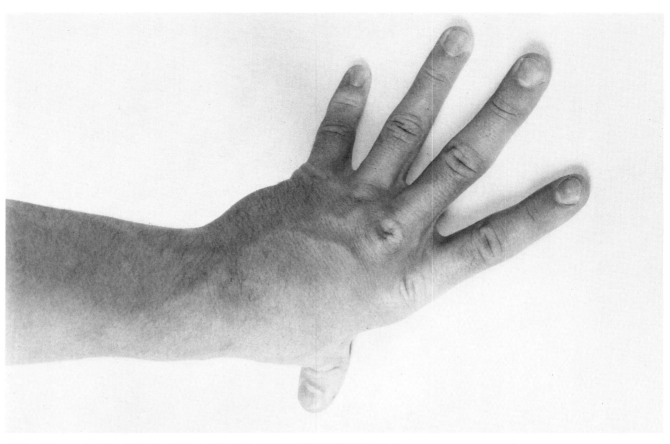

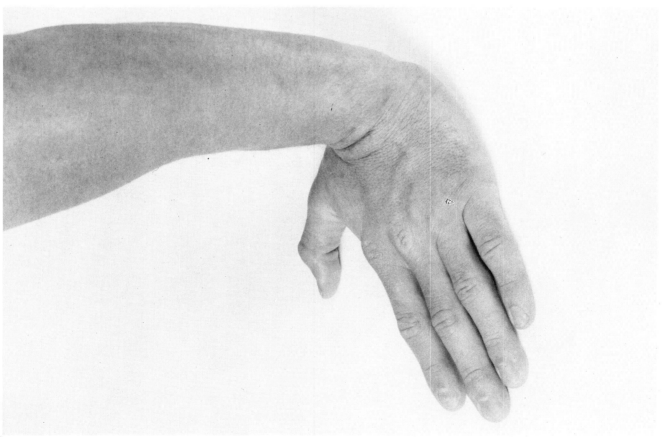

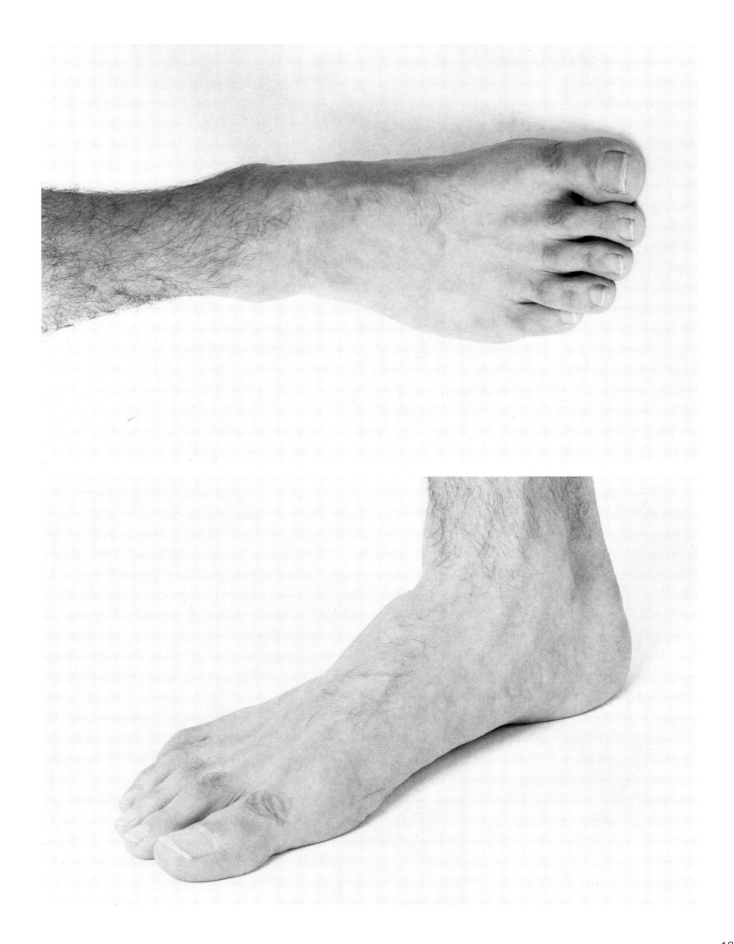

127

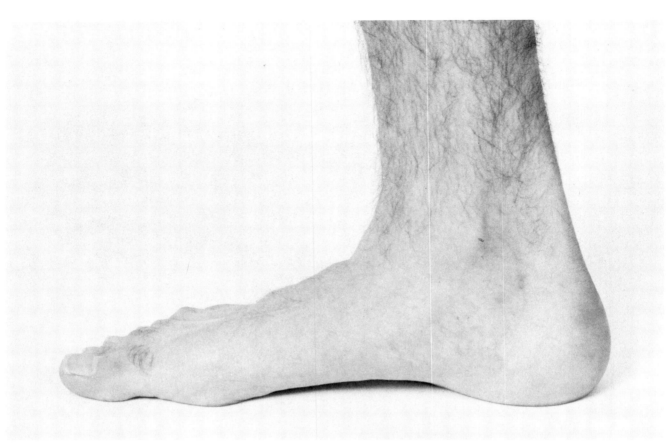

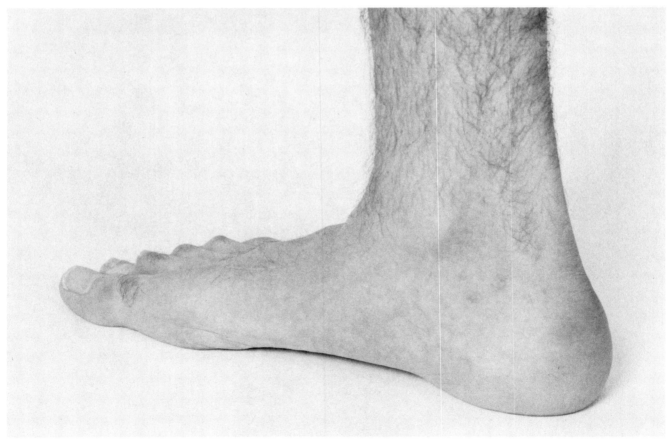

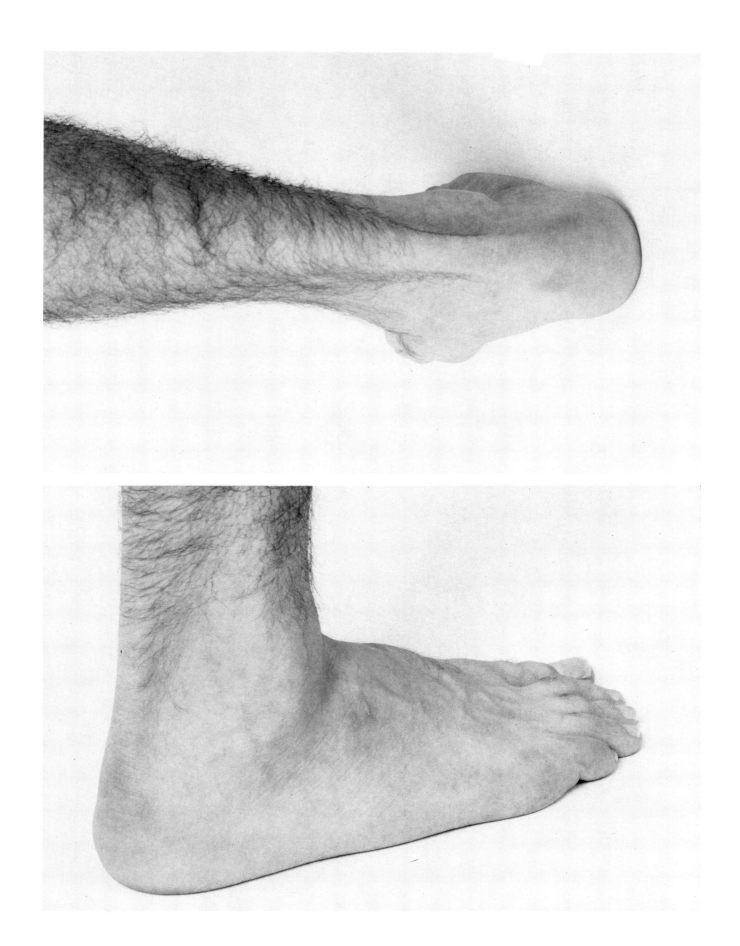

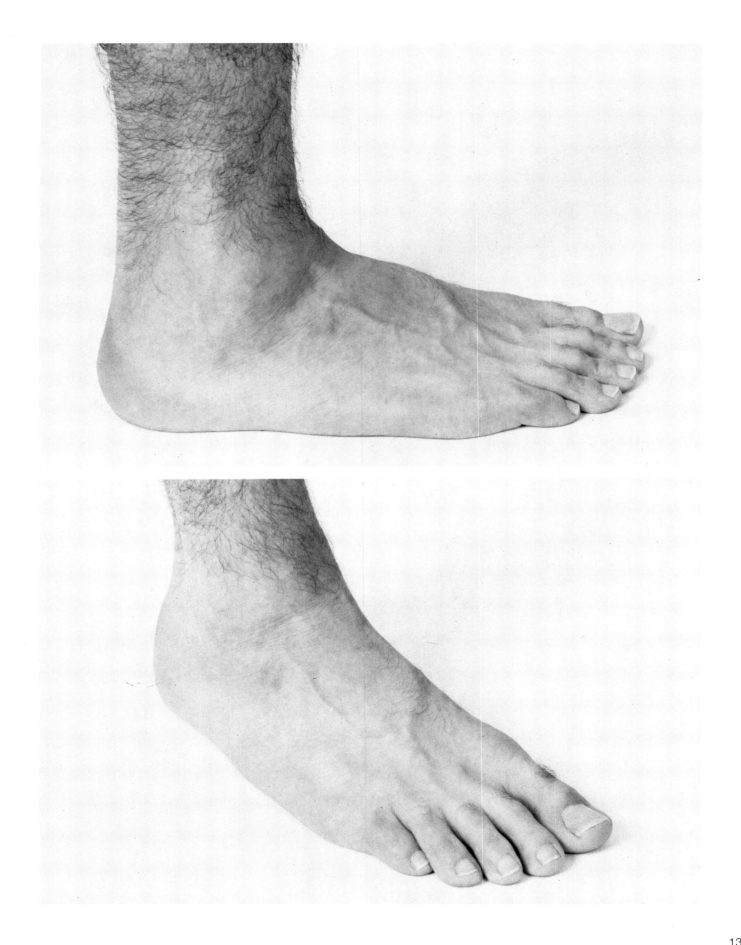

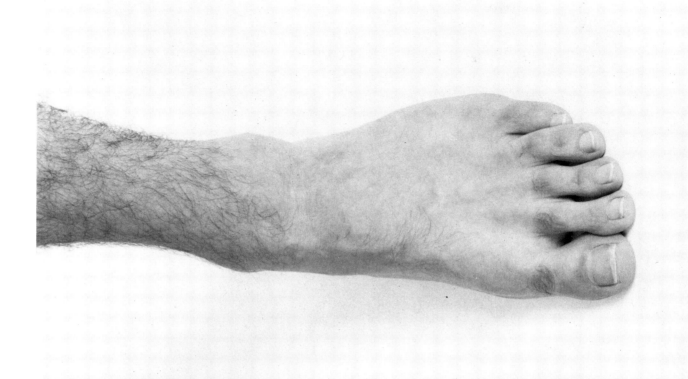

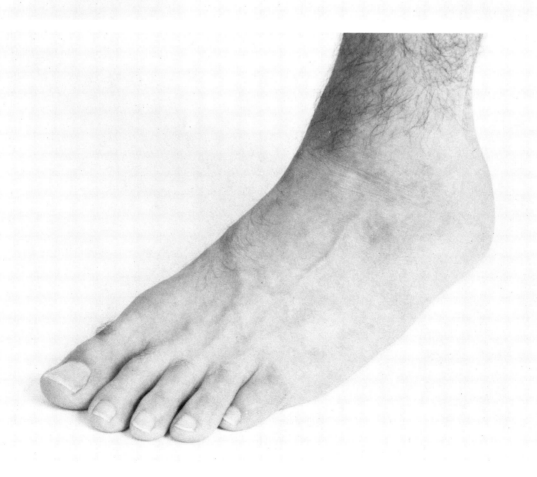

131

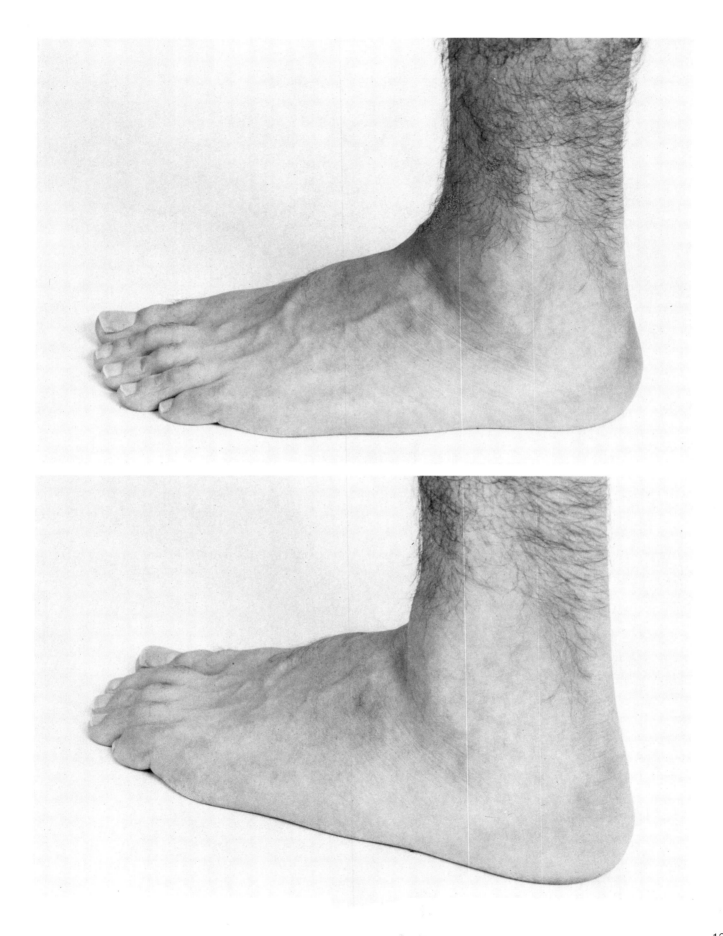

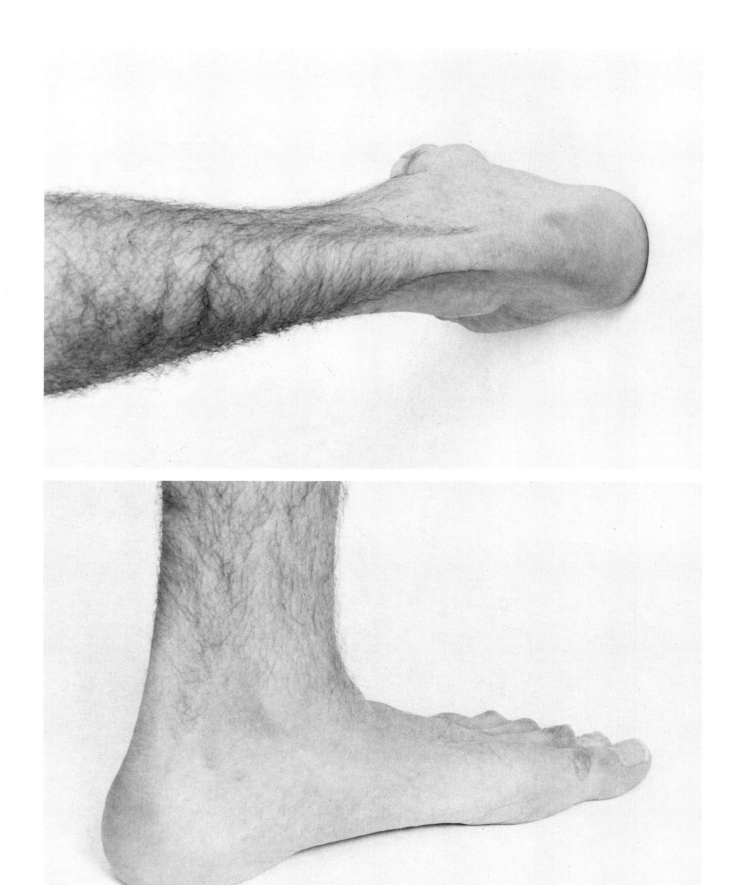

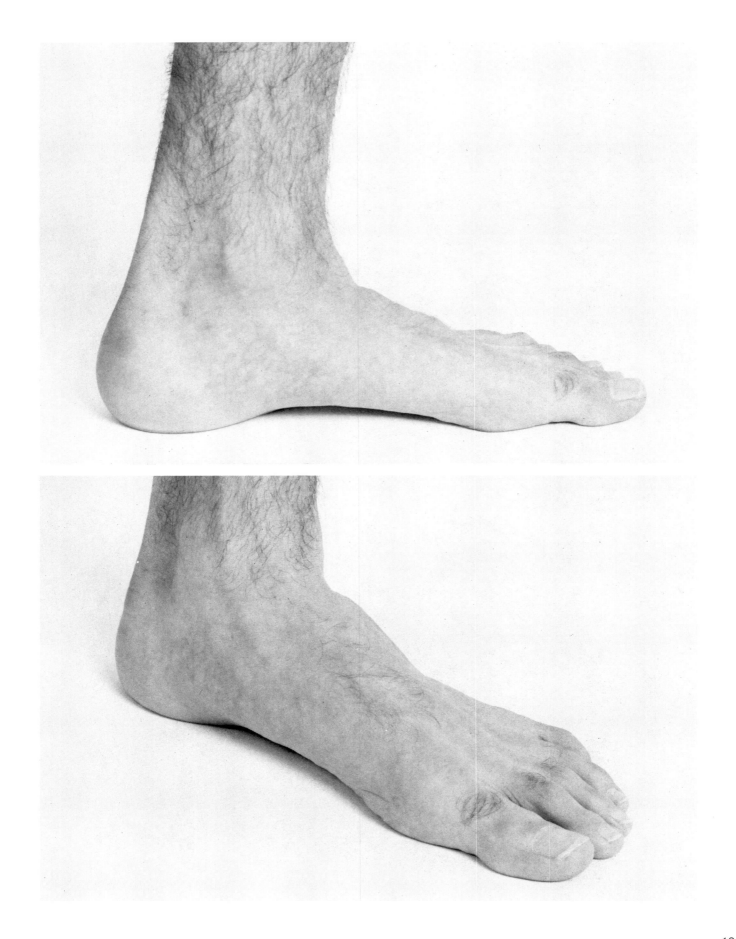

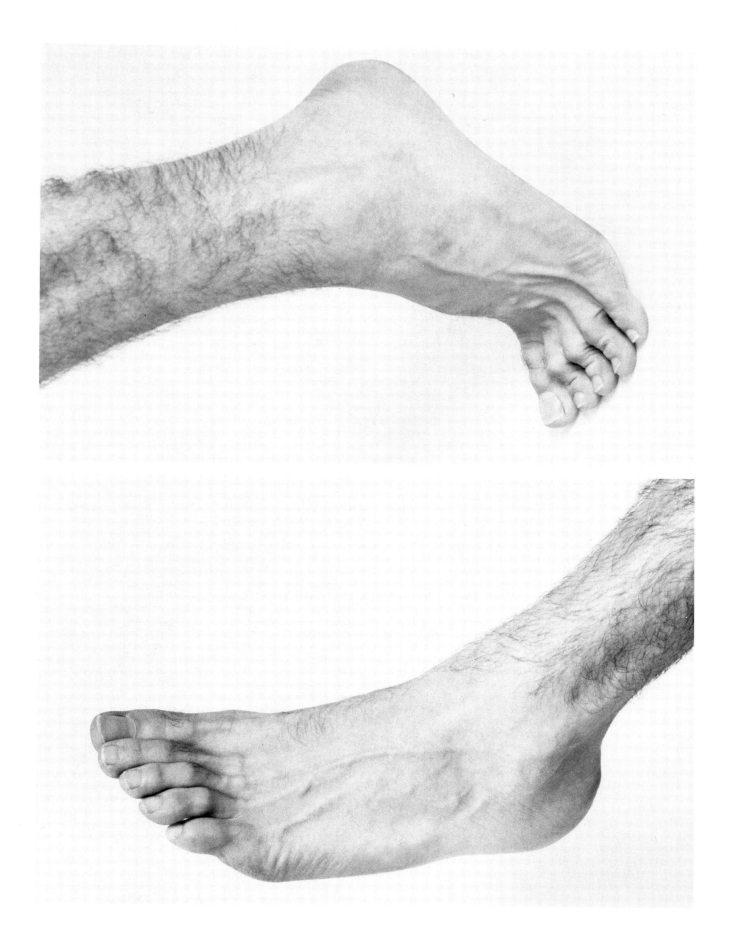

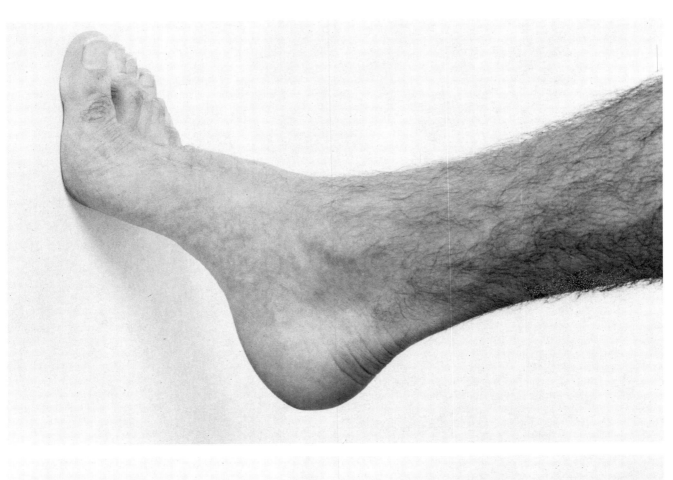

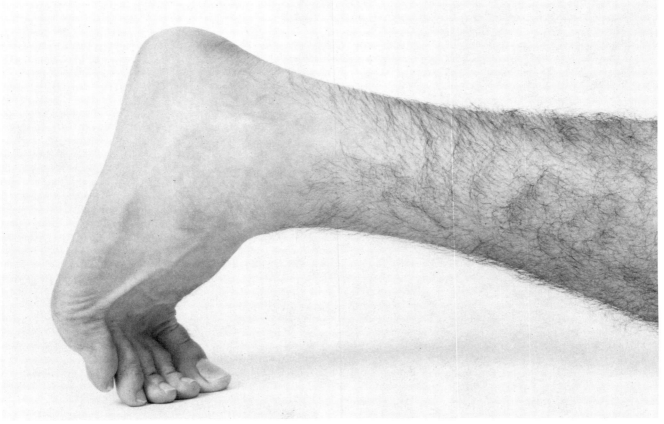

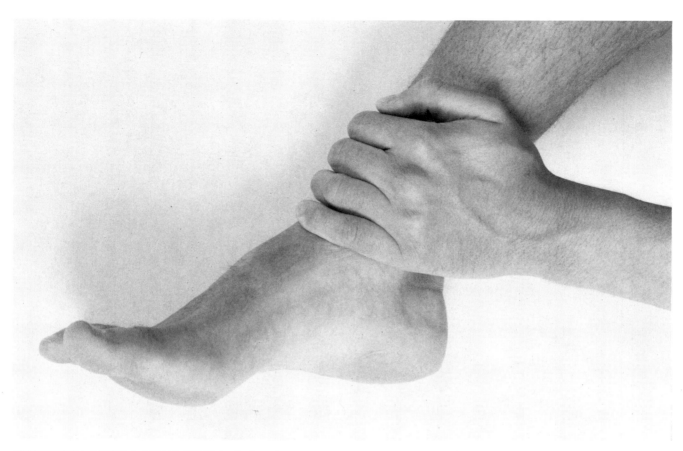

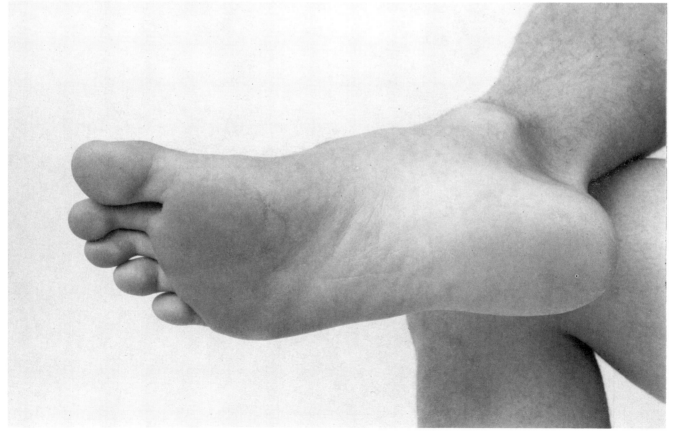

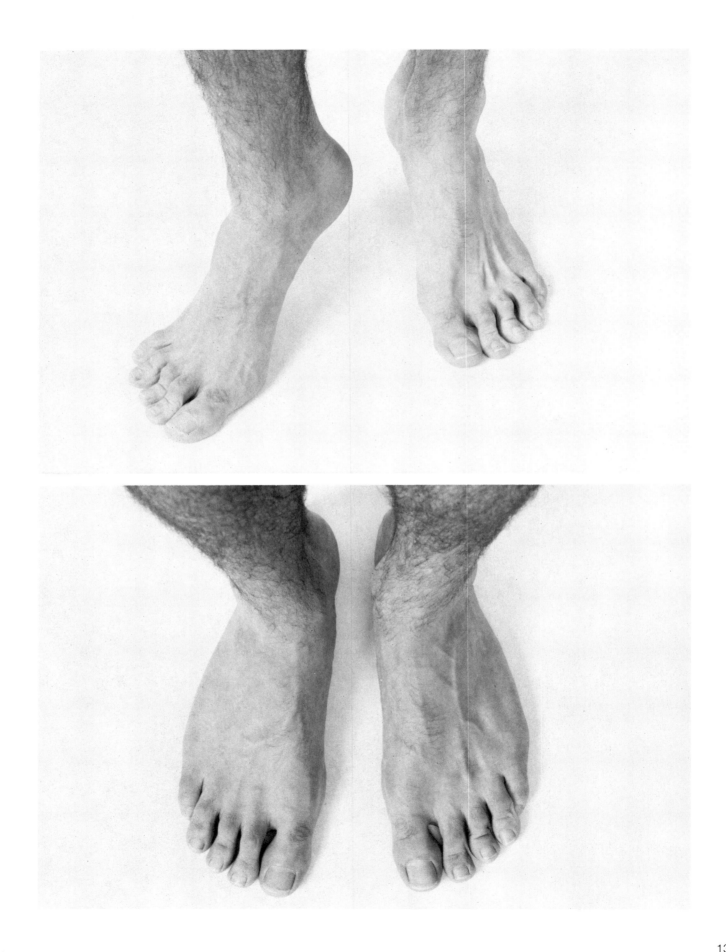

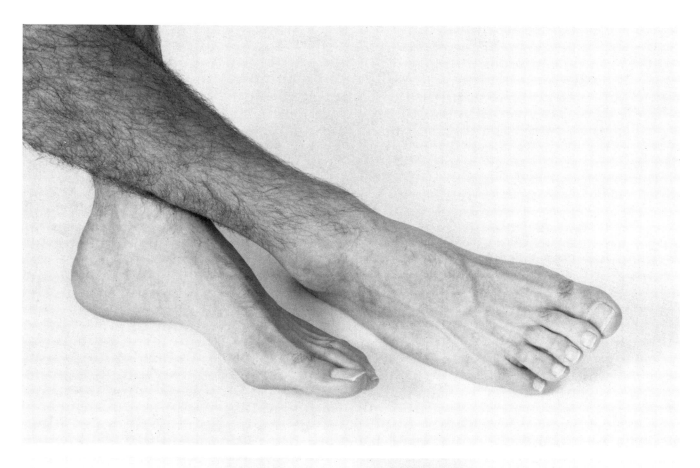

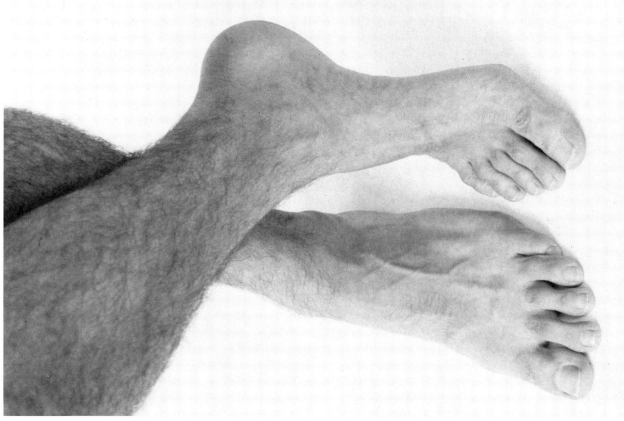

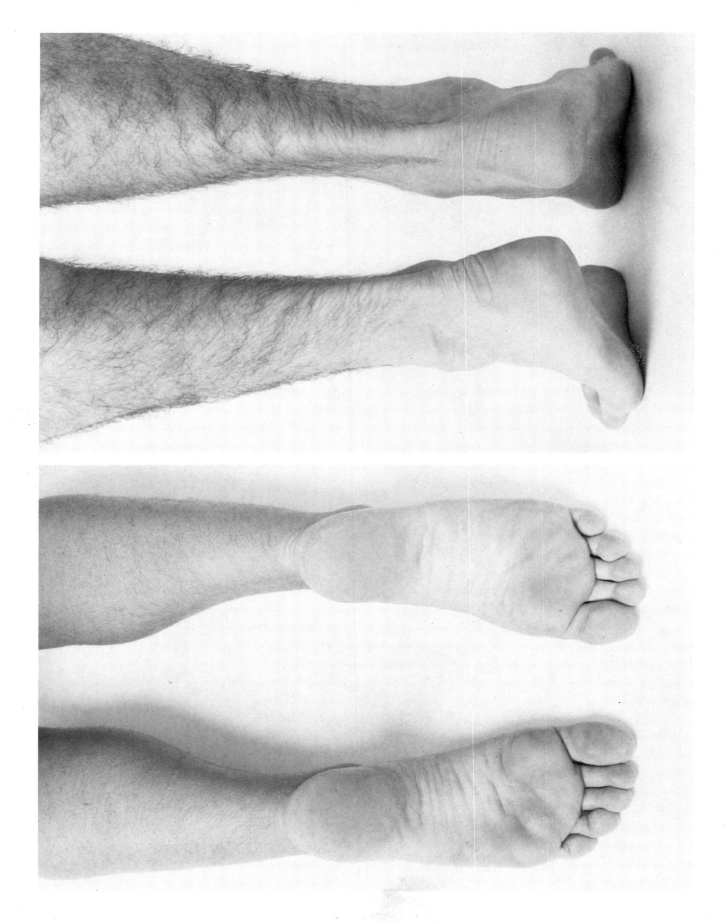

140

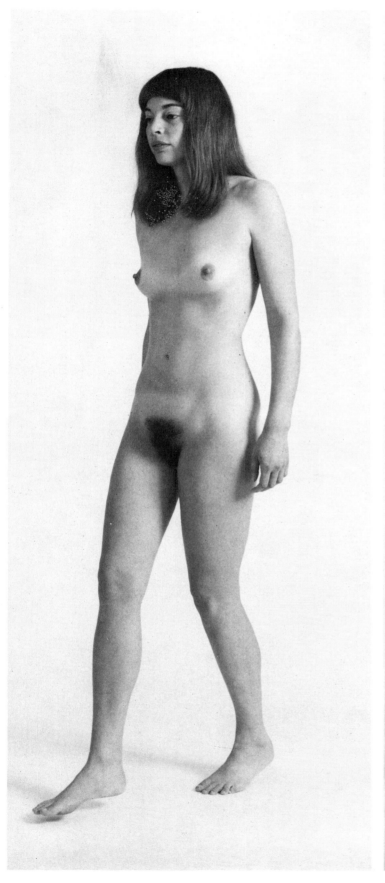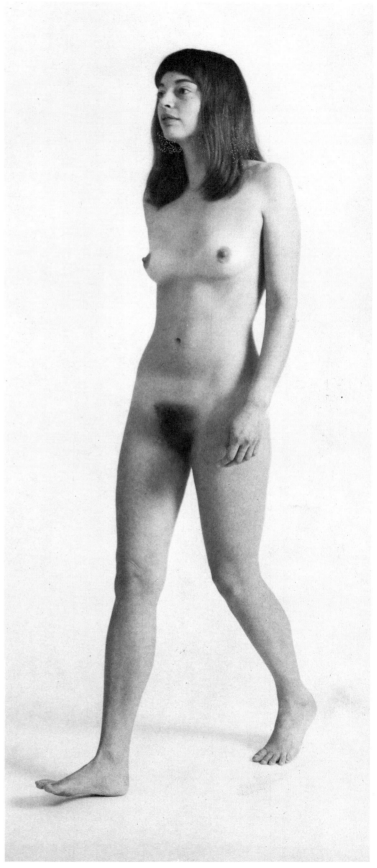

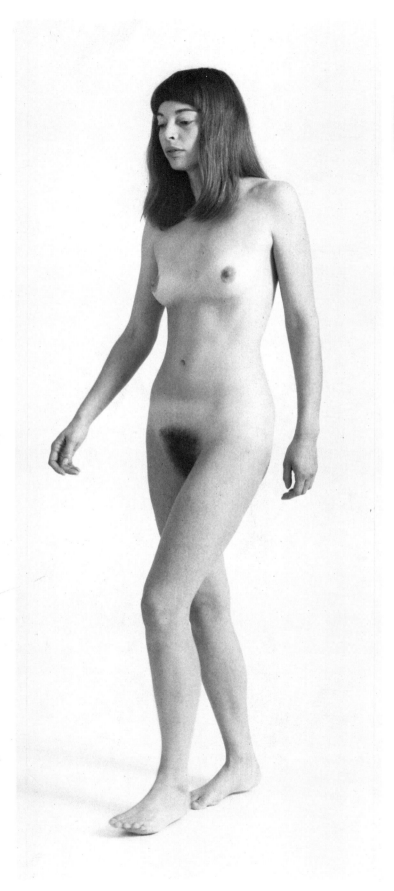
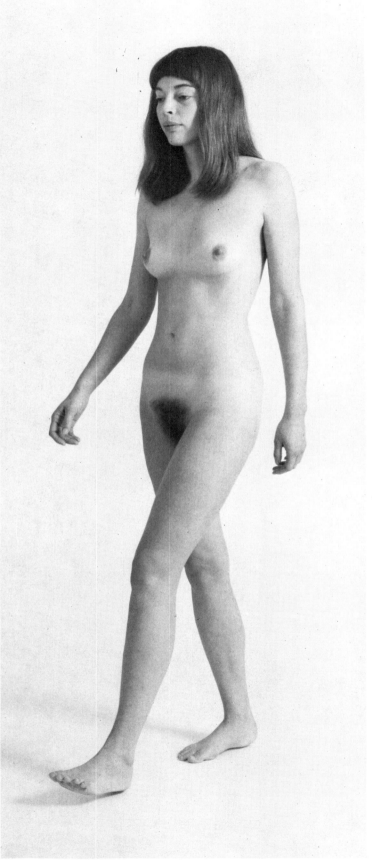

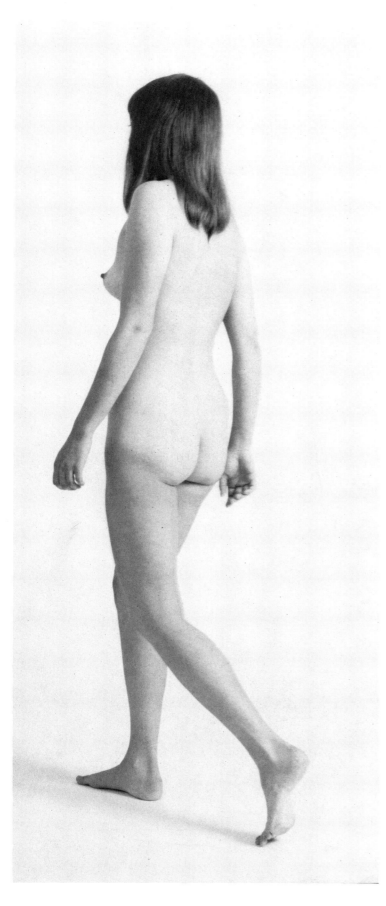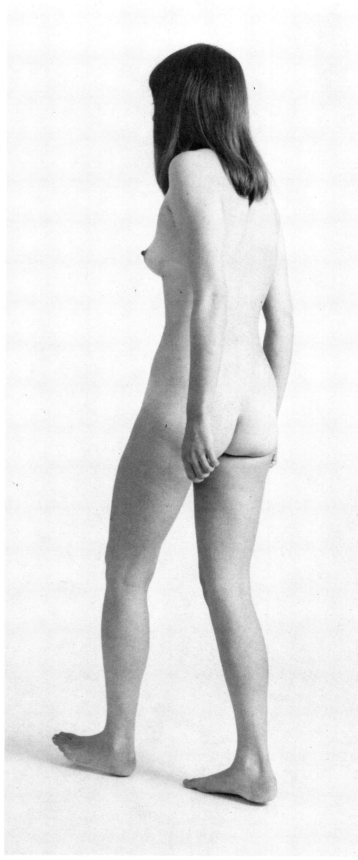

143

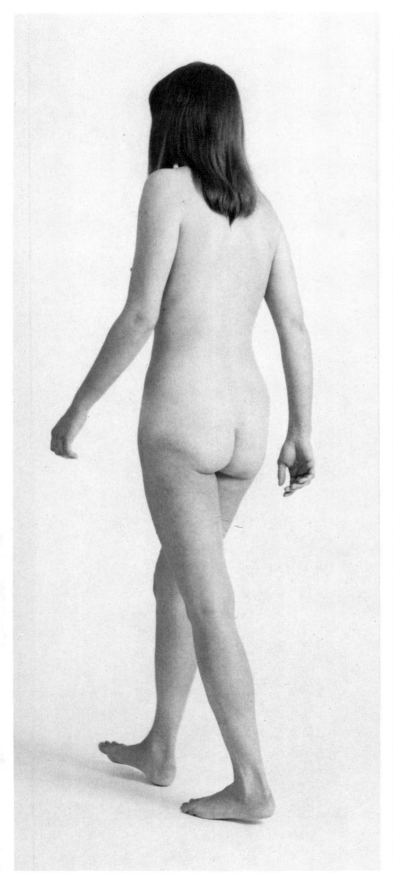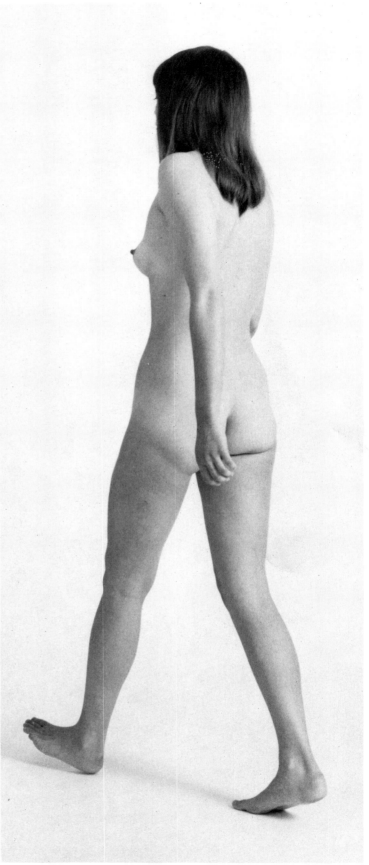

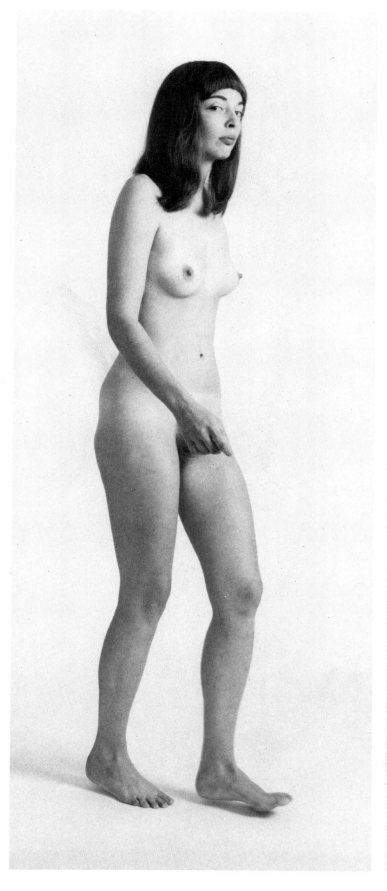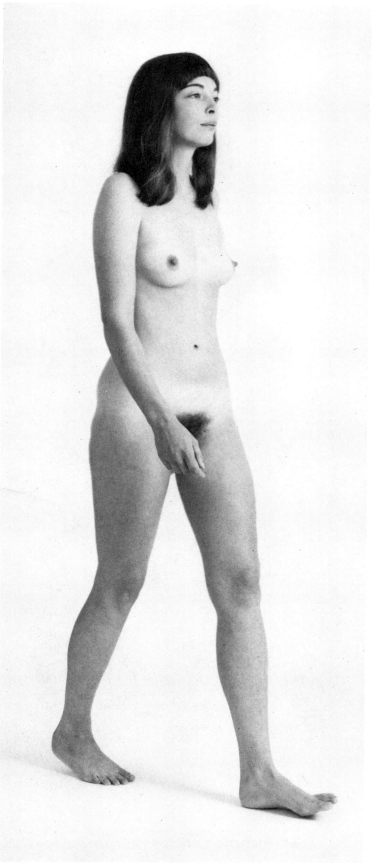

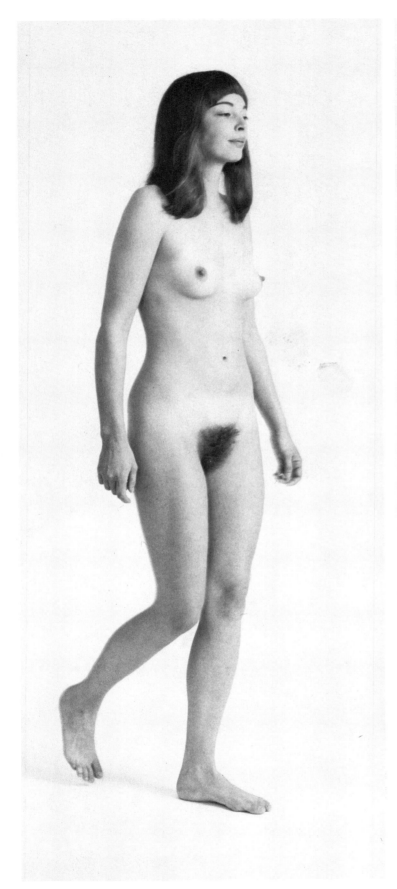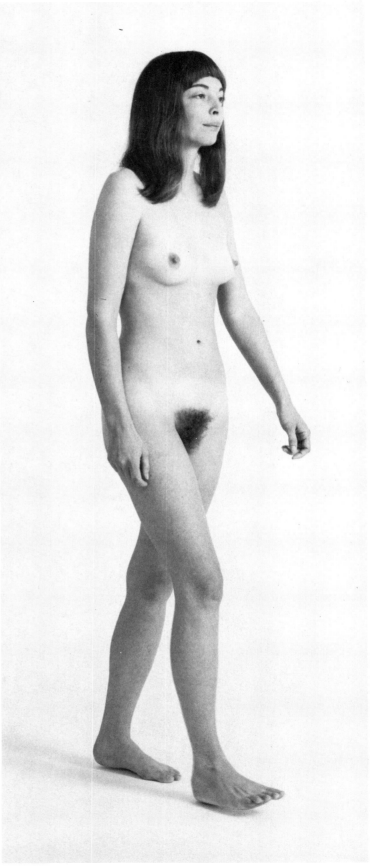

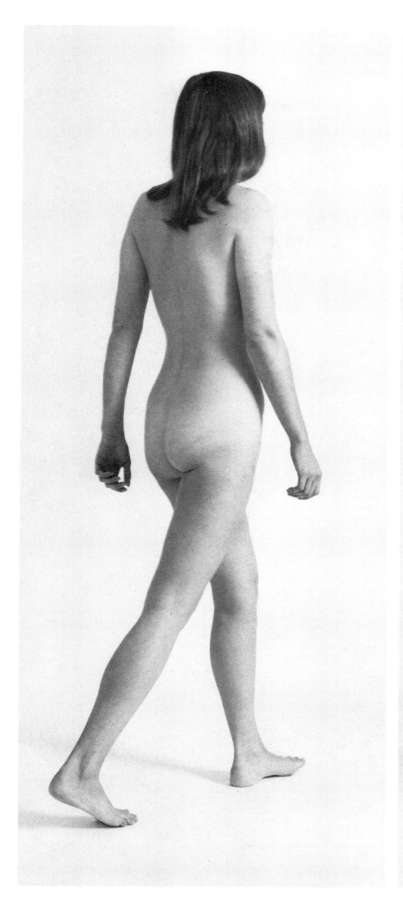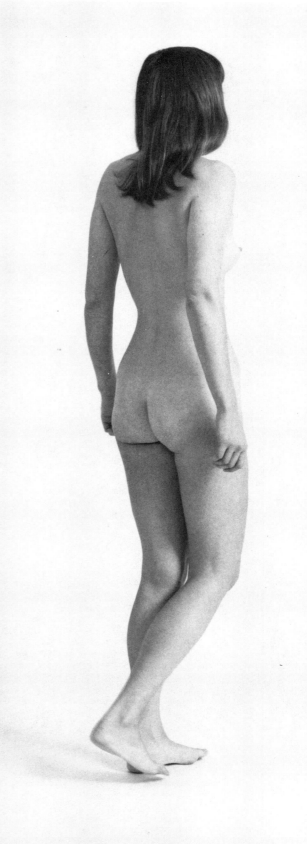

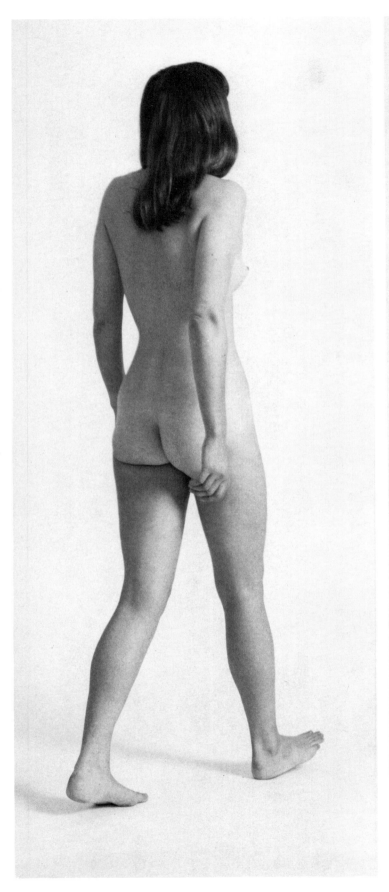
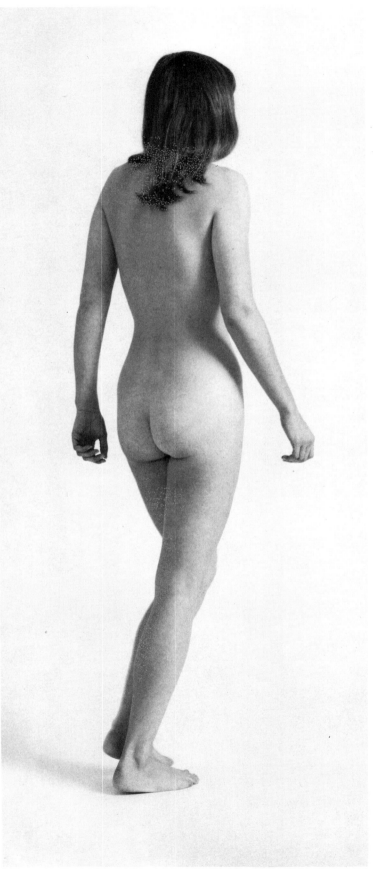

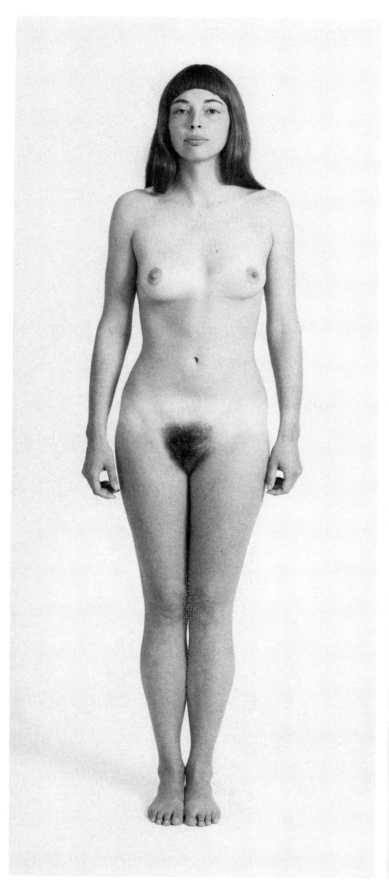
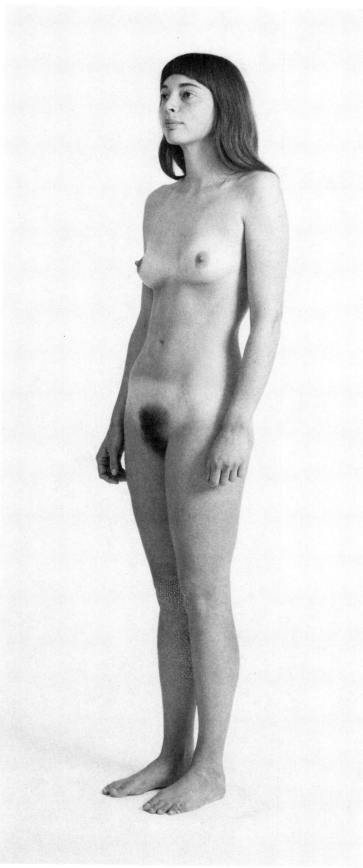

149

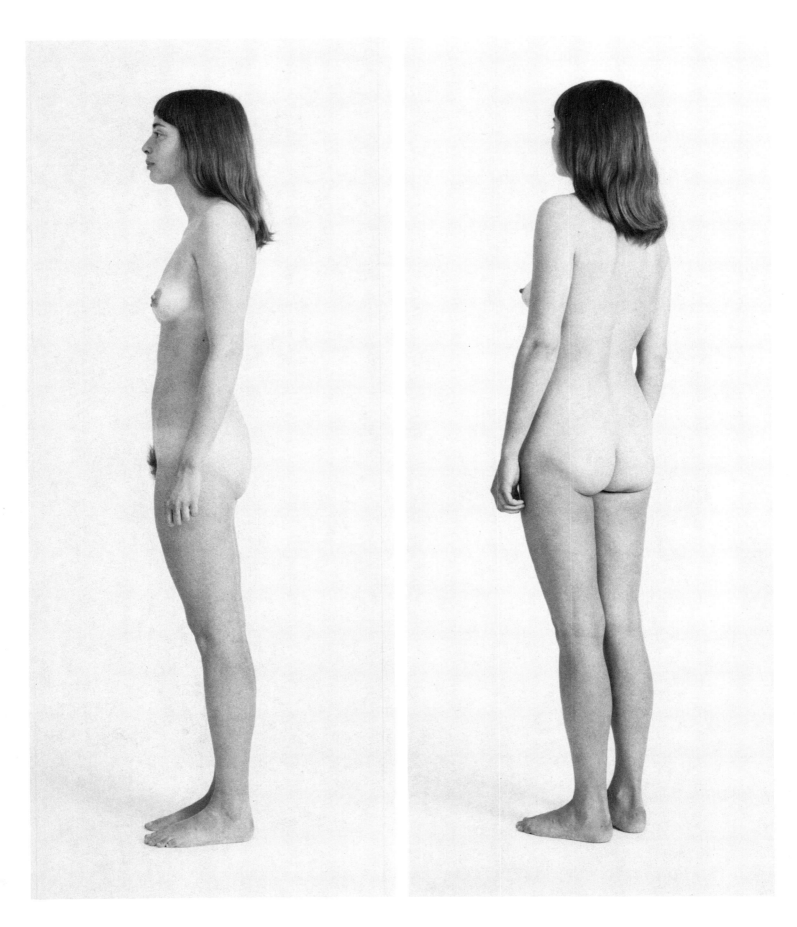

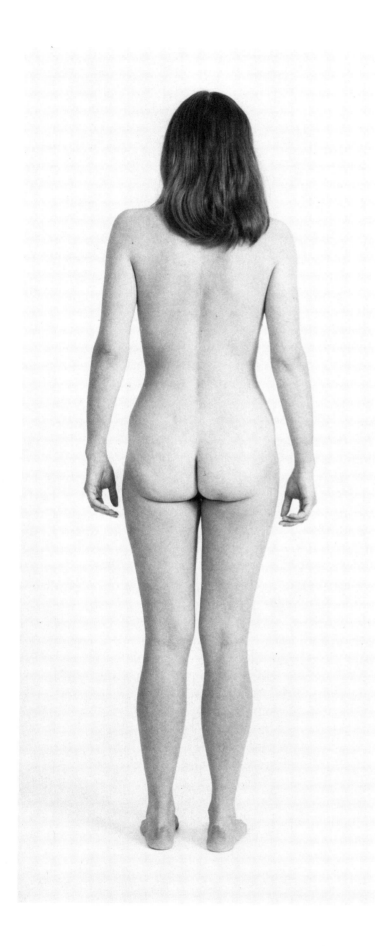
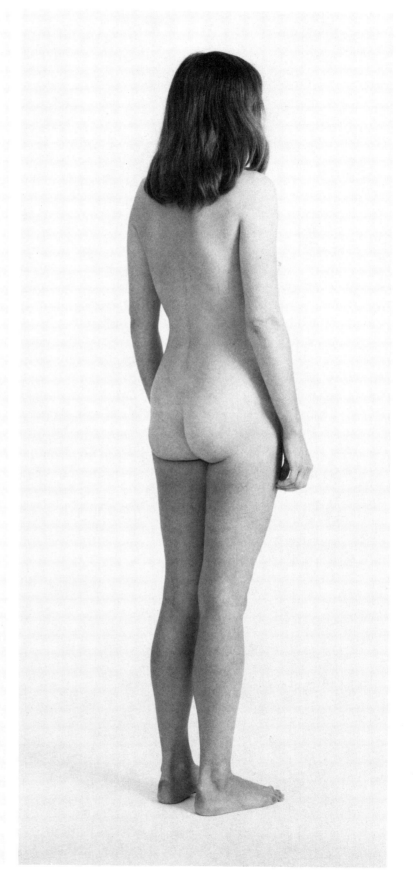

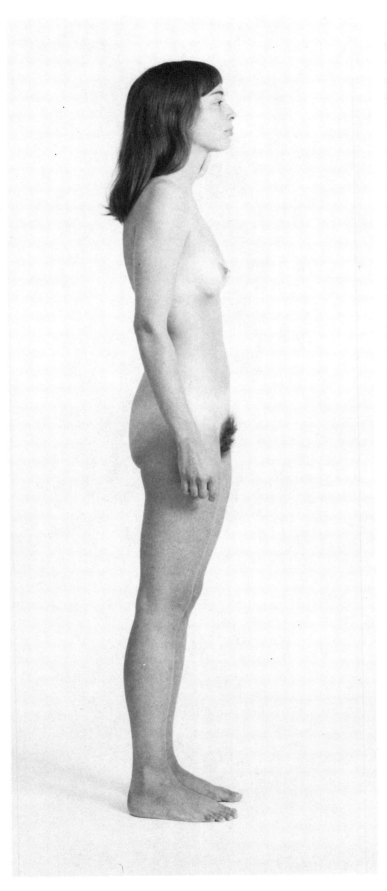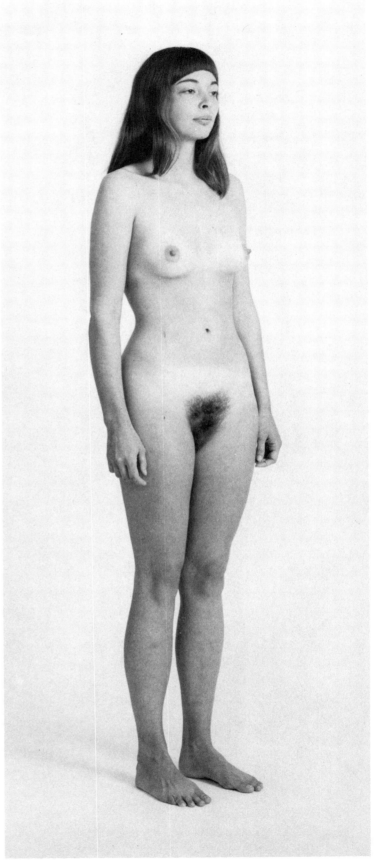

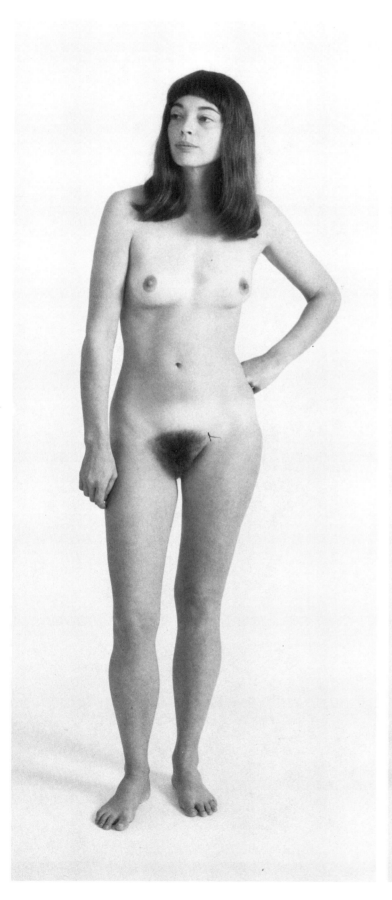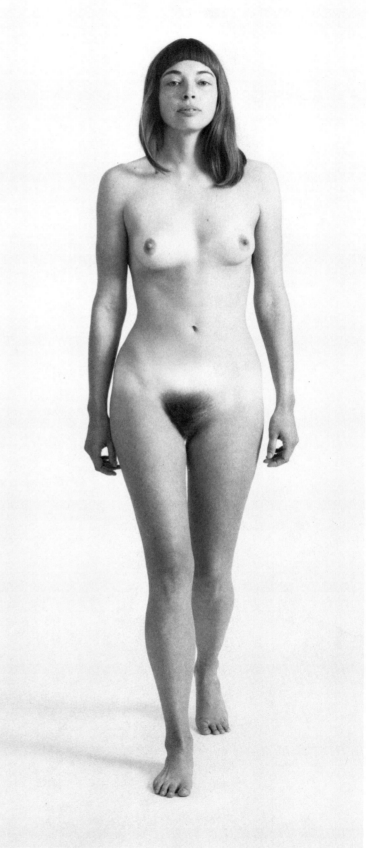

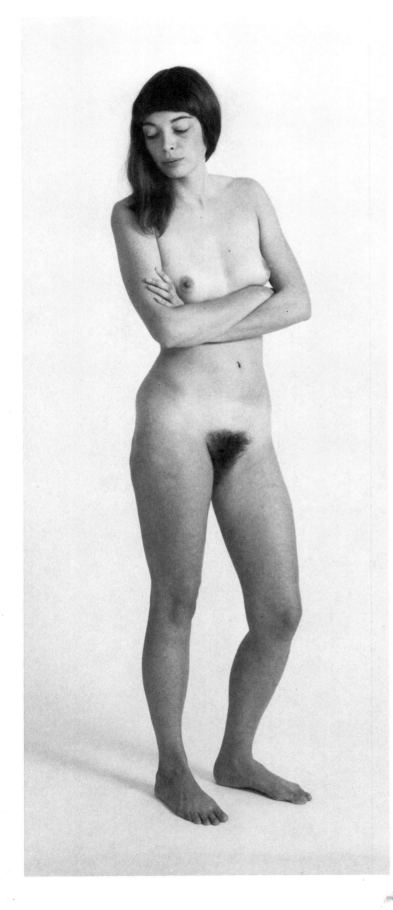
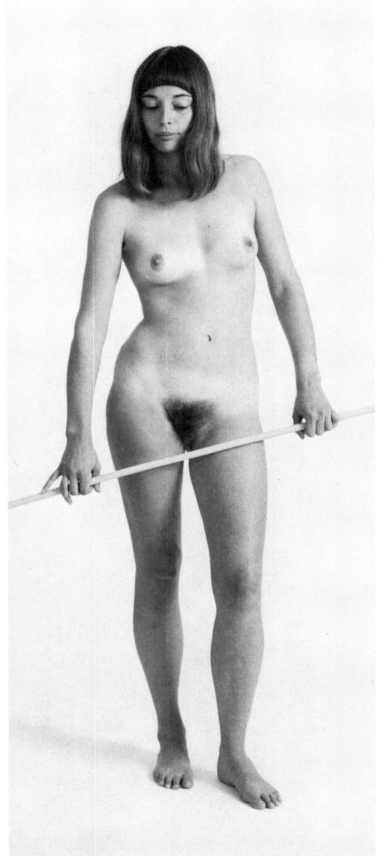

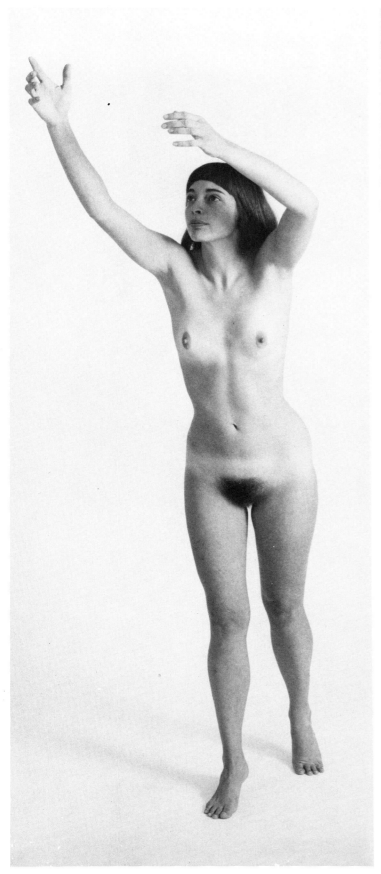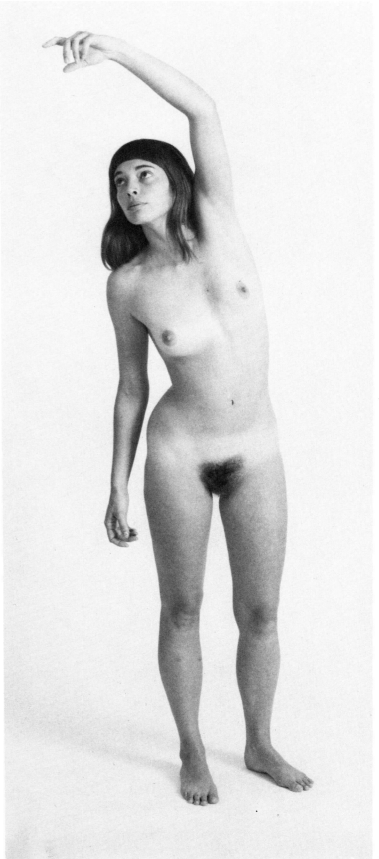

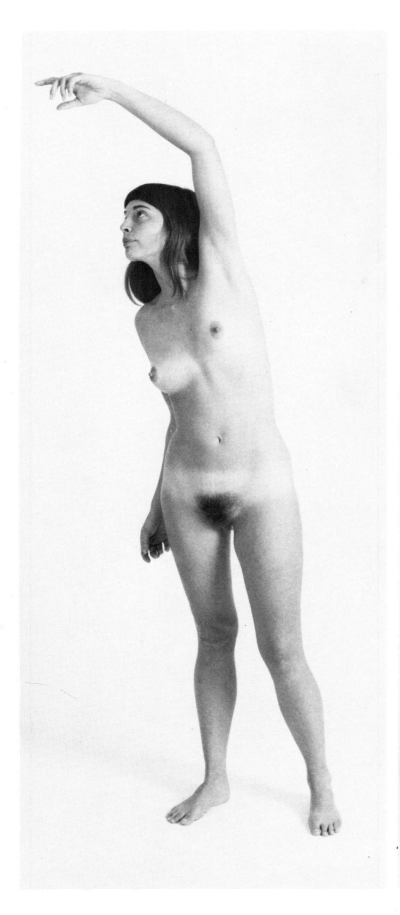
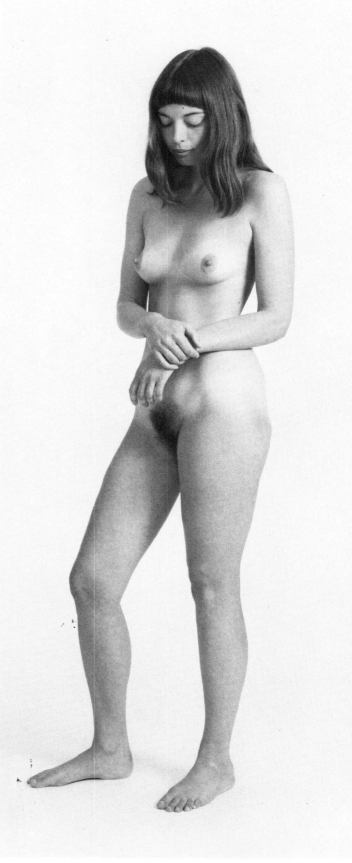

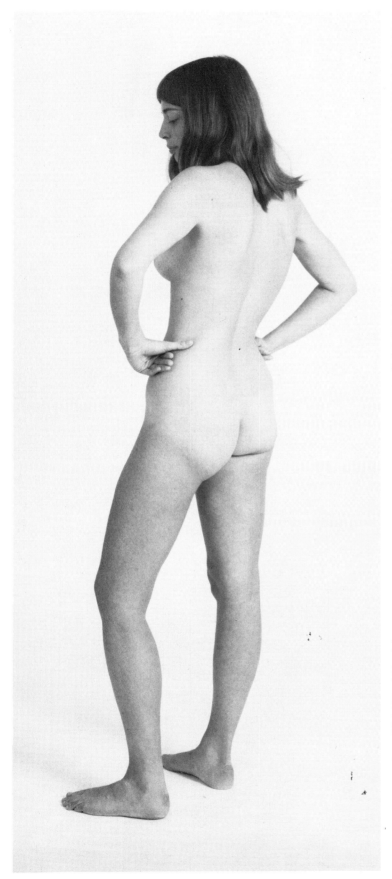
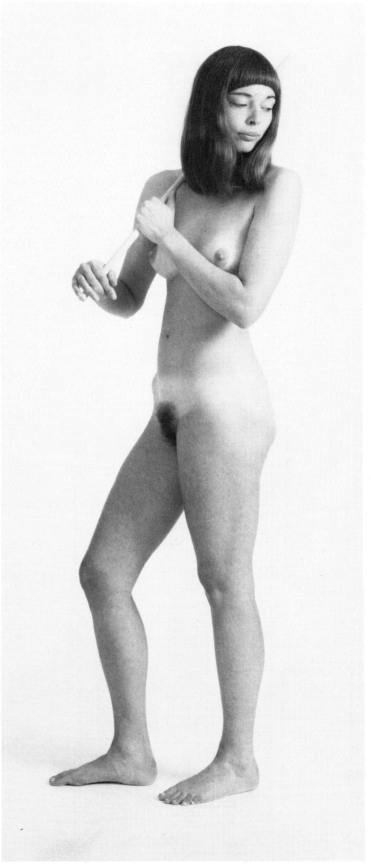

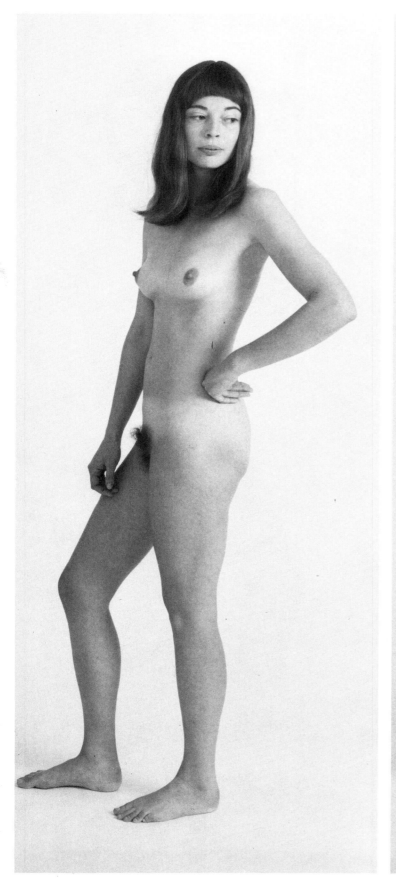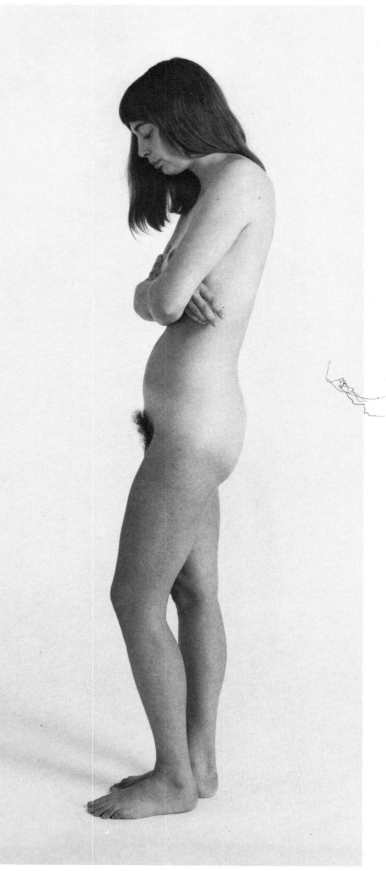

158

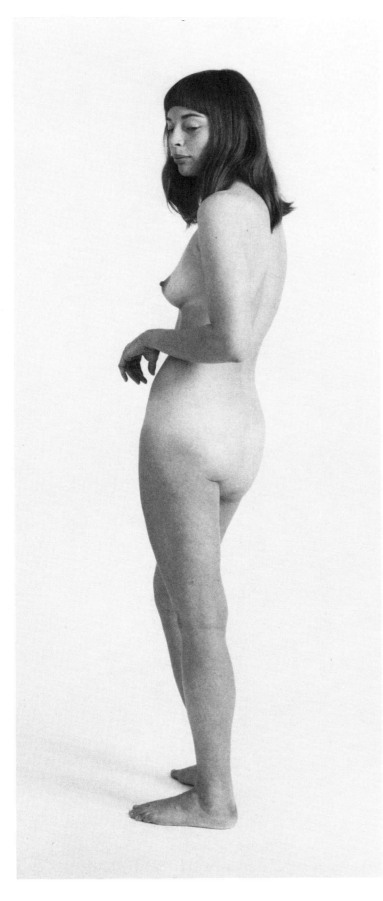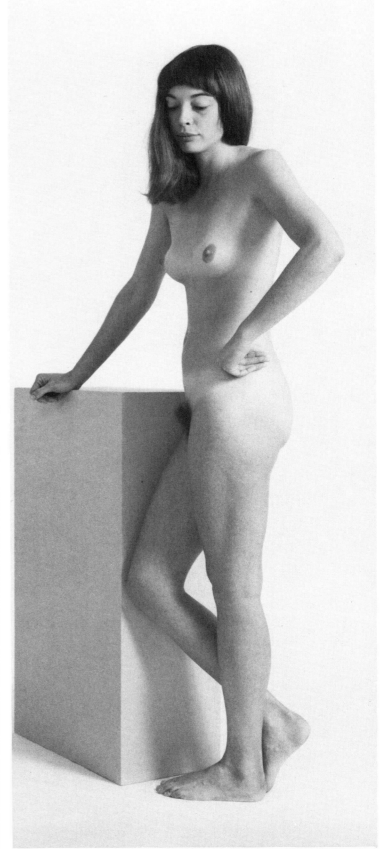

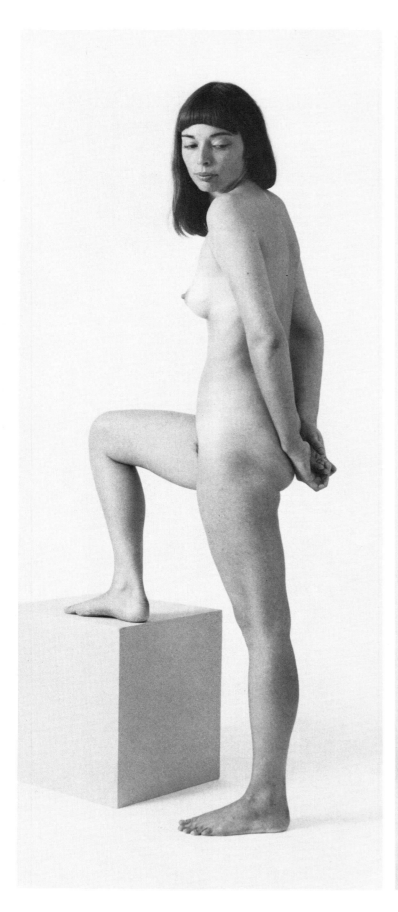
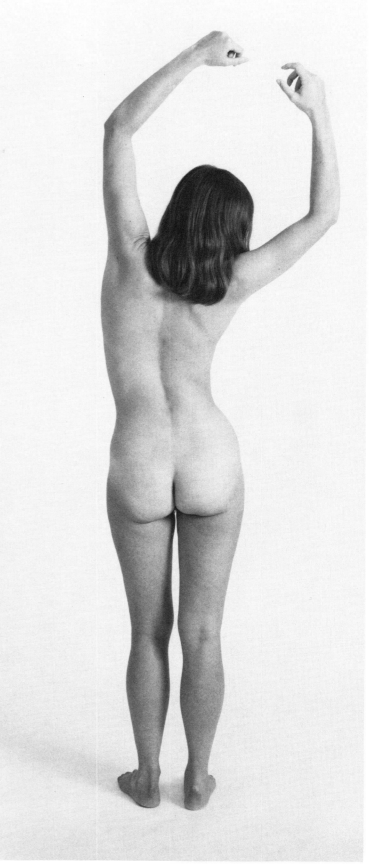

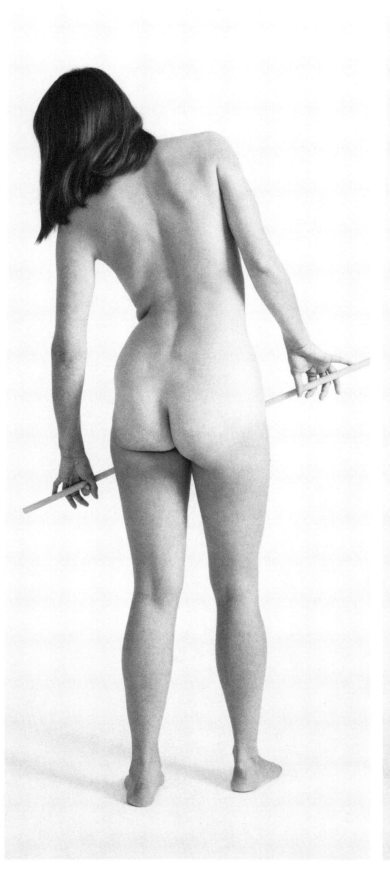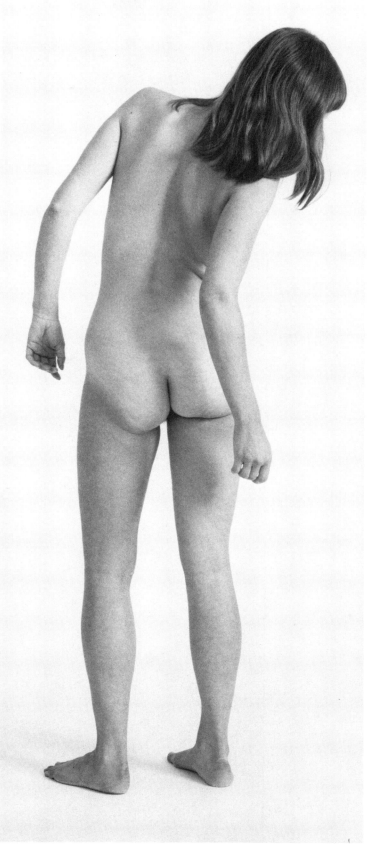

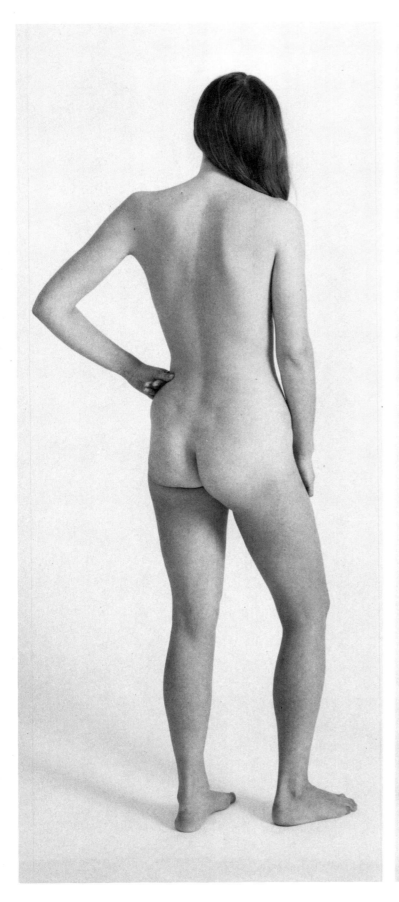
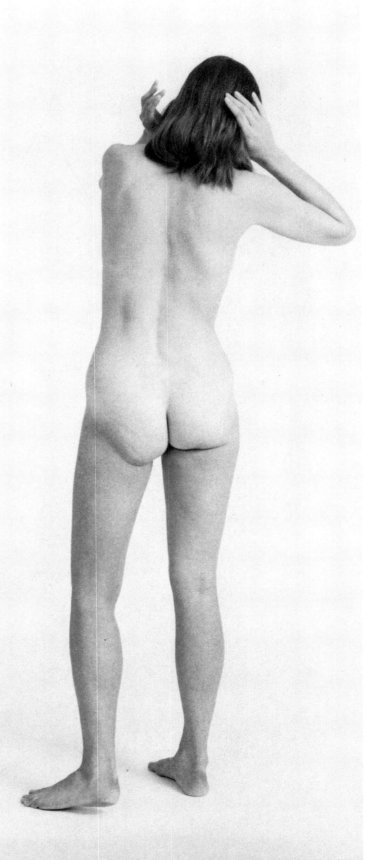

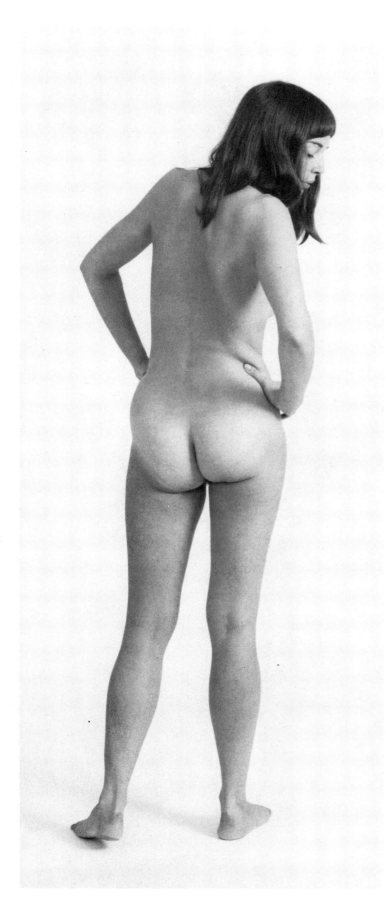
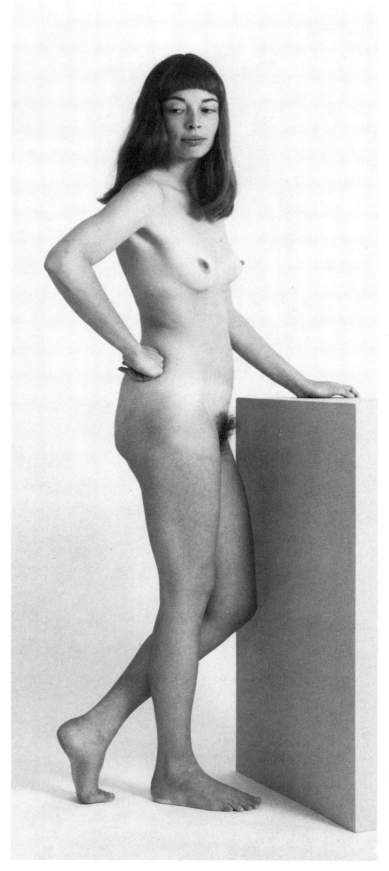

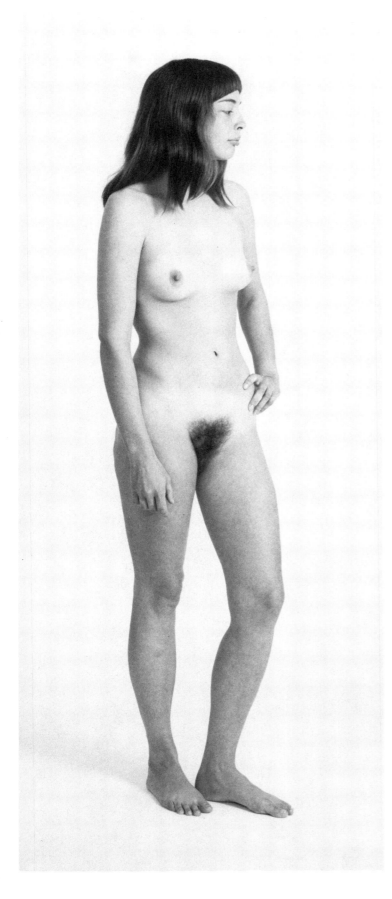

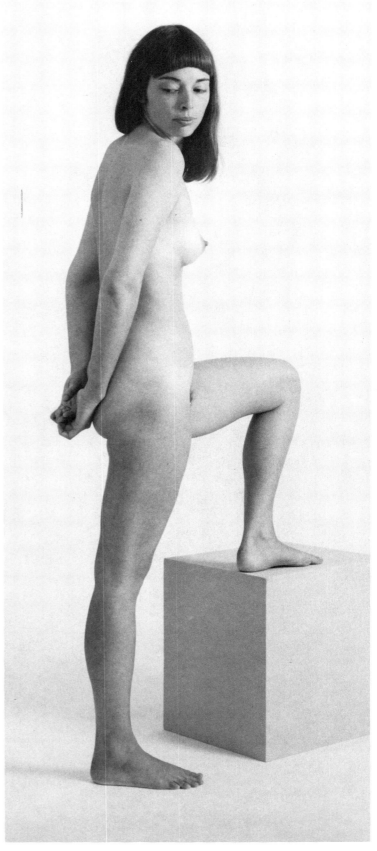

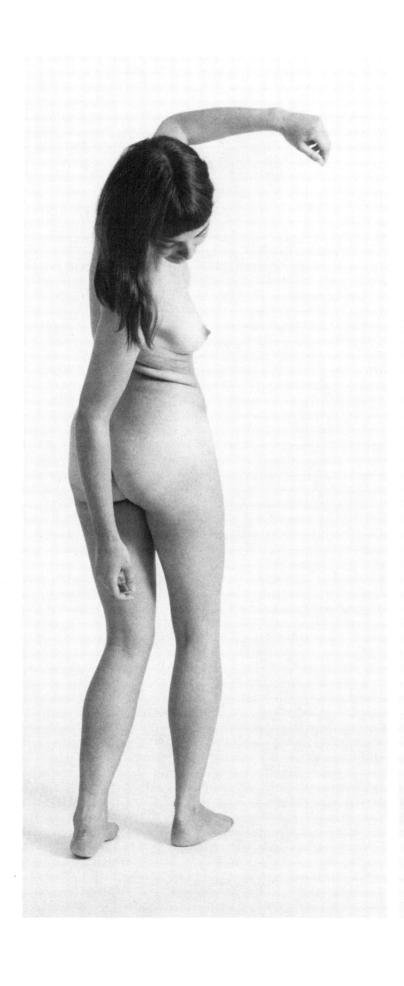
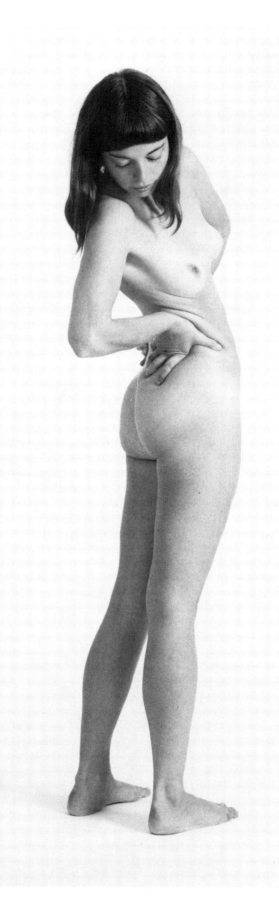

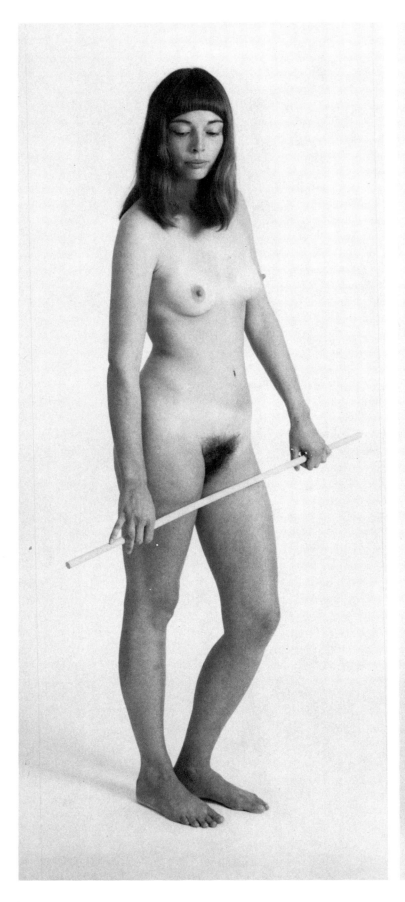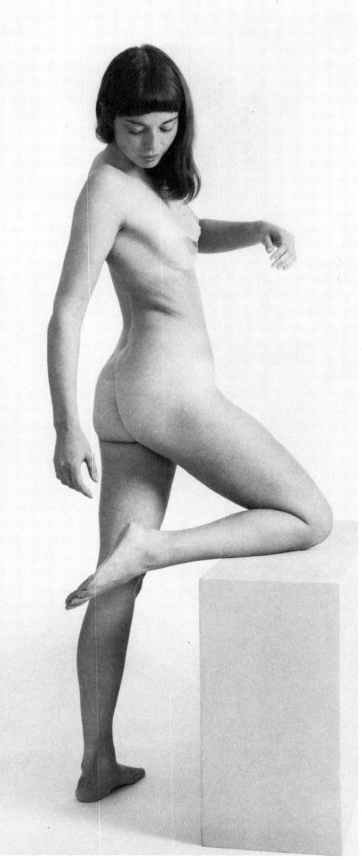

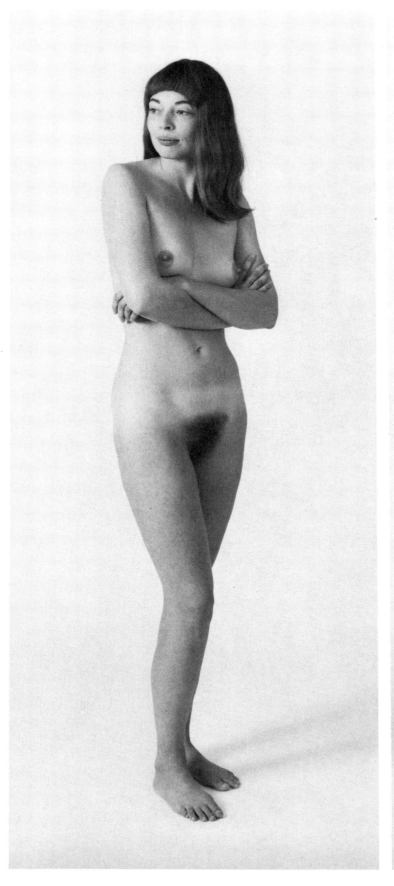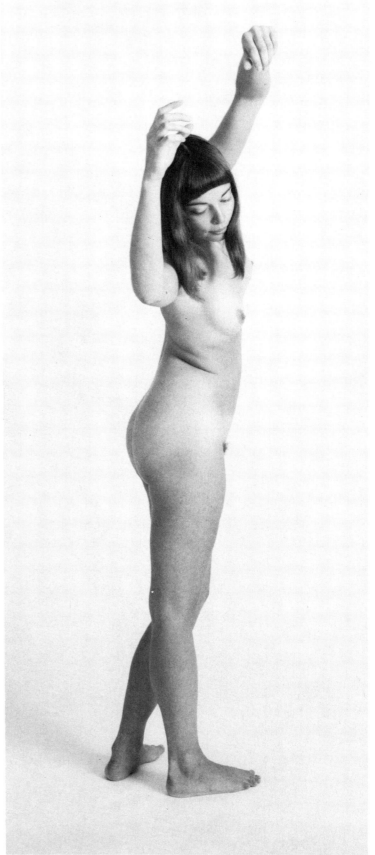

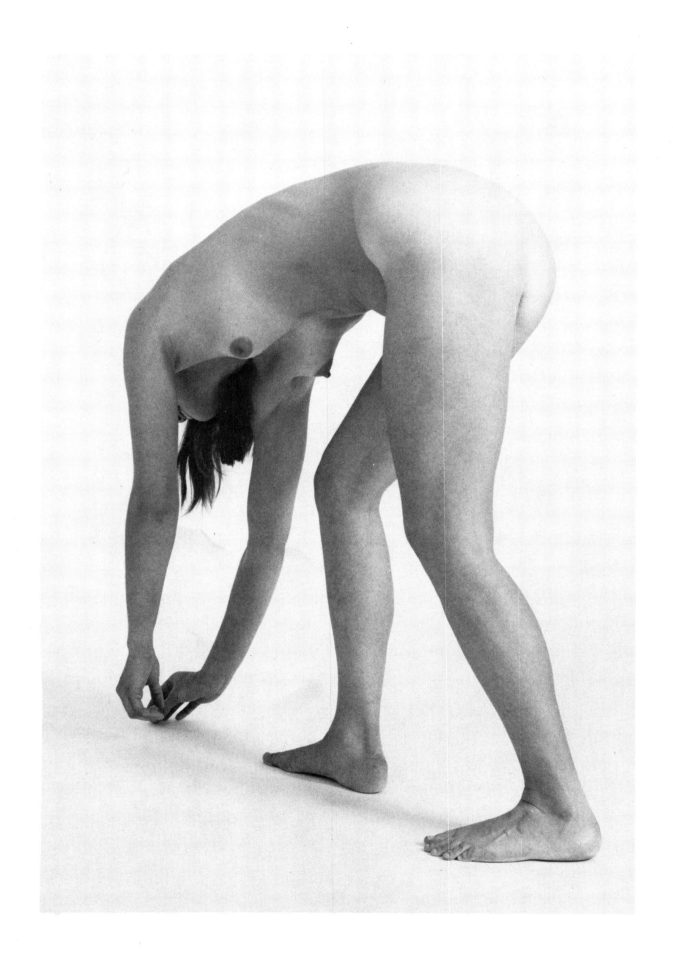

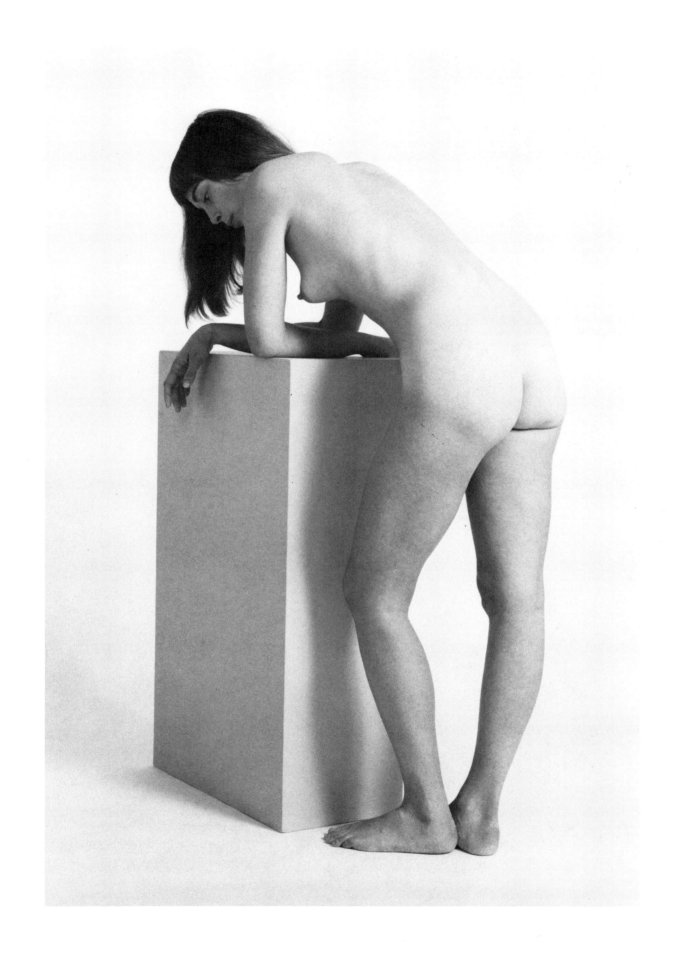

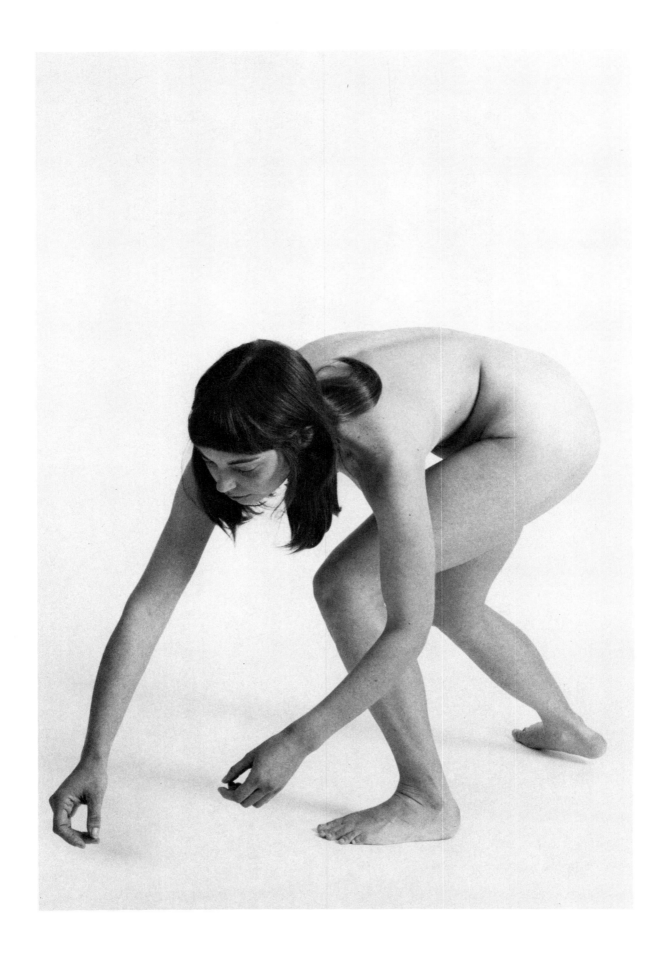

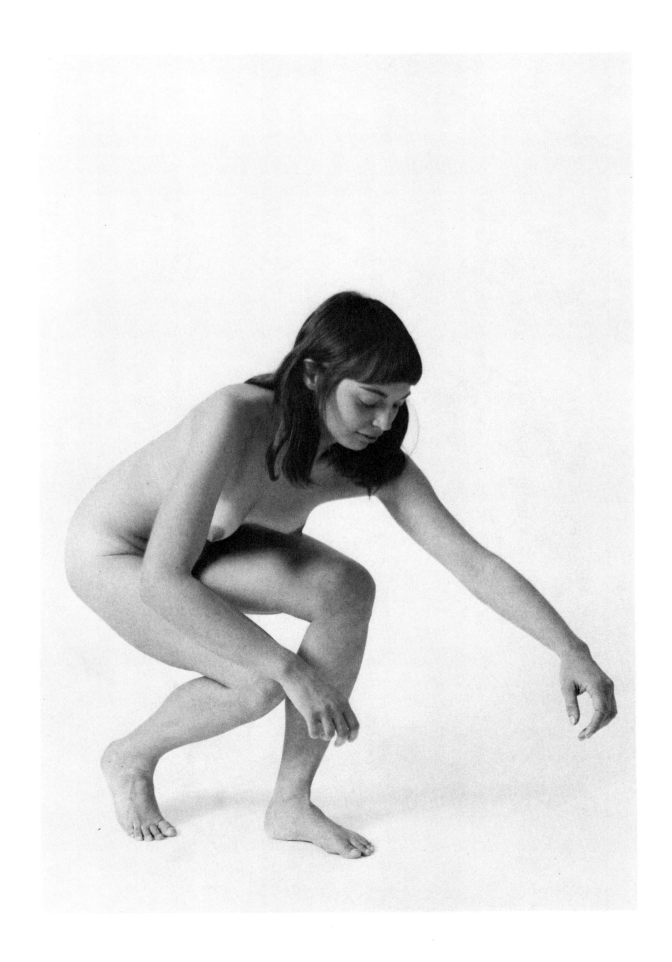

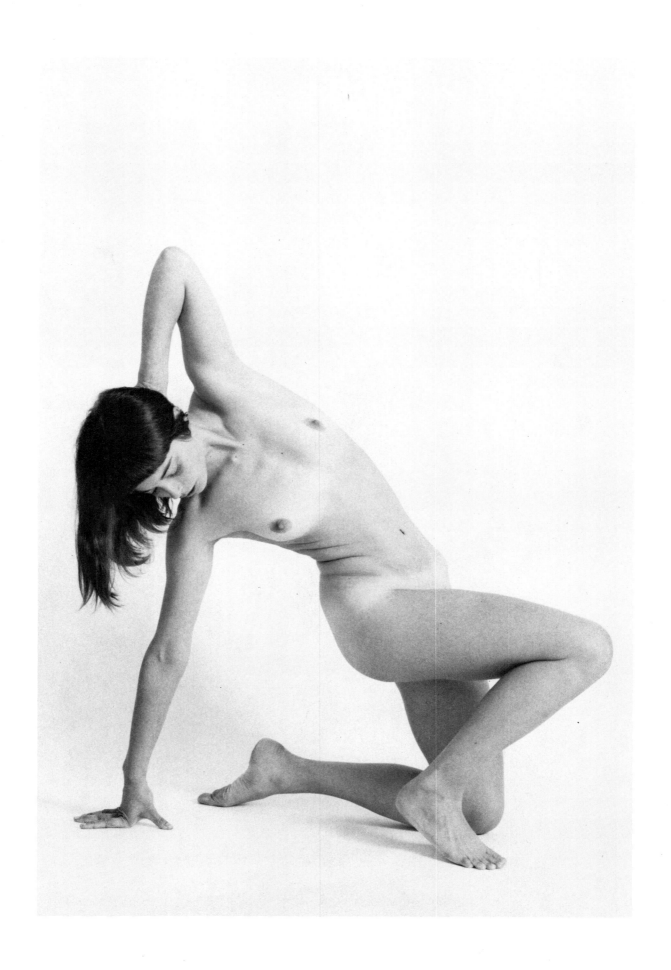

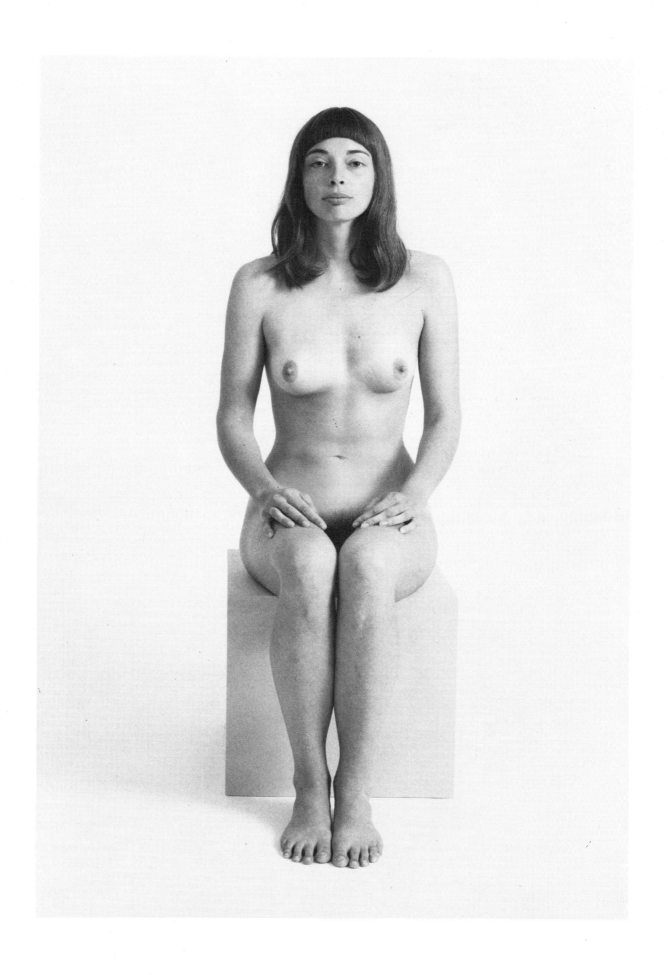

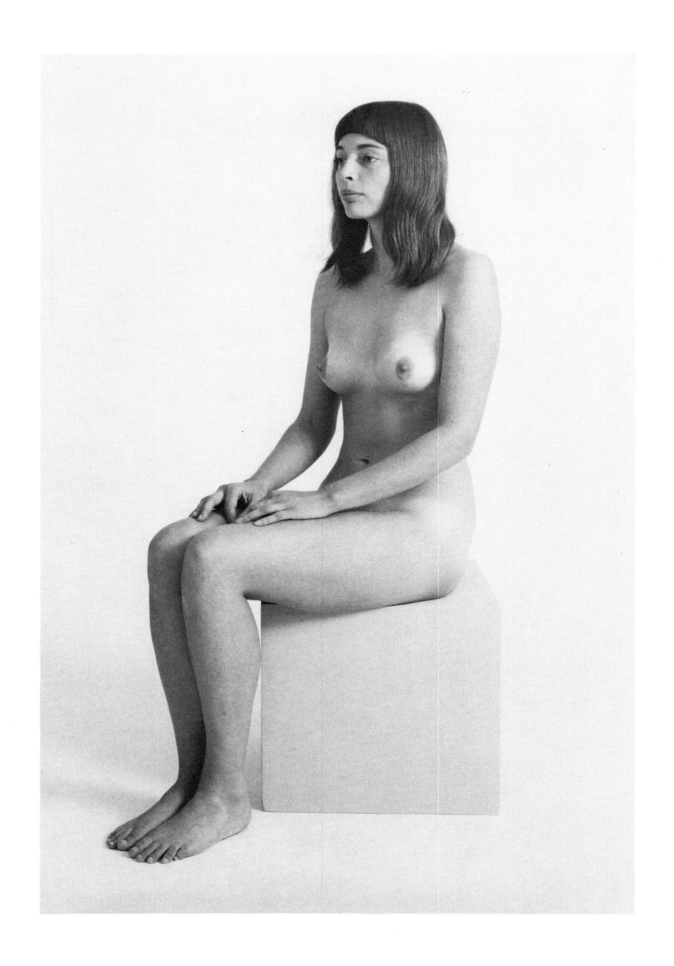

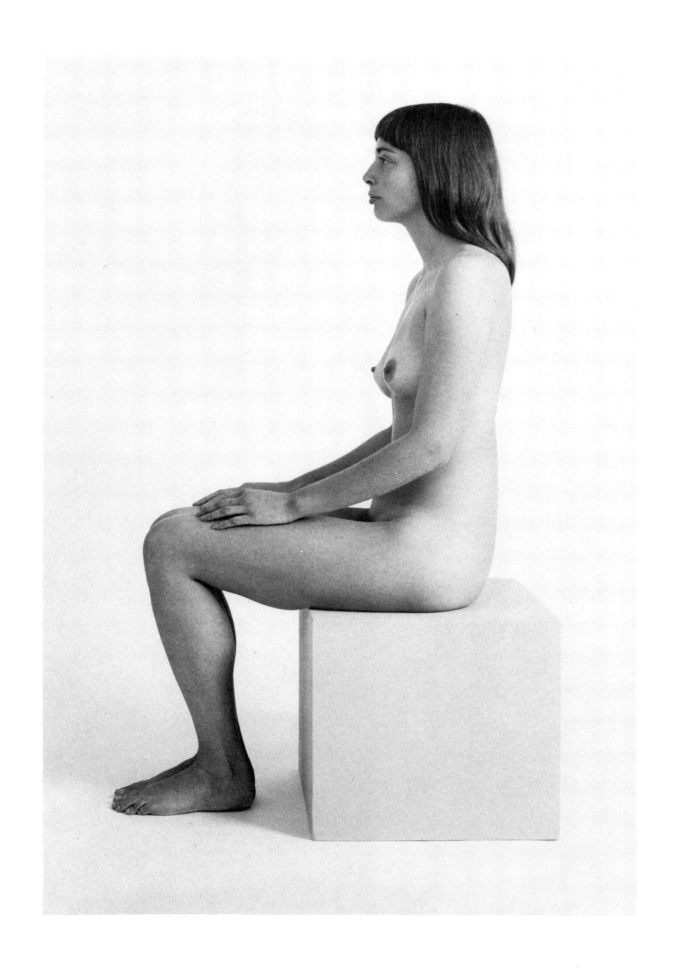

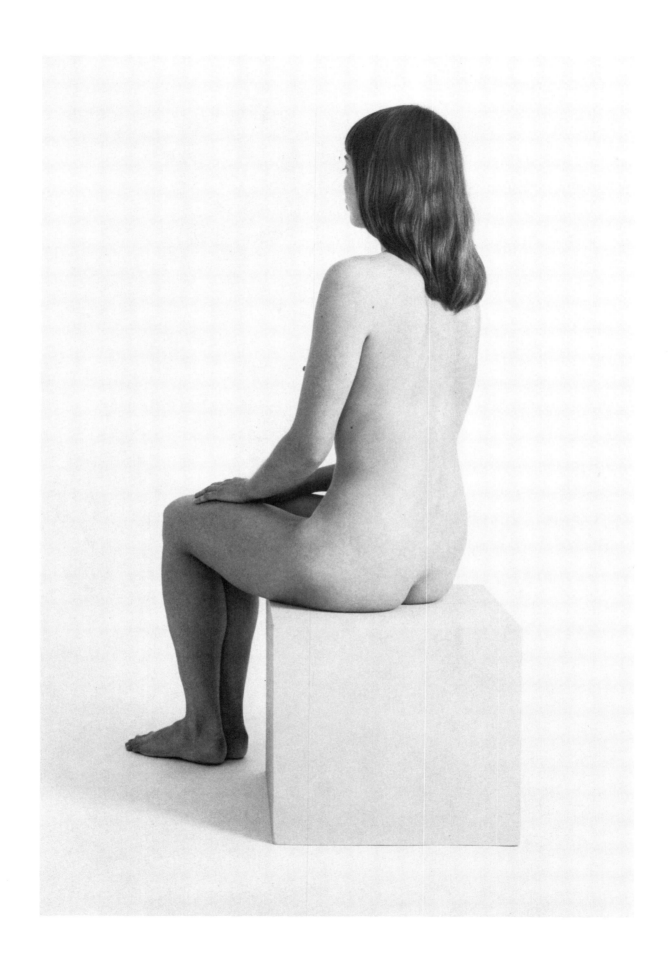

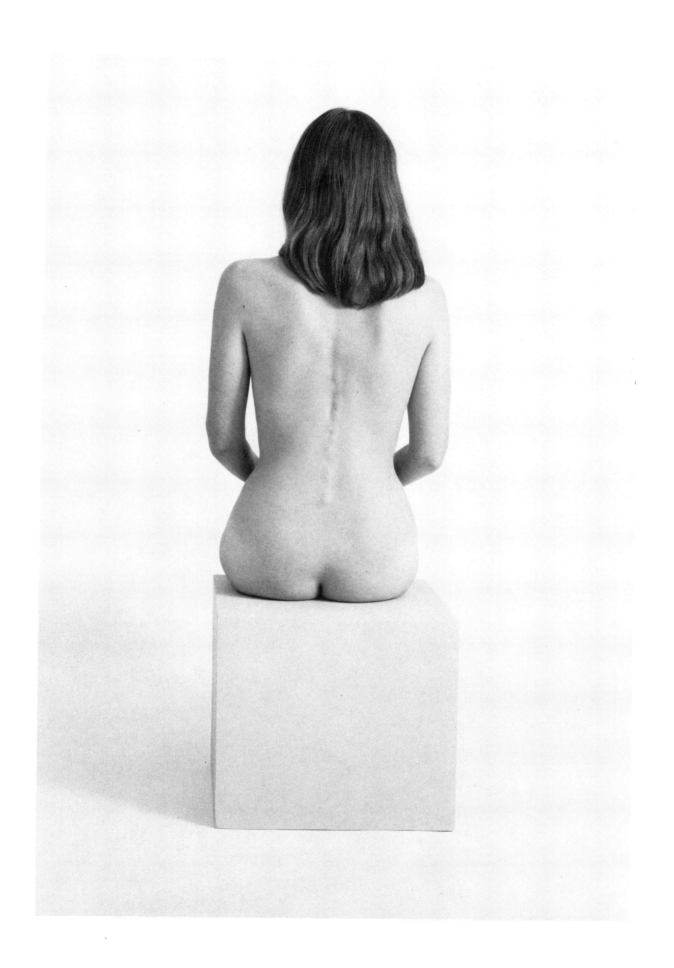

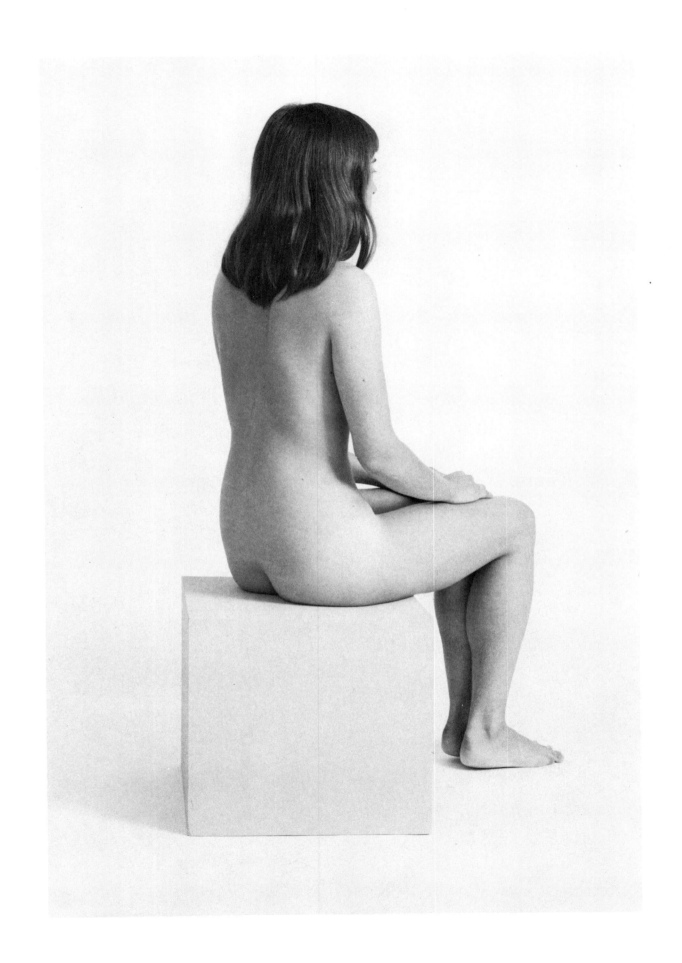

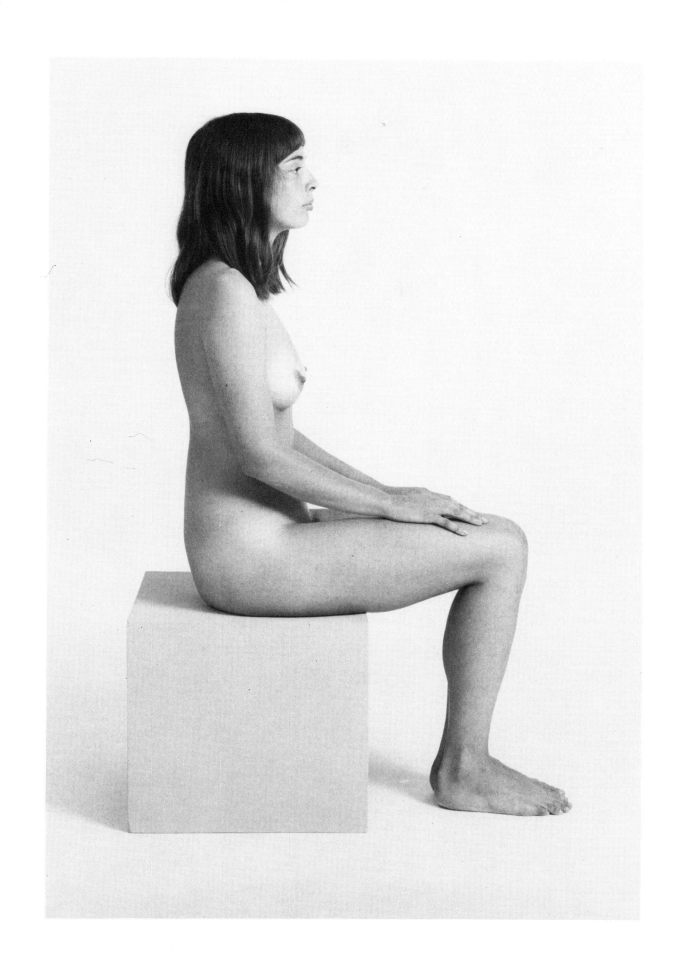

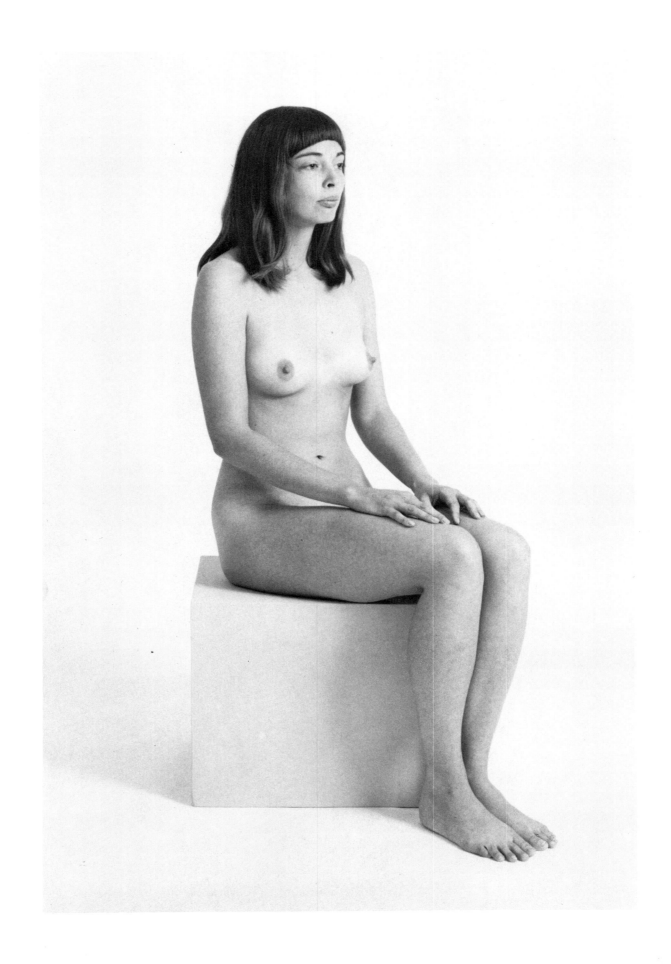

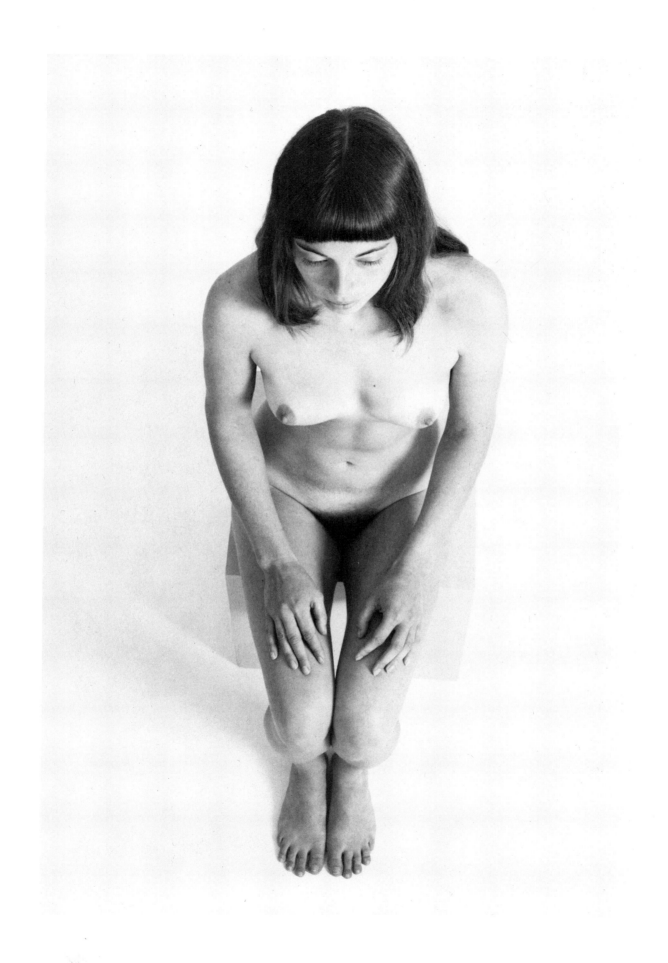

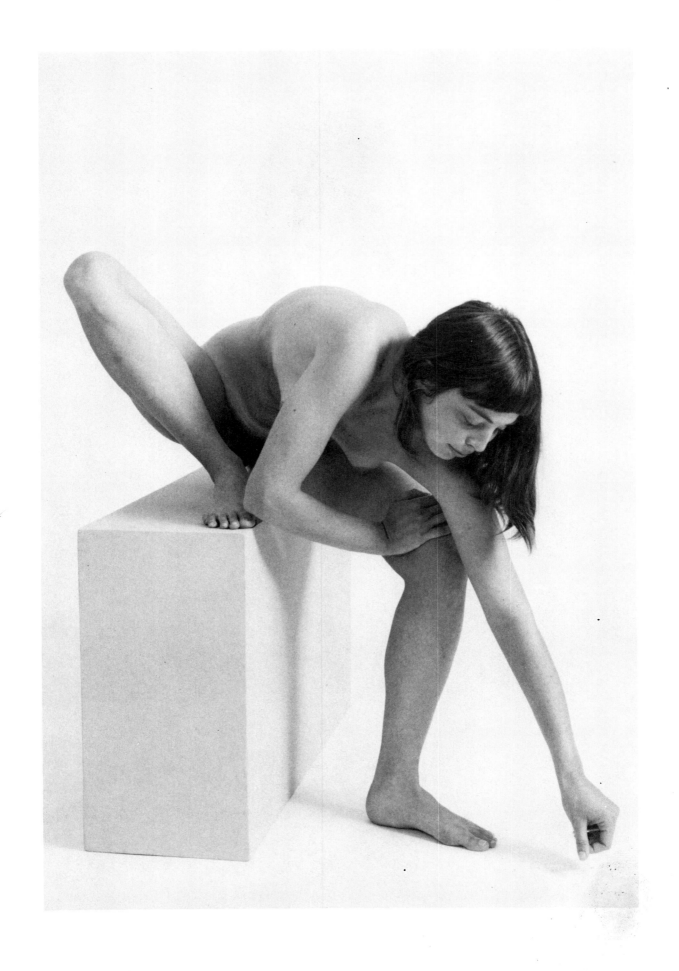

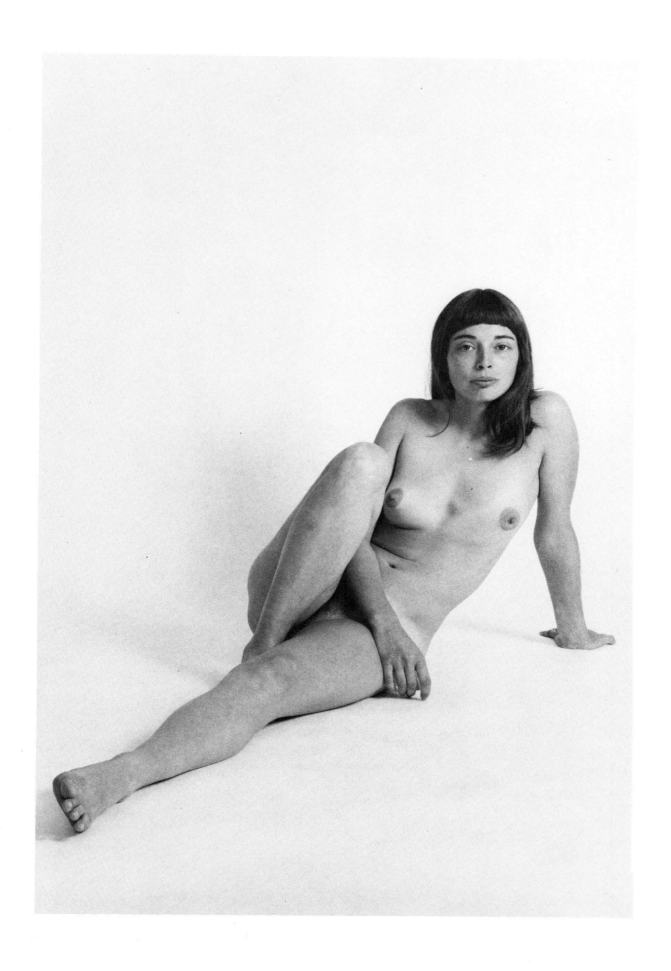

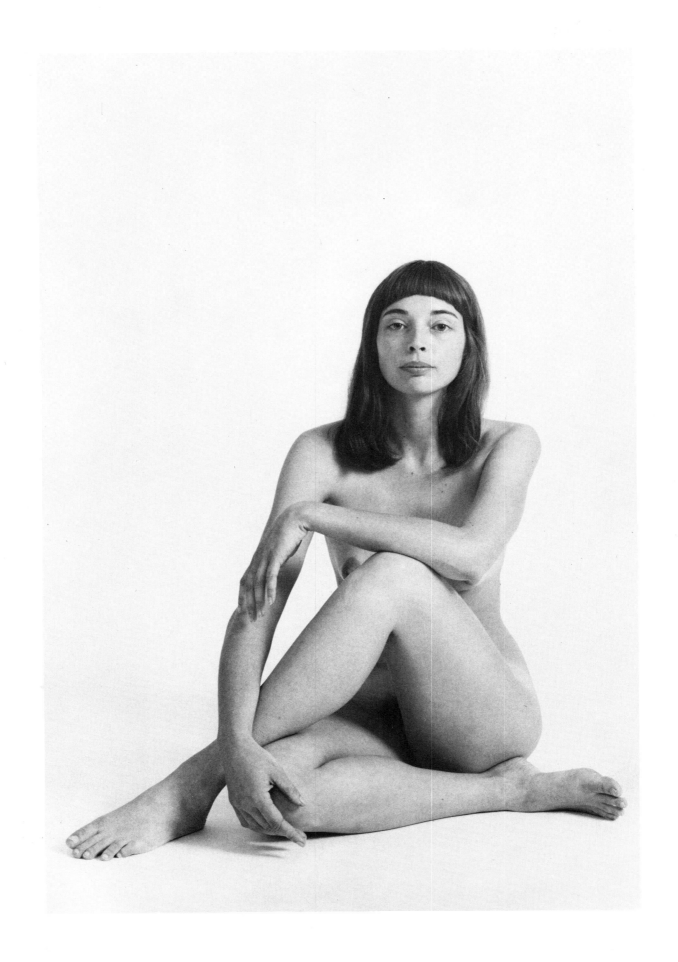

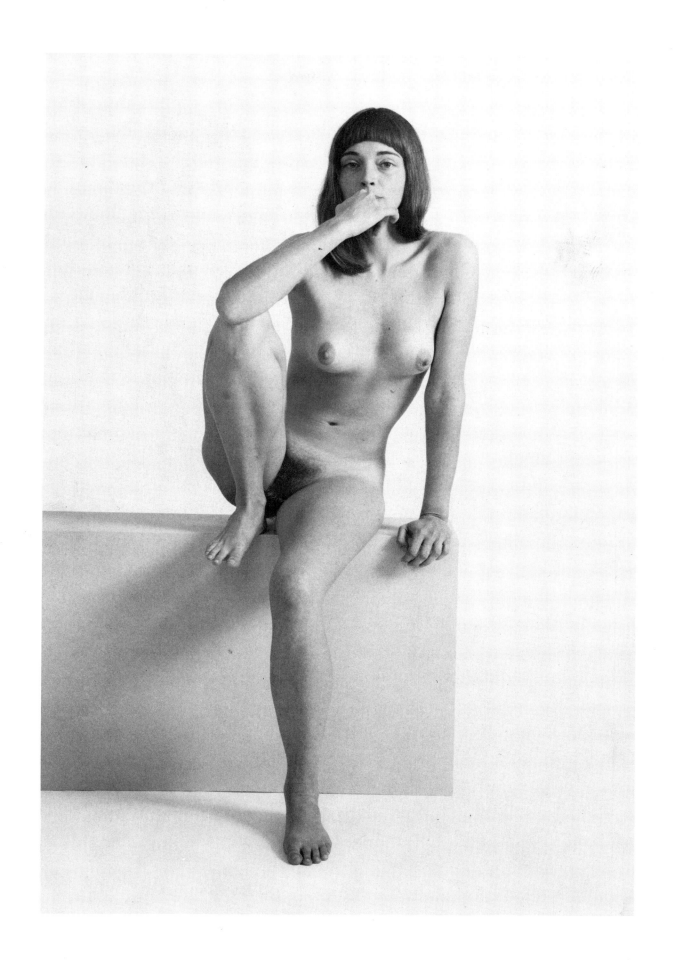

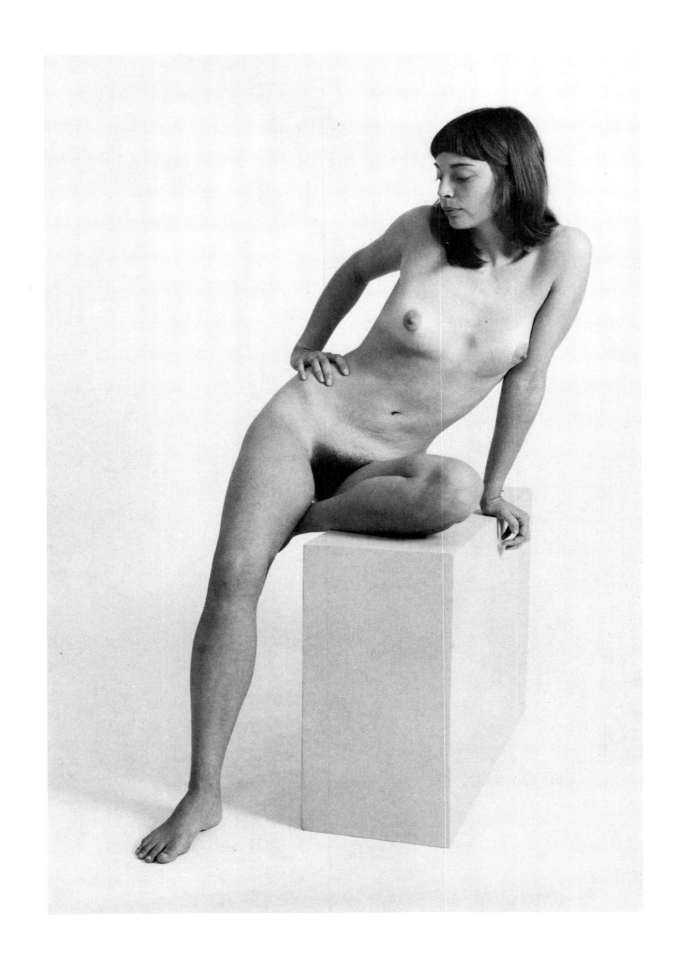

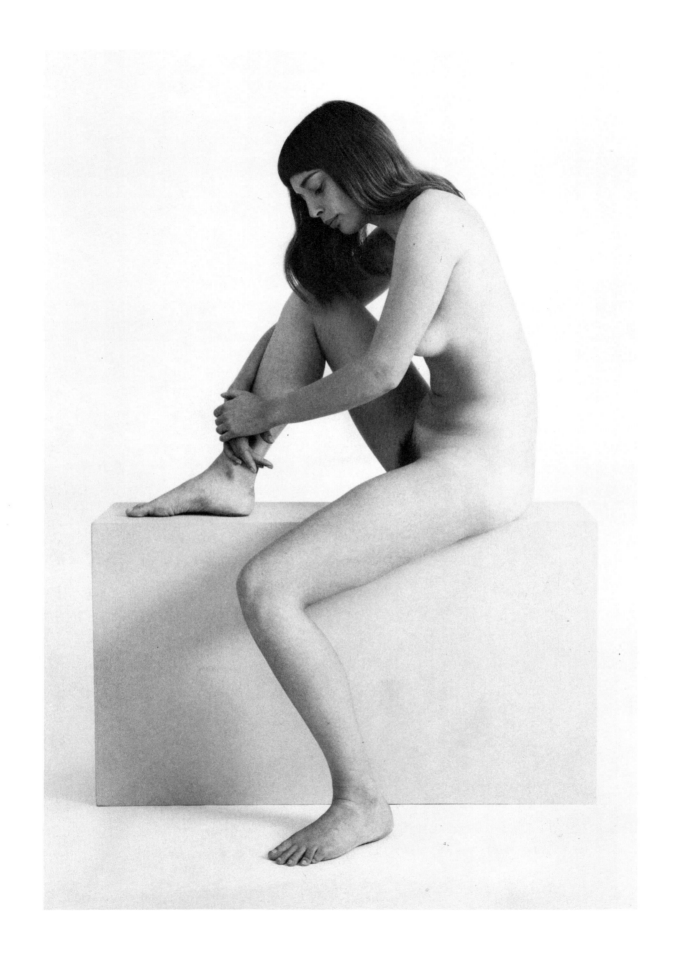

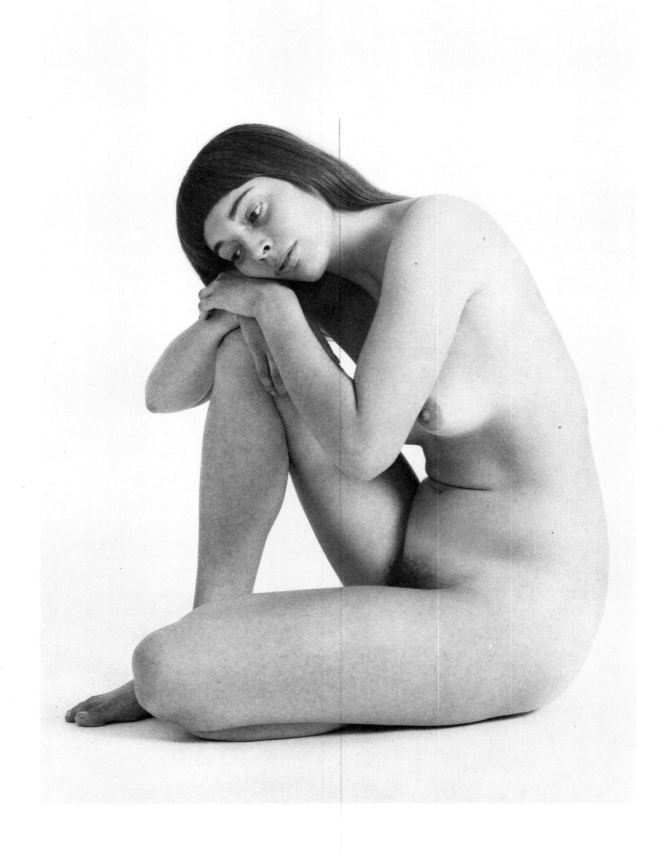

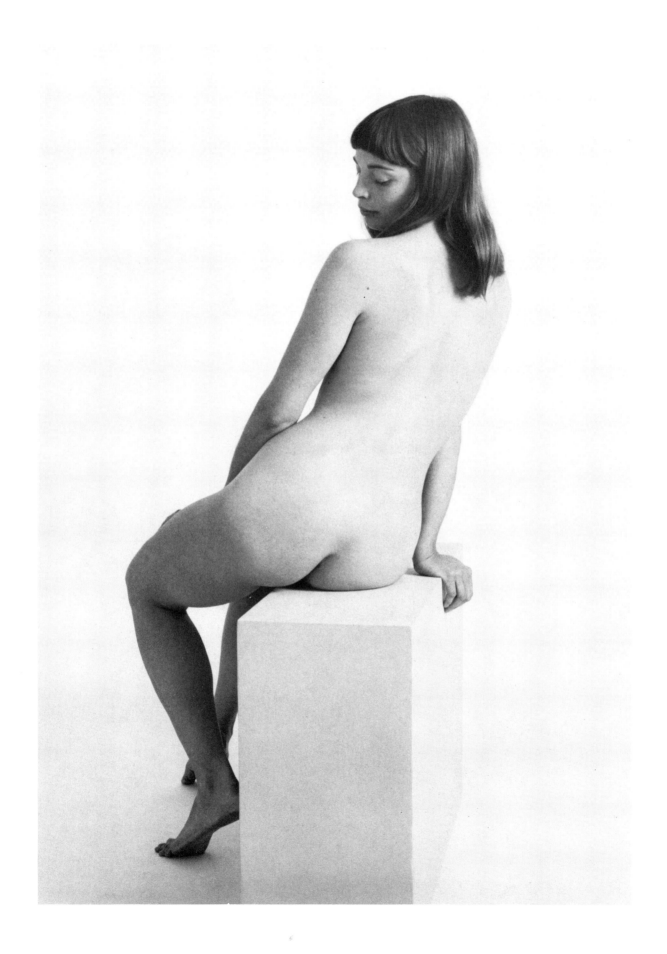

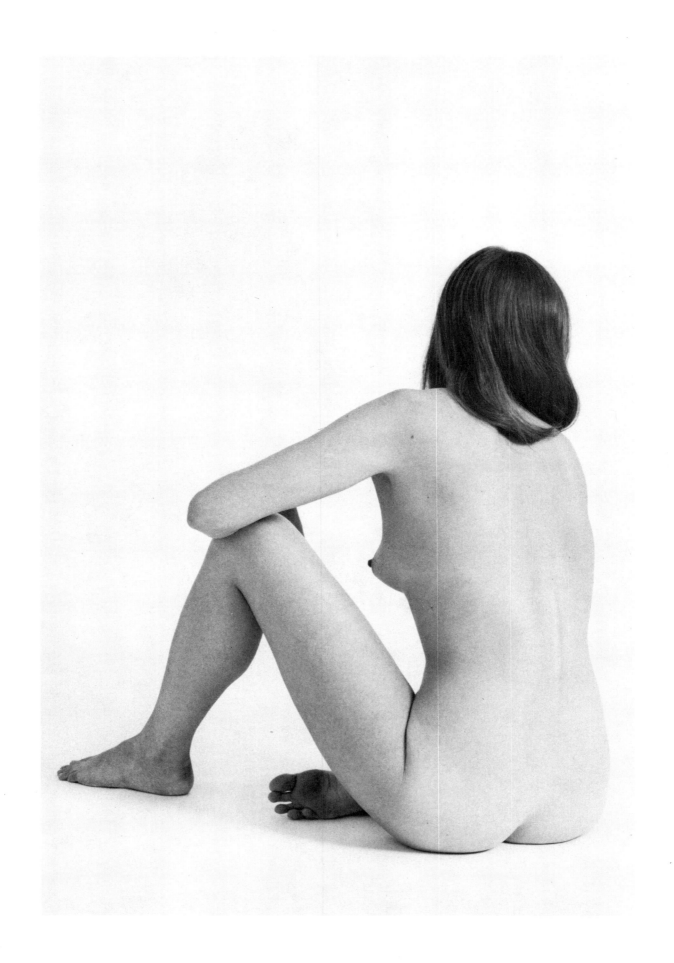

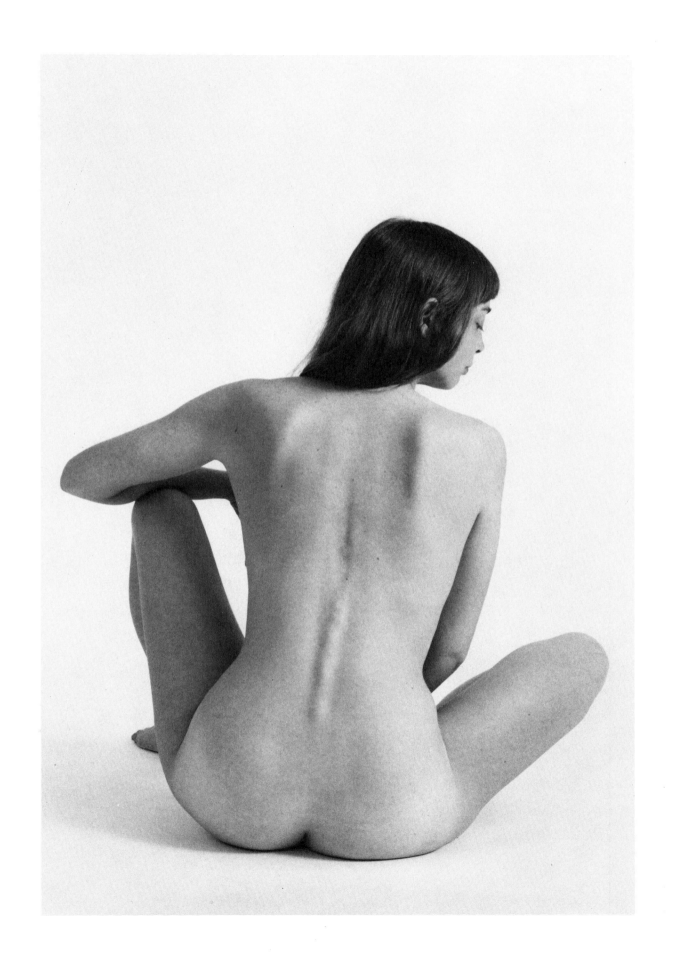

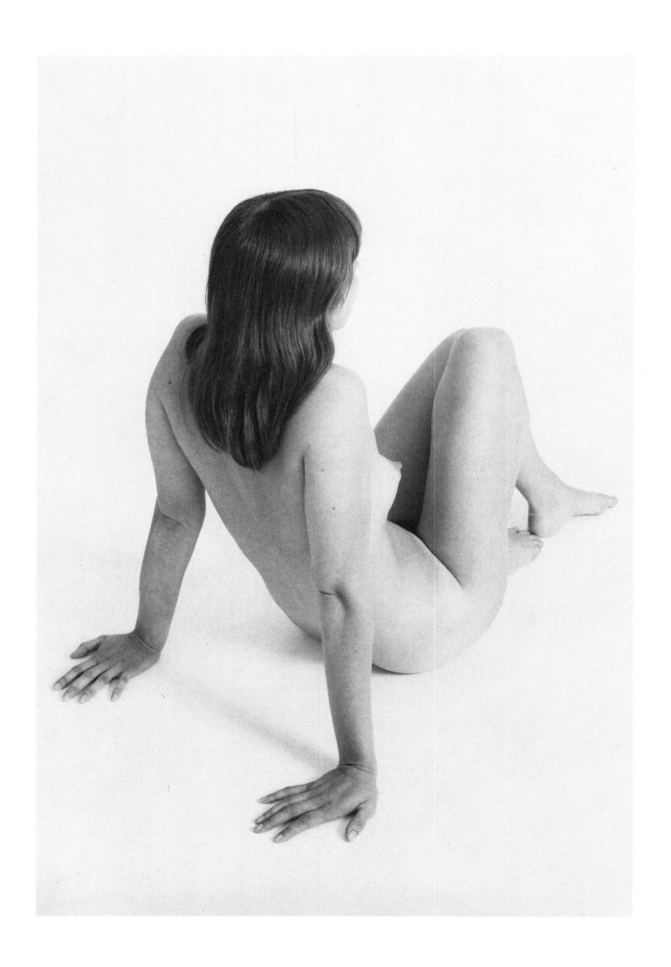

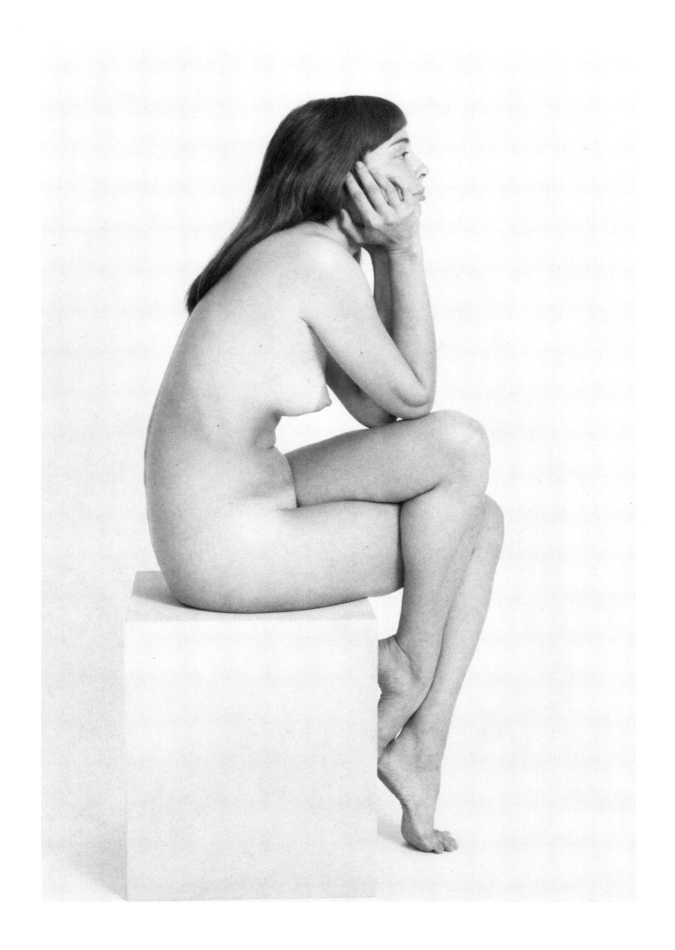

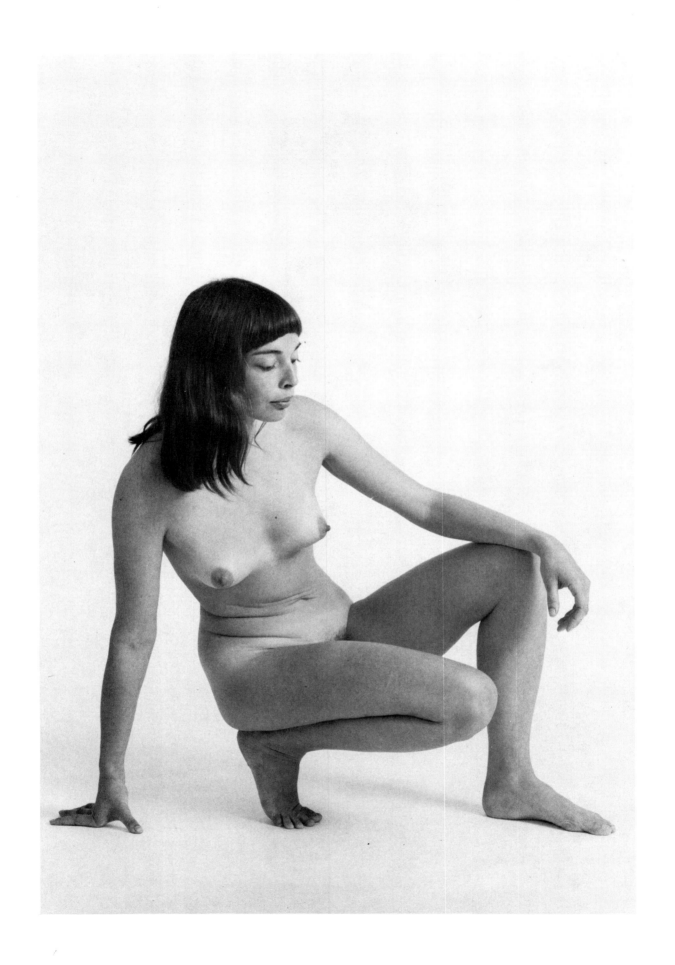

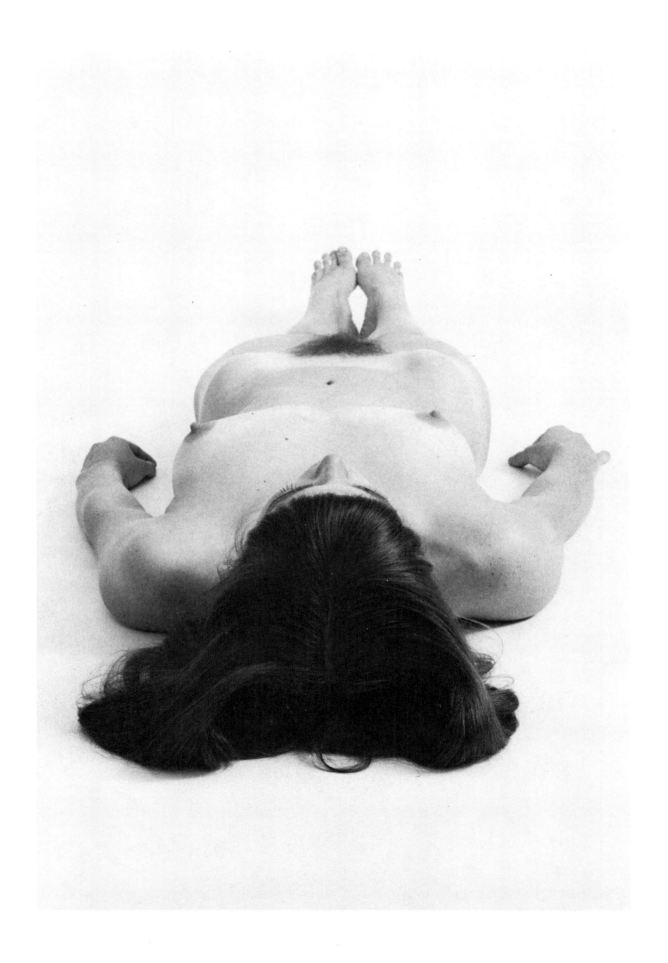

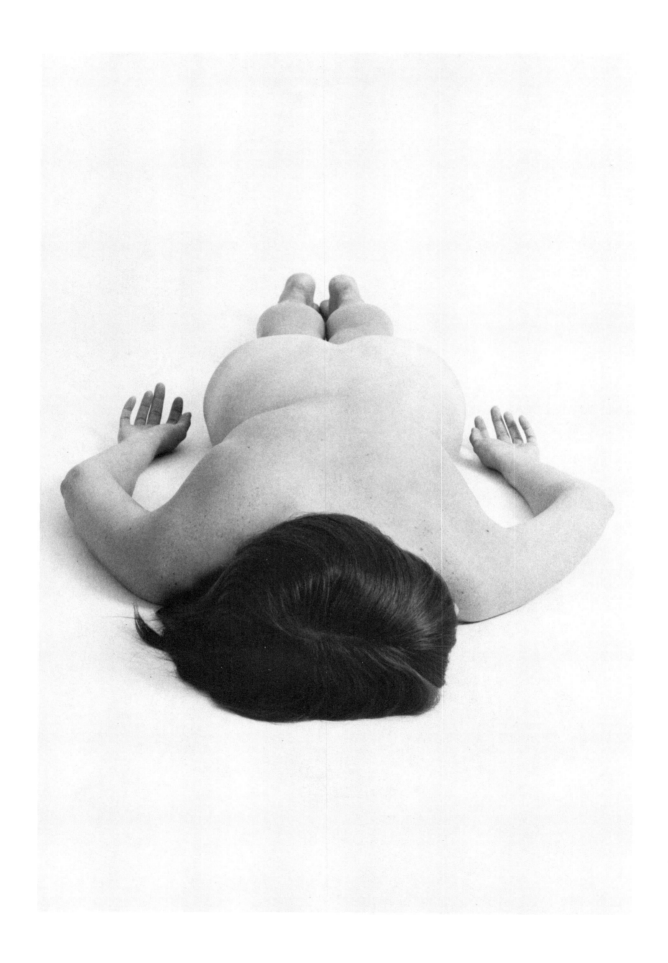

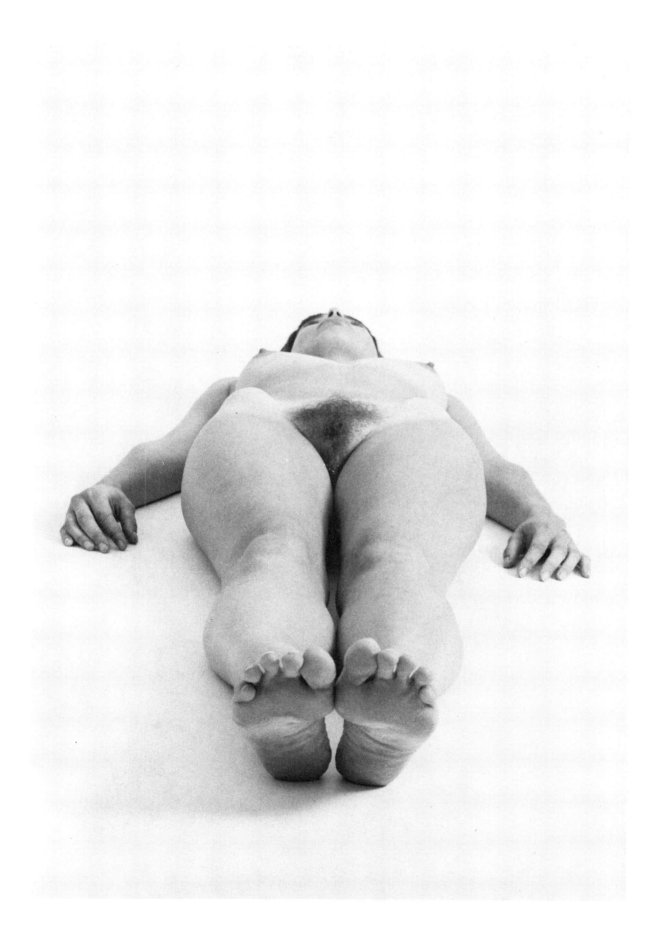

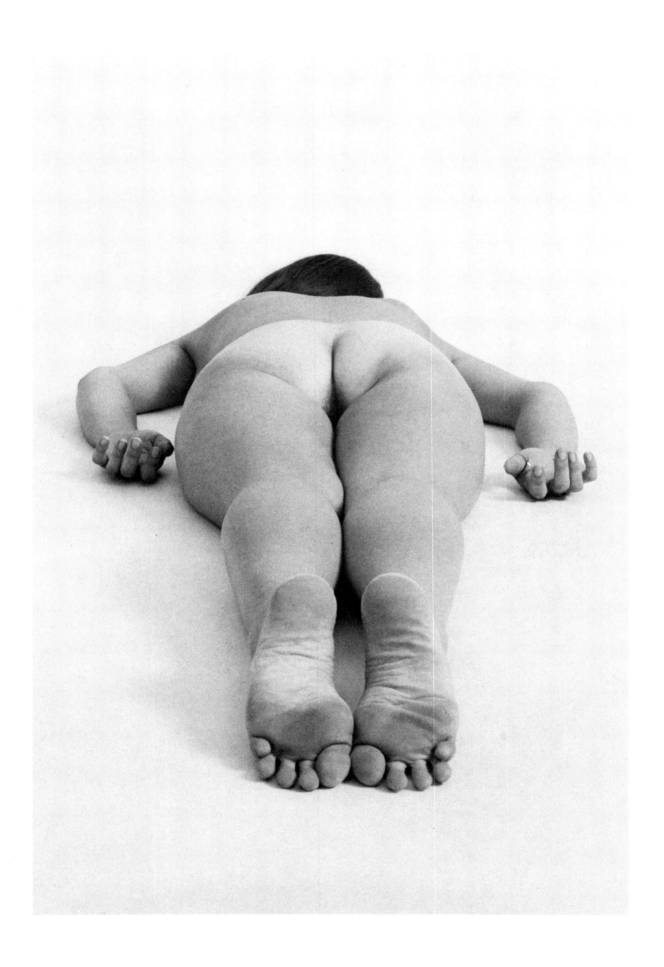

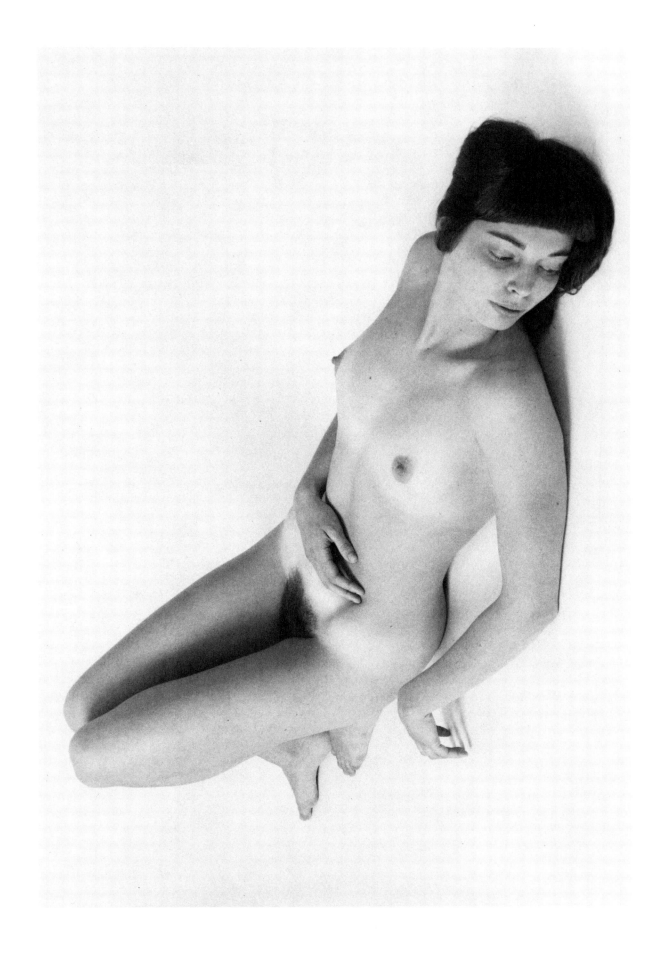

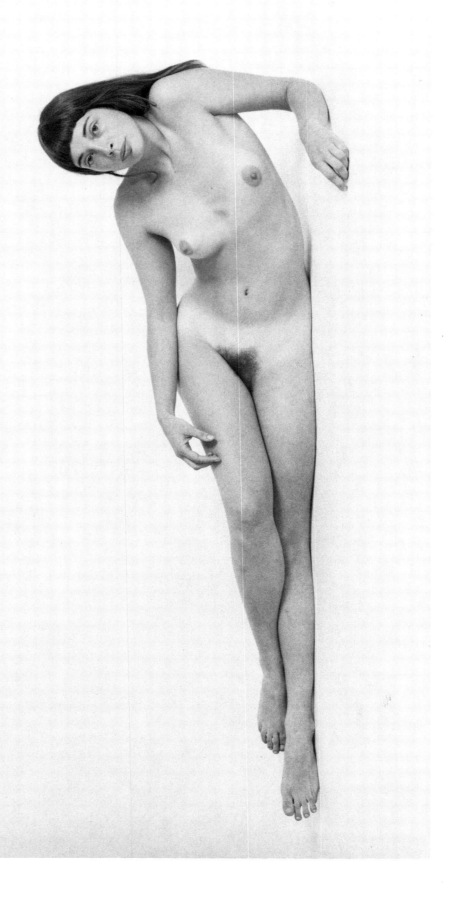

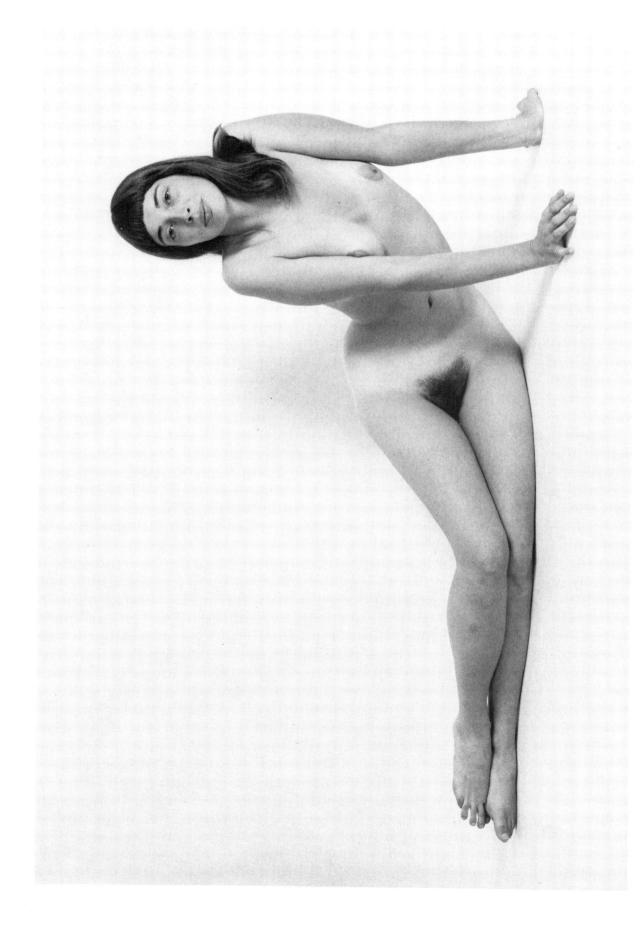

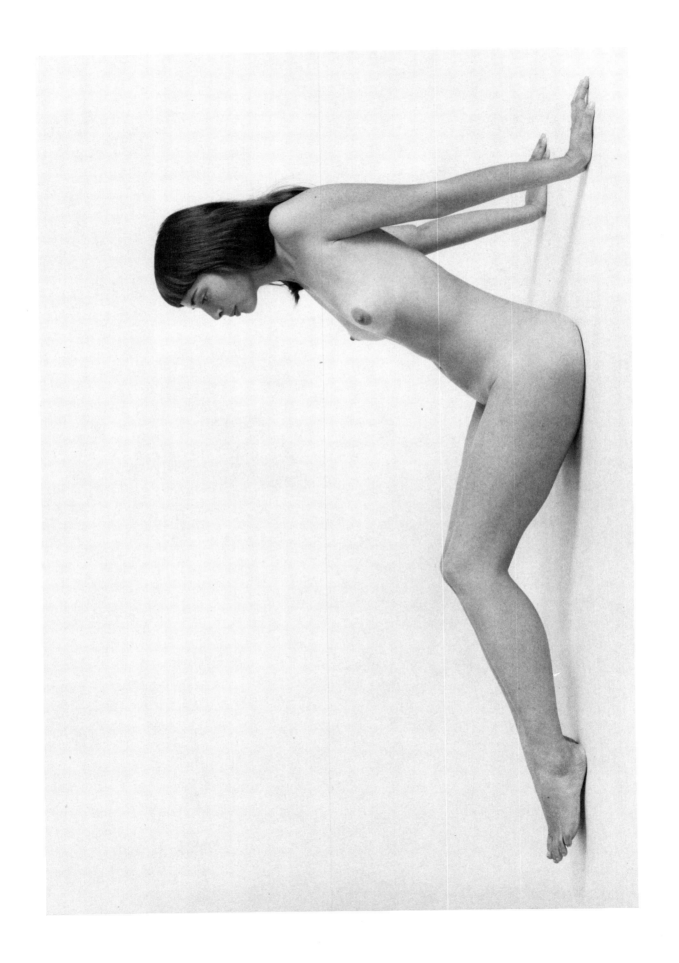

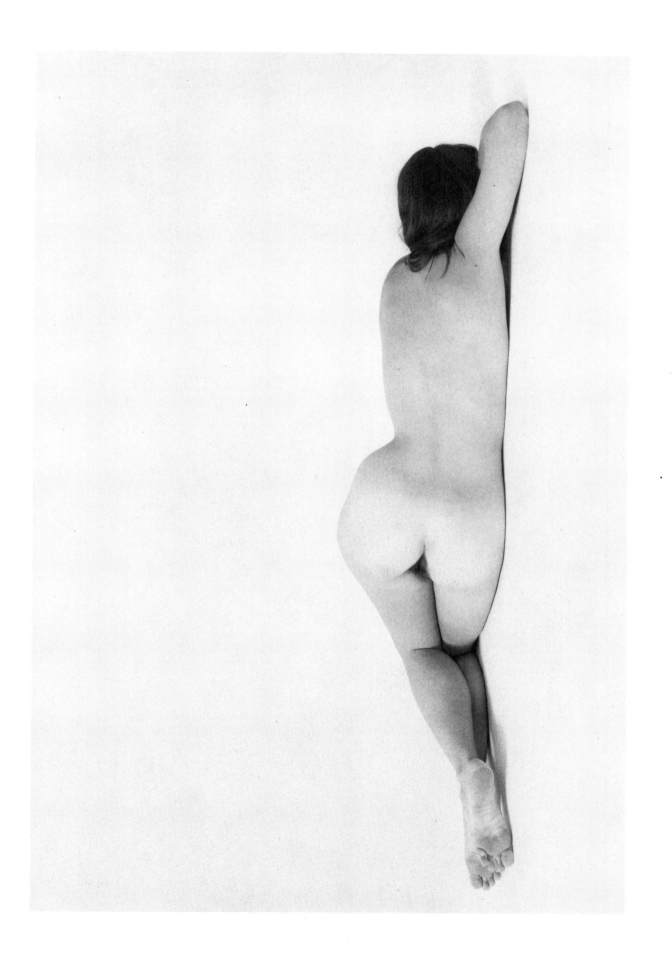

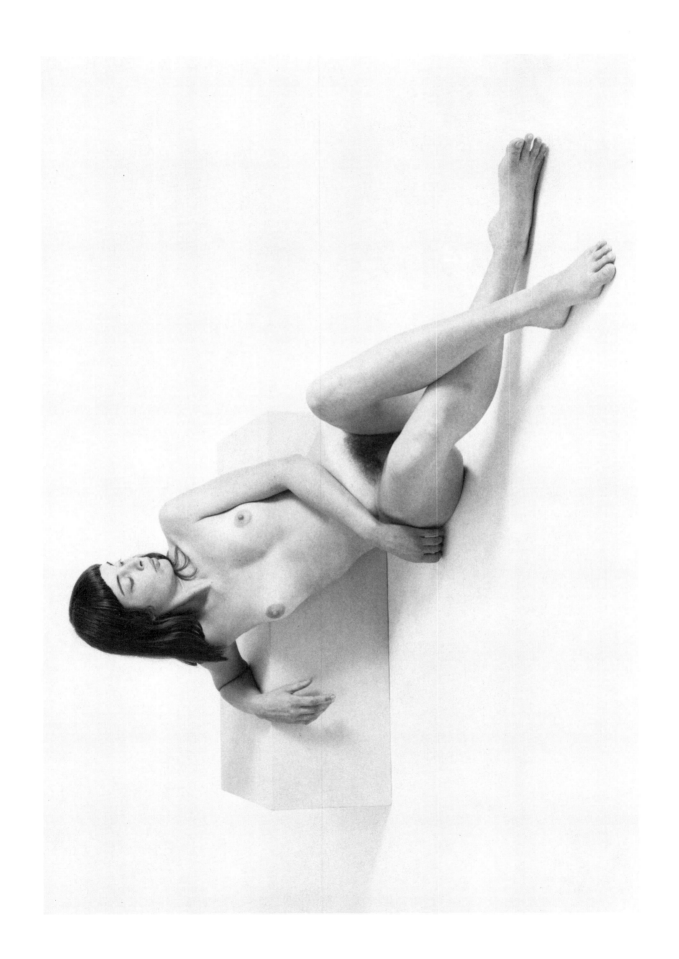

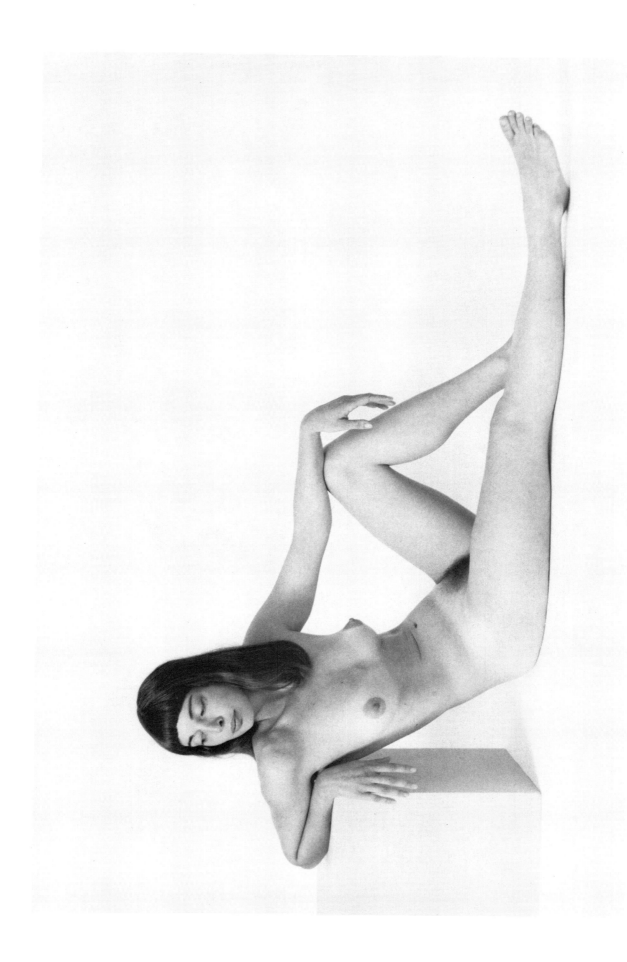

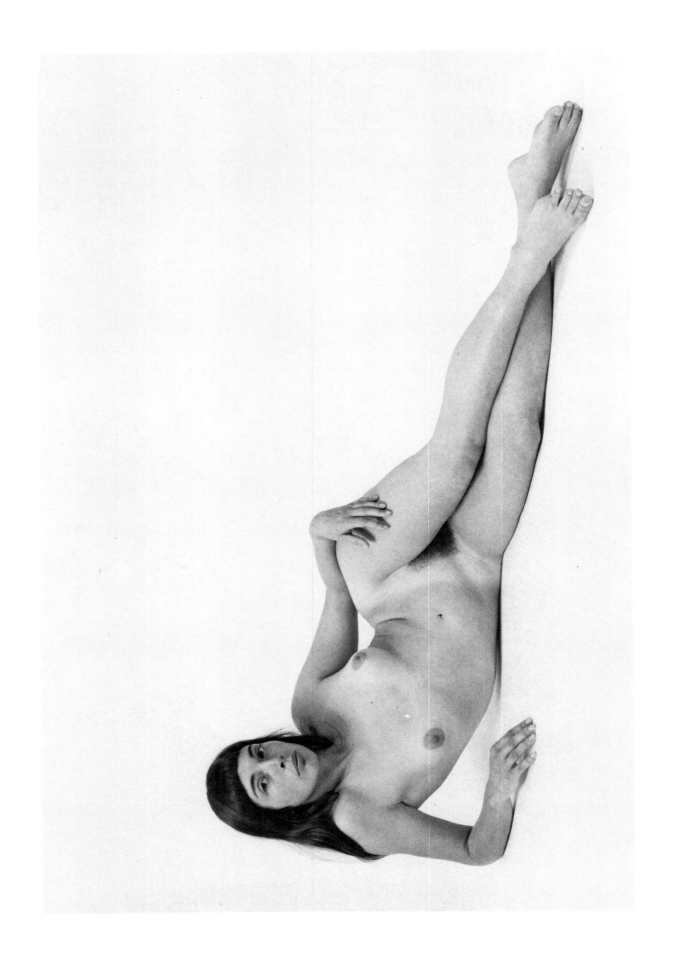

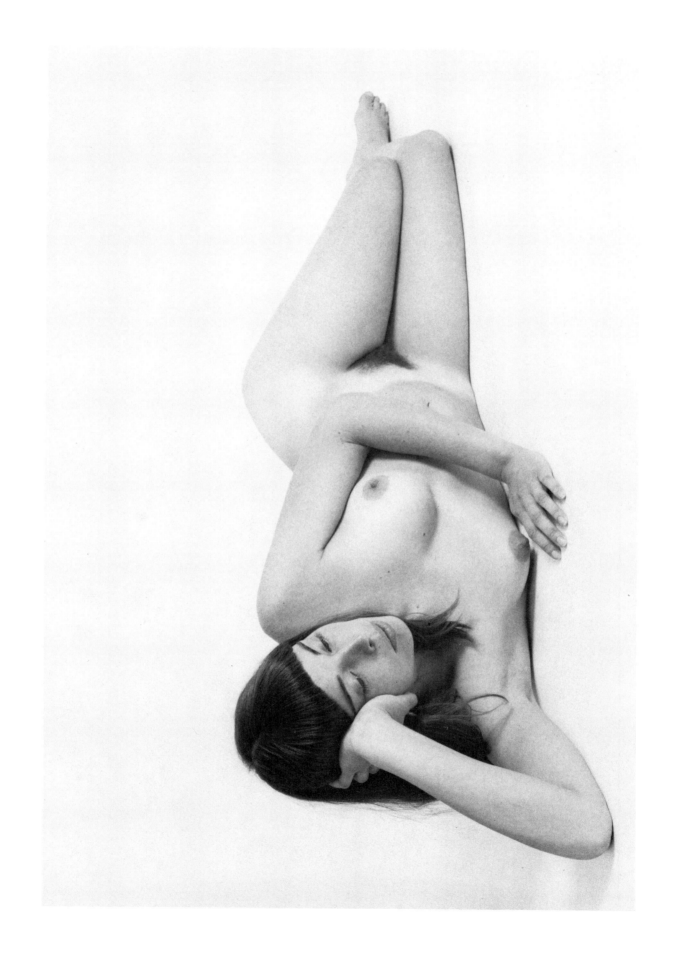

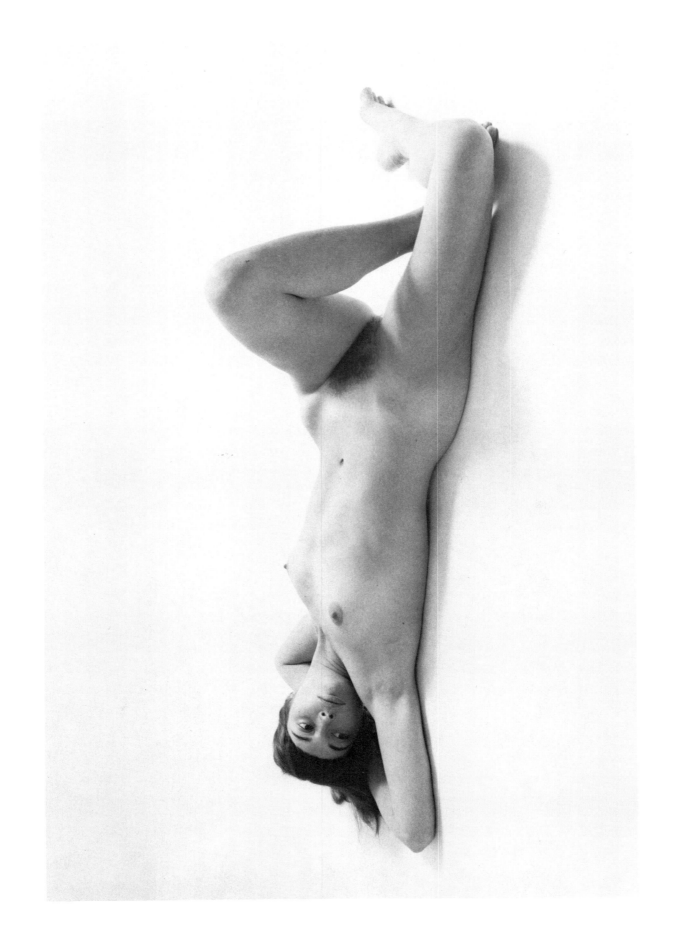

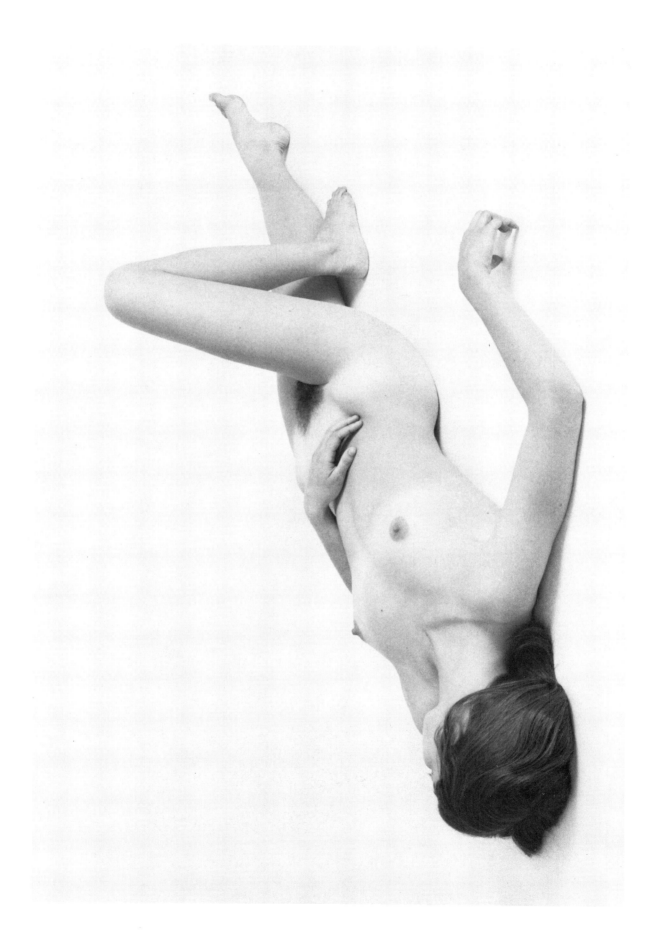

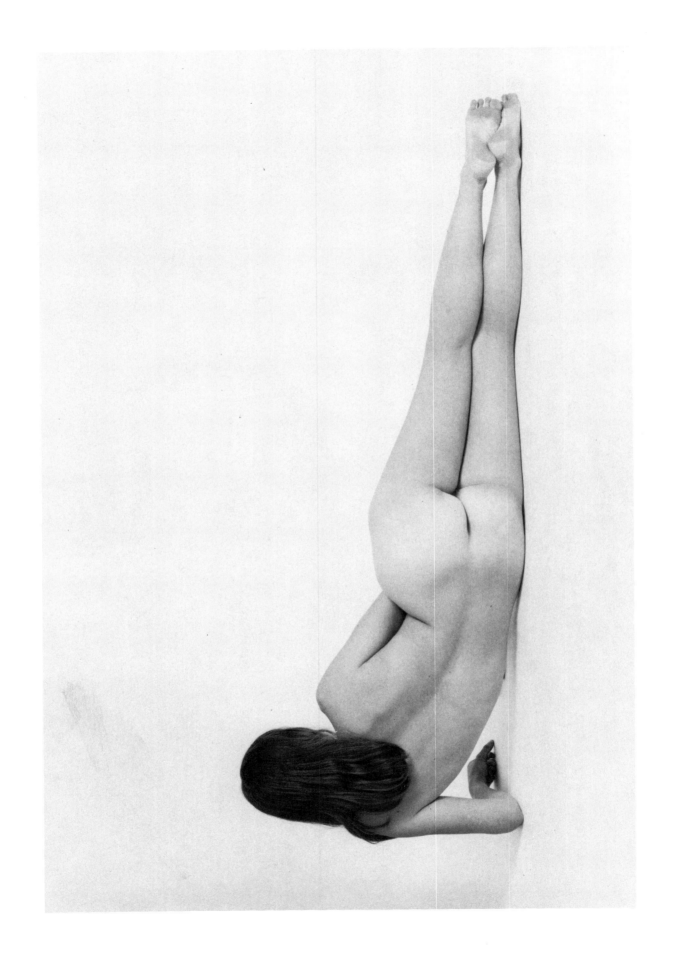

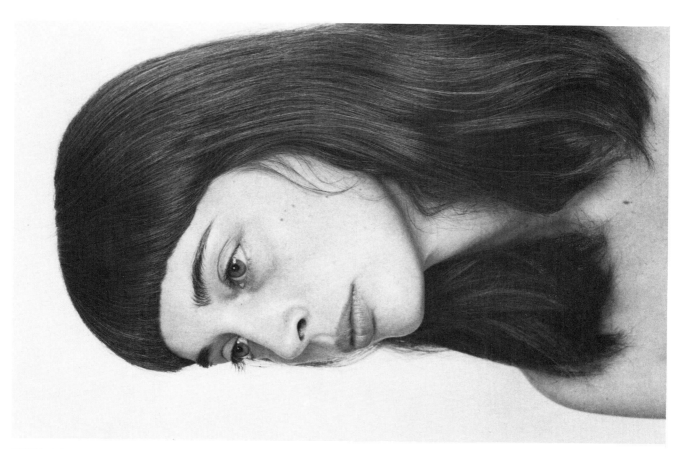

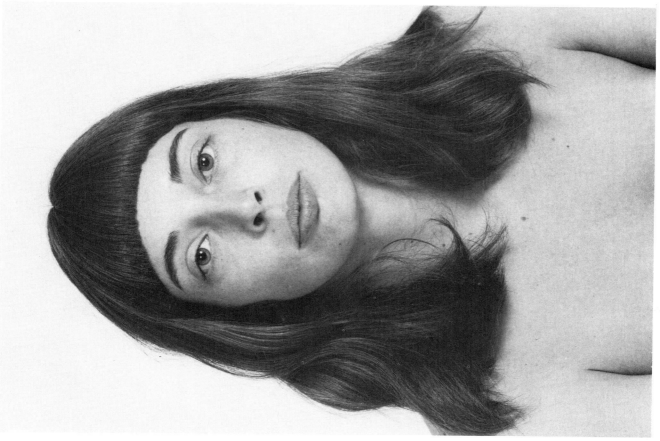

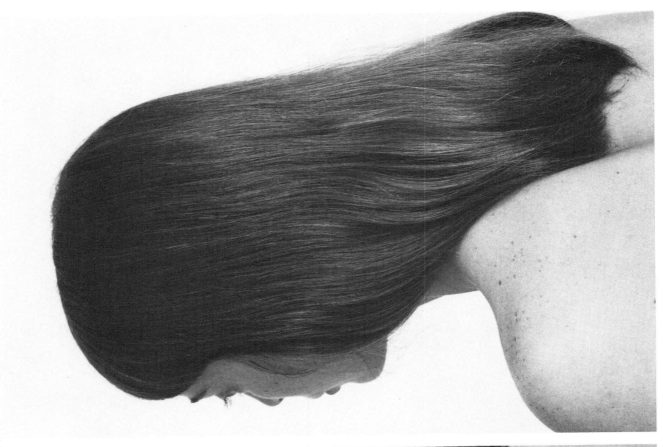

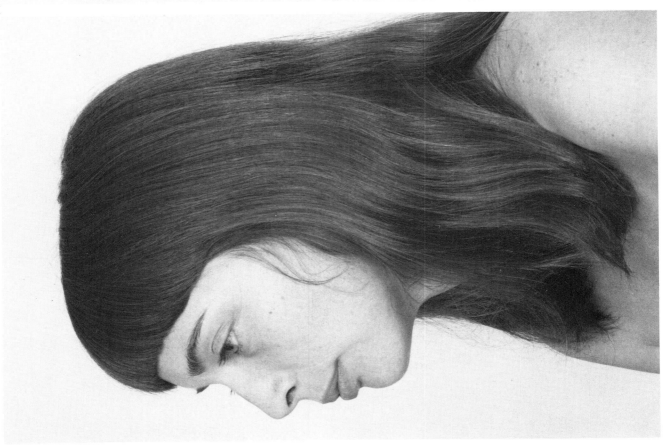

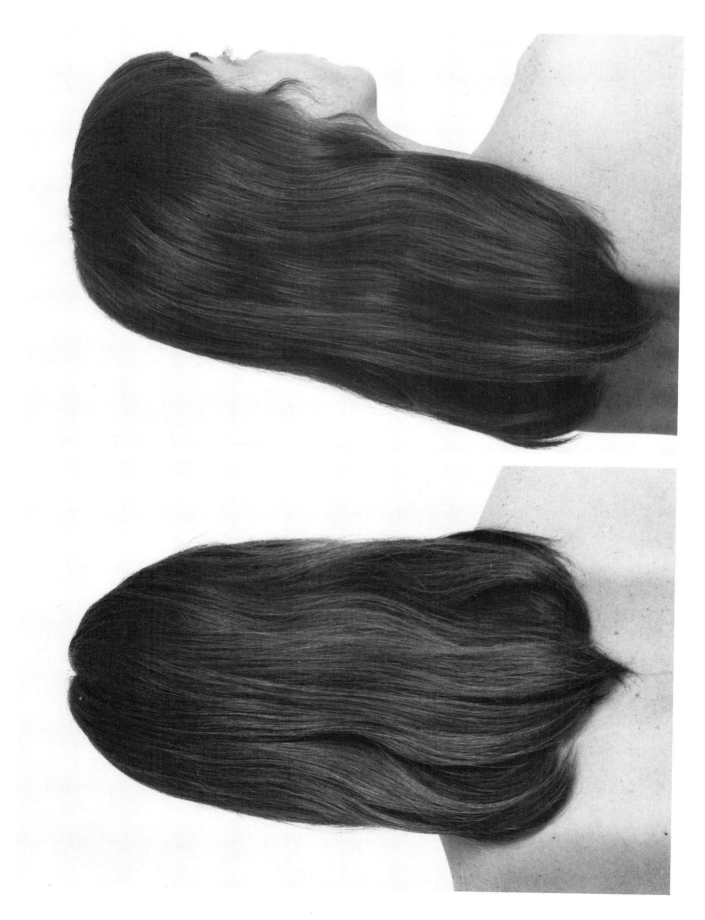

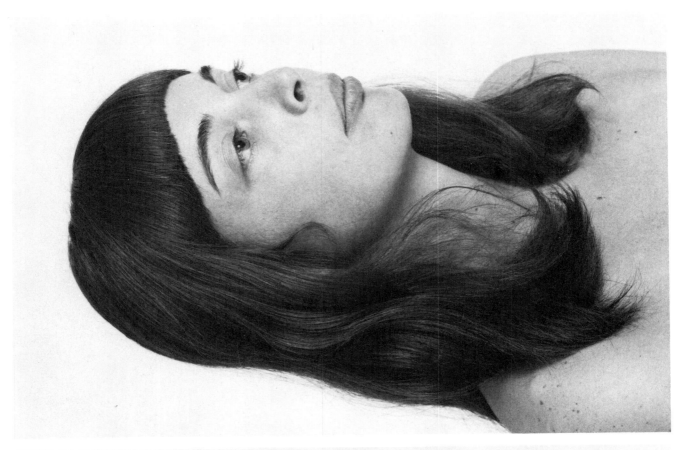

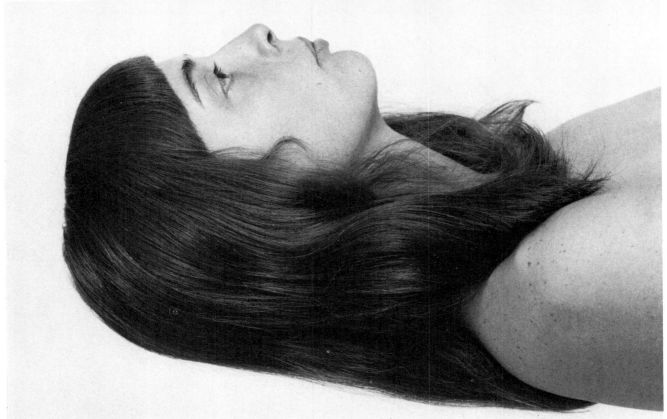

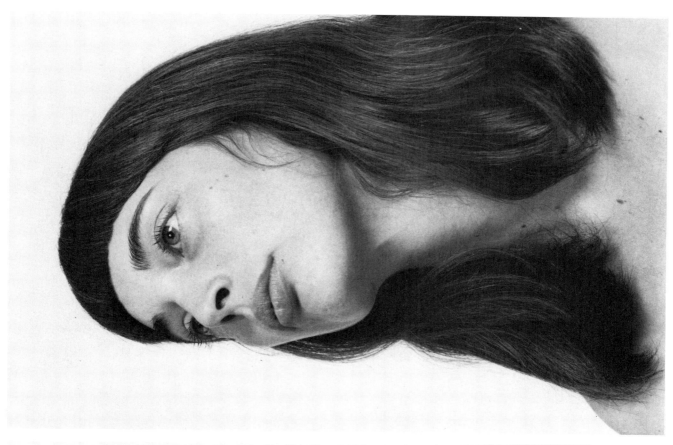

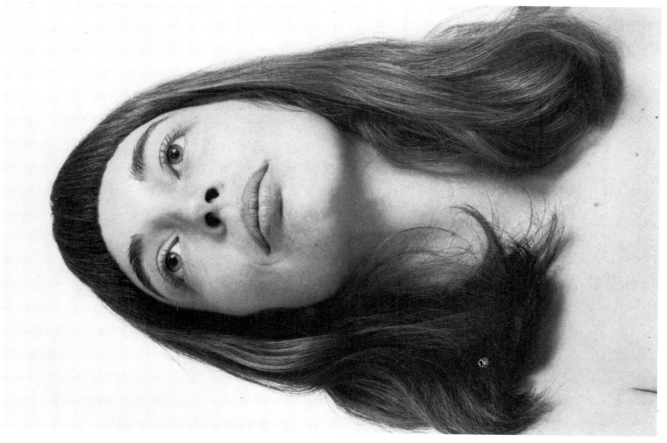

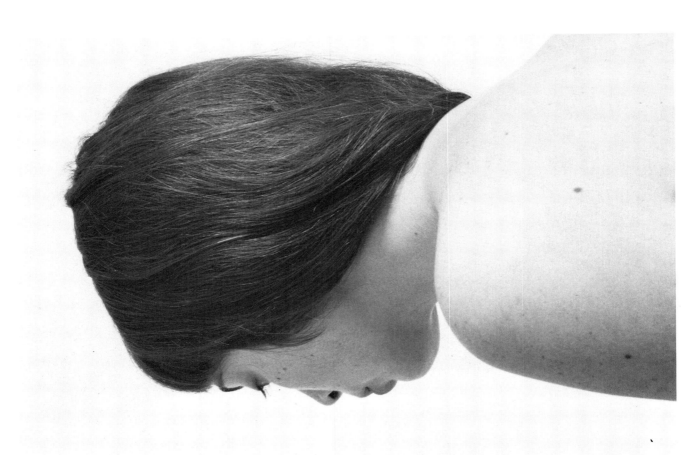

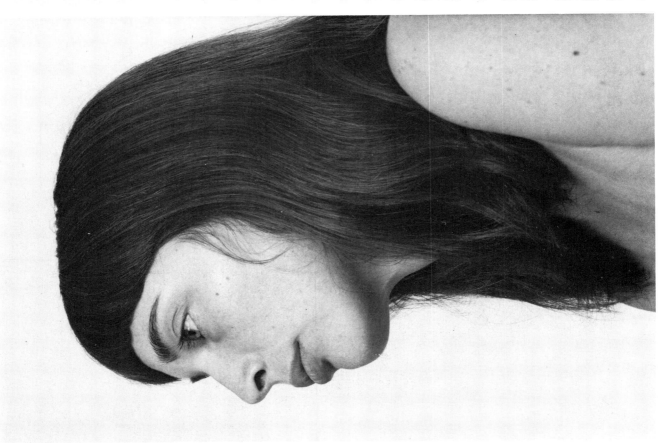

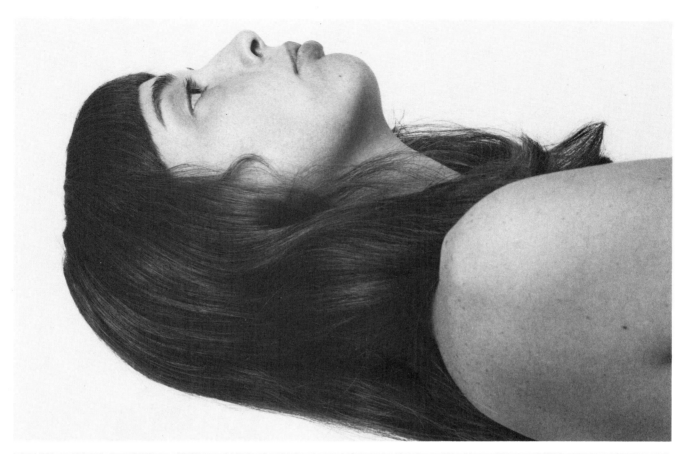

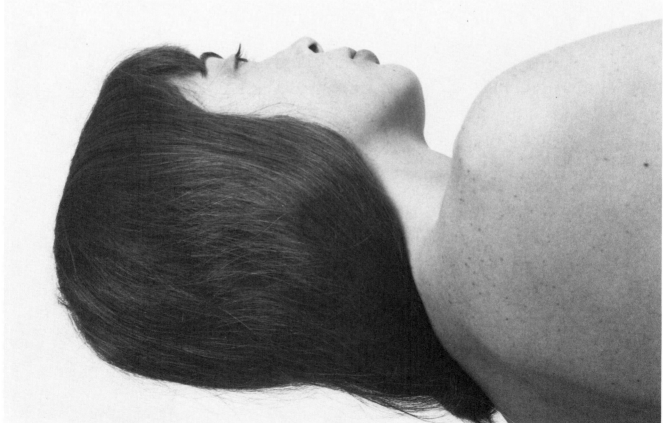

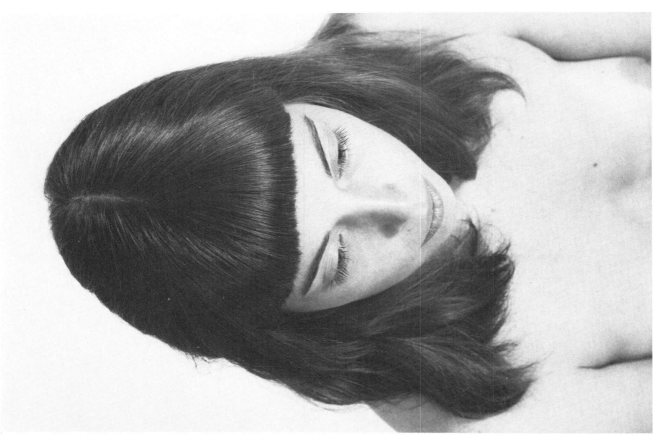

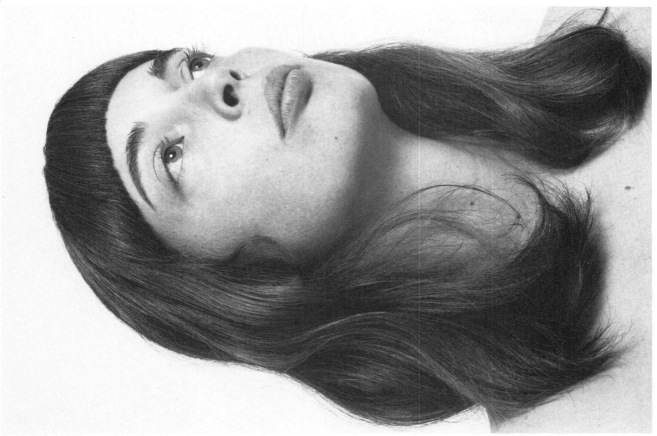

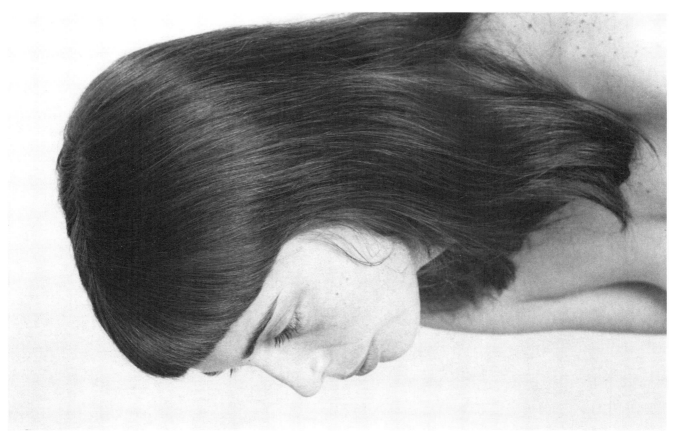

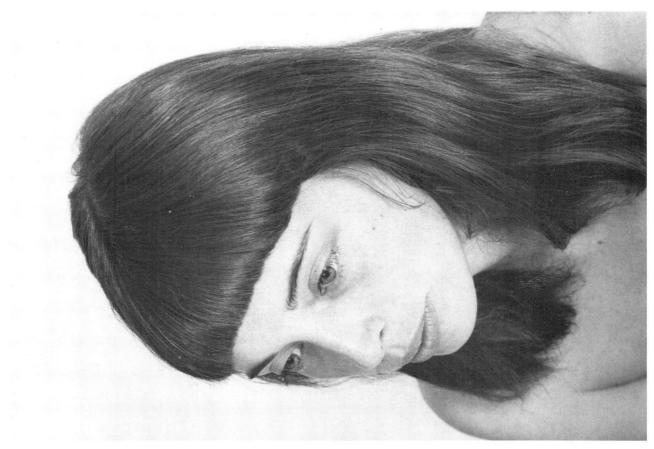

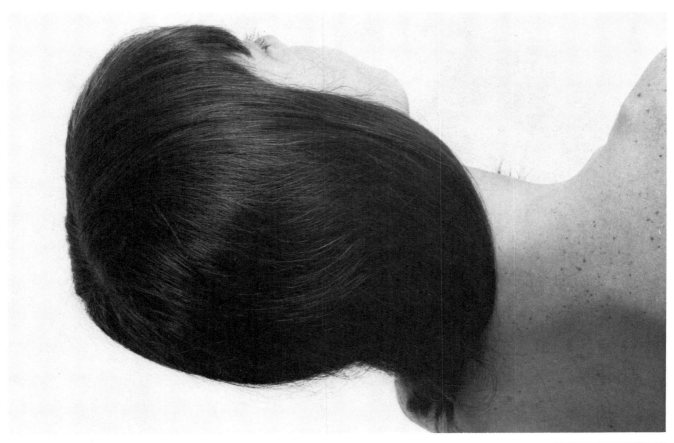

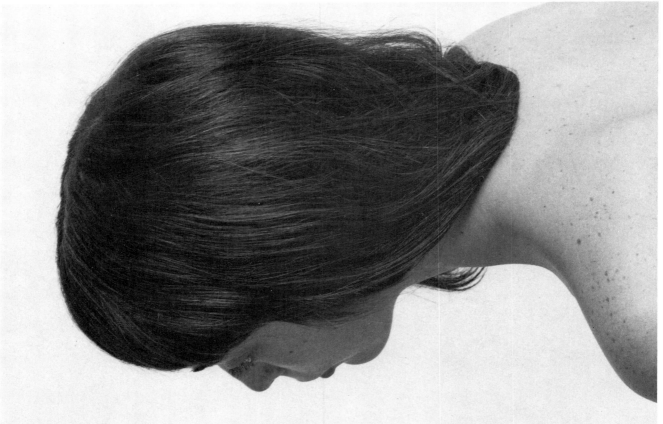

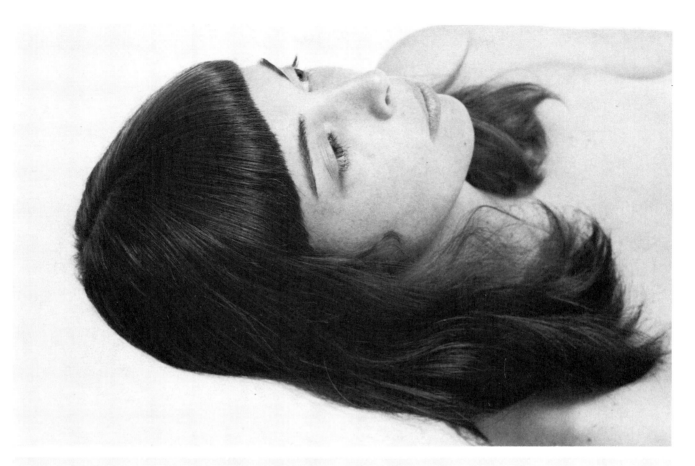

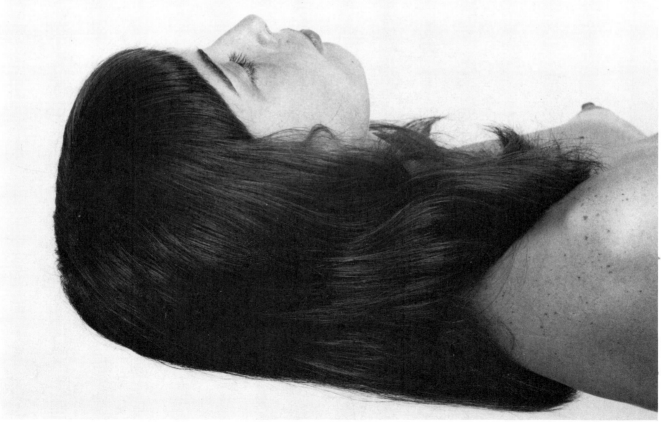

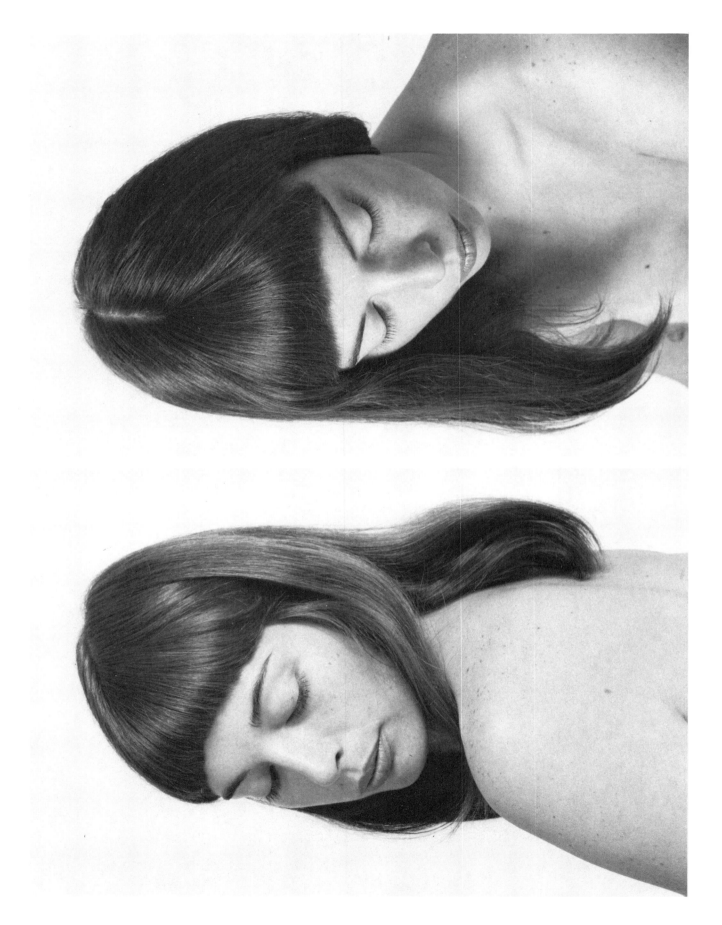

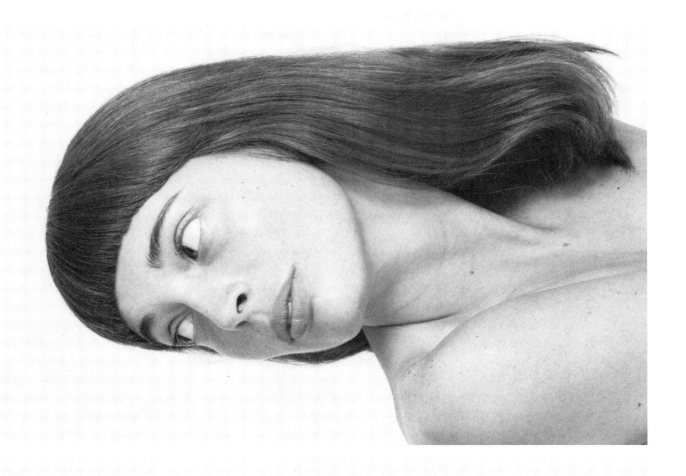

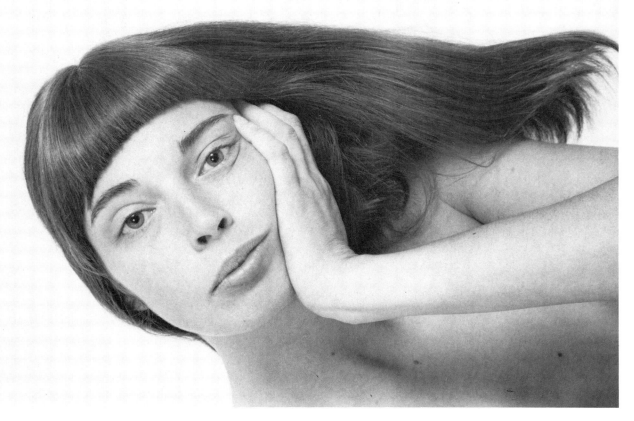

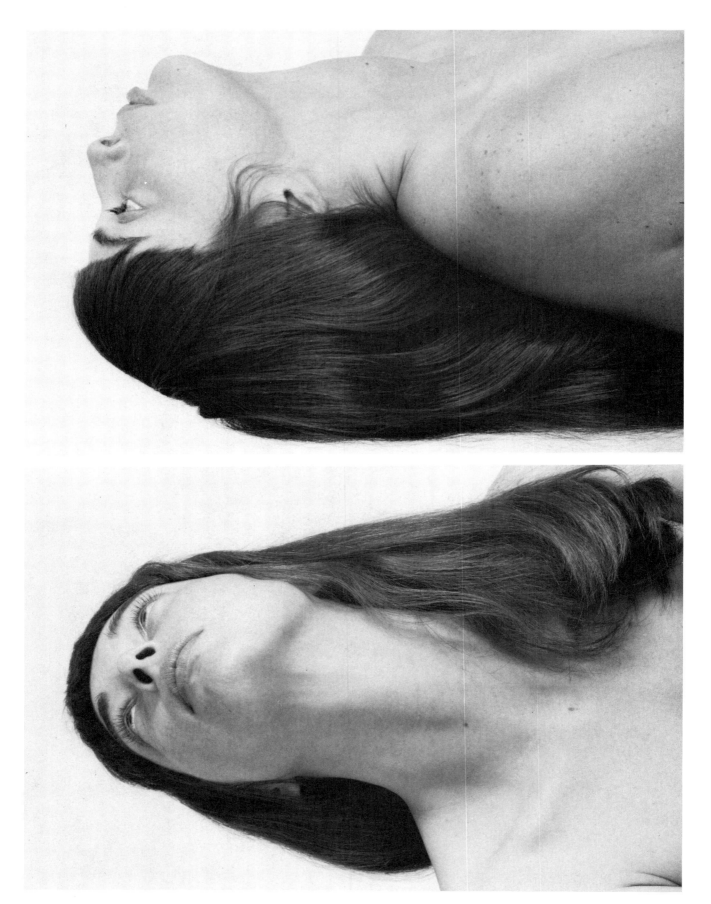

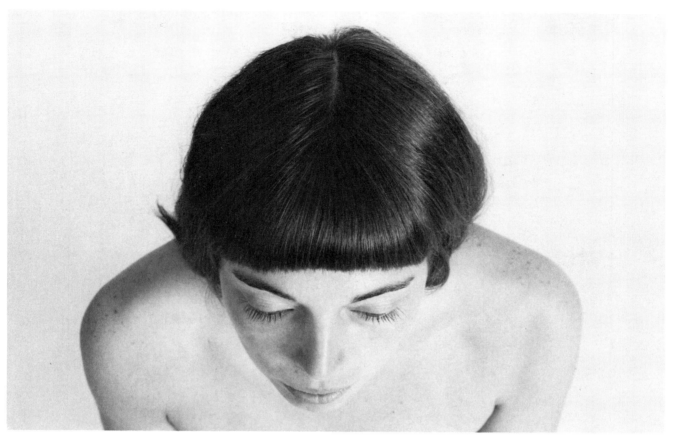

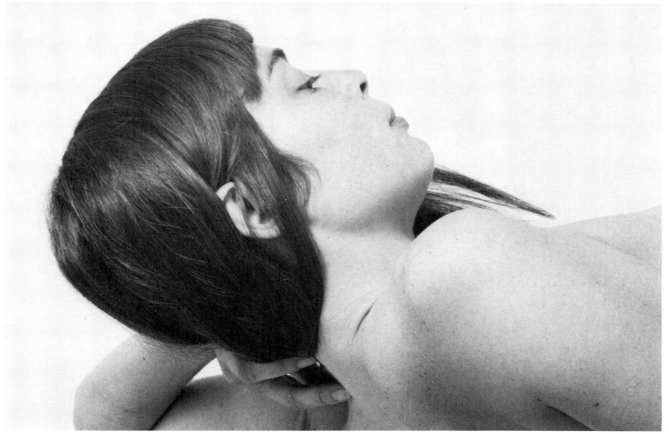

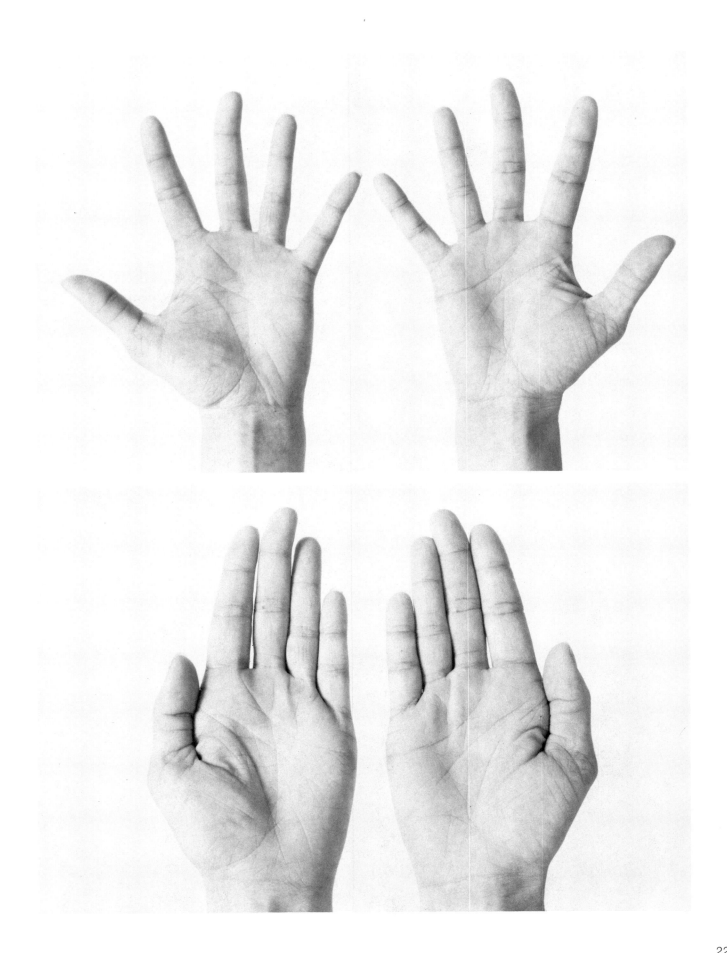

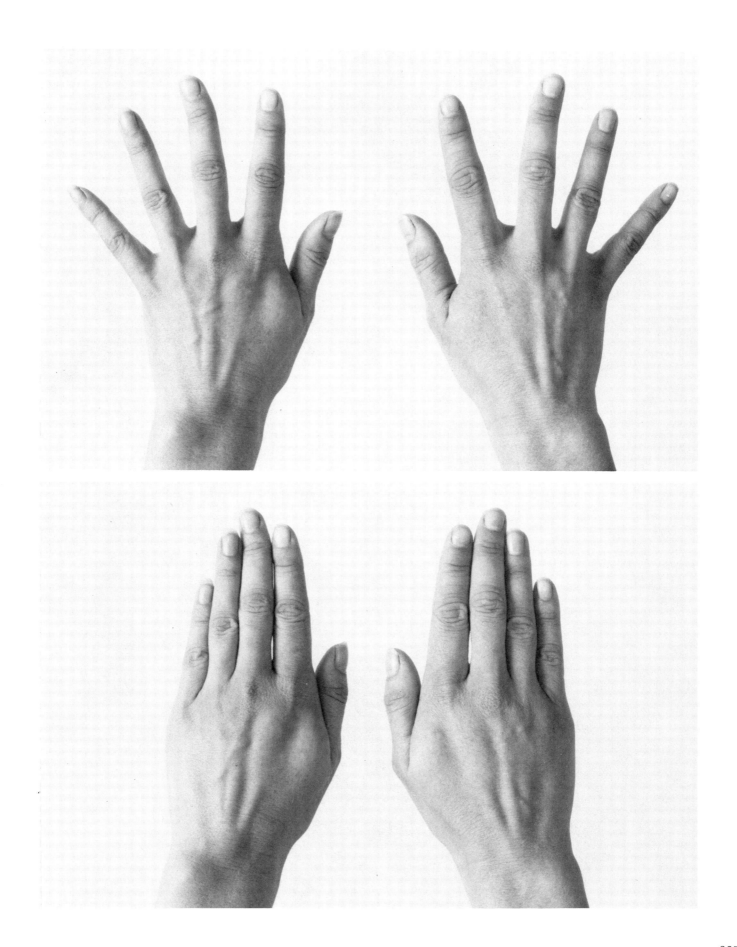

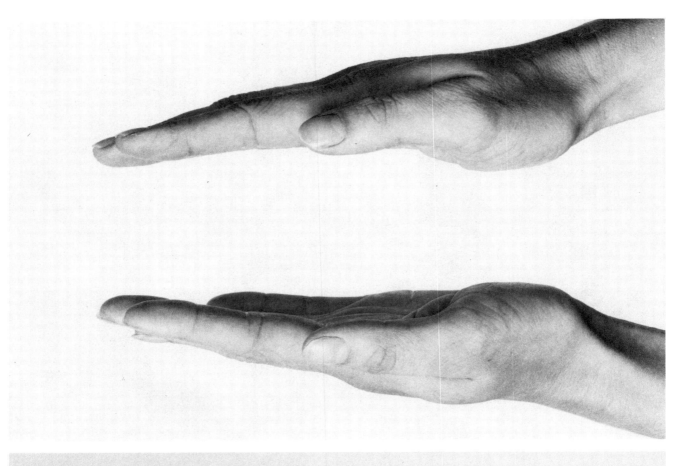

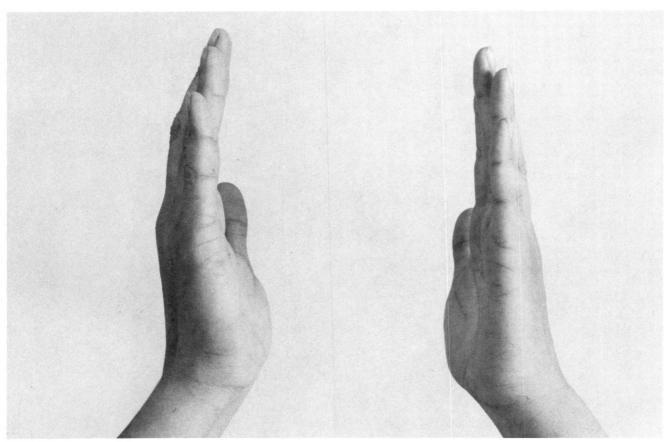

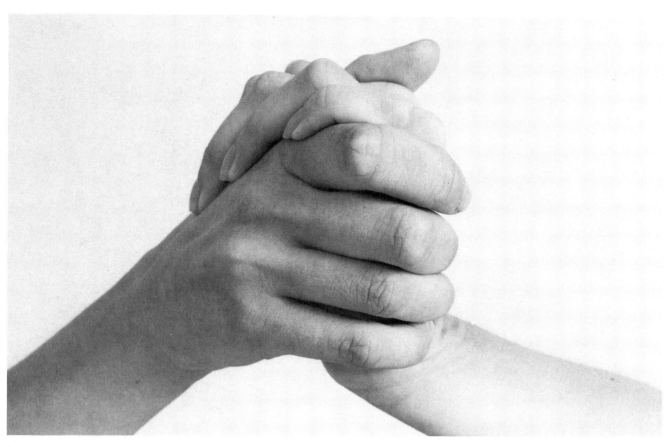

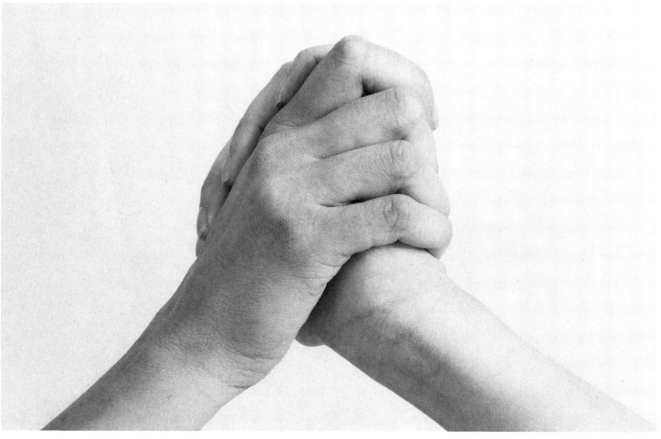

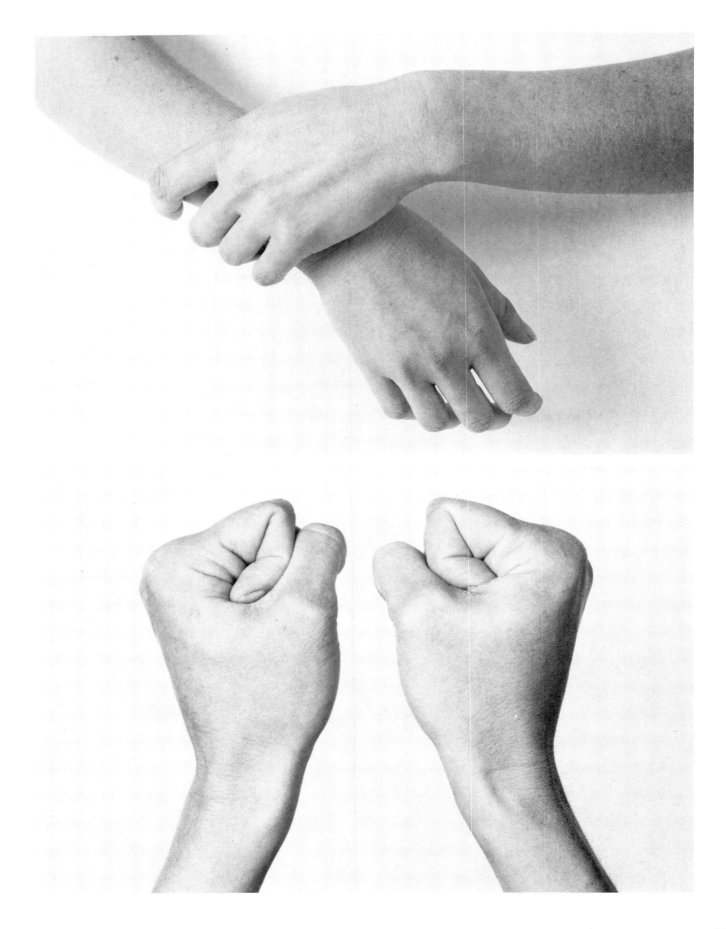

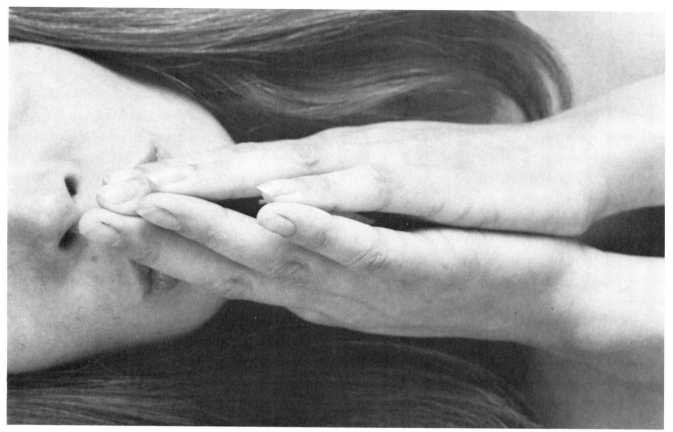

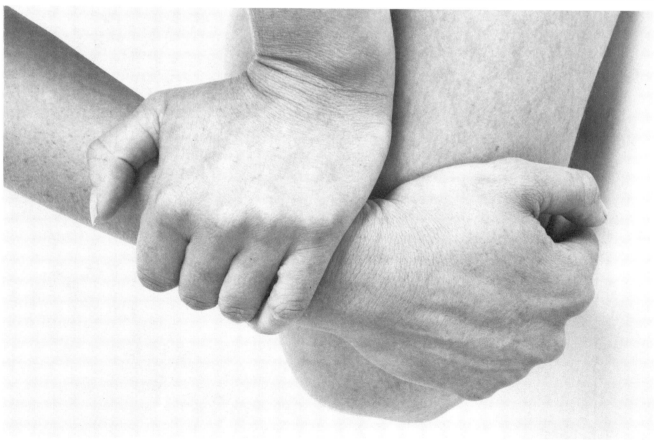

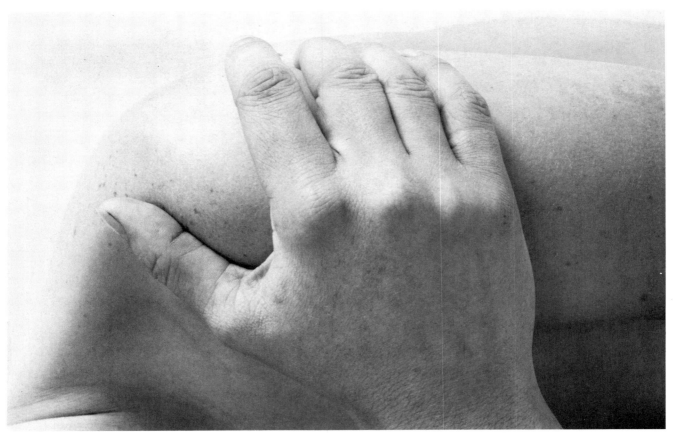

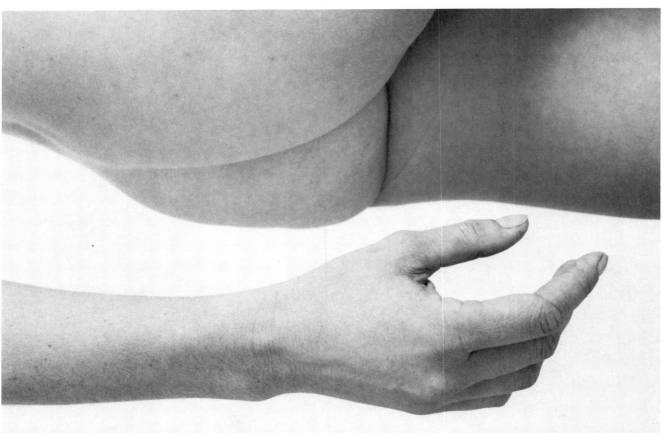

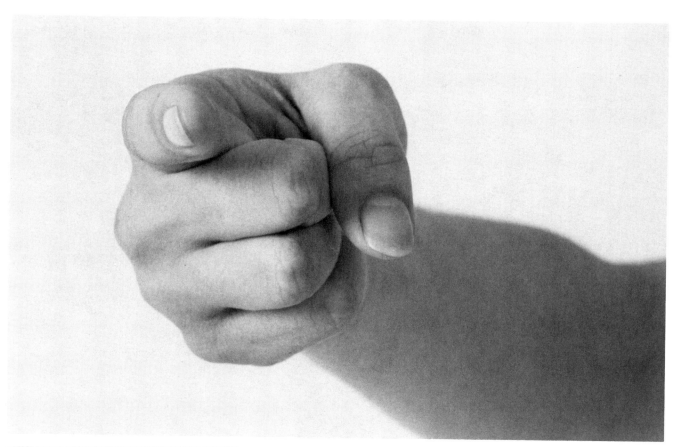

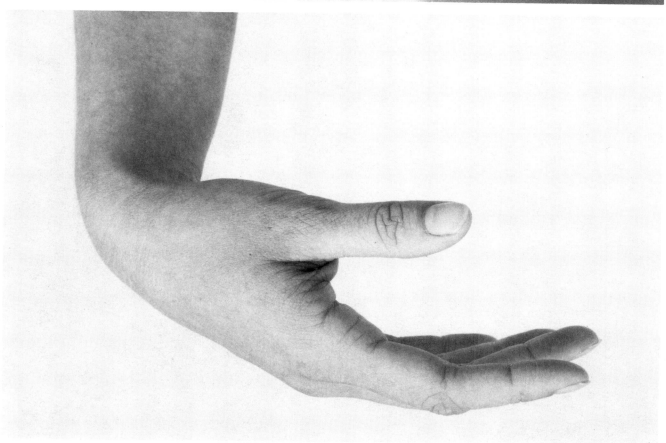

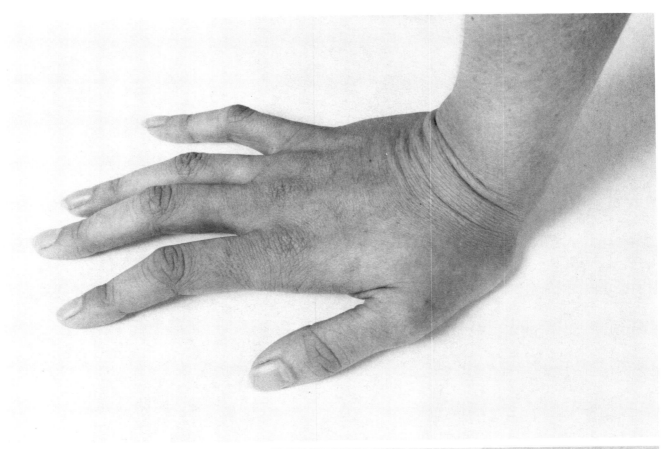

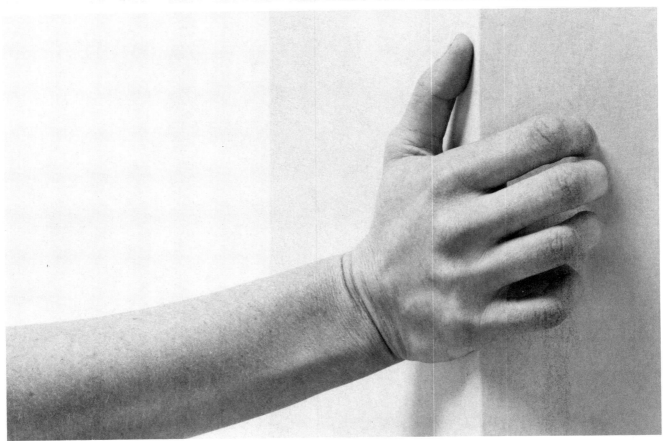

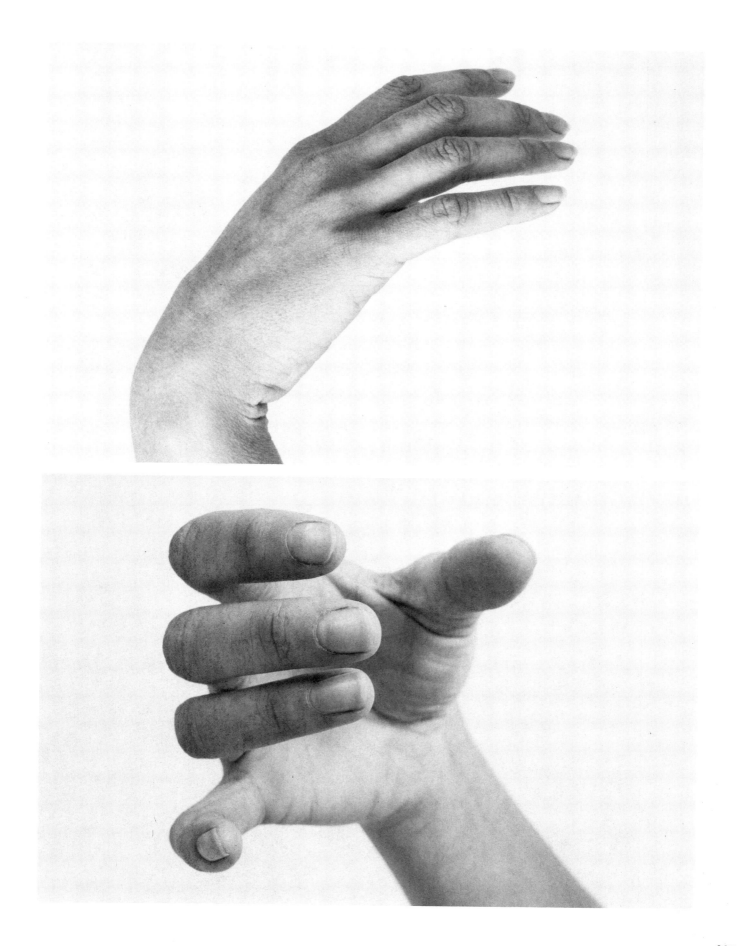

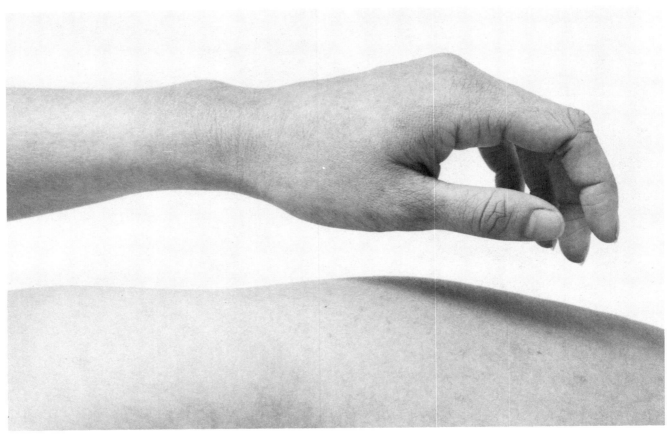

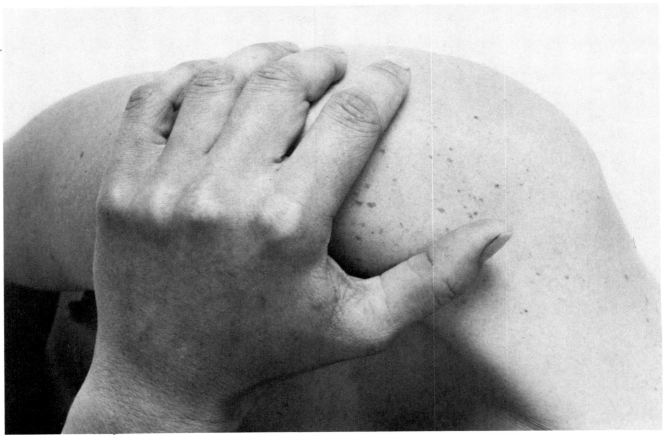

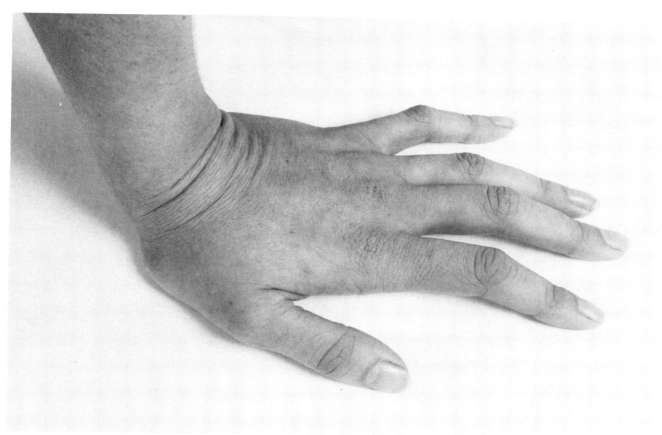

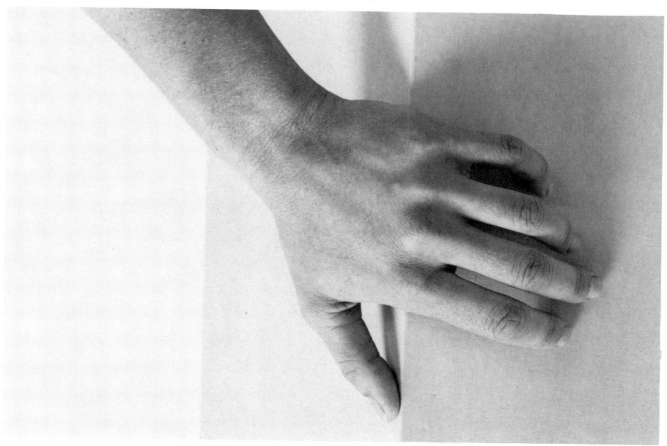

237

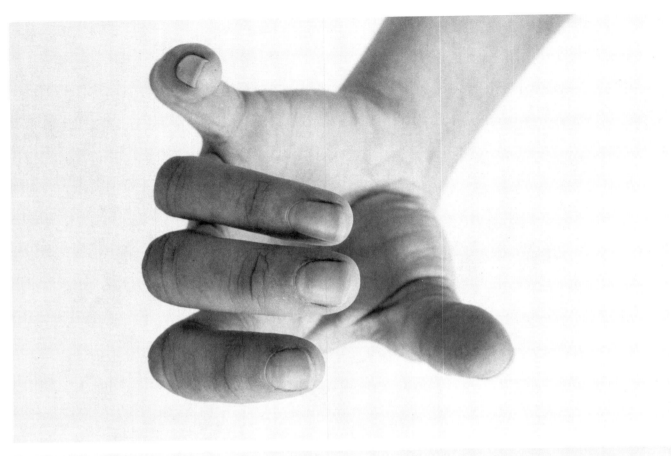

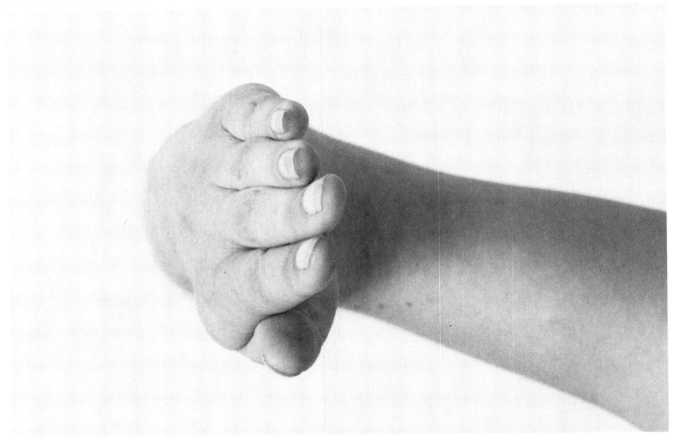

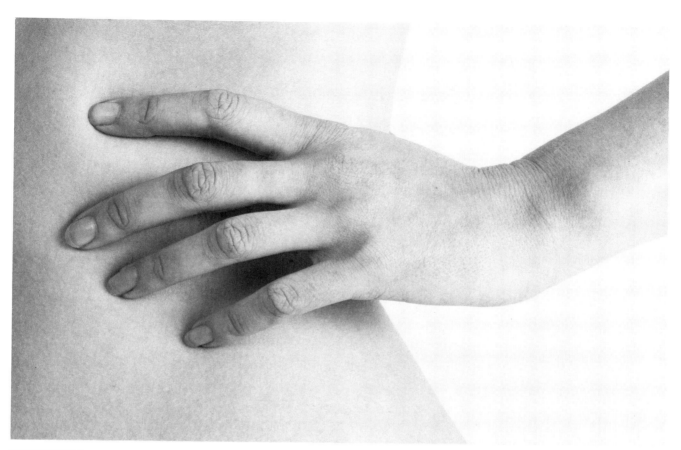

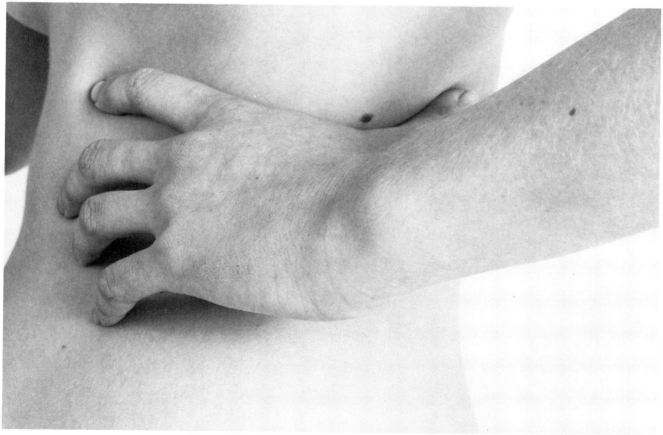

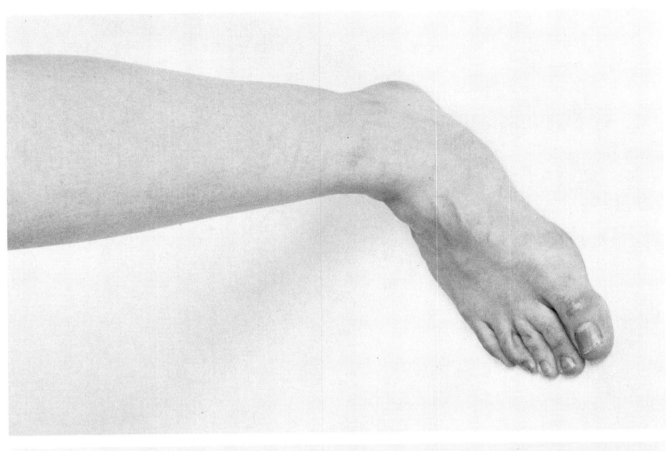

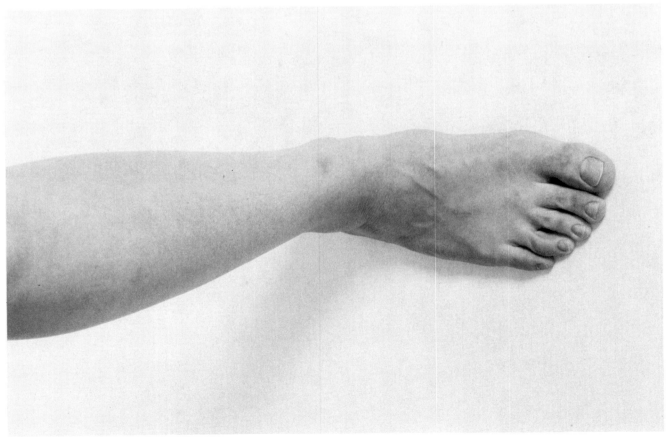

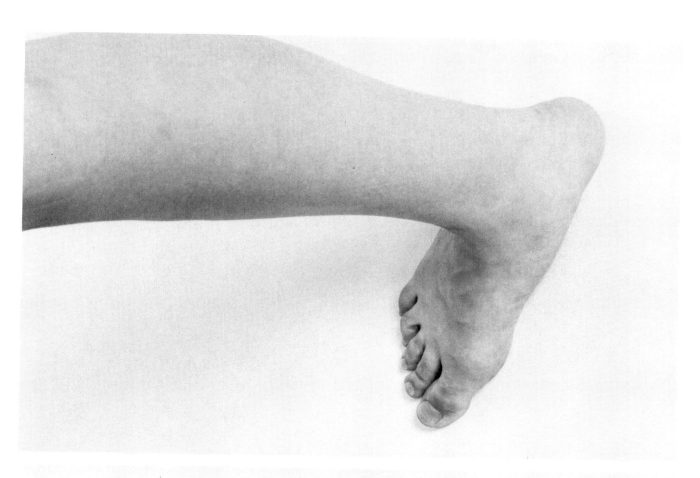

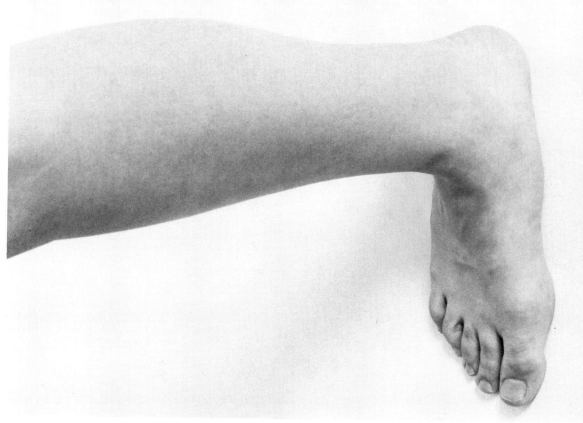

241

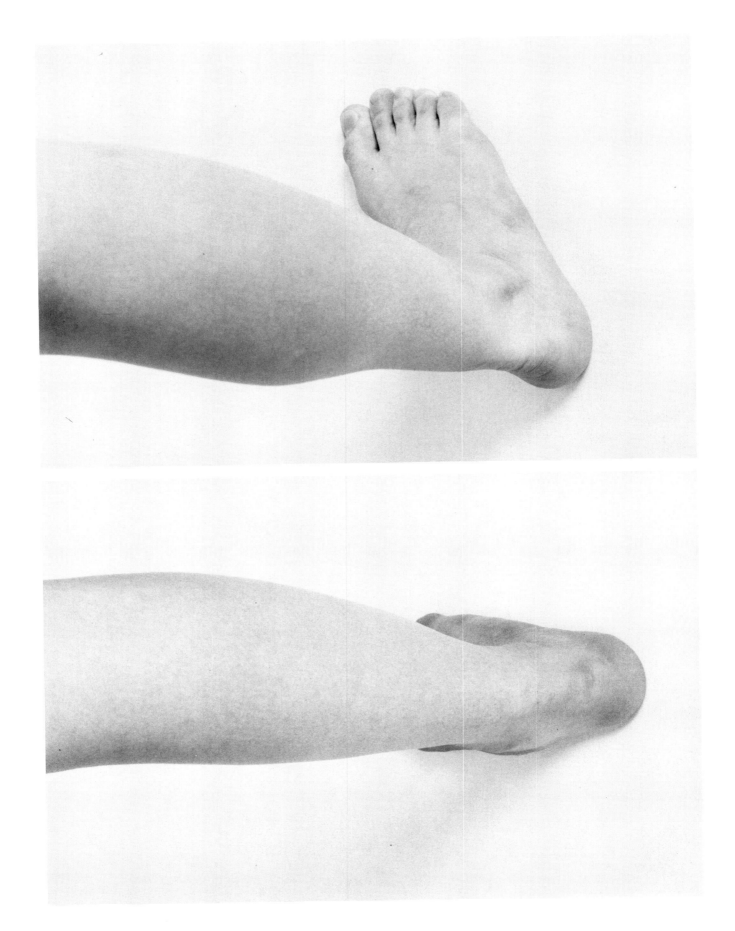

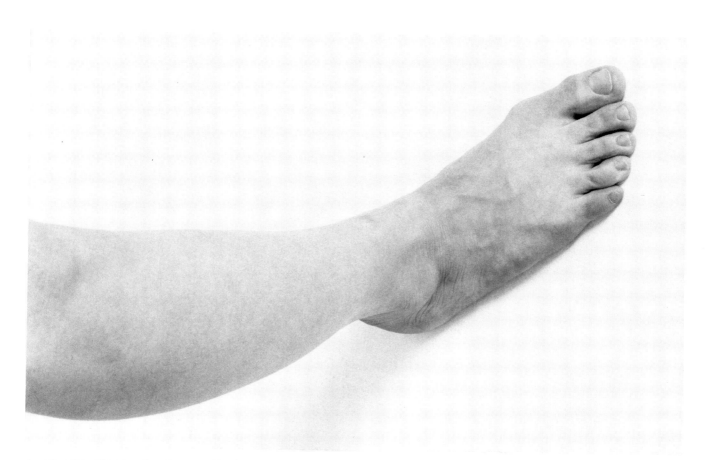

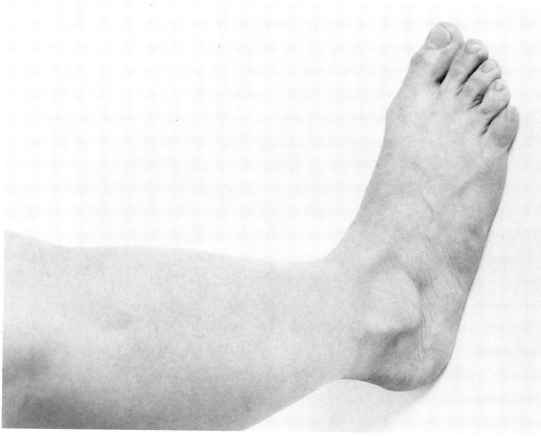

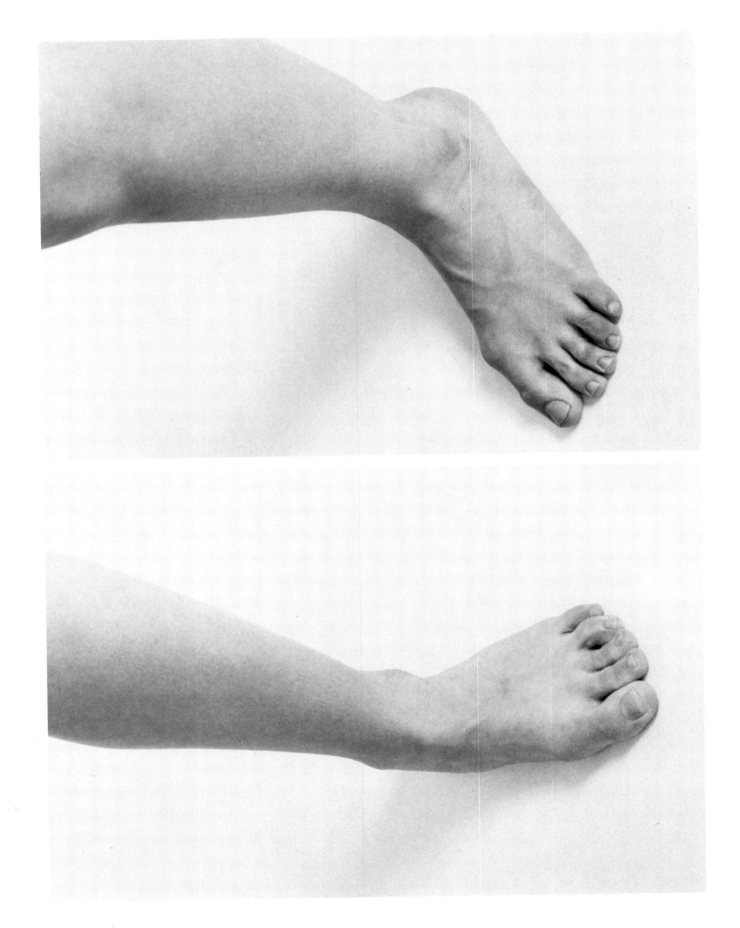

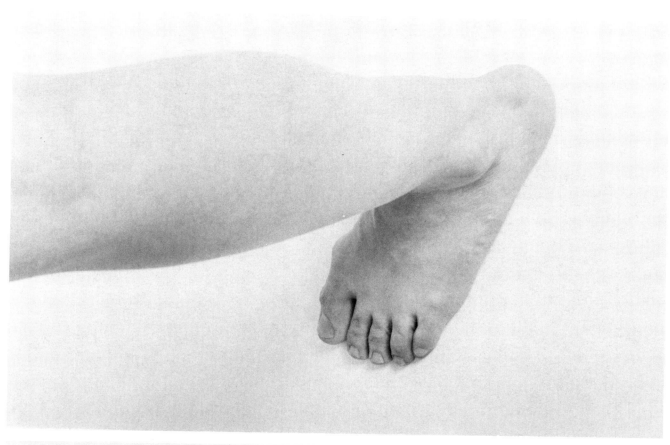

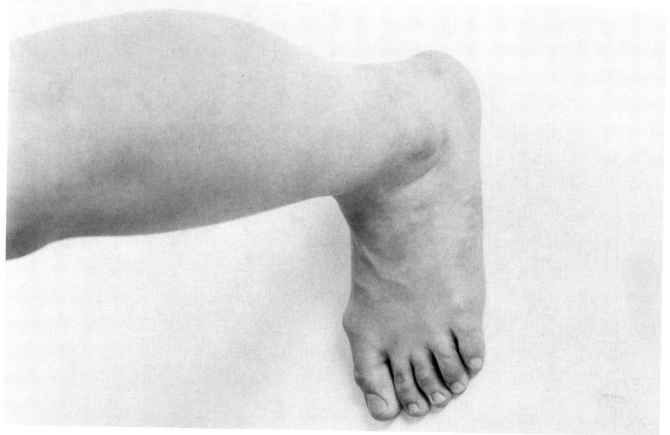

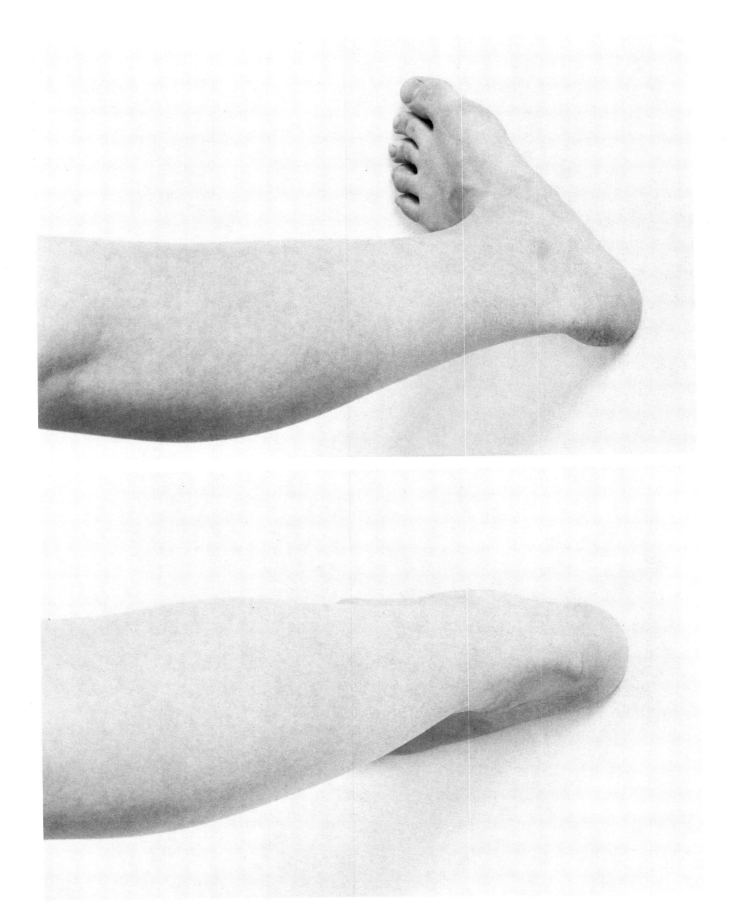

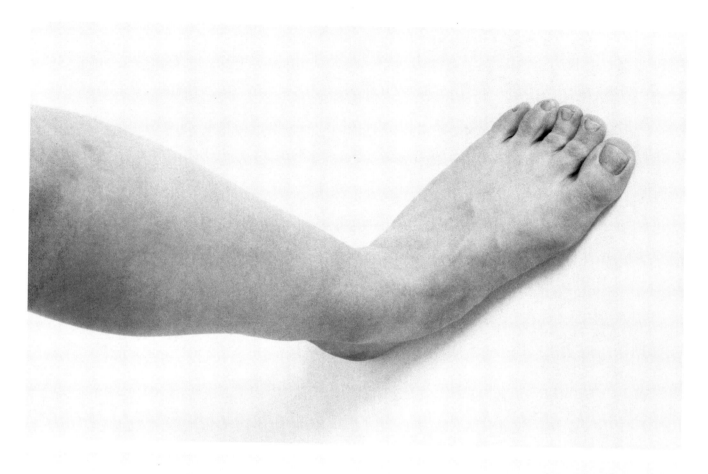

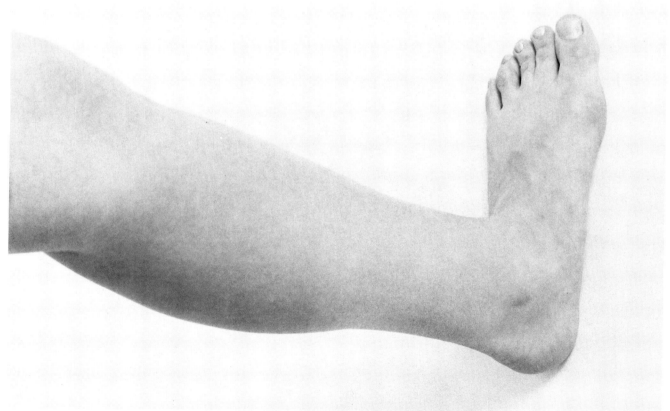

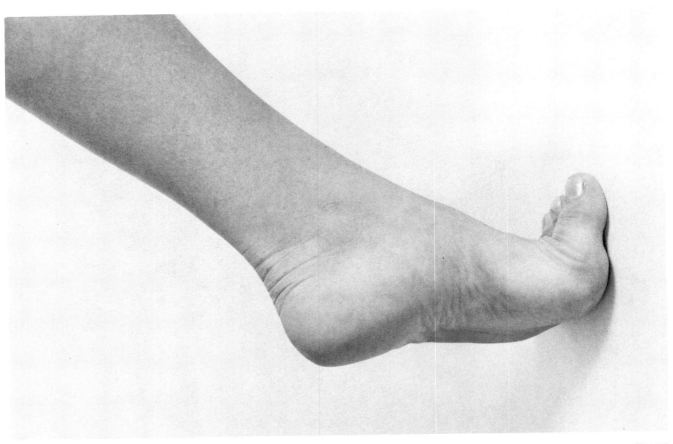

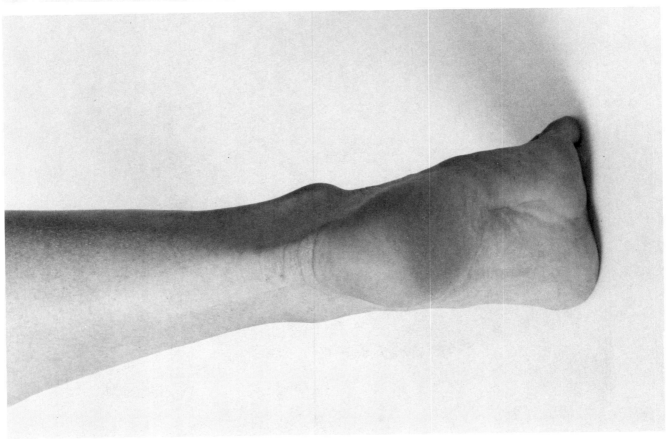

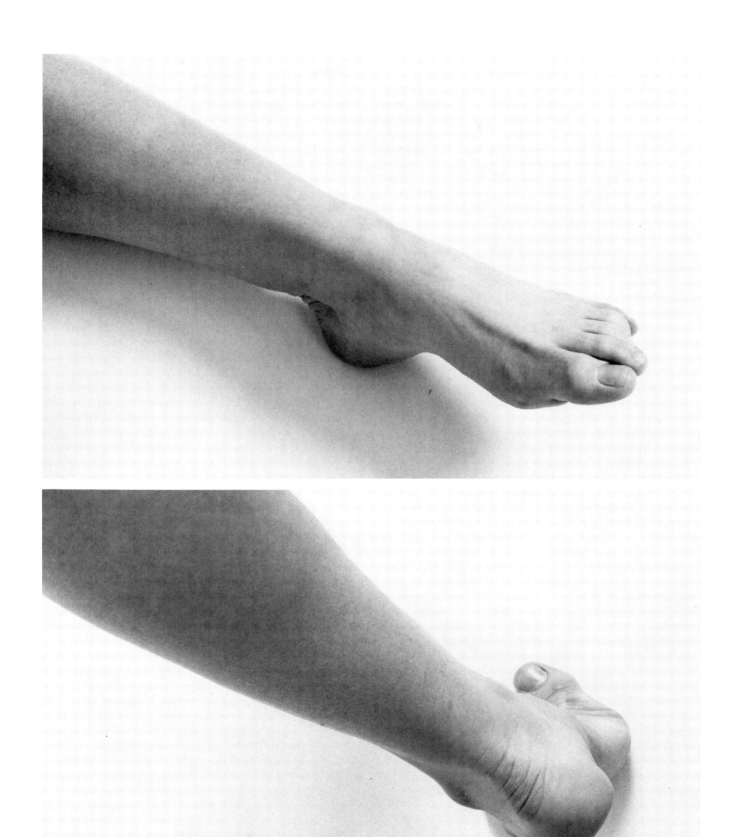

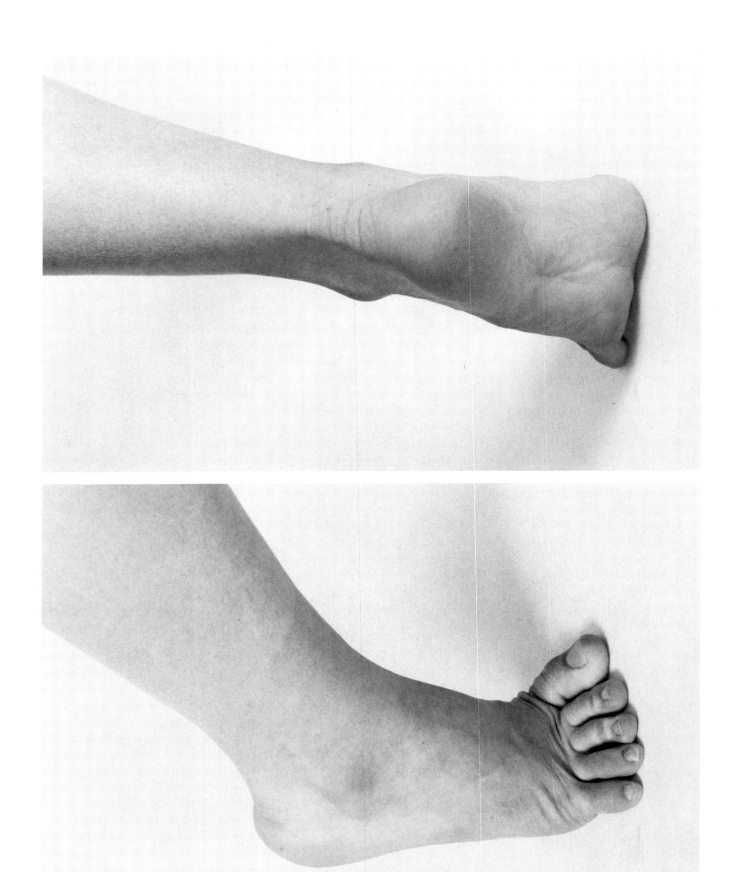

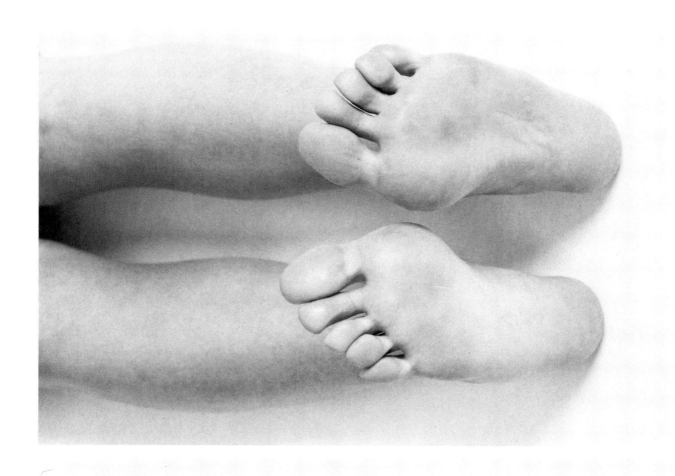

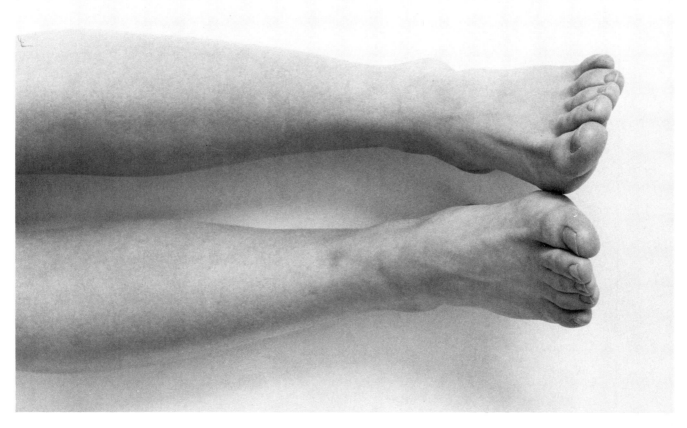

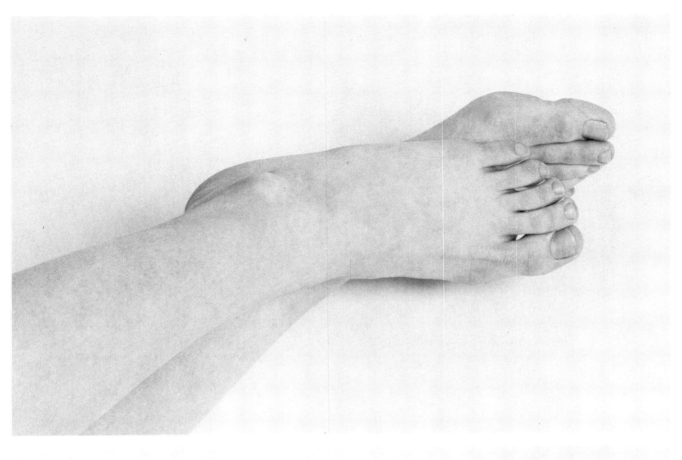

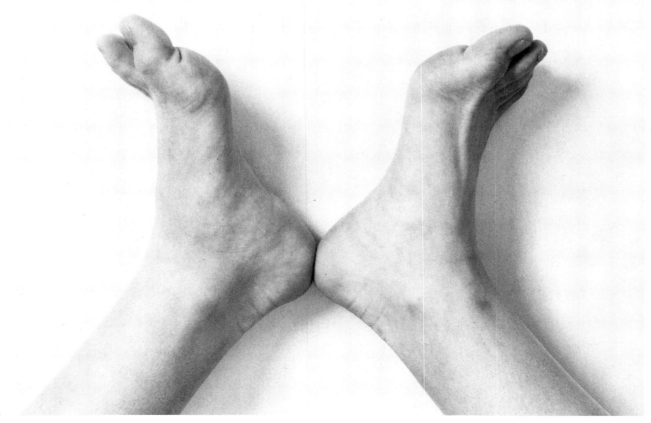

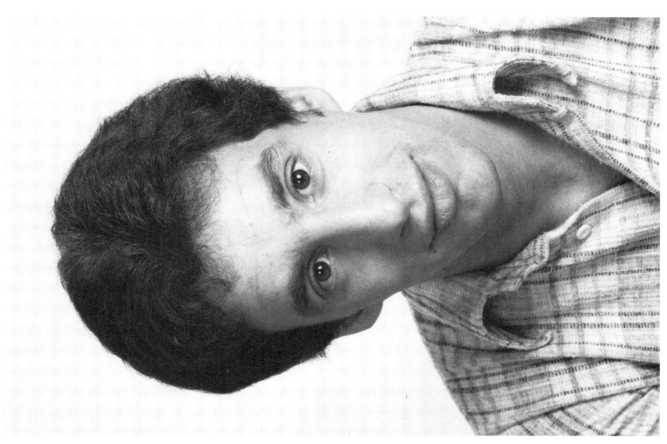

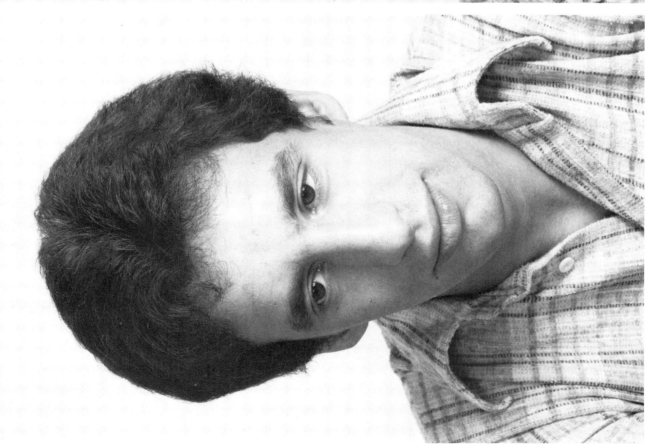

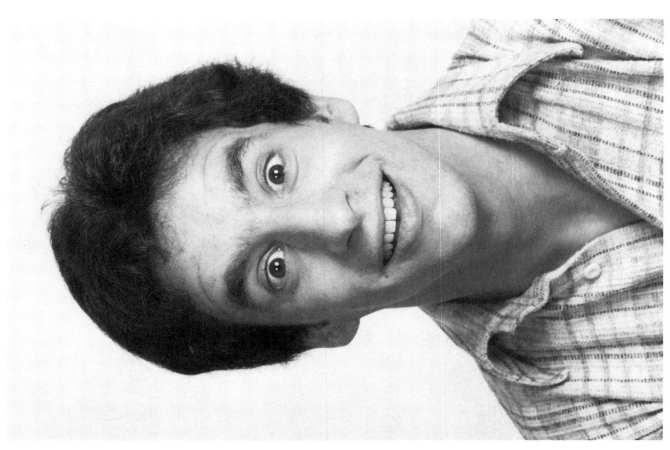

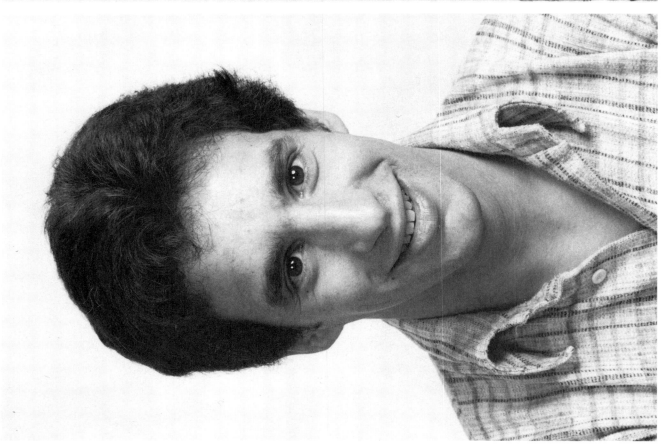

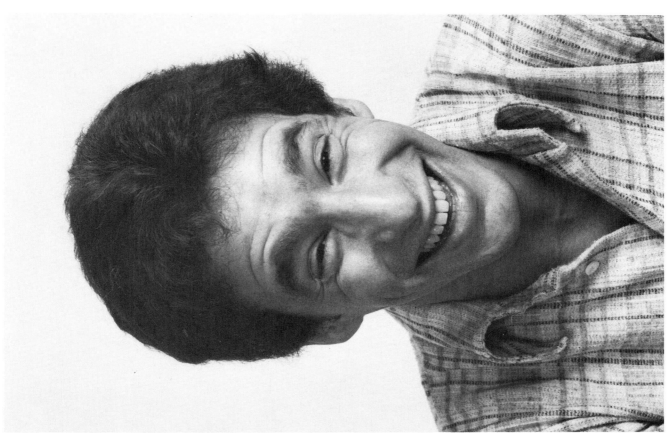

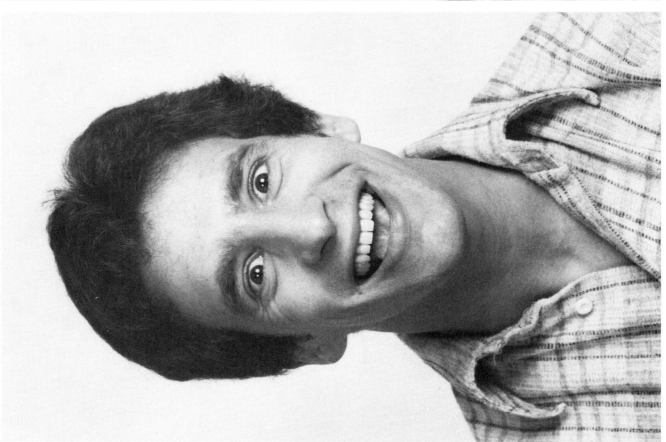

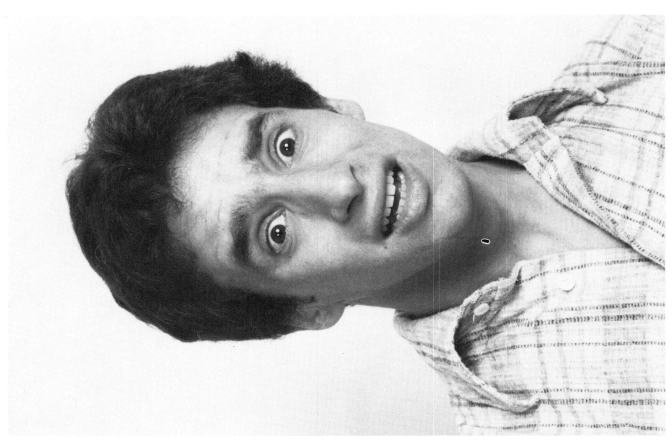

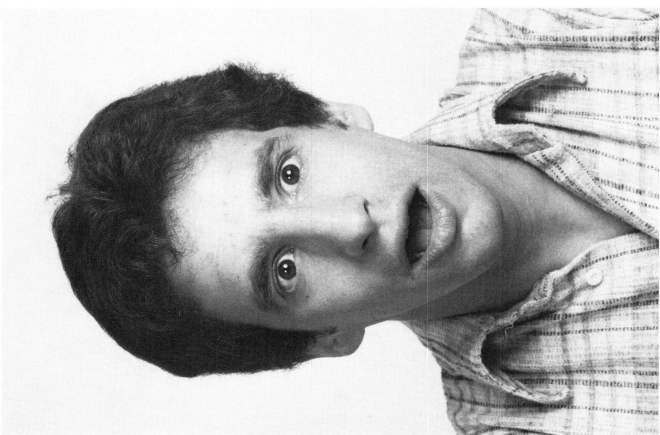

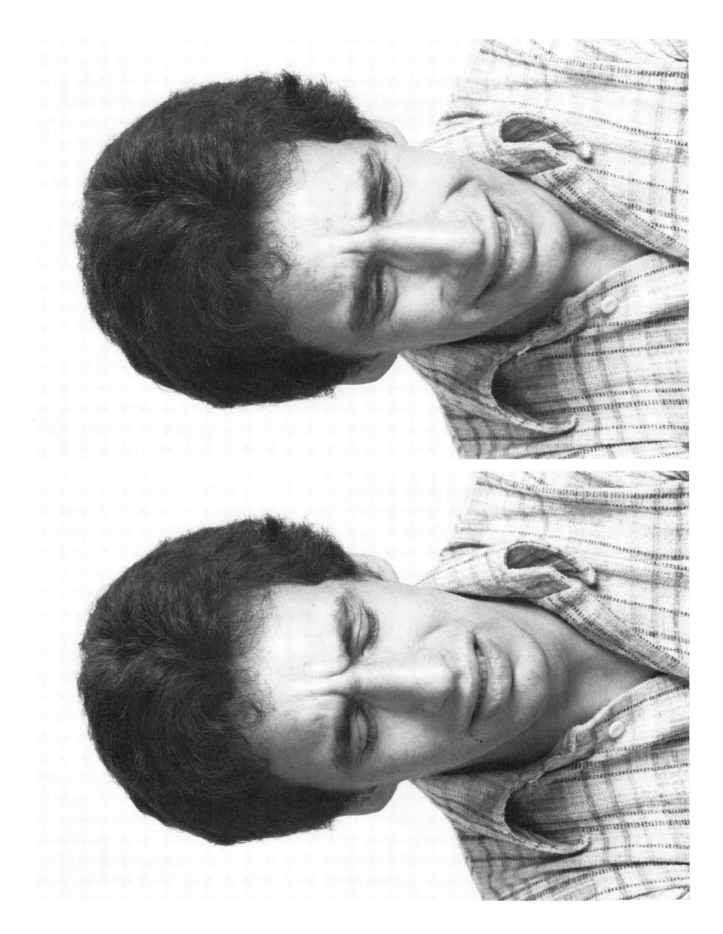

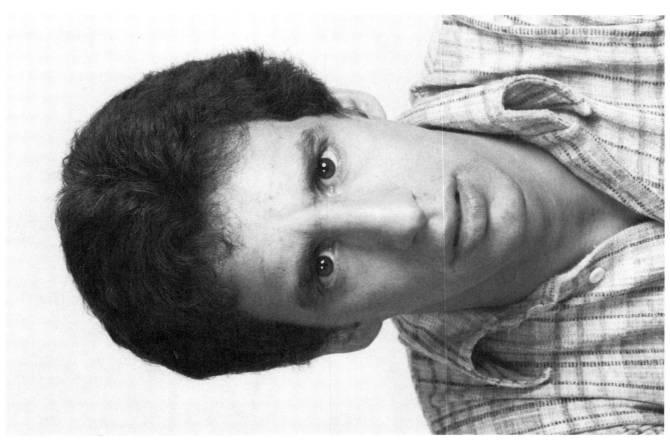

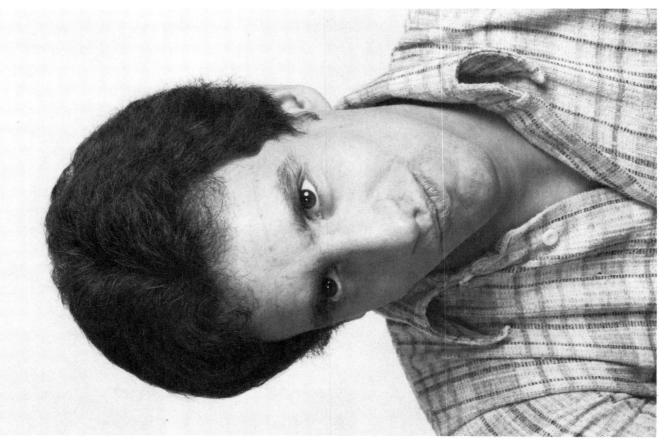

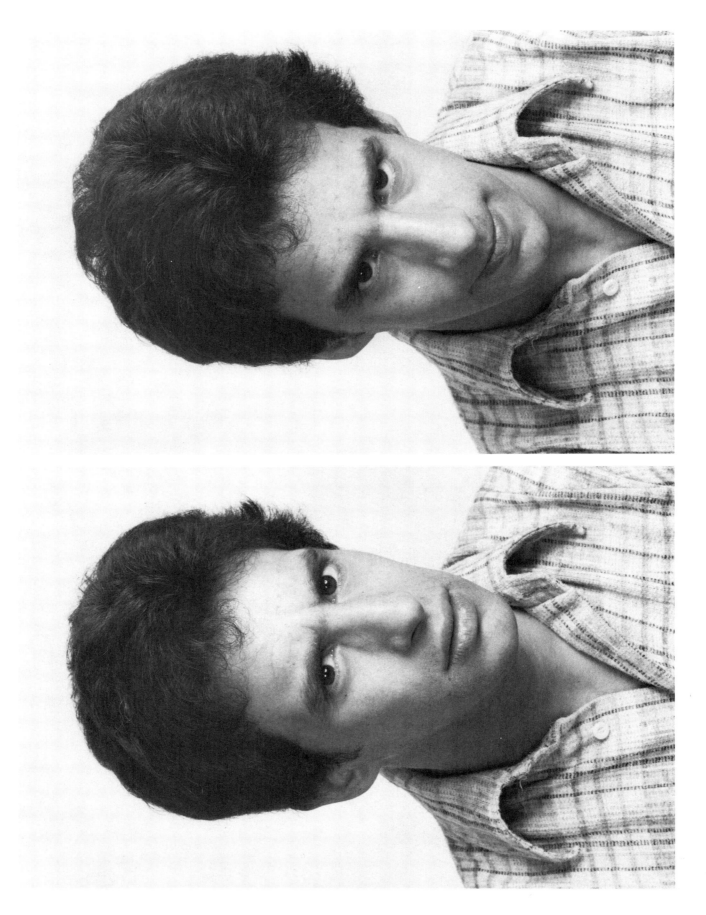

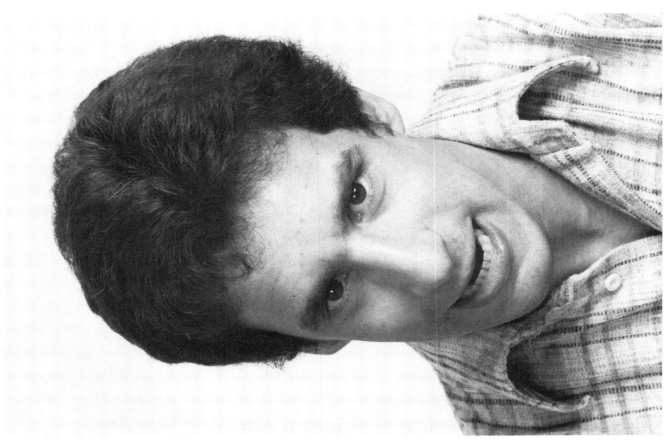

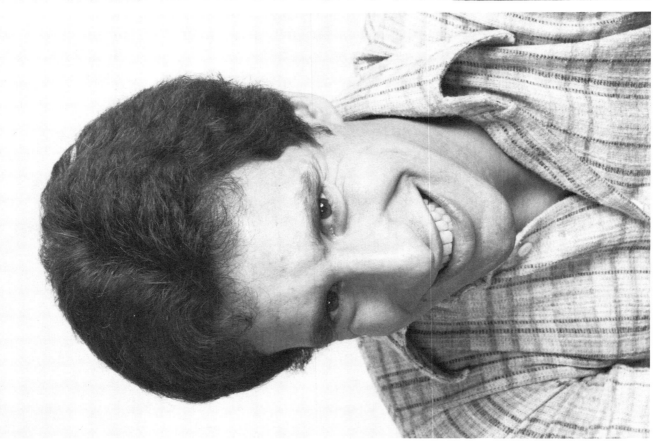

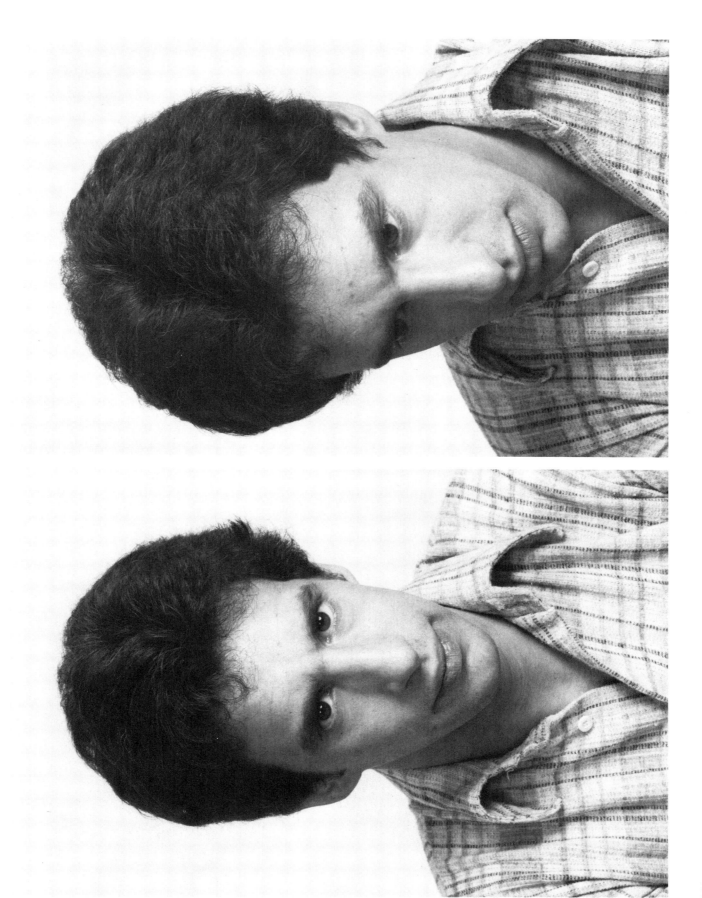

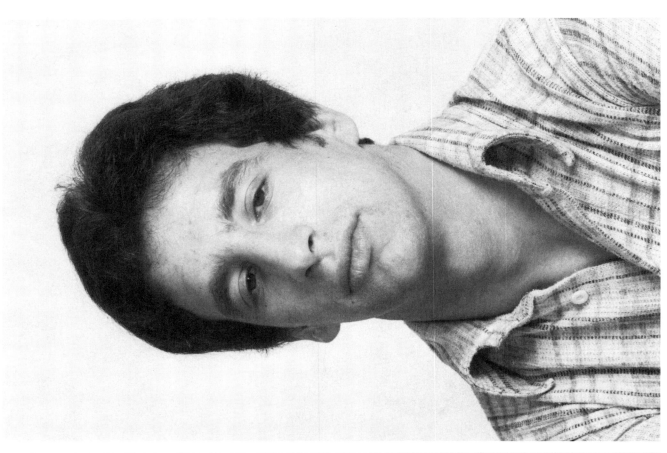

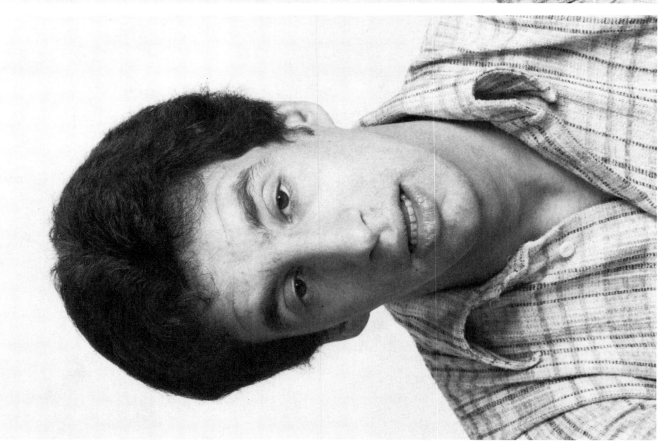

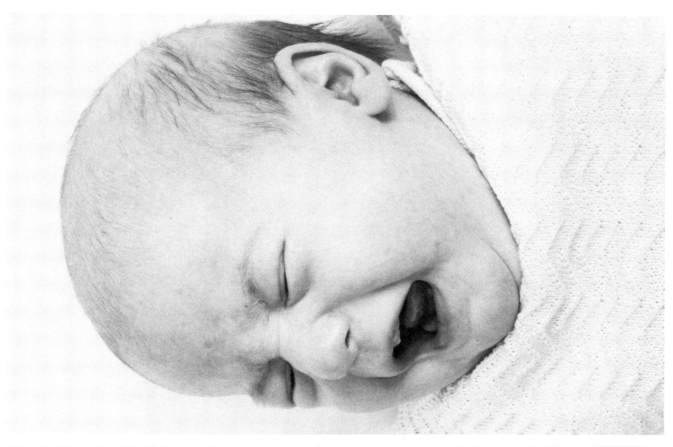

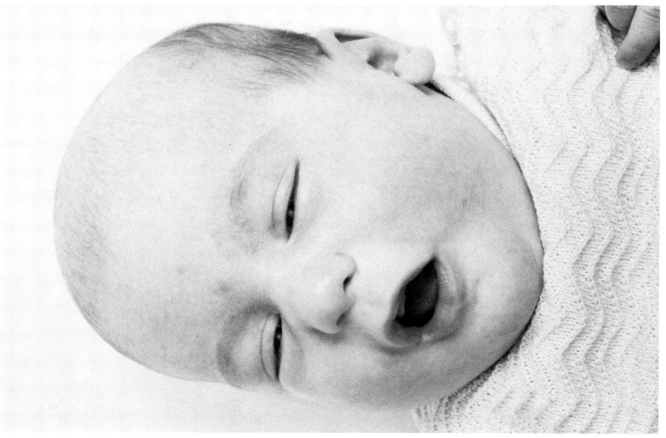

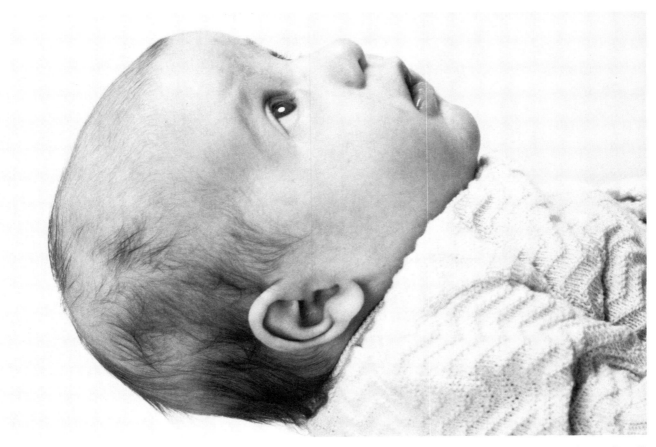

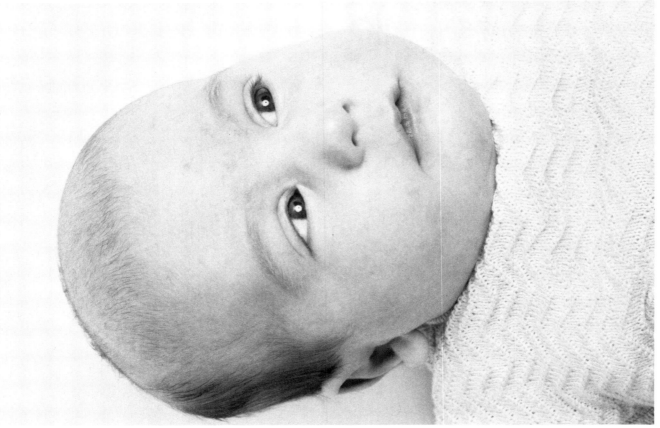

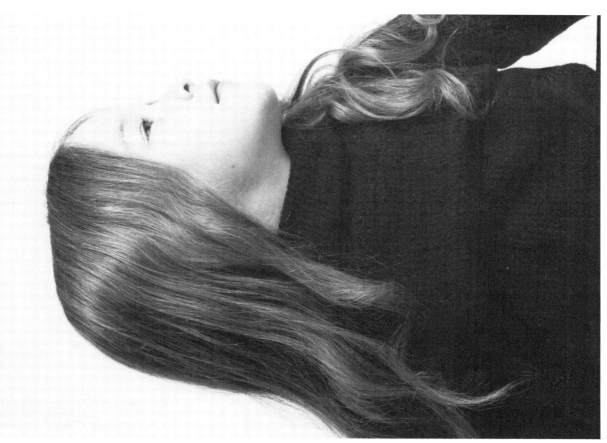

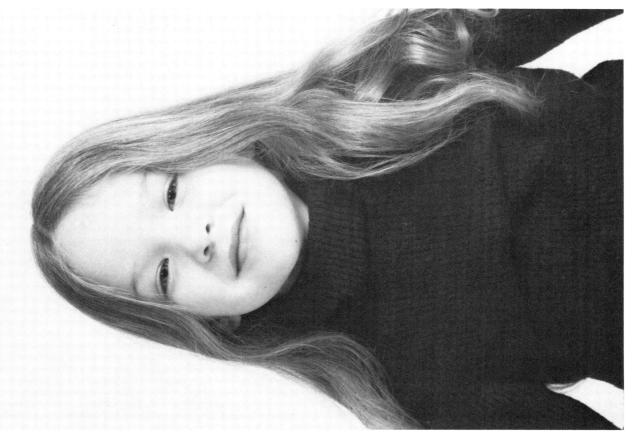

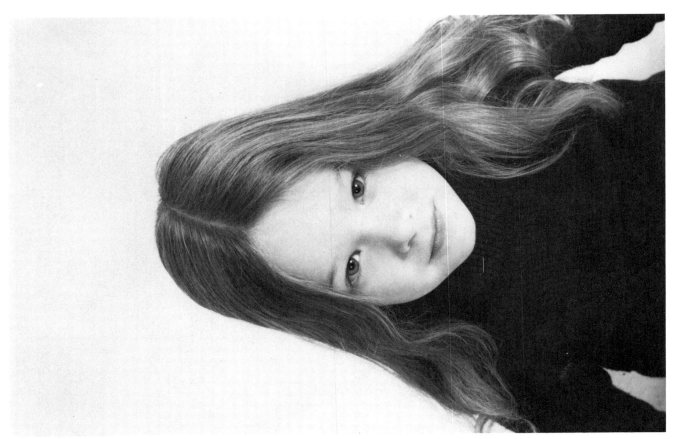

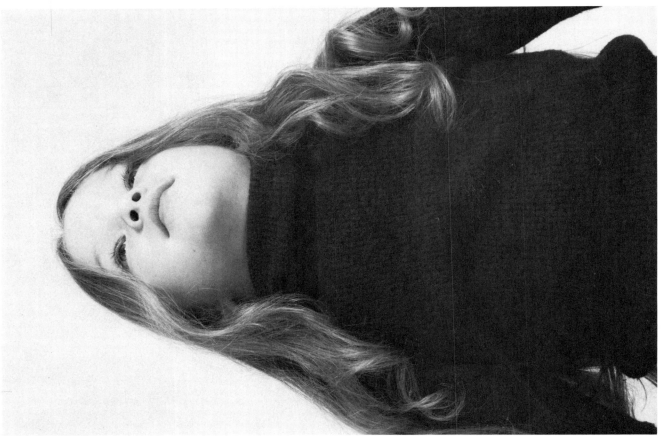

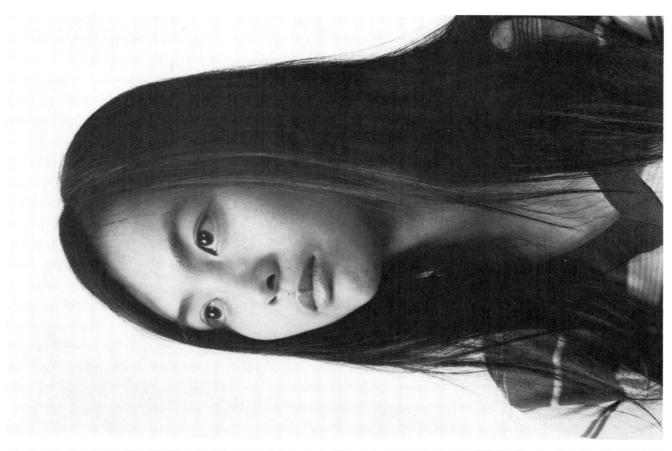

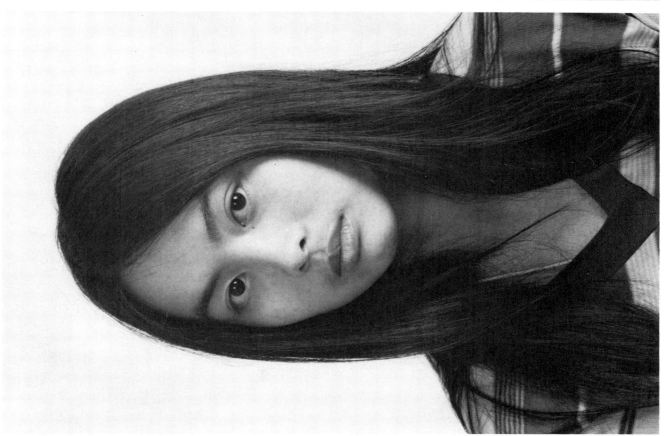

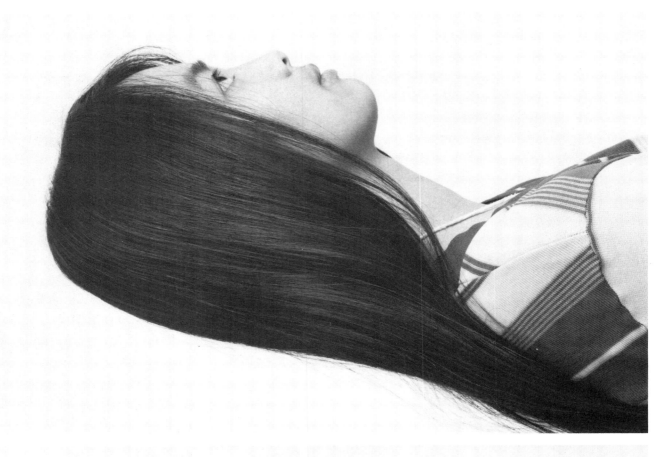

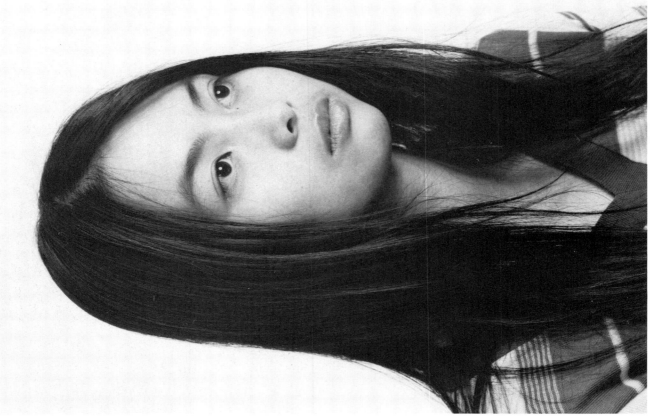

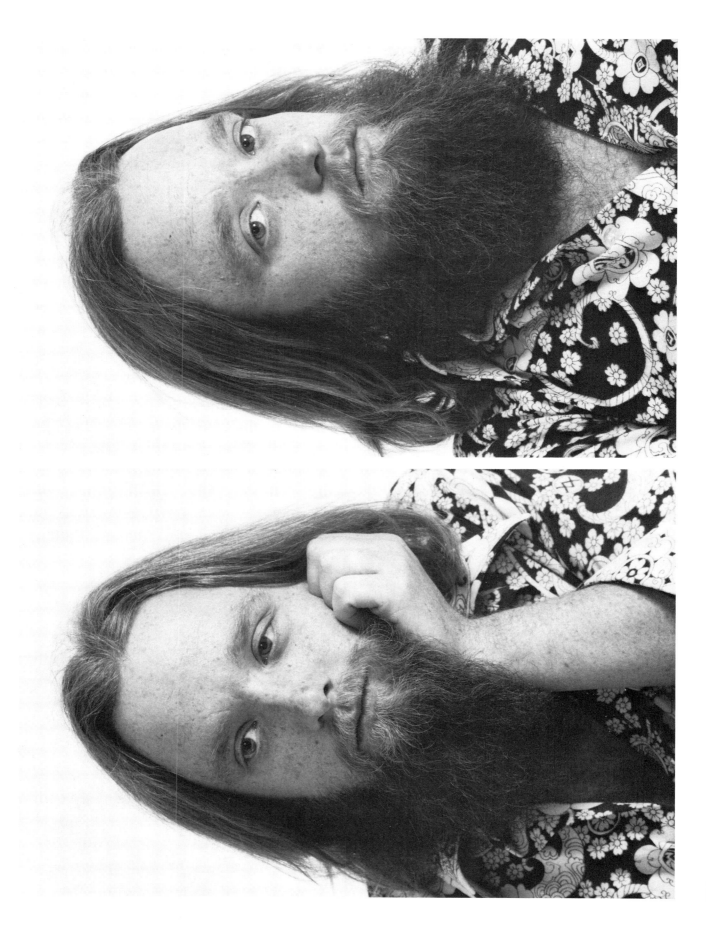

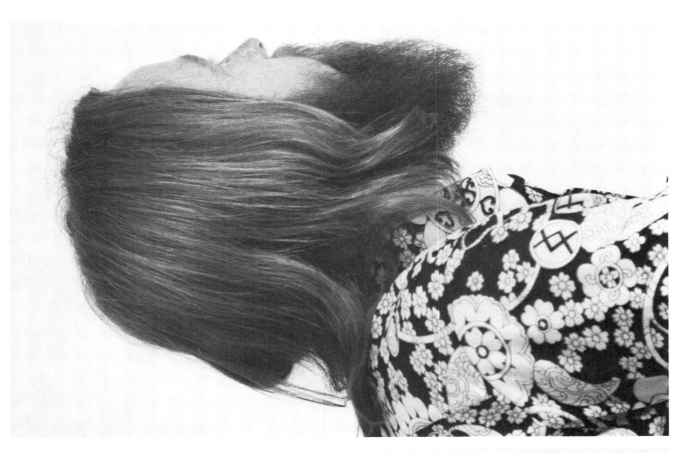

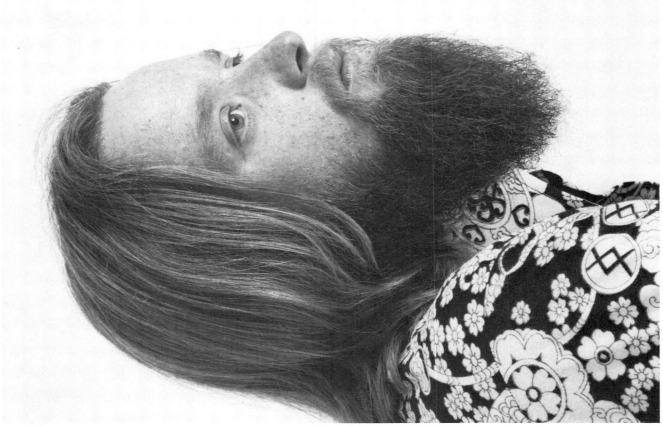

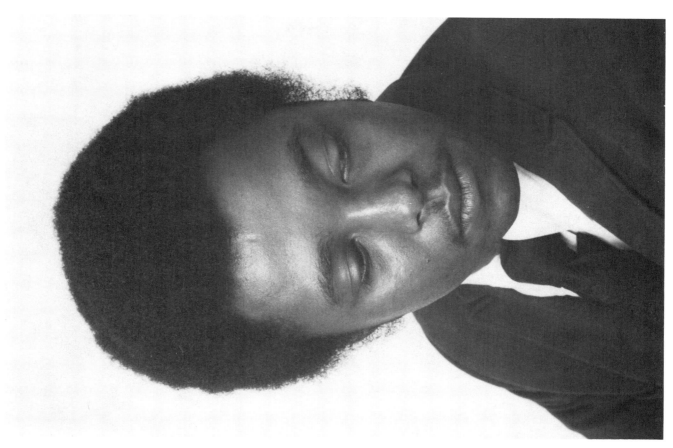

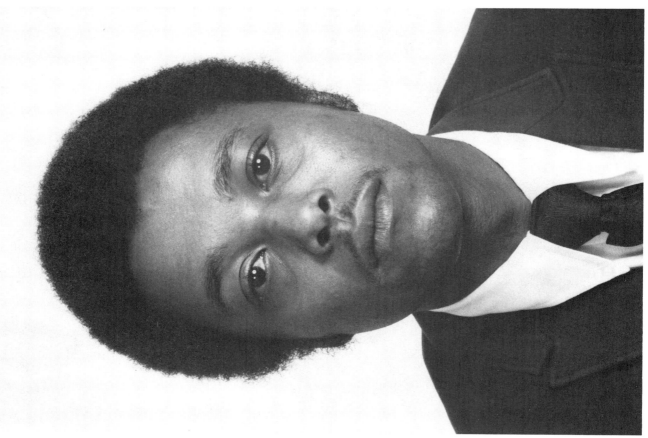

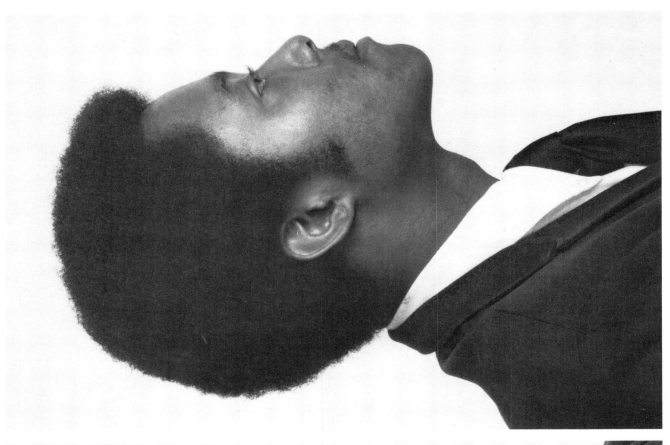

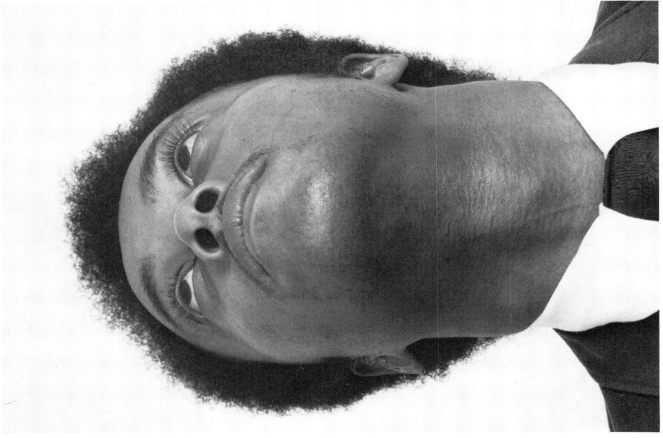

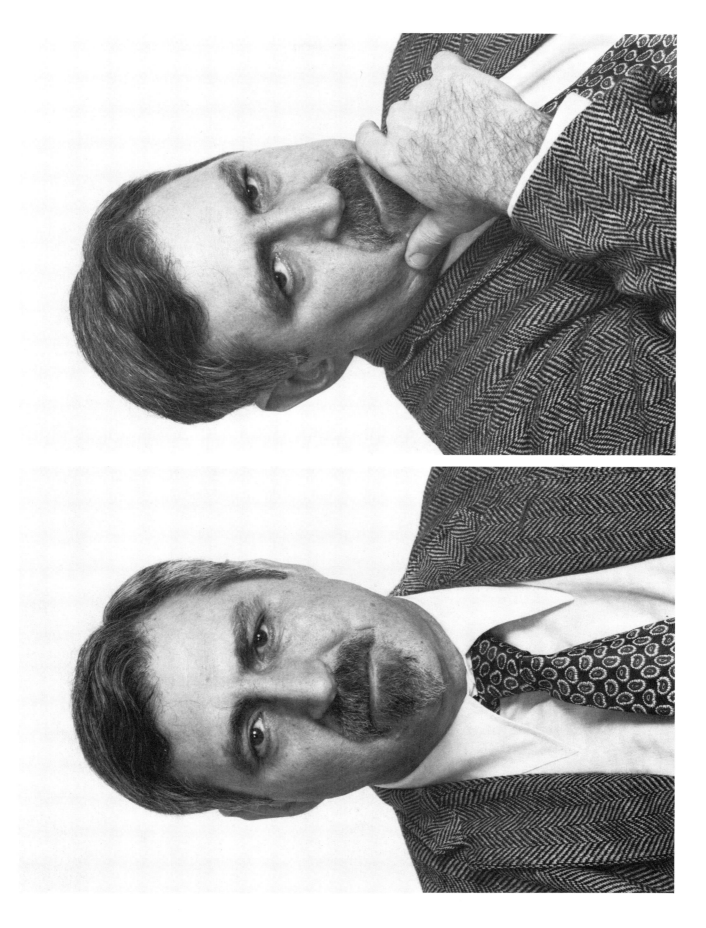

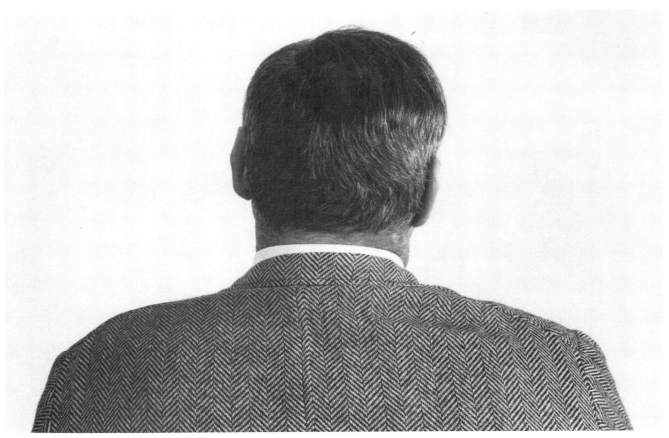

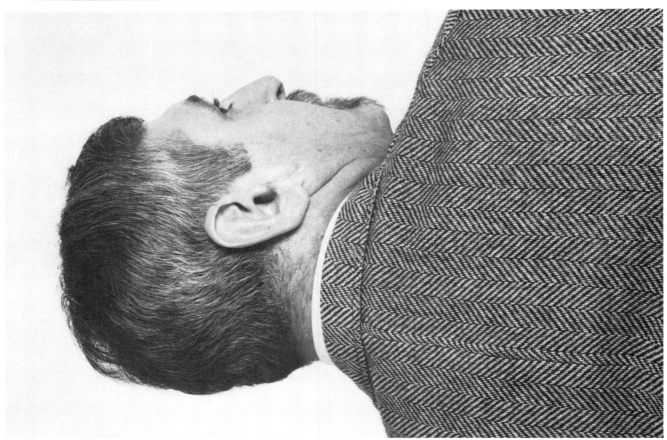

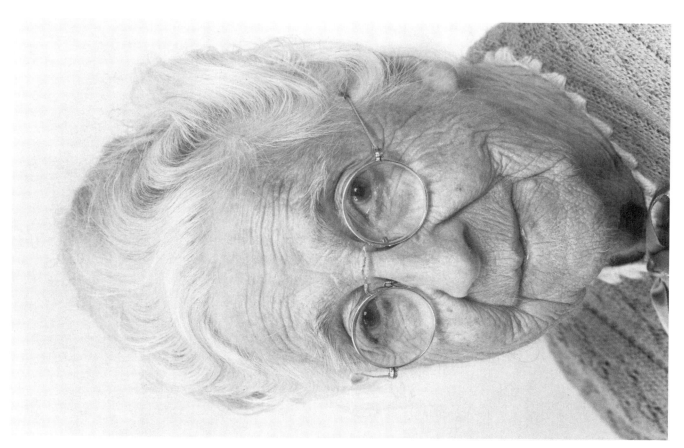

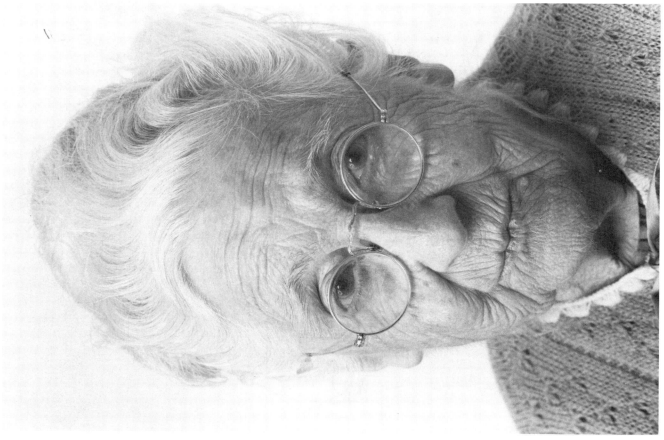

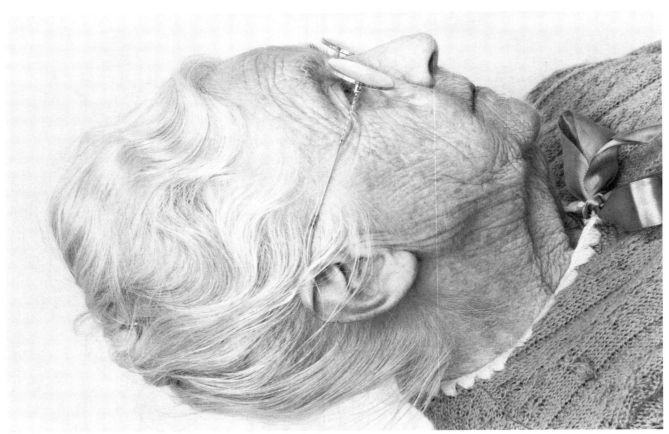

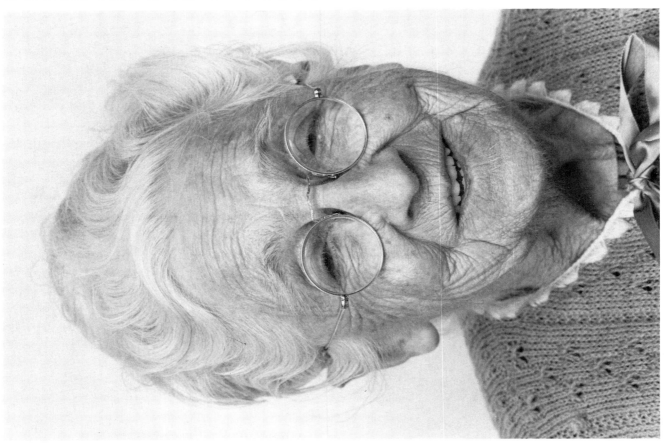

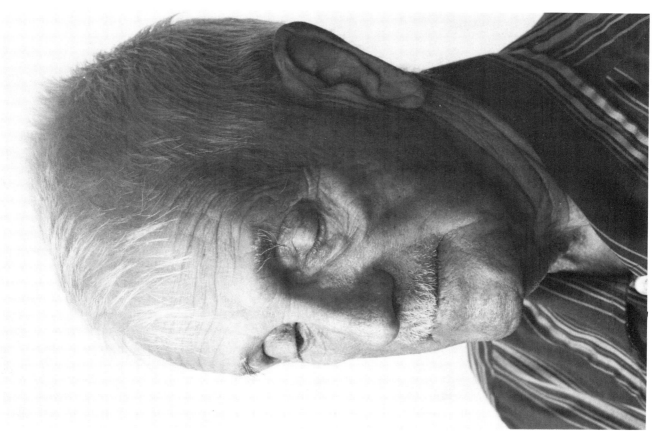

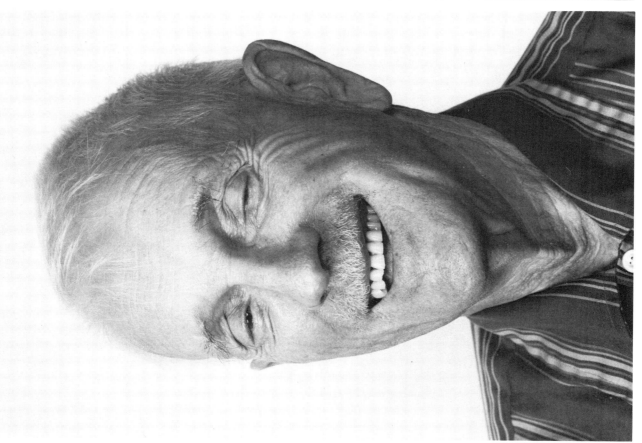

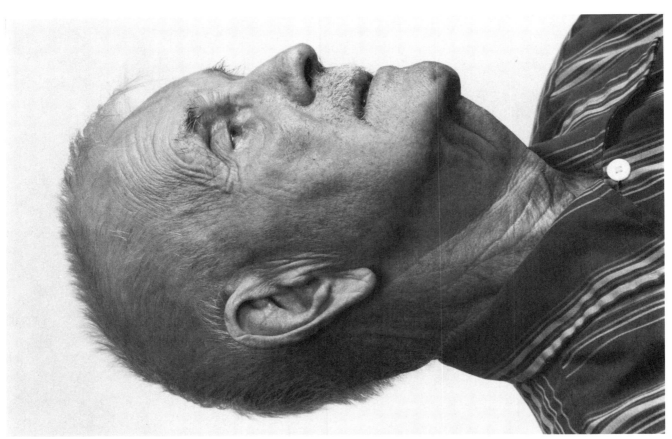

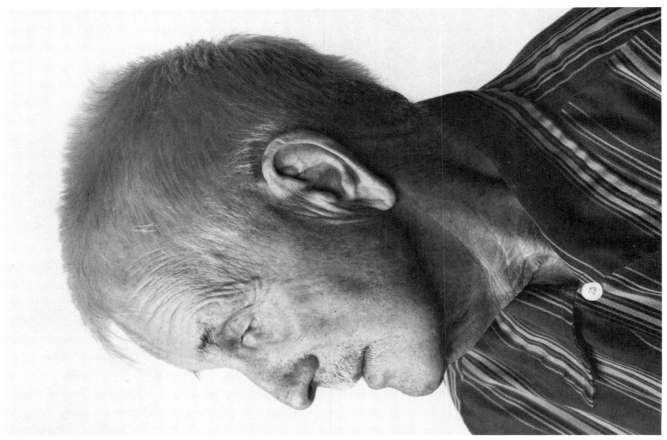

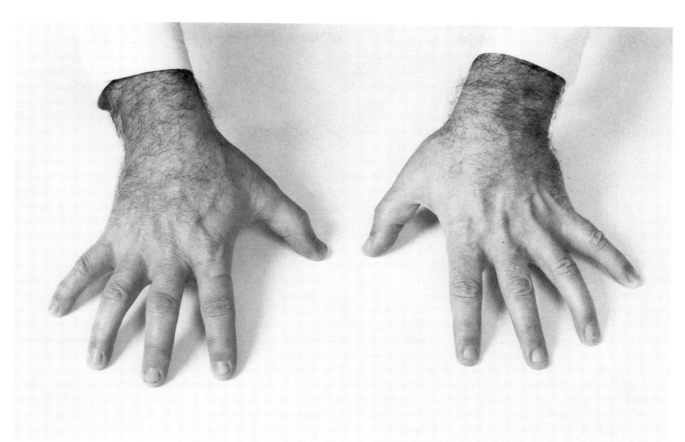

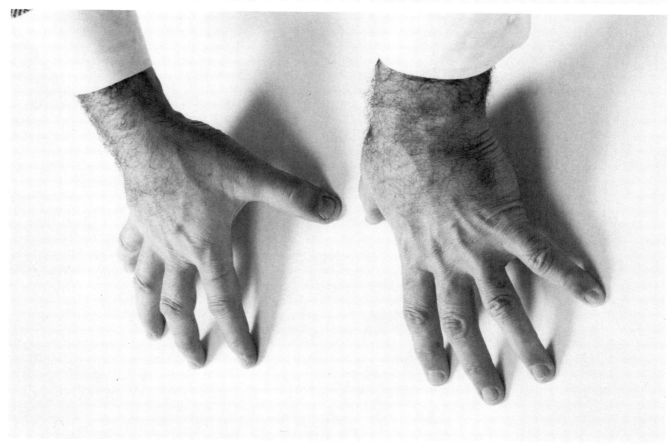

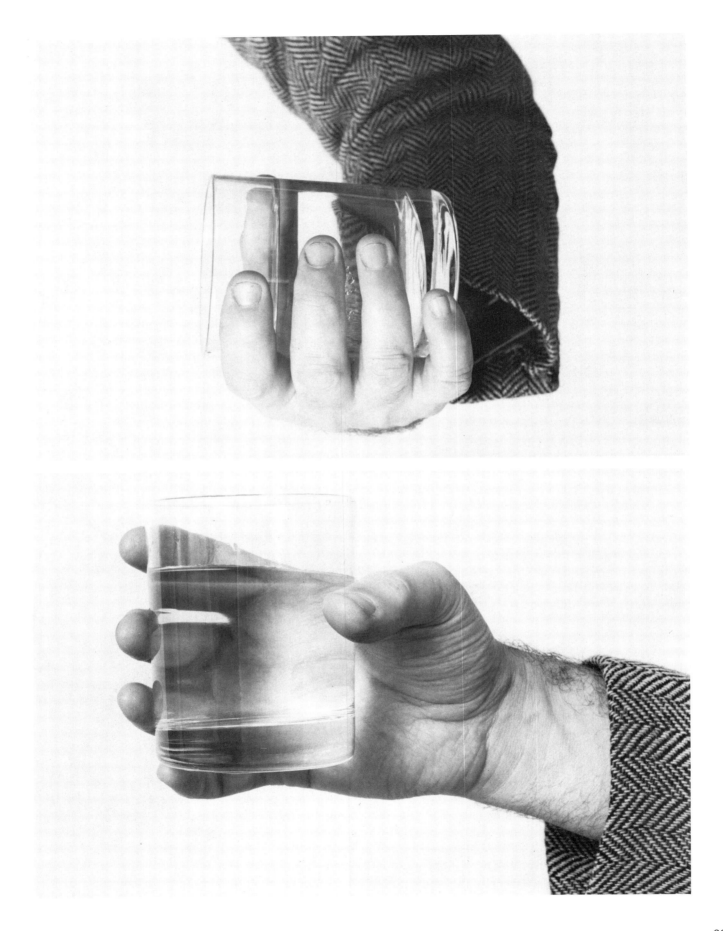

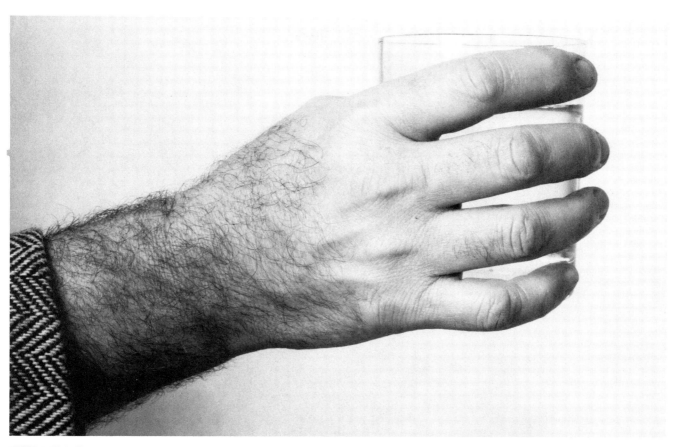

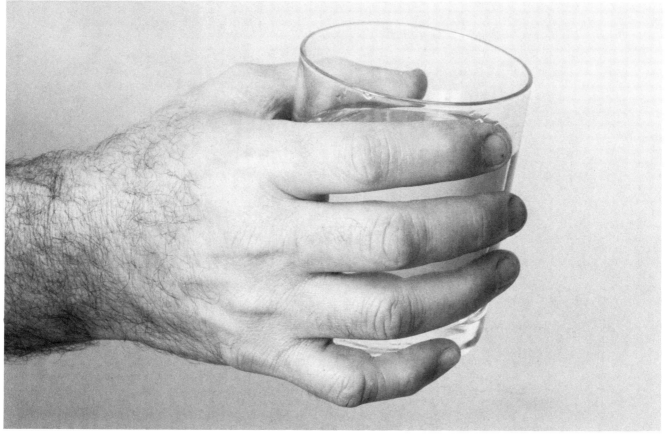

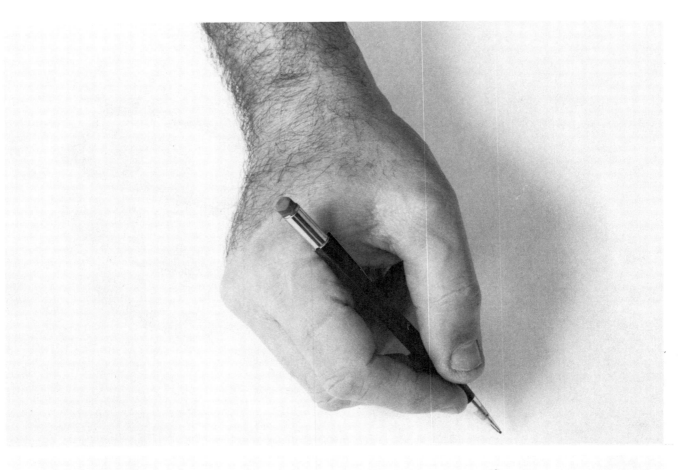

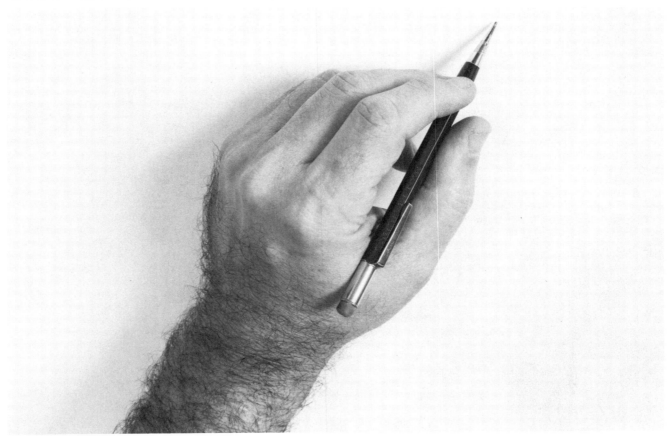

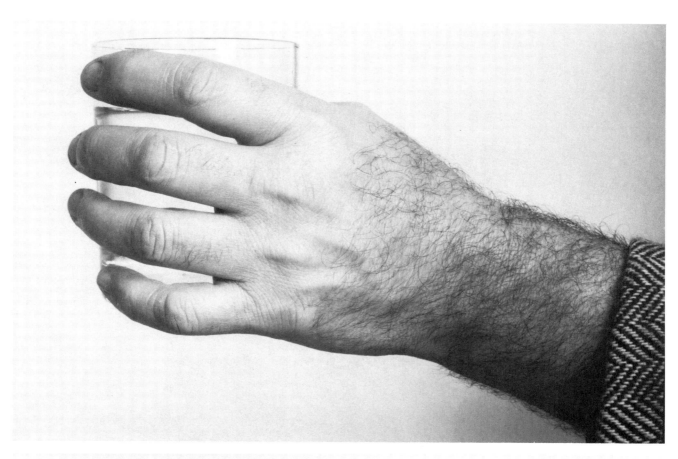

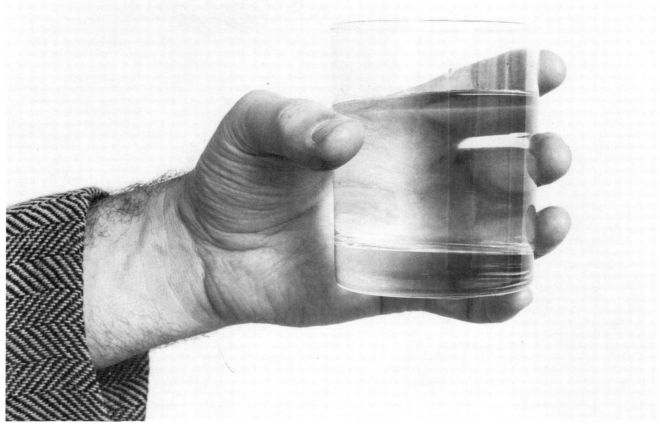

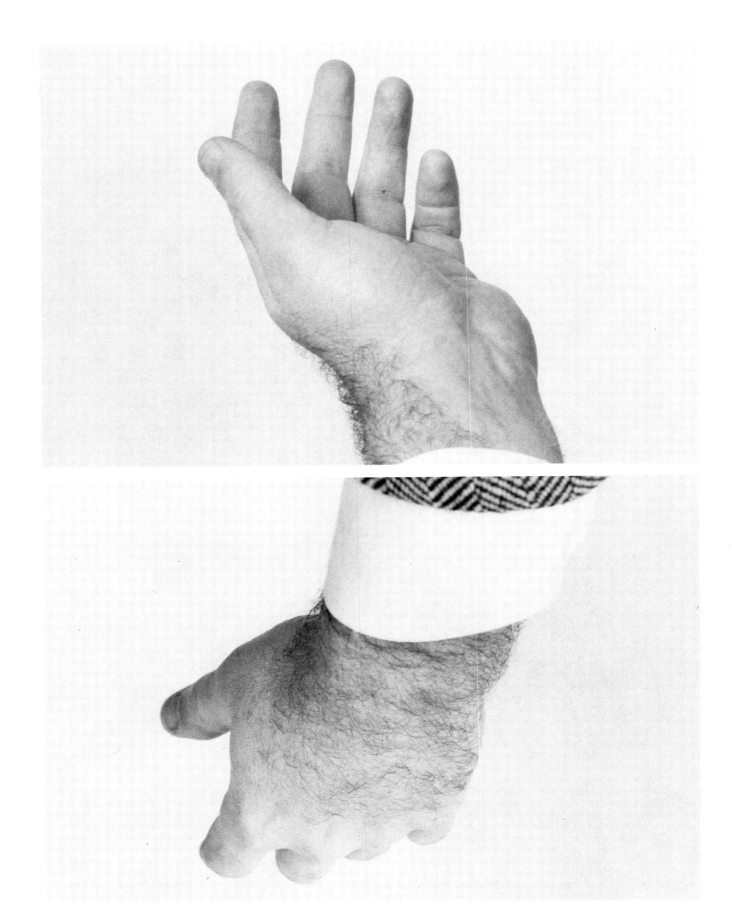

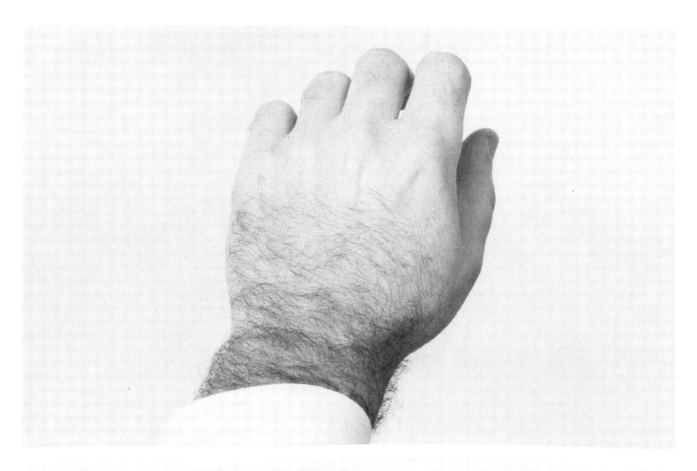

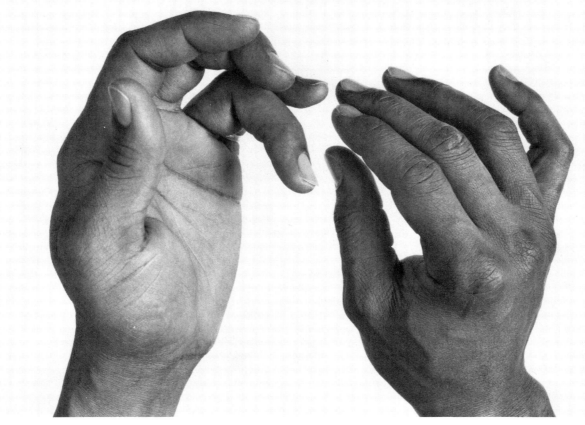

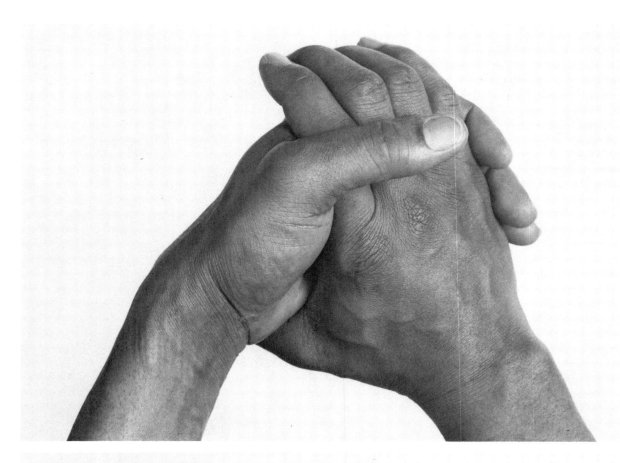

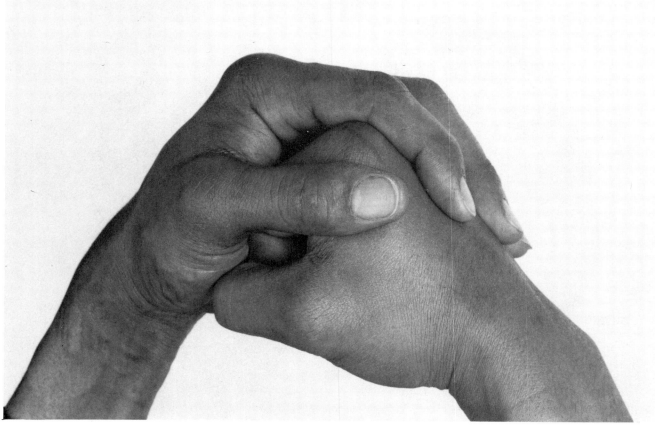

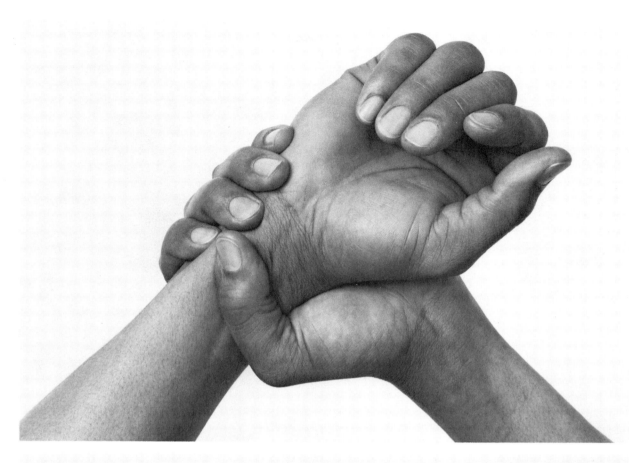

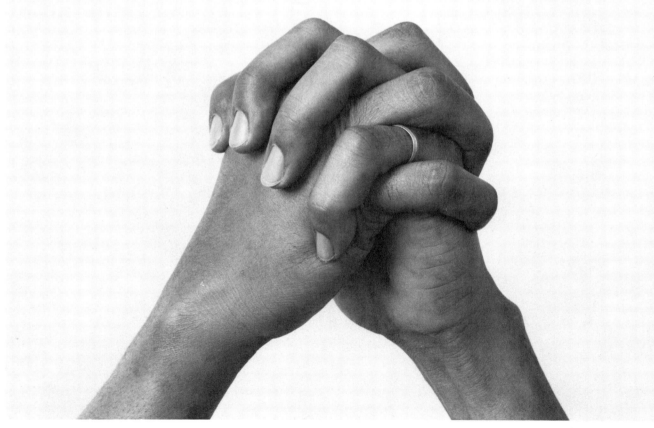

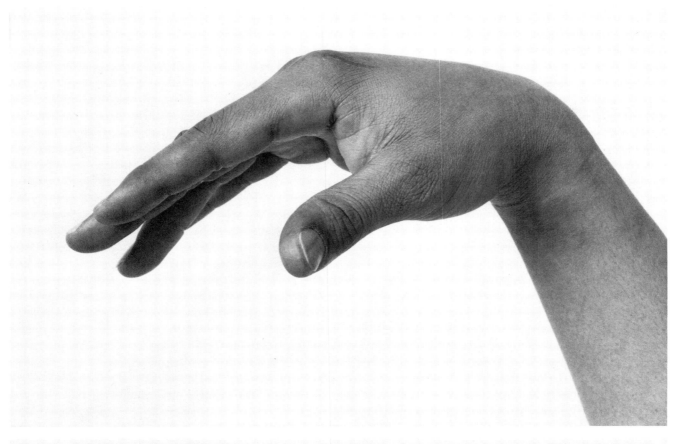

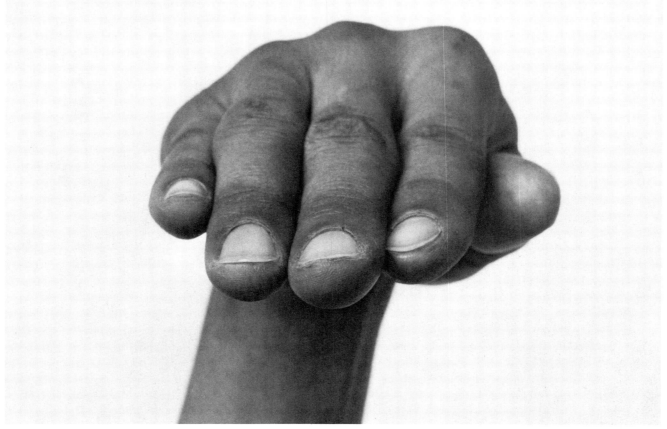

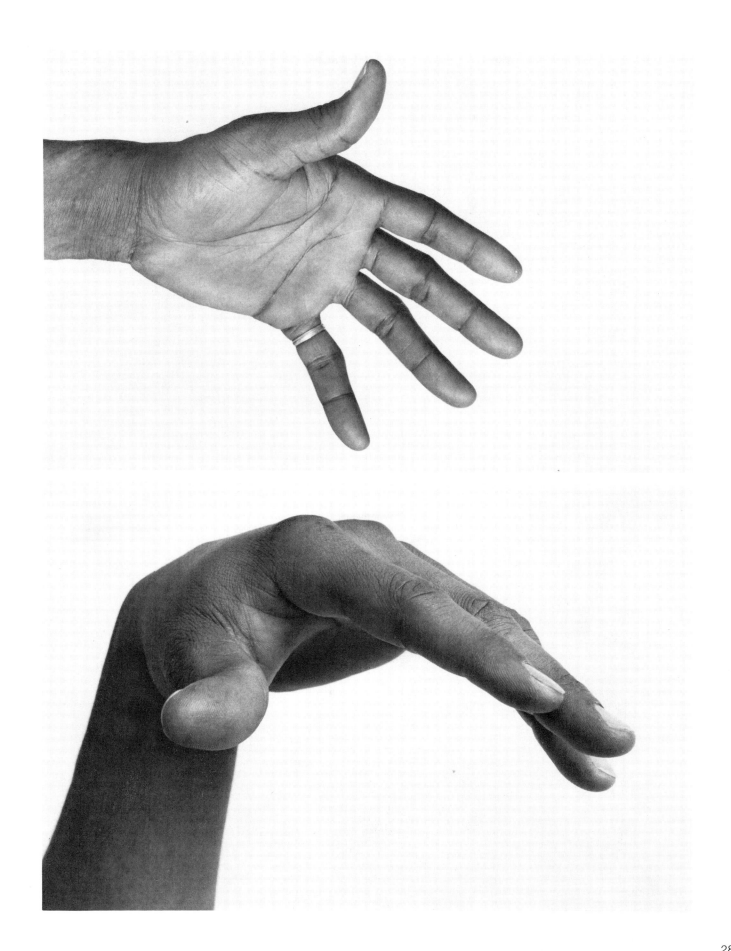

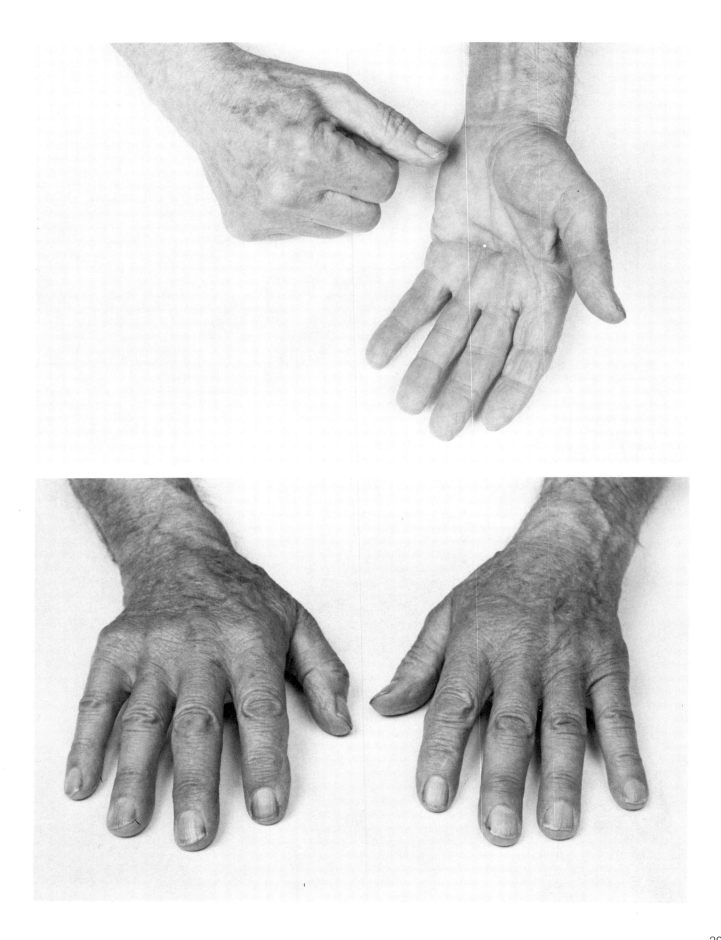

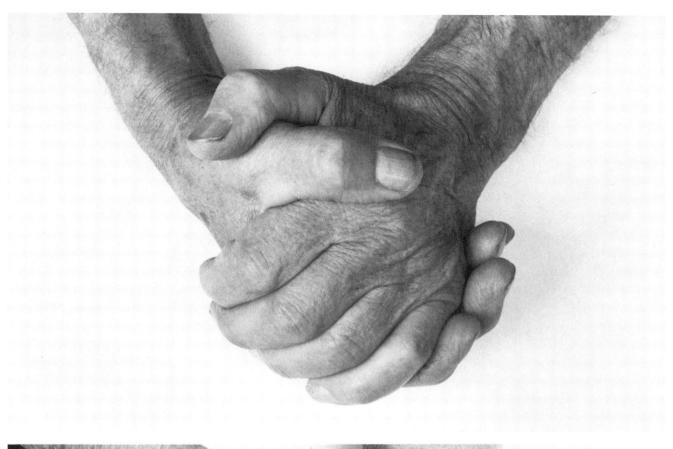

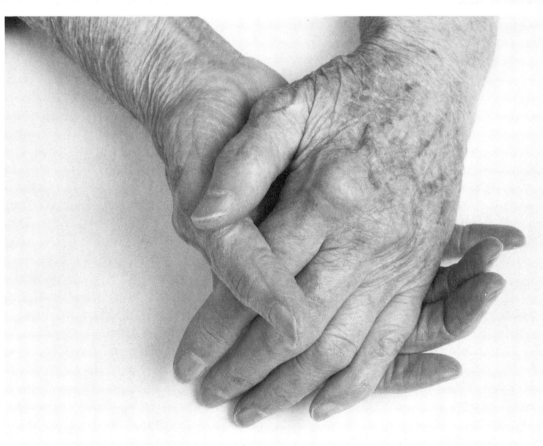

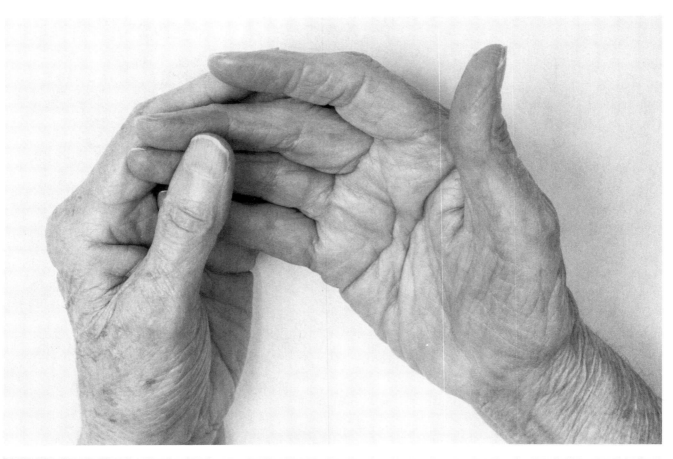

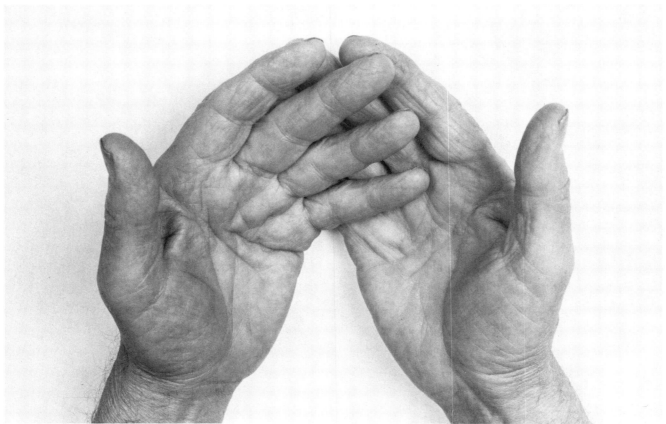

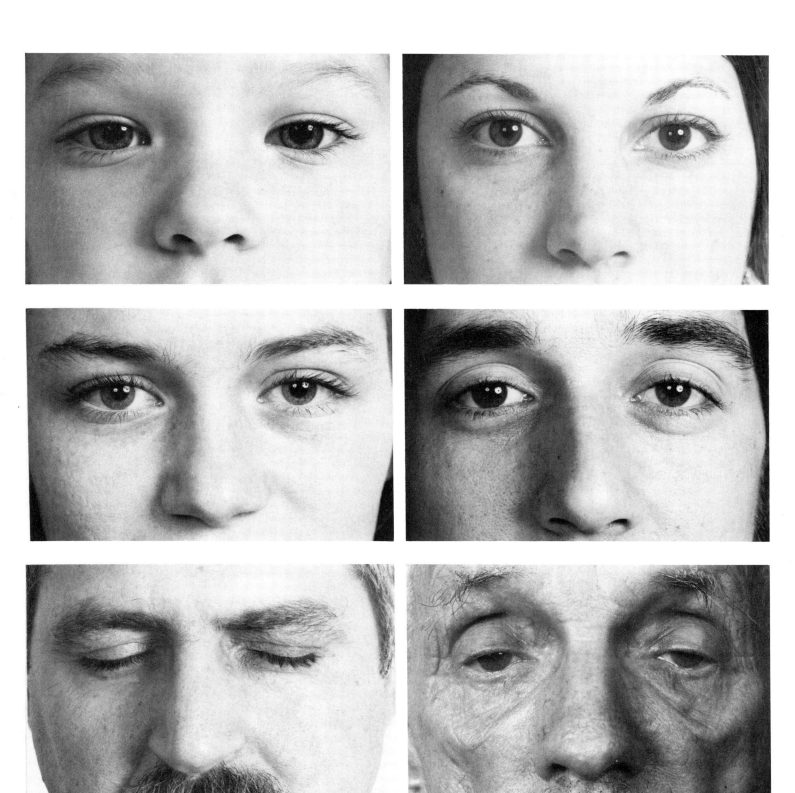

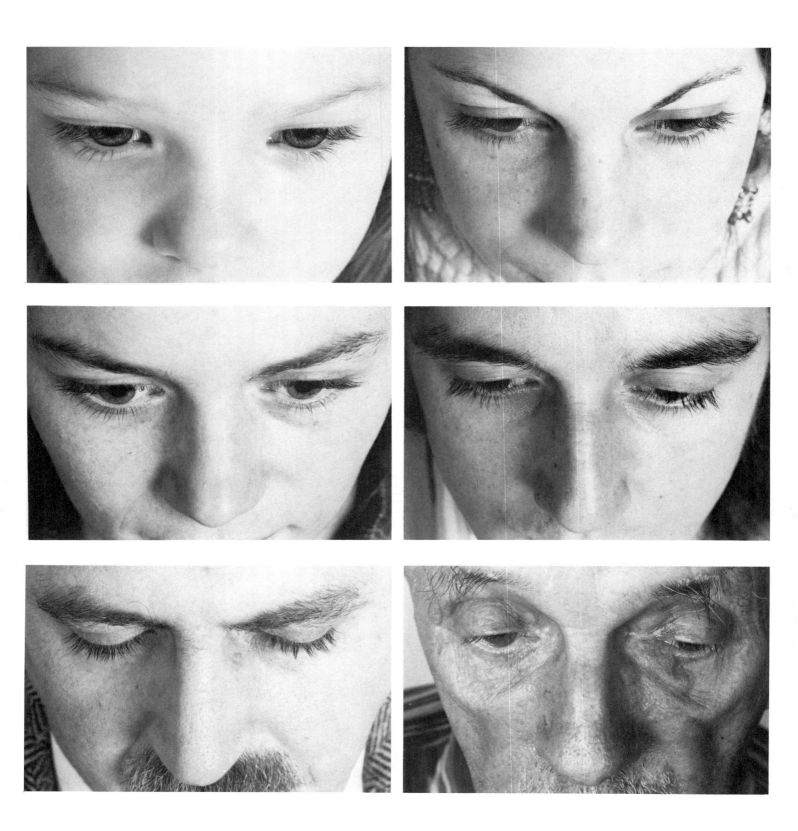

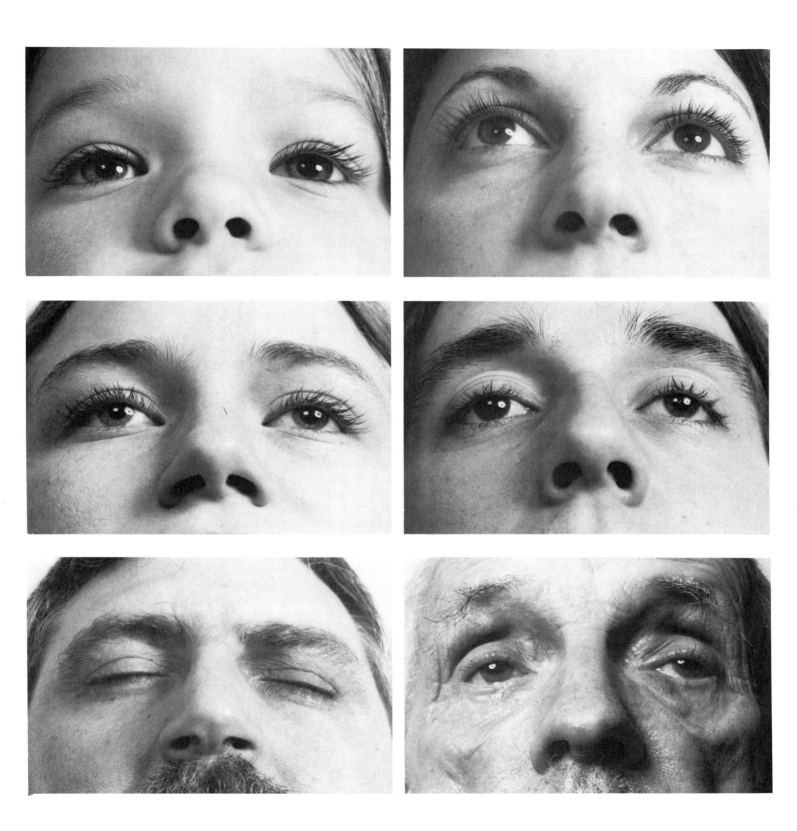

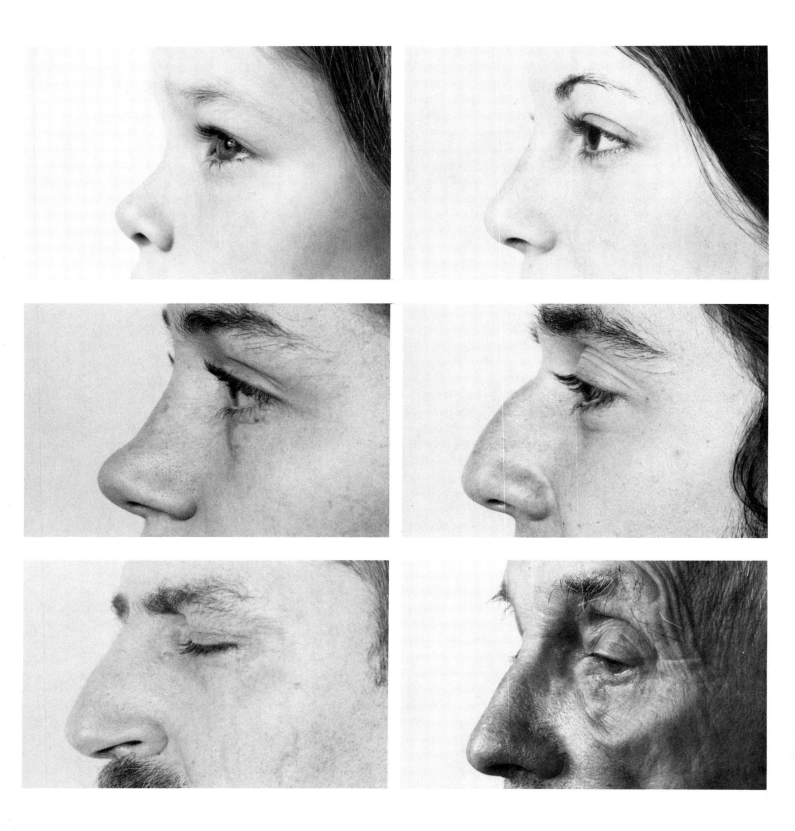

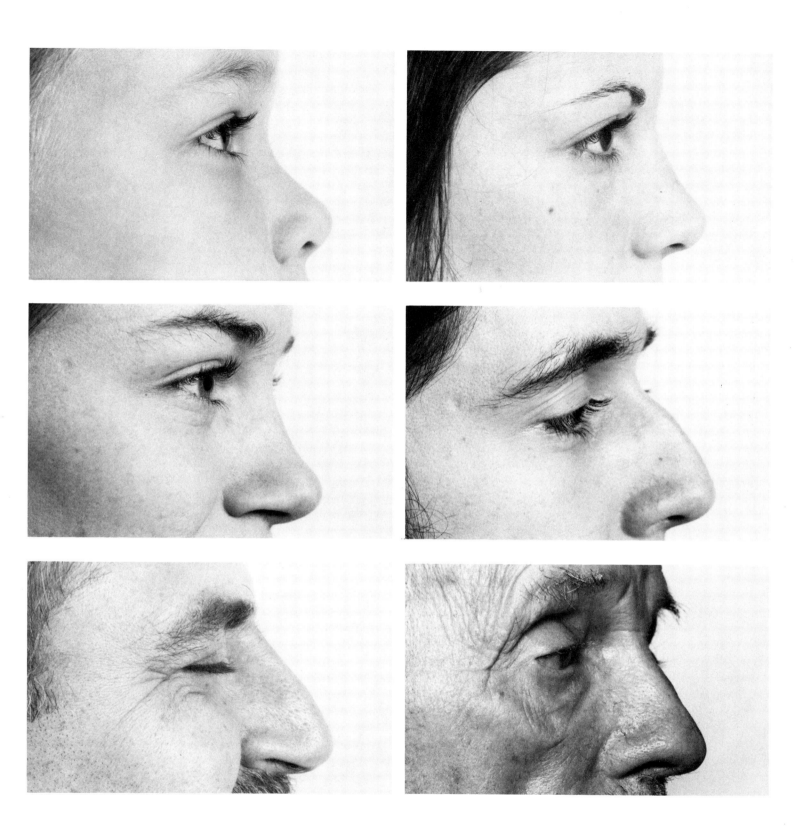

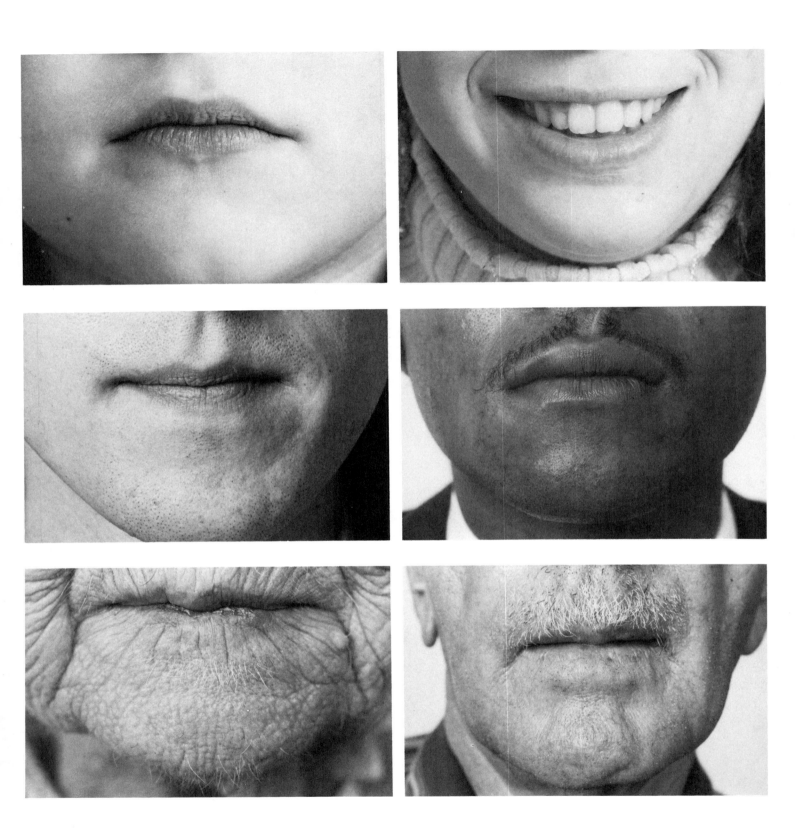

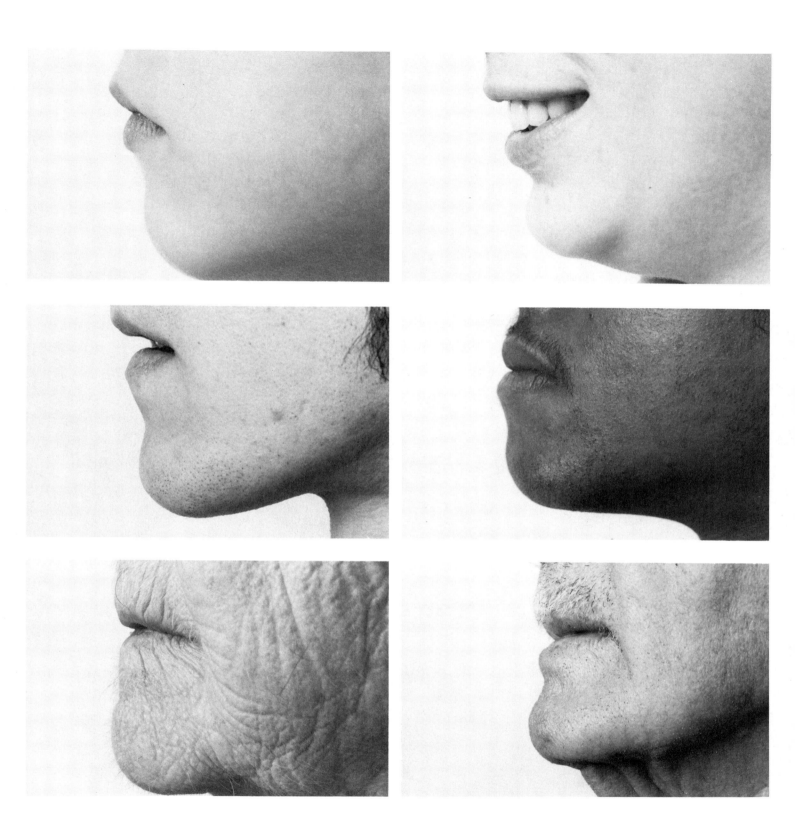

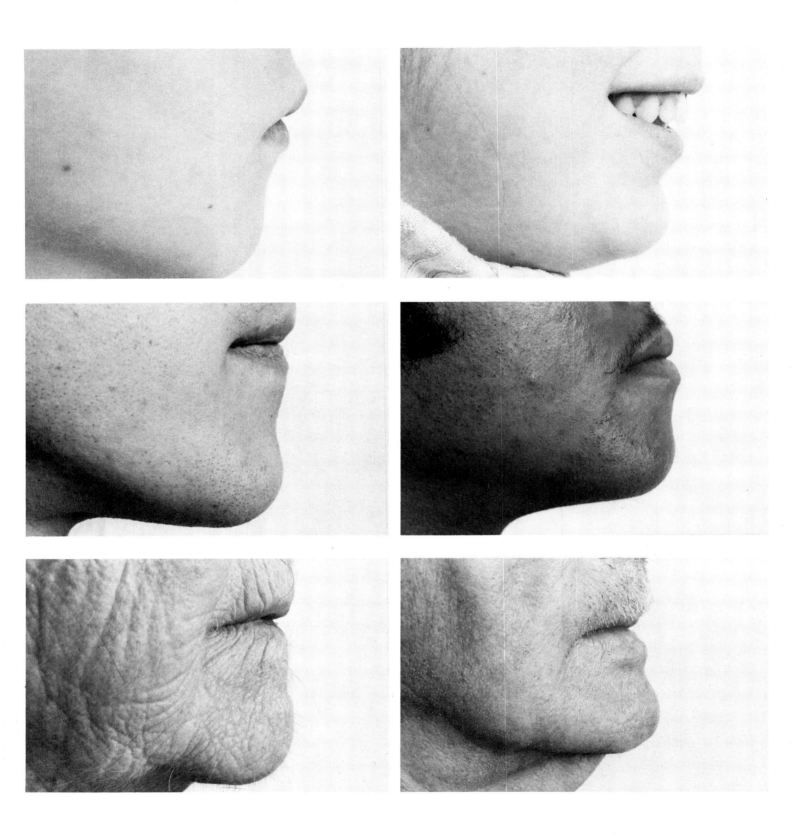

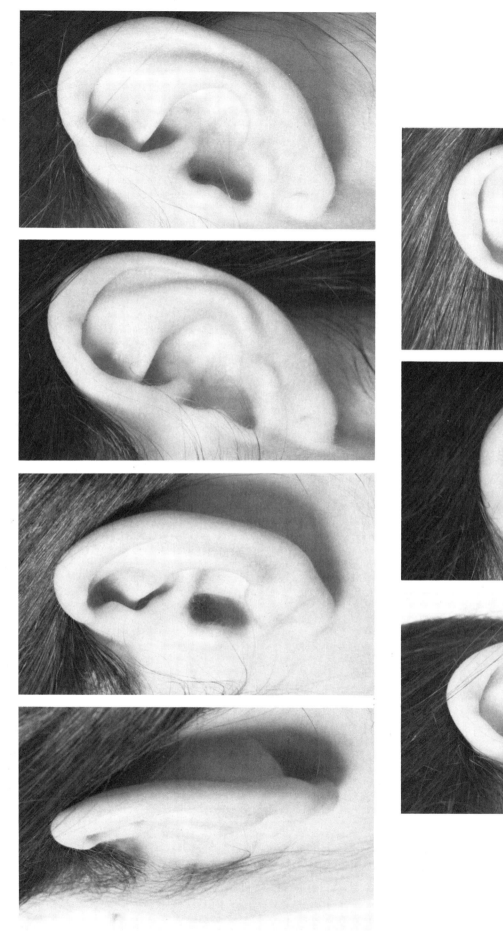

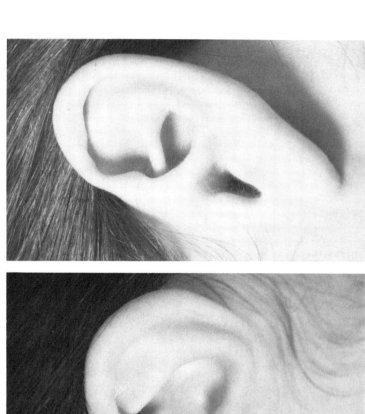

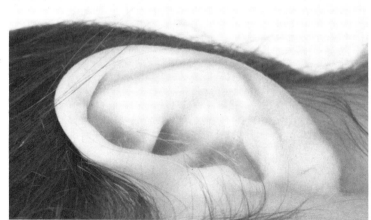

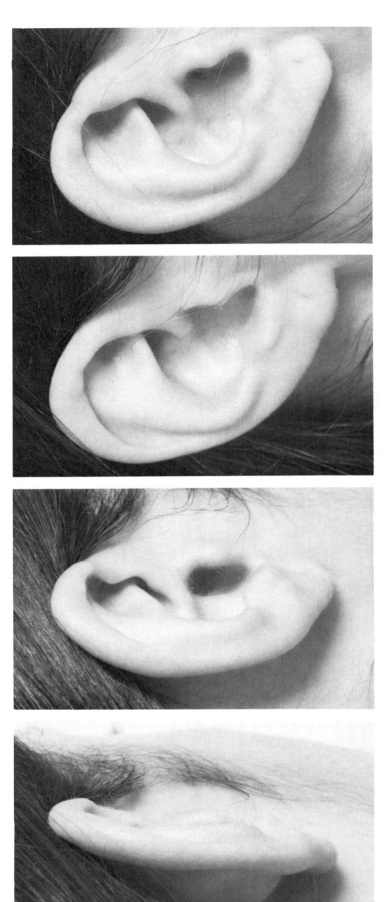

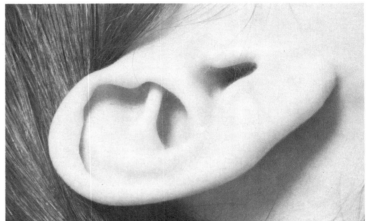

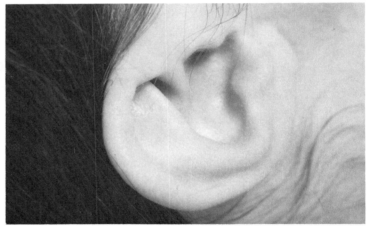

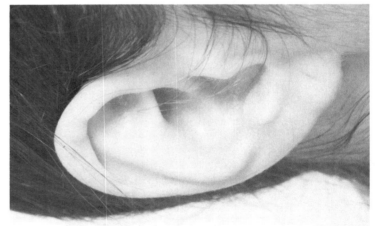

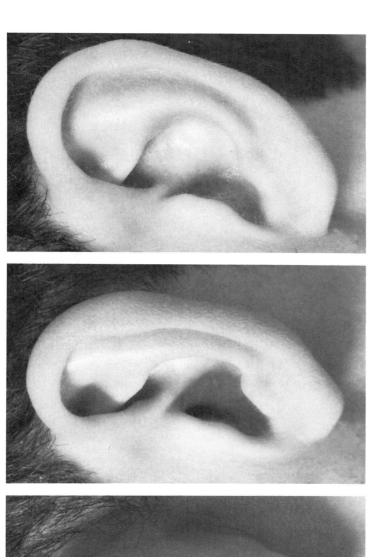

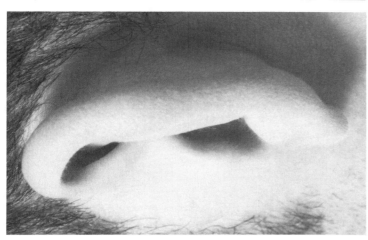

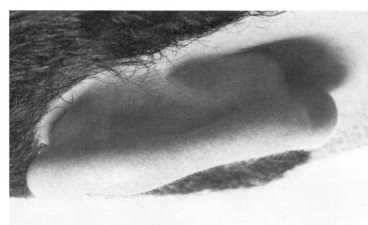

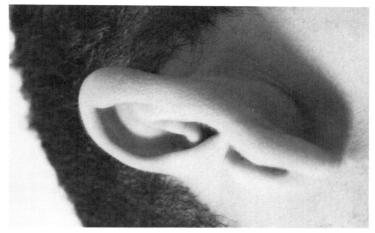

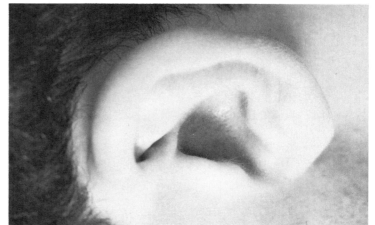

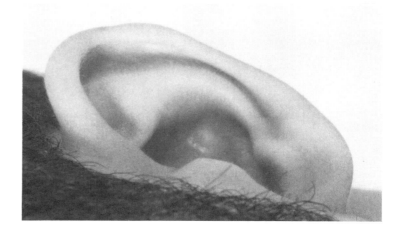

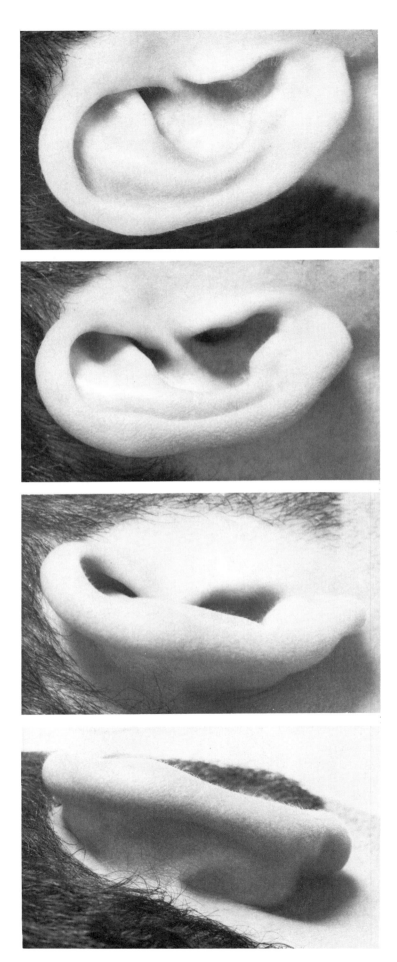

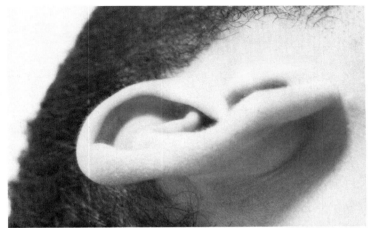

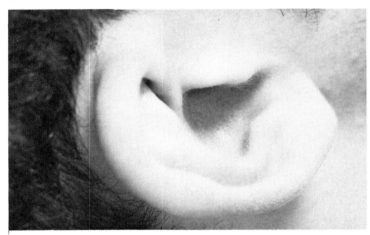

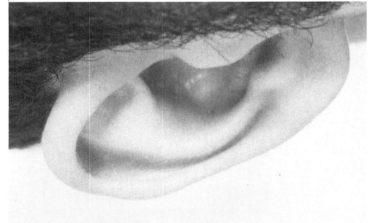

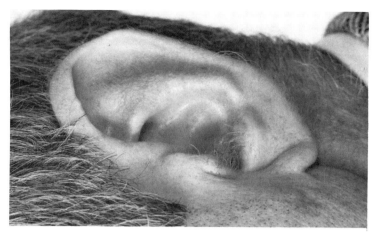

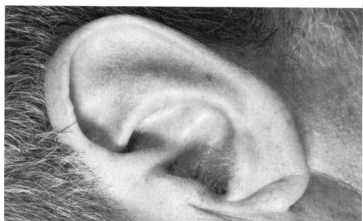

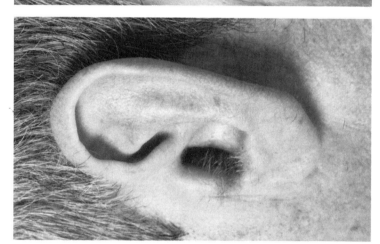

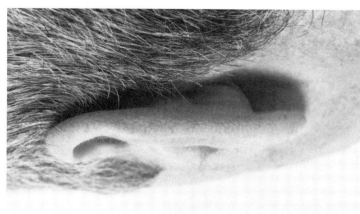

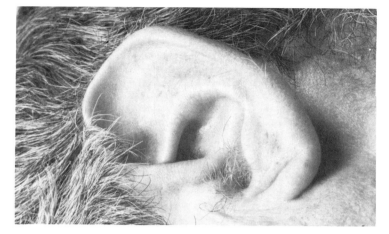

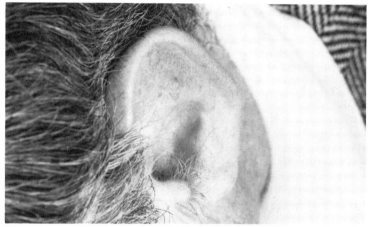

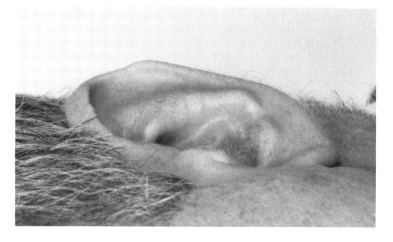

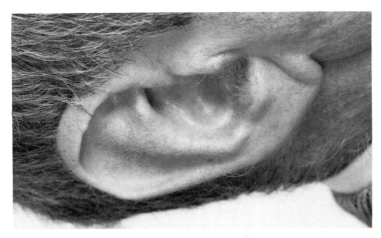

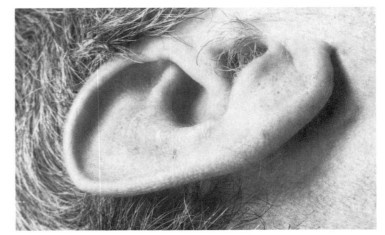

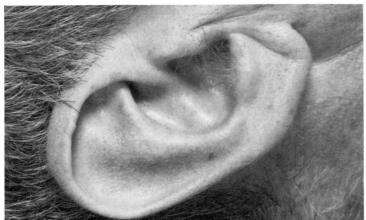

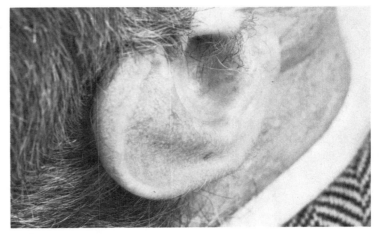

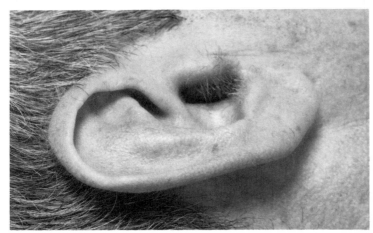

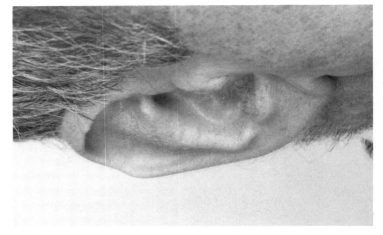

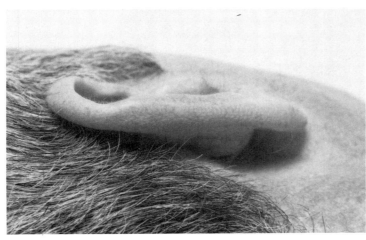

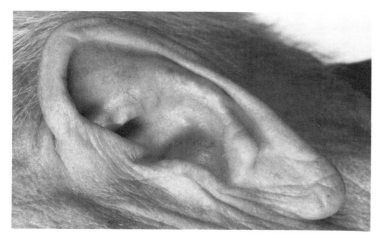

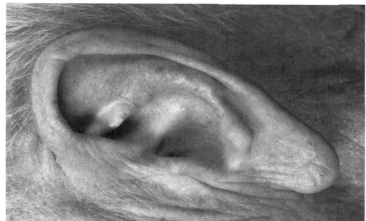

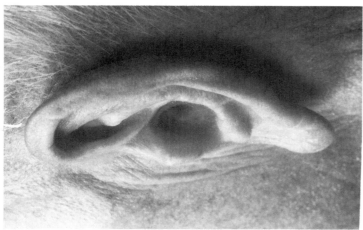

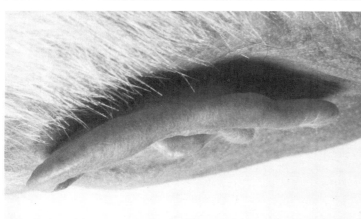

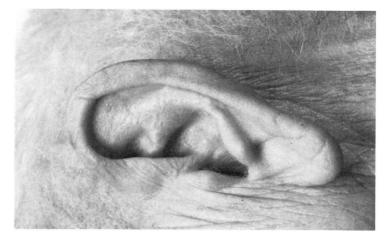

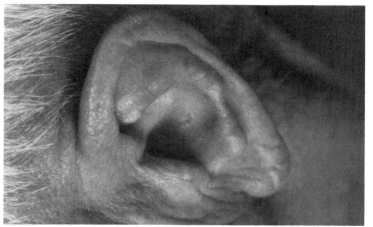

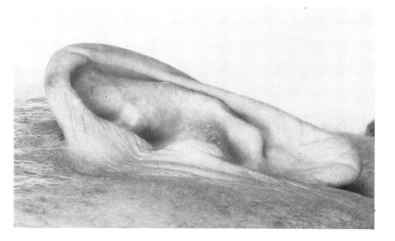

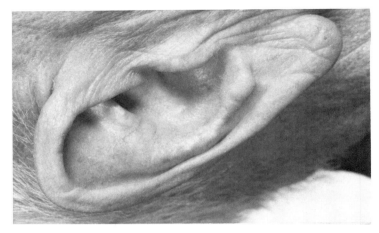

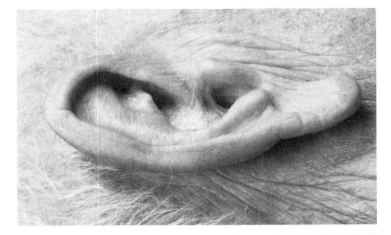

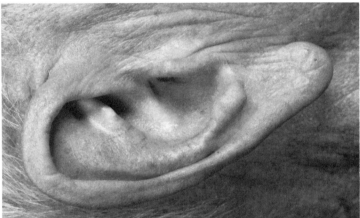

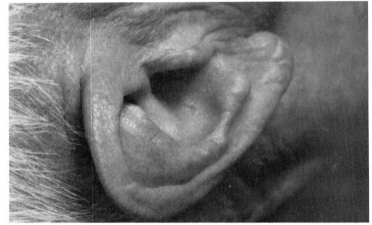

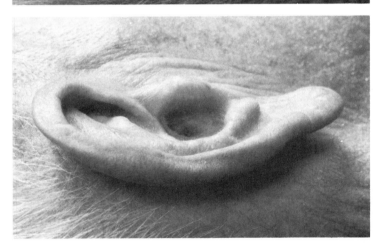

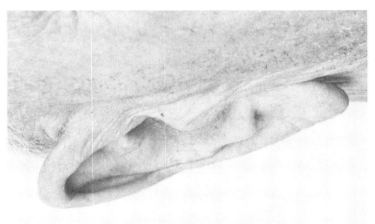

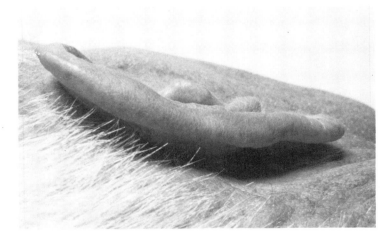

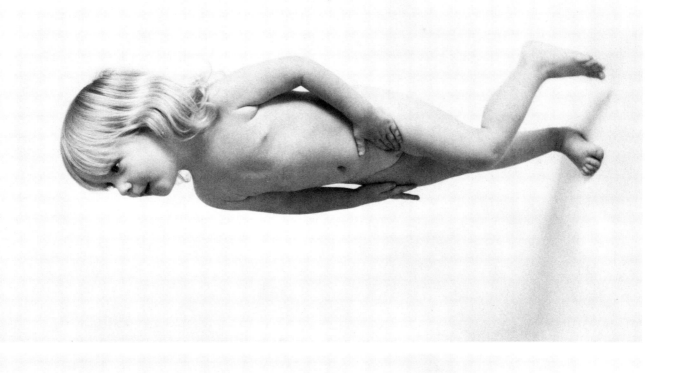

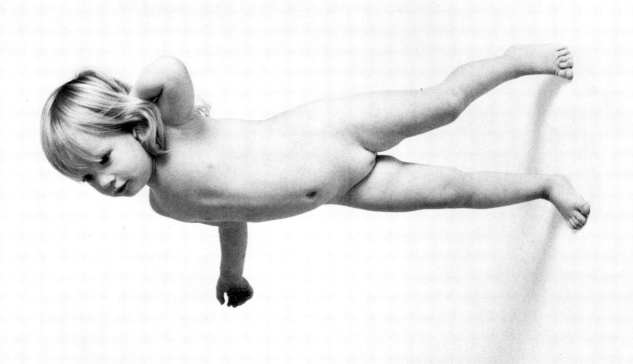

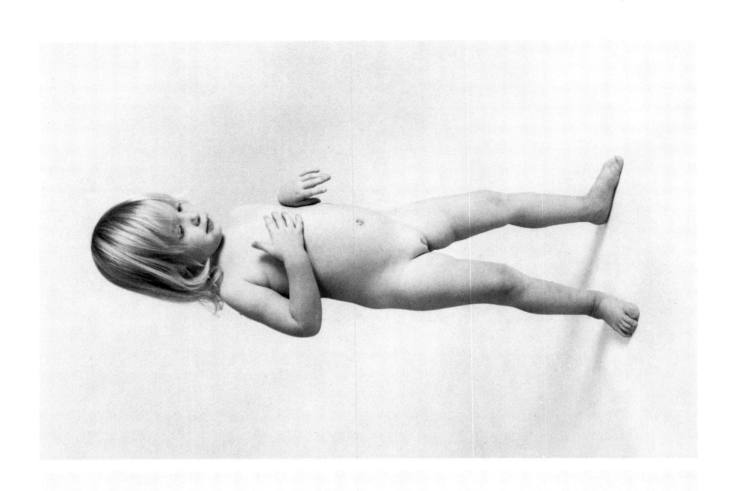

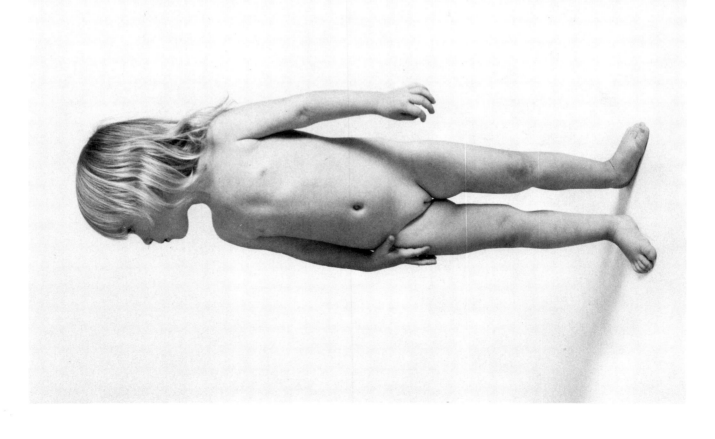

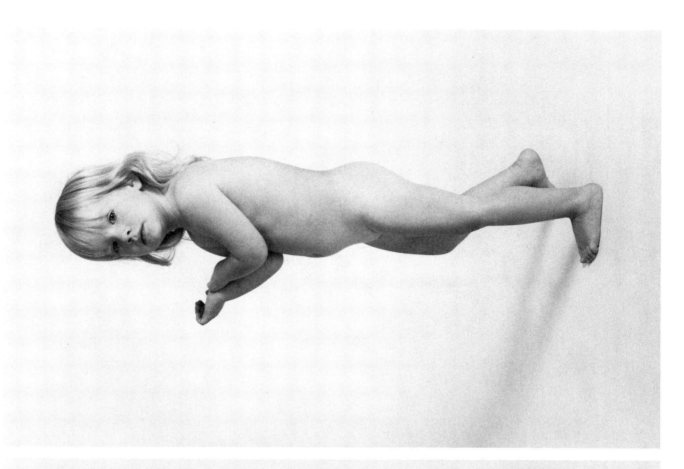

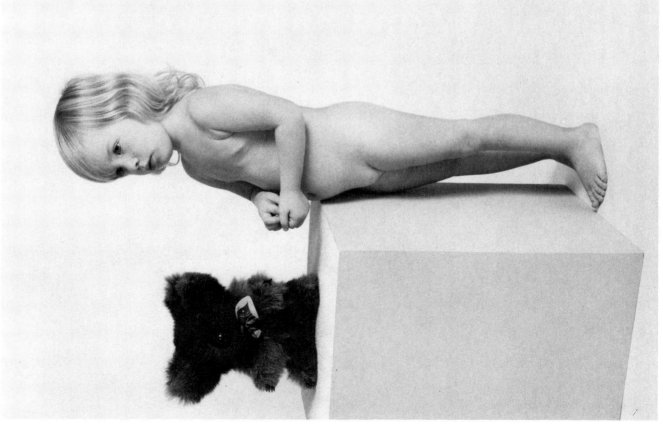

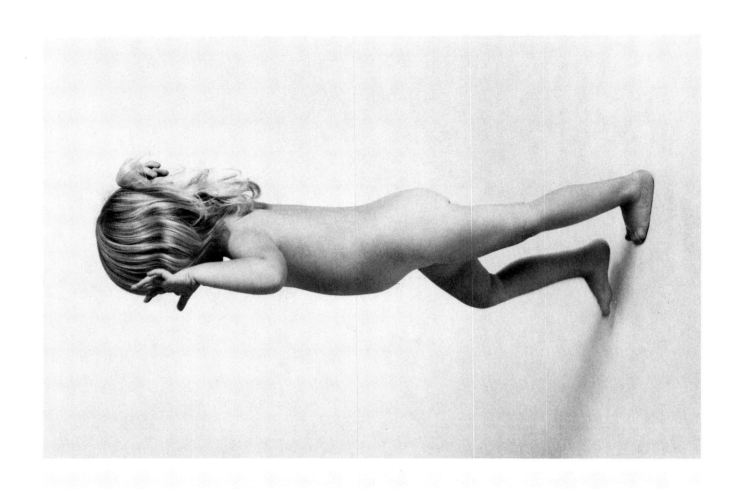

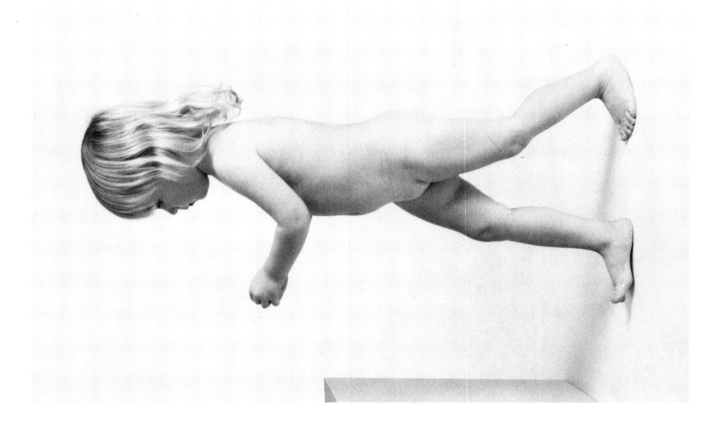

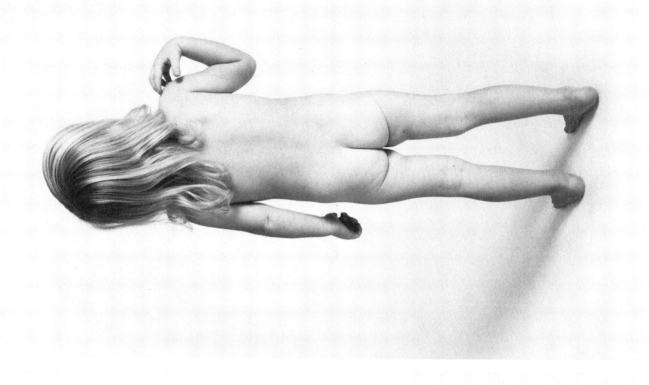

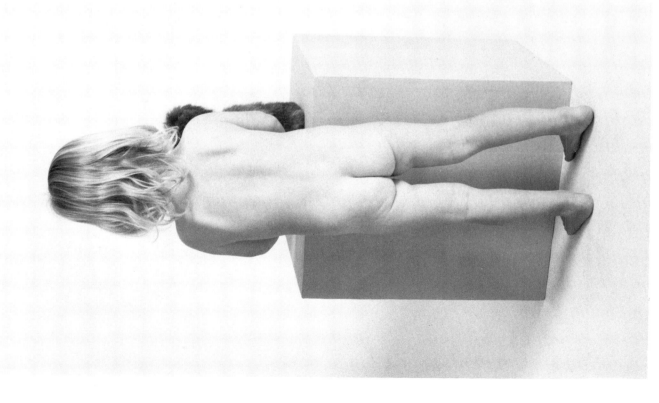

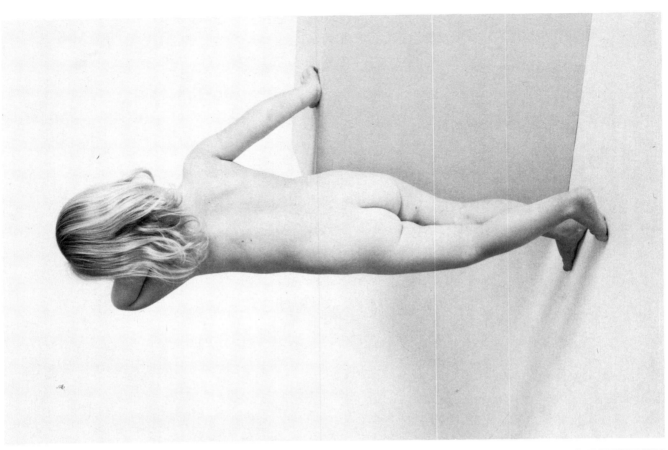

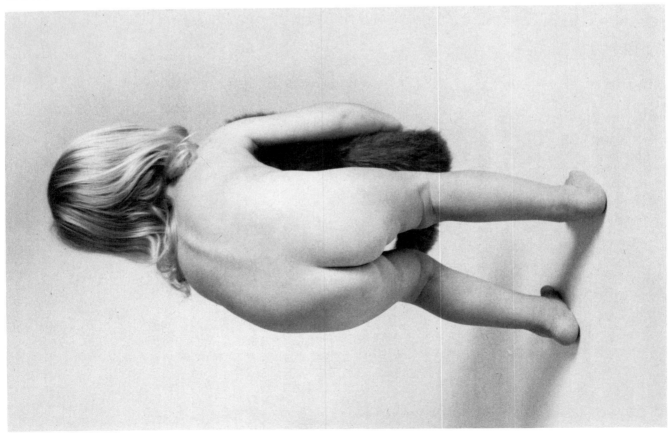

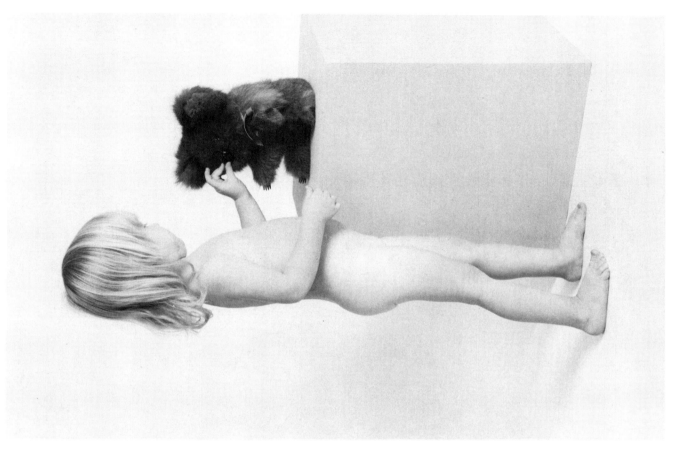

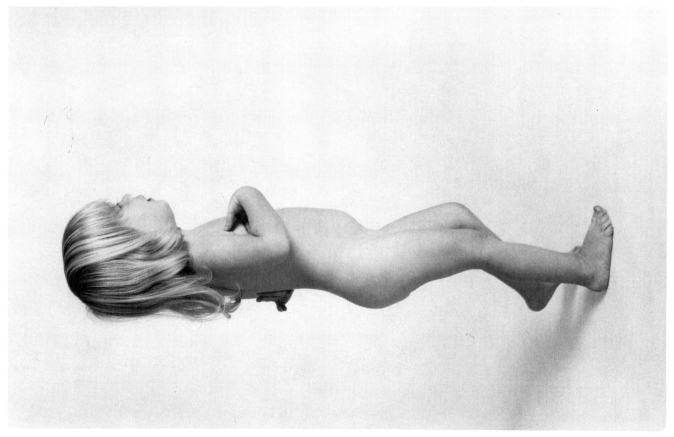

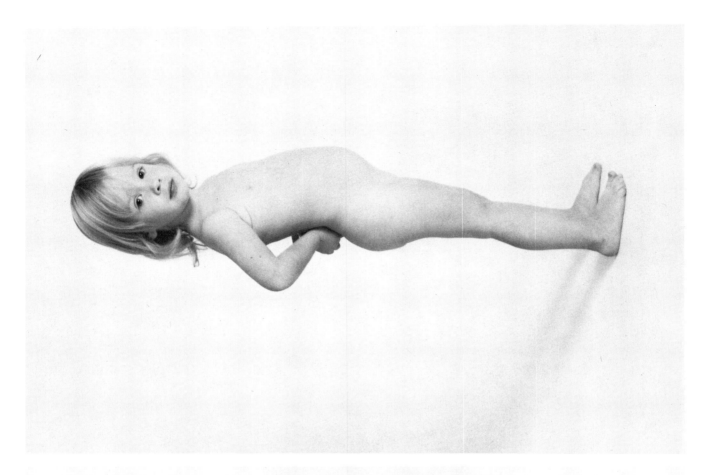

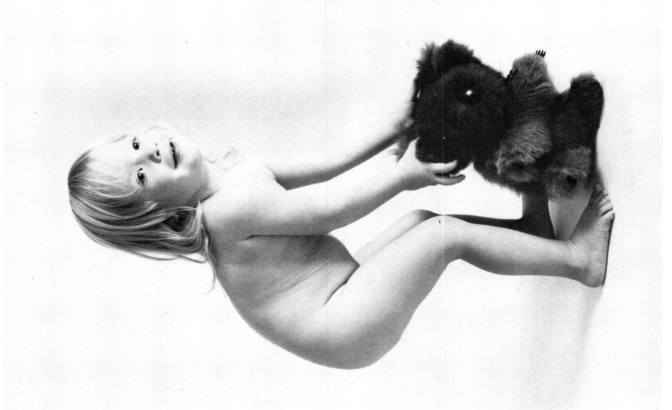

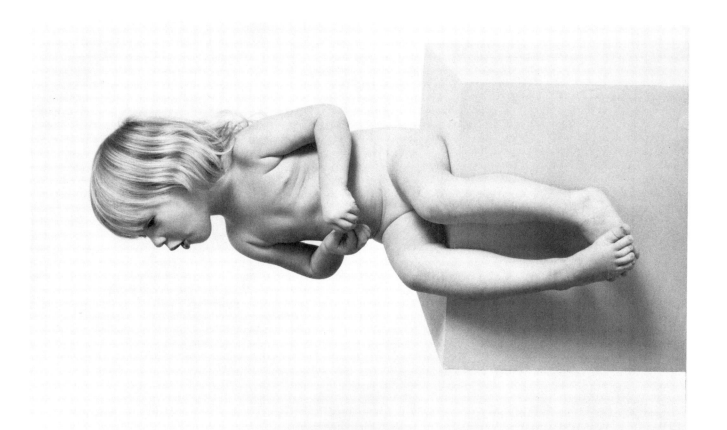

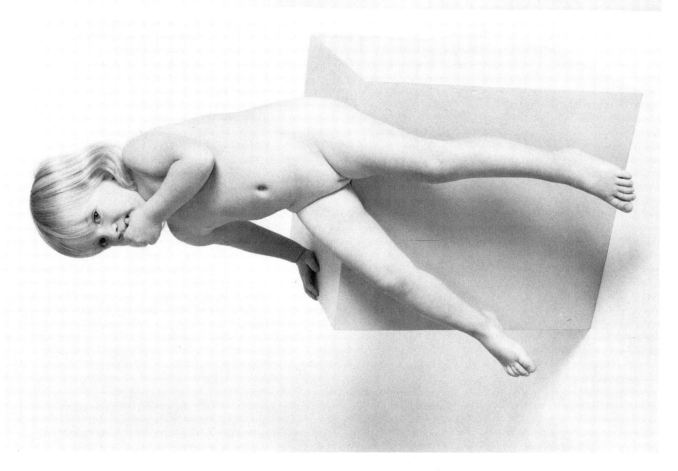

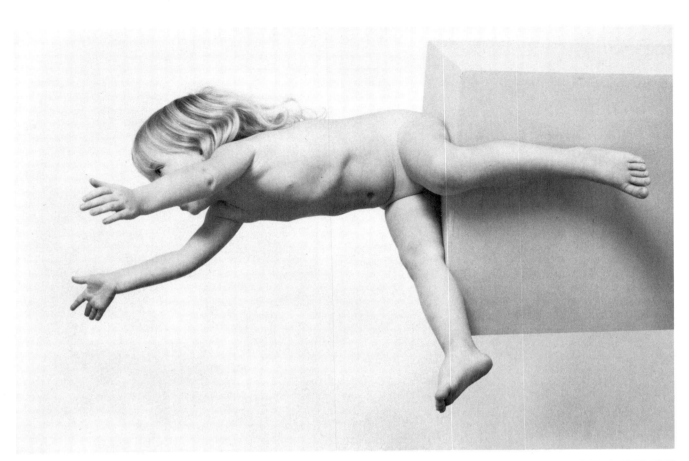

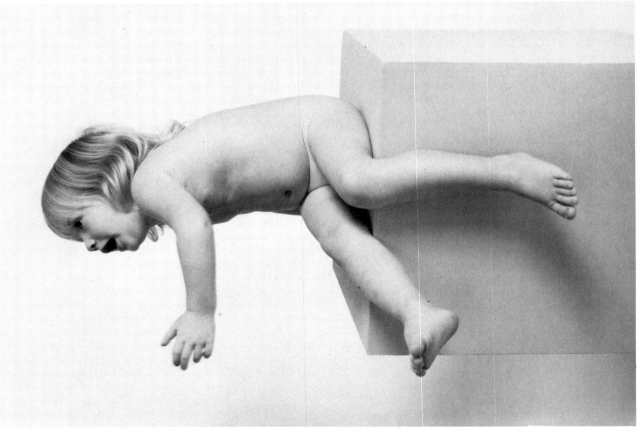

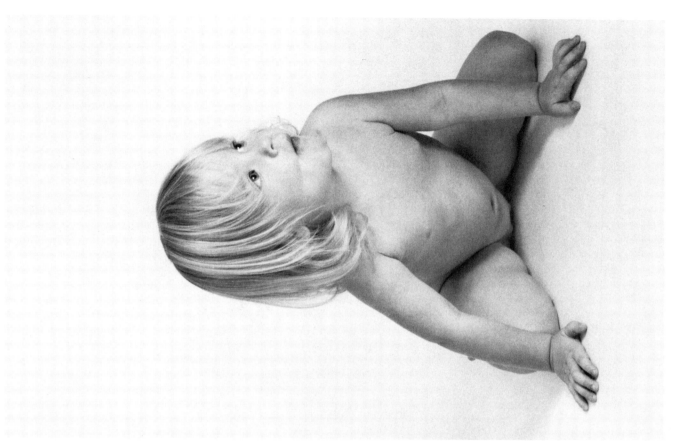

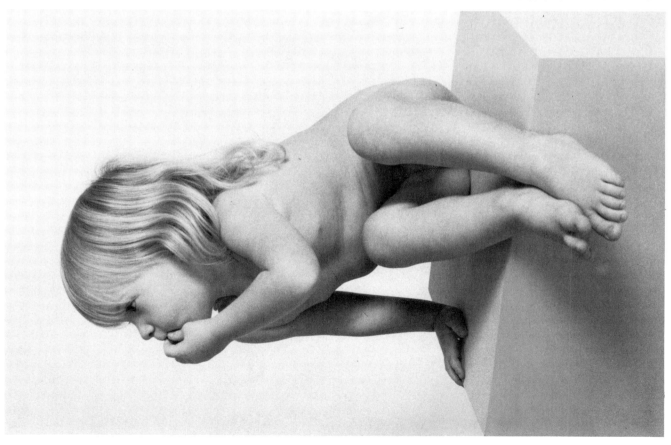

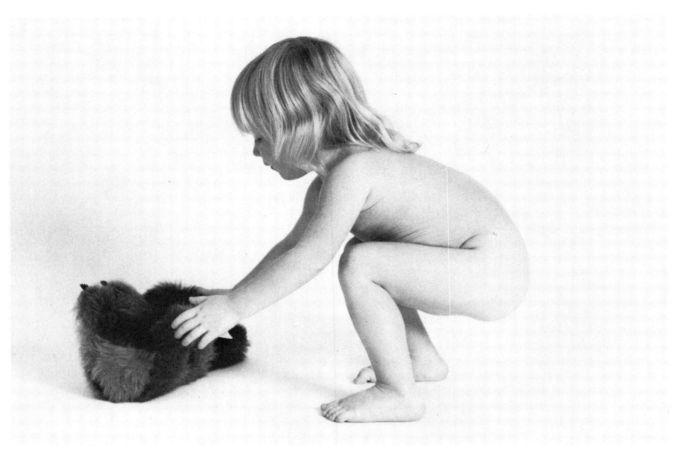

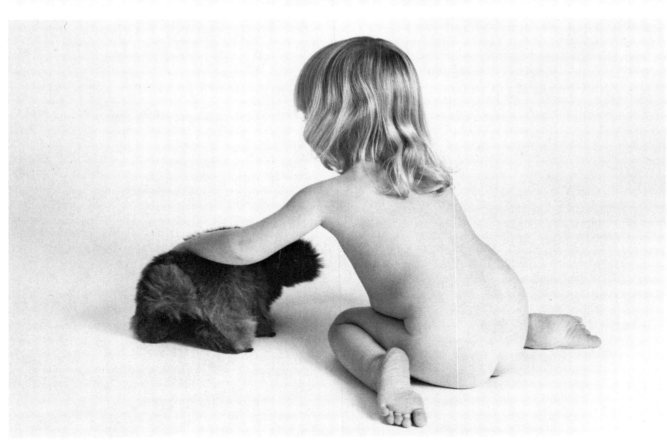

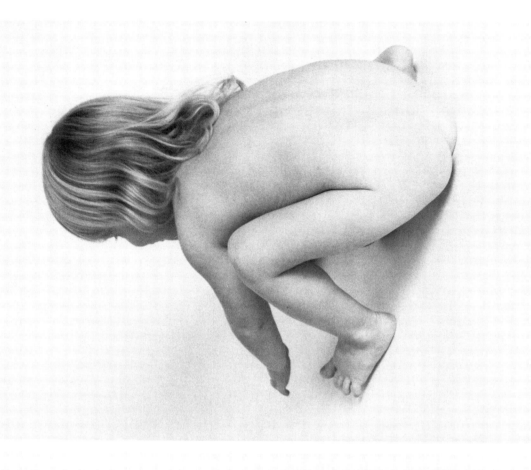

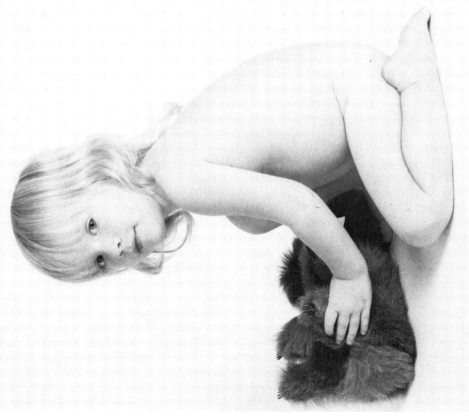

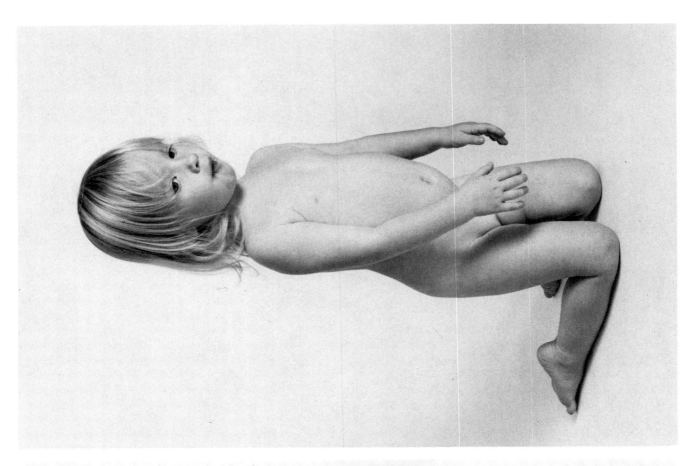

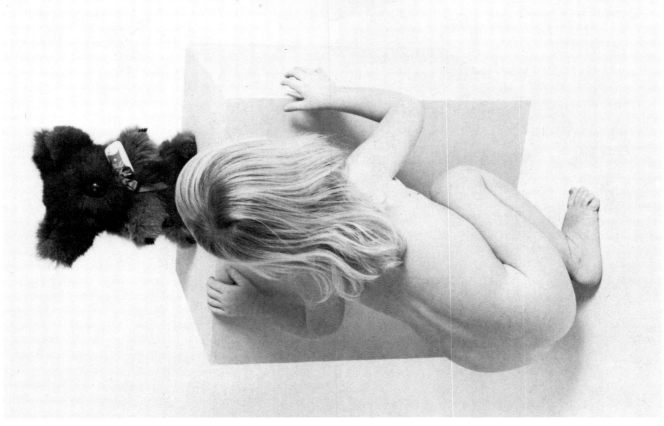

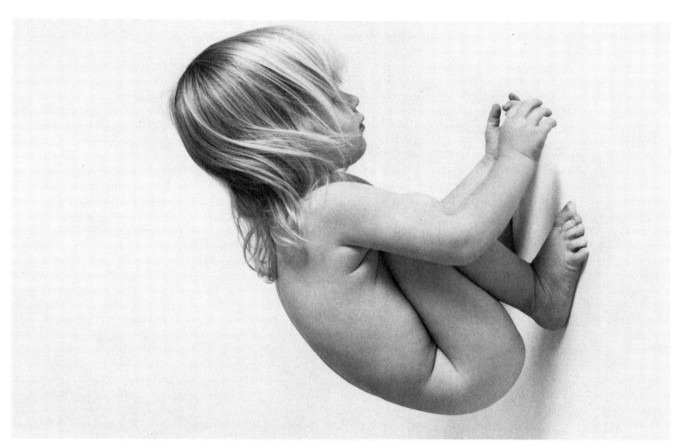

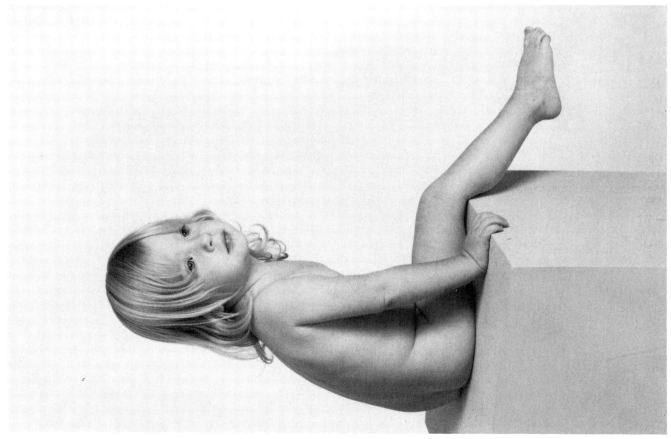

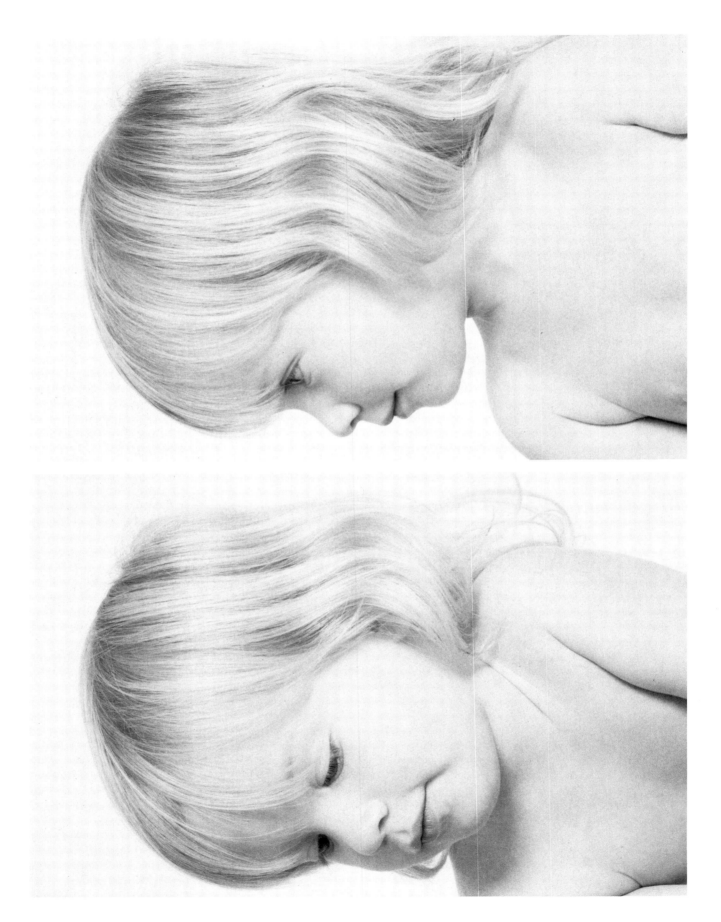

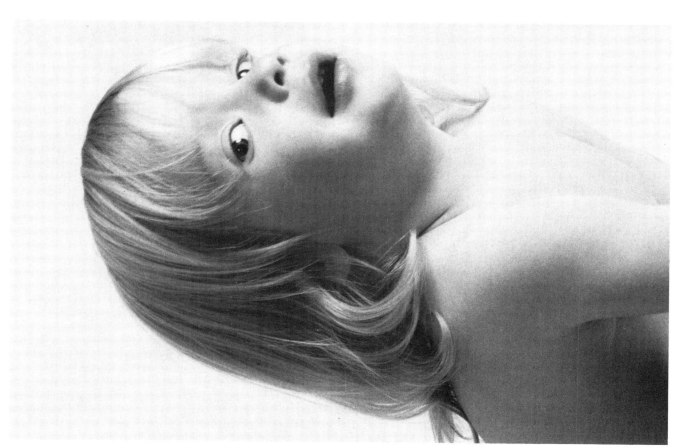

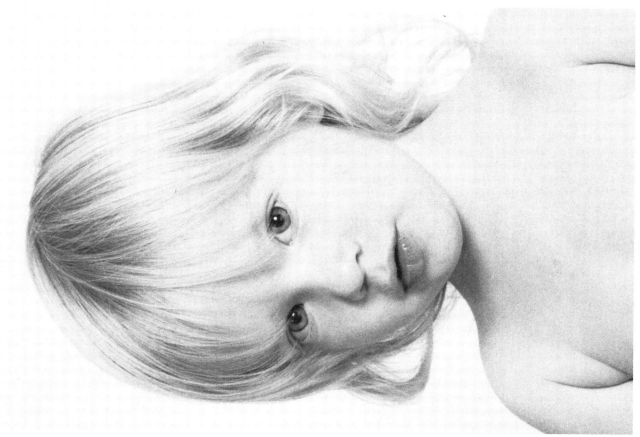

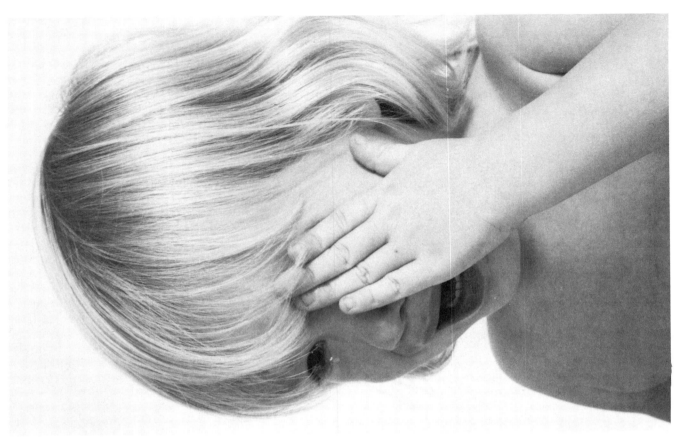

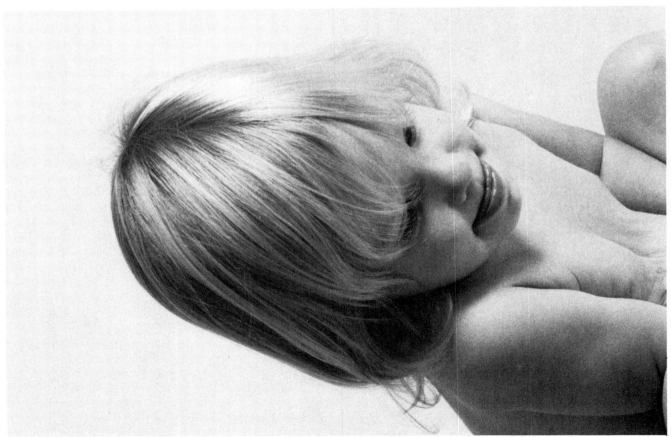

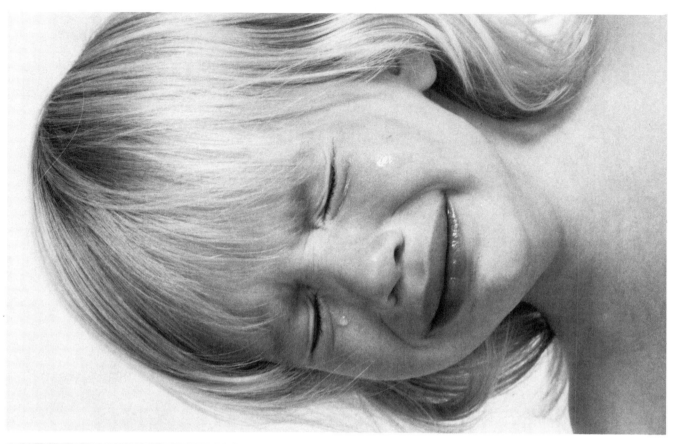

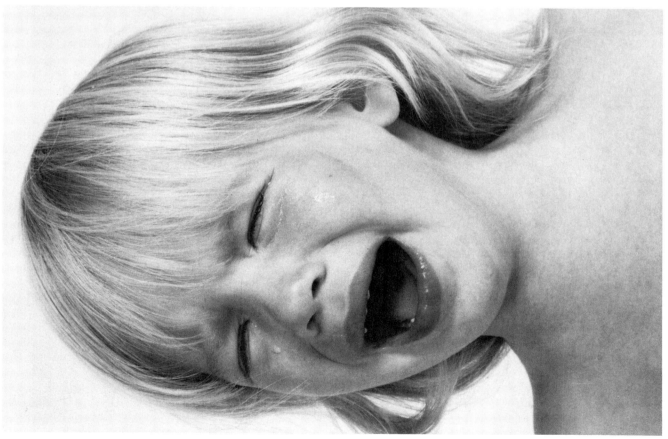

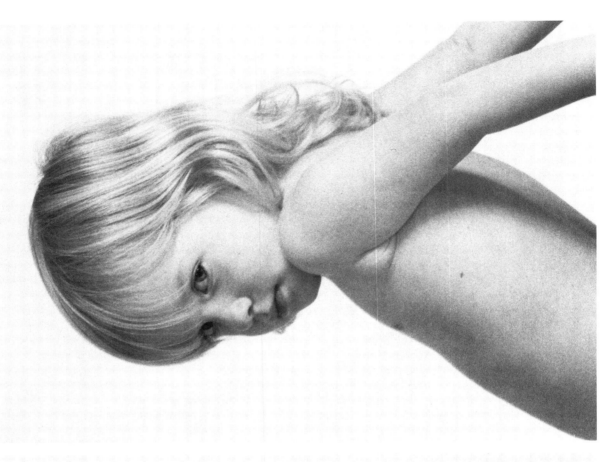

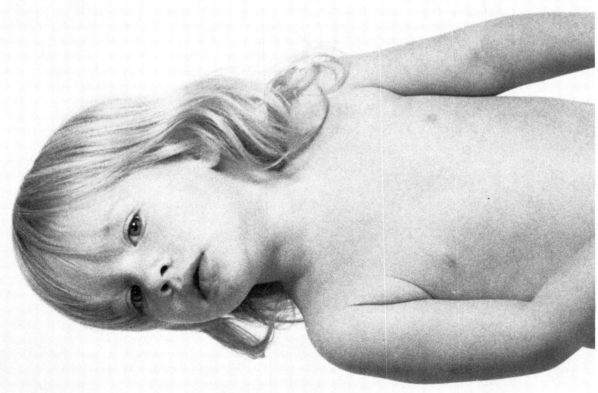

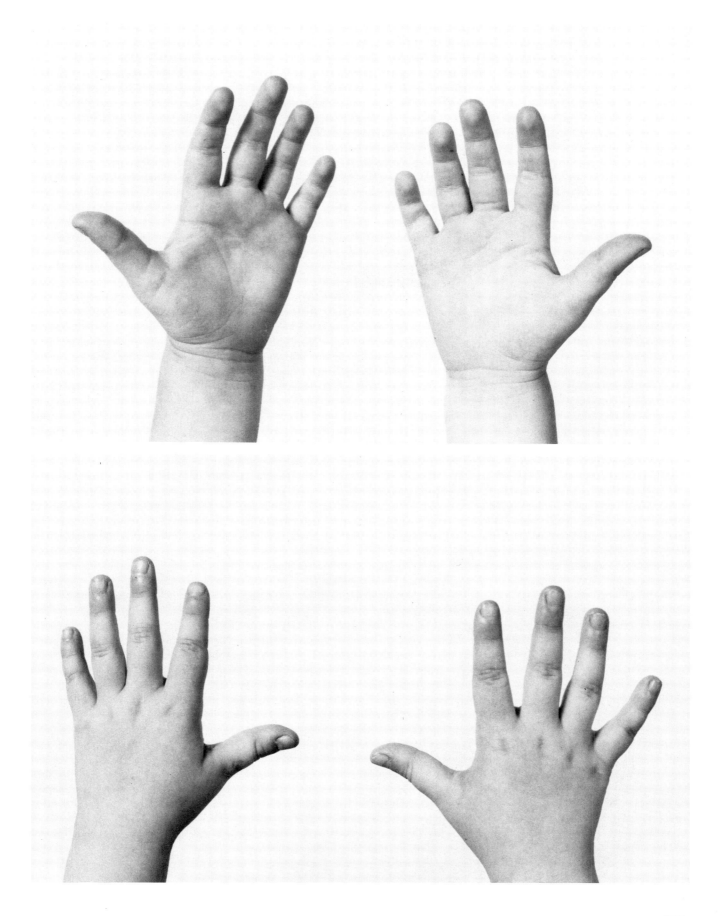

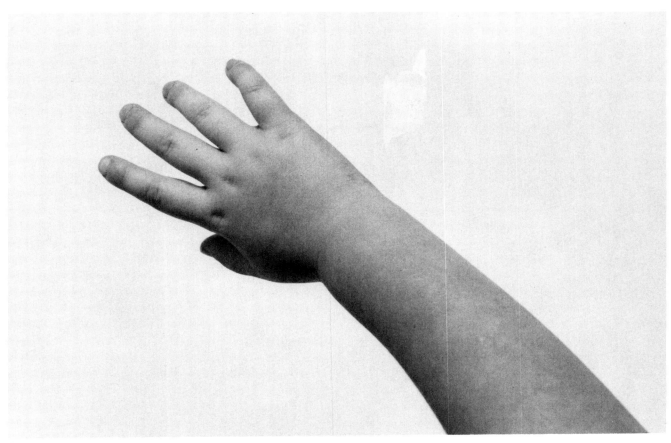

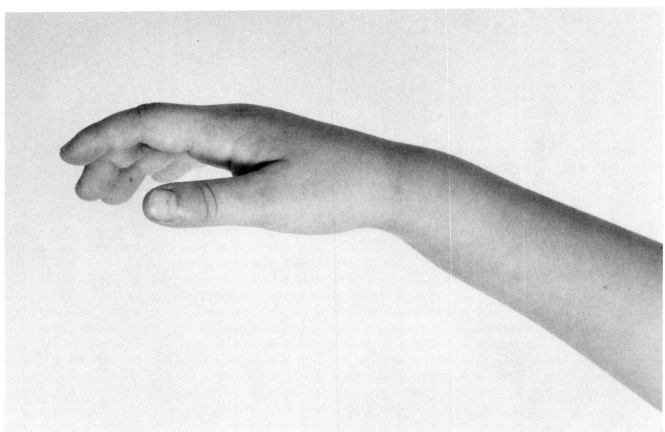

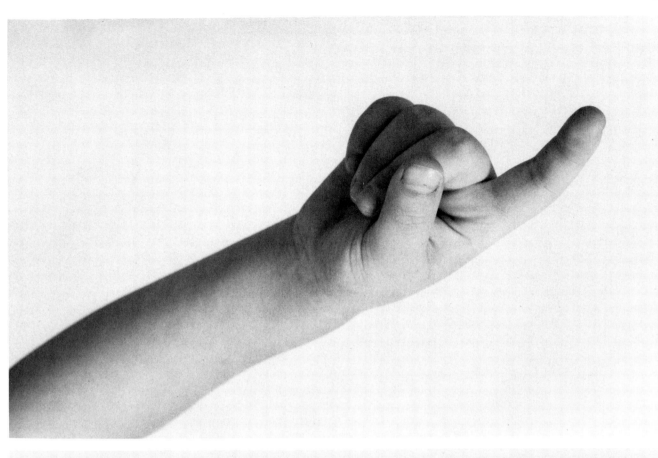

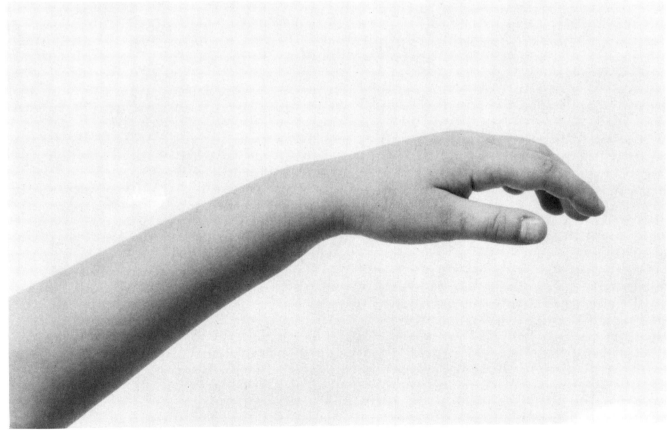

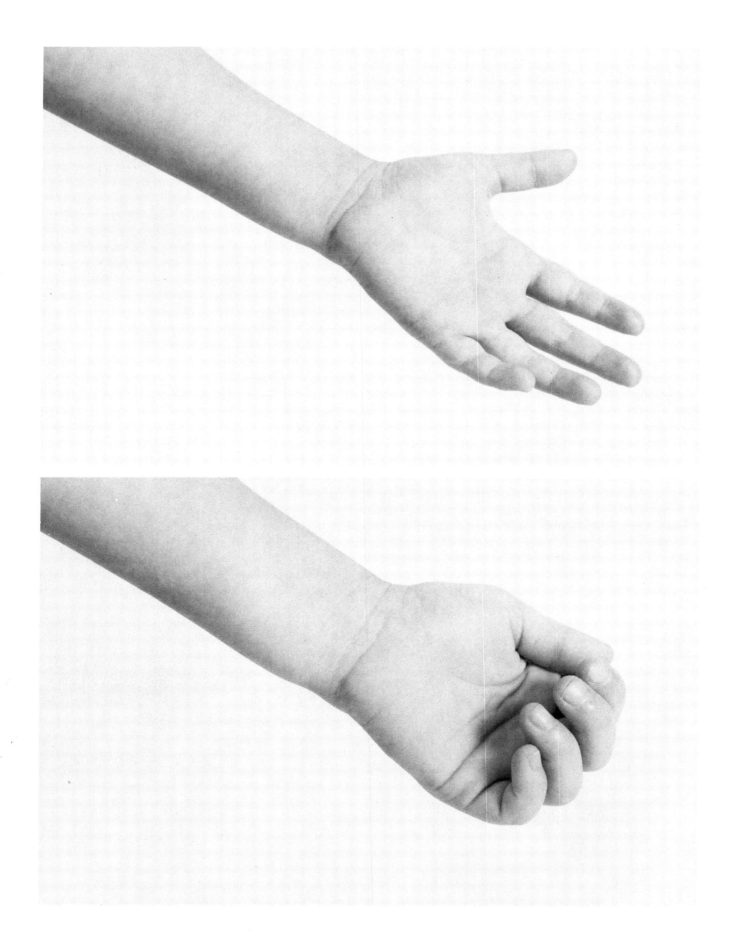

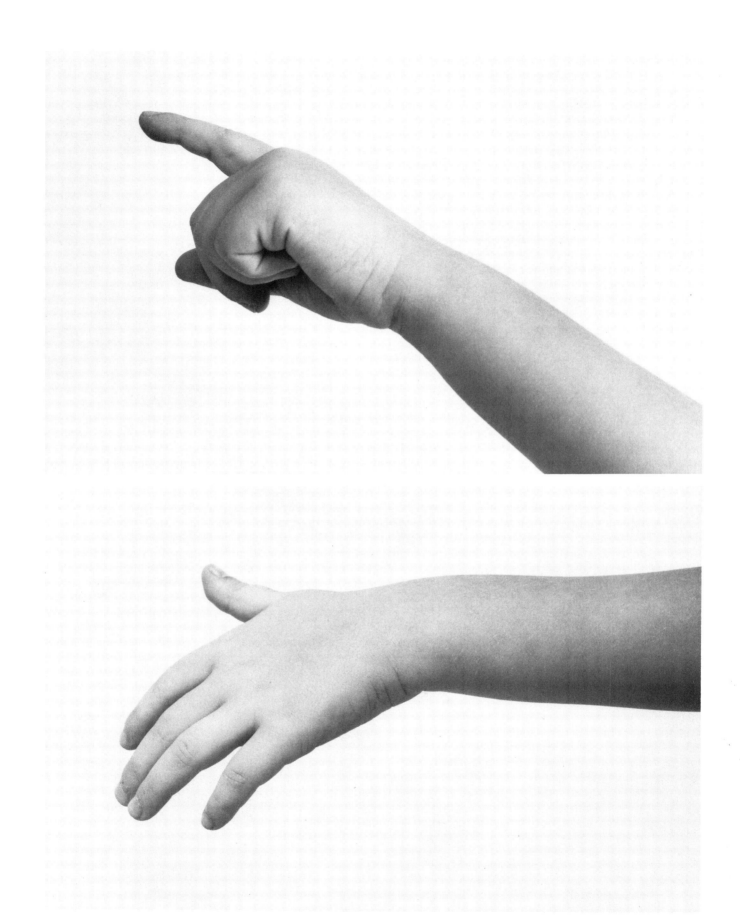

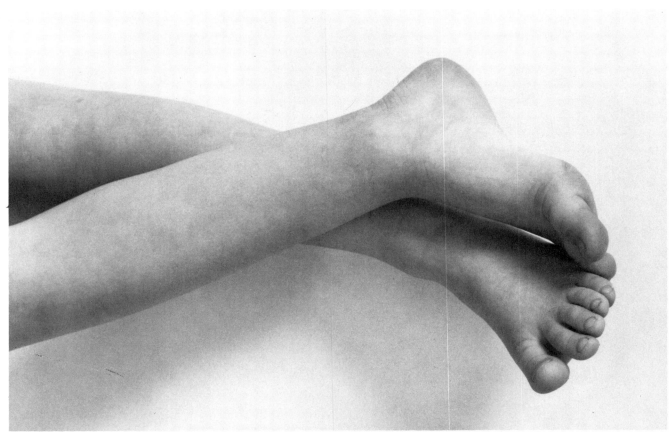

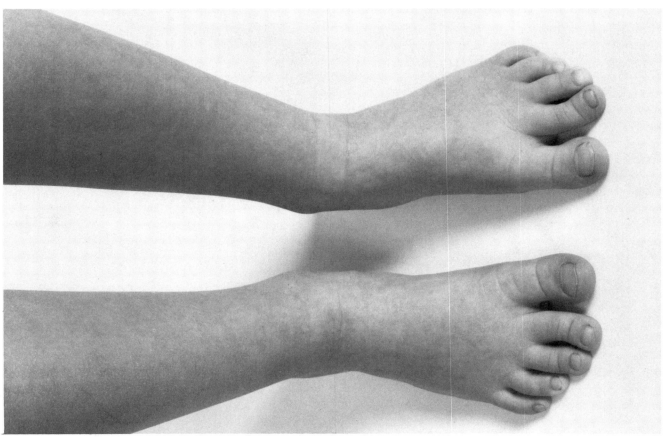

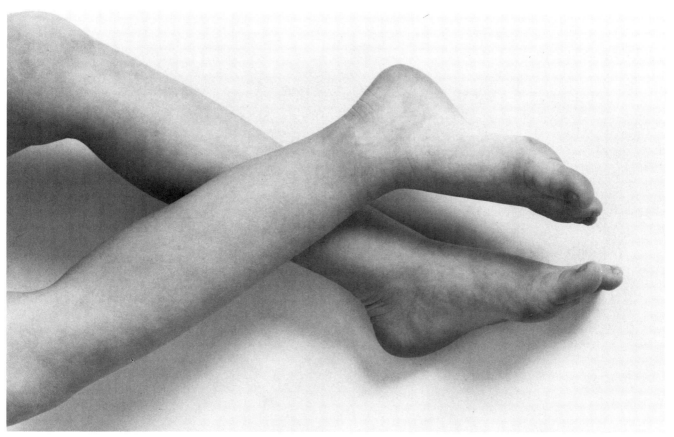

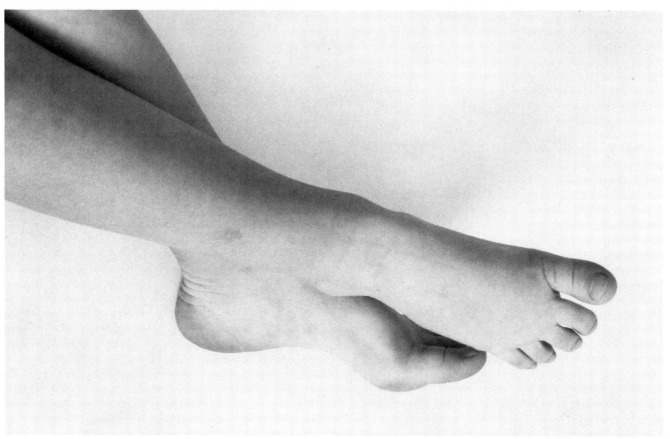

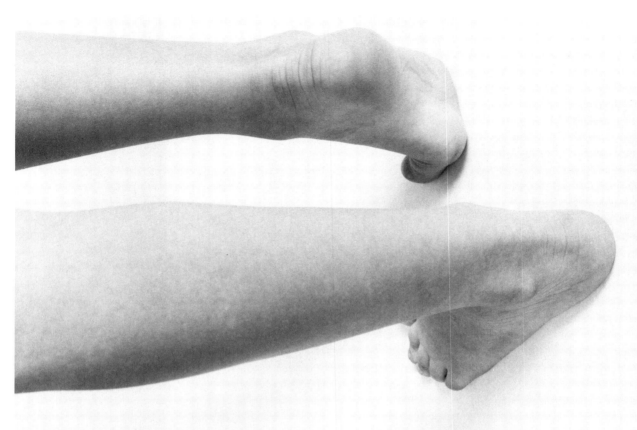

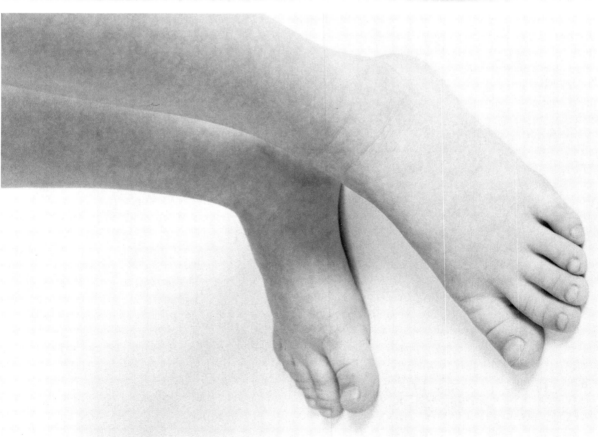

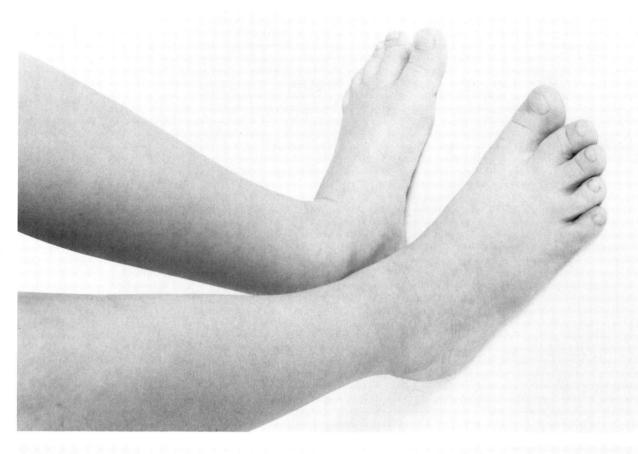

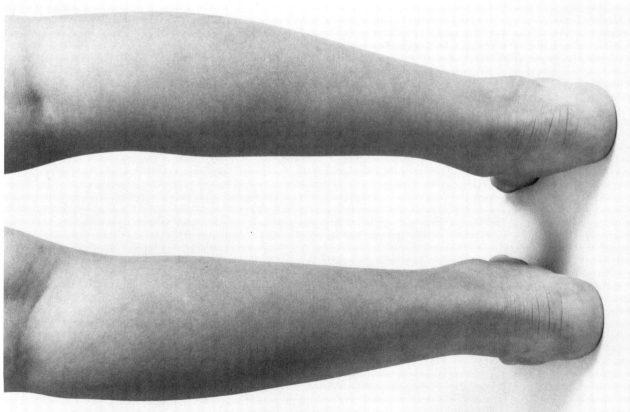

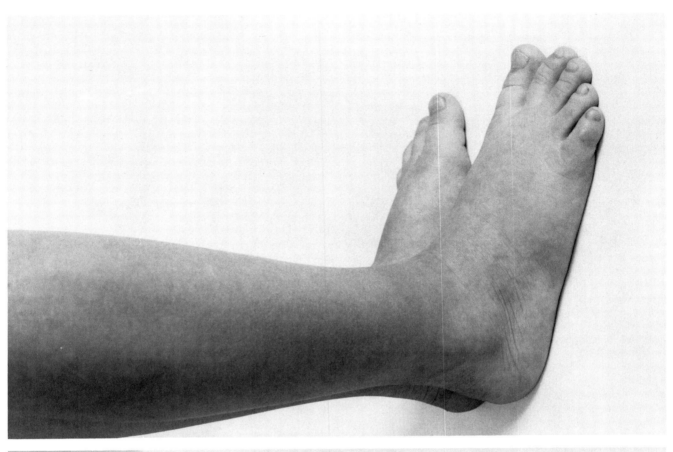

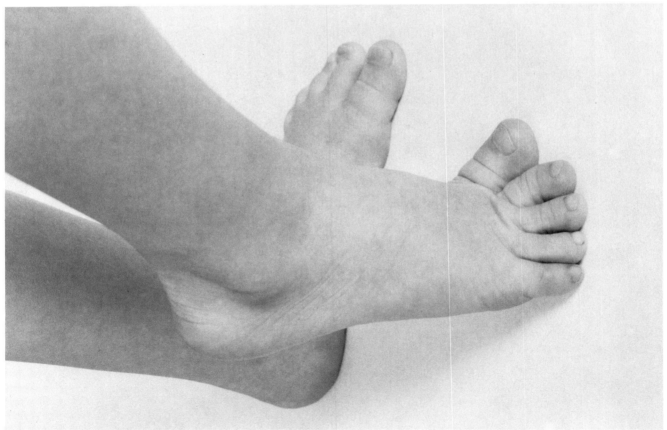